Valuations, mergers *&acquisitions*

Valuations, mergers *& acquisitions*

GREG BEECH DAVE THAYSER

OXFORD
UNIVERSITY PRESS
SOUTHERN AFRICA

OXFORD
UNIVERSITY PRESS

Oxford University Press is a department of the University of Oxford. It furthers the University's objective of excellence in research, scholarship, and education by publishing worldwide. Oxford is a registered trade mark of Oxford University Press in the UK and in certain other countries.

Published in South Africa by
Oxford University Press Southern Africa (Pty) Limited

Vasco Boulevard, Goodwood, N1 City, P O Box 12119, Cape Town, South Africa

First published 2015

Valuations, mergers and acquisitions

ISBN 978 0 19 905277 6

Typeset in Utopia Std 9.5pt on 12pt
Printed on 70 gsm woodfree paper

Acknowledgements
Publishing Manager: Alida Terblanche
Publisher: Marisa Montemarano
Commissioning Editor: Ilse Groenewald
Development Editor: Ilse Groenewald
Project Manager: Kelly Williams
Editor: Angela Voges
Designer: Gisela Strydom
Indexer: Tanya Paulse
Typesetter: Equire
Cover design: Judith Cross
Printed and bound by ABC Press, Cape Town
124024

The authors and publisher gratefully acknowledge permission to reproduce copyright material in this book. Every effort has been made to trace copyright holders, but if any copyright infringements have been made, the publisher would be grateful for information that would enable any omissions or errors to be corrected in subsequent impressions.

Abridged contents

Contents

Chapter 12 Concluding thoughts on valuations

PART 2 Mergers and acquisitions

Chapter 13 Why consider mergers and acquisitions as part of your growth strategy?

Chapter 14 Pricing the deal

Foreword

One of the areas with which prospective Chartered Accountants have always experienced difficulties is the acquisition of Financial Management knowledge and understanding.

Over the years, we as SAICA have worked extensively with one of the authors, Greg Beech, in the setting of professional examination questions on these topics.

He has a clear understanding of what students at university struggle with and we believe that he is best placed to co-author such a book, which should go a long way towards assisting our students to gain an understanding of these difficult concepts.

A book of this nature is long overdue.

Chantyl Mulder
Senior Executive: Professional Development, Transformation and Growth, SAICA

Preface

This book was conceived to address a perceived gap in the South African and African educational market. Numerous international textbooks and practical reference guides cover the valuation of companies, debt instruments, derivative instruments, intellectual capital and assets and liabilities for financial reporting purposes. Some of these are superb for practical use and teaching purposes. Unfortunately, most are tailored for the USA and Europe and lack the African flavour. Many South African textbooks tend to be too academic in nature and lack practical insights into valuations and deal-making.

Valuations is an important skill in business whether you are a corporate finance executive, company director, business owner or financial manager. Chapters 1 through 4 cover the foundations of valuing a business and should be helpful to undergraduate students and non-accountants. Thereafter, the practical aspects of valuations will be covered; hopefully this book will serve as a useful reference tool when dealing with issues such as how to value private companies, apply discounts and premiums at the end of the valuation, and interrogate valuation results. The book uses numerous practical examples to illustrate principles.

The conventional theory in performing valuations is sound, with academics and mathematical geniuses having made profound contributions to valuation theory over the past six decades. The likes of Harry Markowitz, Merton Miller, William Sharpe, Franco Modigliani, Eugene Fama and Robert Shiller have been recognised for their contributions to developing robust valuation models and theories to assist students and practitioners. Unfortunately, some of these theories are being challenged in practice. The practical application of conventional valuation theory sometimes produces unrealistic results. The world is constantly evolving: its only constant is change. Valuations are forward-looking, which can be terrifying in itself. Who would have predicted the disruptive nature of social media 20 years ago? Today, the likes of Google, Apple Inc. and Facebook, to mention a few global businesses, have changed, and are changing, the business landscape. Whenever there is disruption and change, some industries falter and others benefit from the evolving environment. Google and Facebook have changed the global advertising market by providing an alternate platform to reach consumers and monitor their needs and aspirations. Apple has been a key mover in the smartphone and music markets. Over 1 billion smartphones were sold in 2014, according to various media reports – given the global population, these numbers are significant. The personal computer market is under threat due to the advances in smartphone technology and other devices that provide connectivity.

A classic example of business disruption is Uber. This membership-based transportation network was launched in 2010, and provided an alternate means of commuting in over 200 cities by 2015. Uber is an app-based service allowing members to request transportation via their smartphones instead of hailing a taxi on a street corner. The Uber business model would not be possible without smartphones or other mobile connectivity. The taxi, car rental and courier industries are facing increasing competition from Uber. Attempting to value any business in these industries is challenging given the disruptive business model of Uber and other currently unknown potential threats.

Valuations occur at a point in time. We are not attempting to be futurists by predicting, for example, whether self-driving flying machines will replace petrol-fuelled vehicles. We can only forecast business performance based on currently available information. However, we need to investigate and consider potential future threats and changes to the industry in which a business operates.

Valuations draw upon multiple financial management skills and business acumen. Implicit in valuing a business is knowledge of finance, mathematics, accounting, costing and strategy. It is a journey of intrigue and discovery that includes:

- analysing the business model of the company being valued;
- reviewing and analysing historical financial information;
- identifying the threats and opportunities facing the business;
- building a valuation model to incorporate financial forecasts;
- researching the industry in which the business operates;
- benchmarking forecast performance against historical results and peers;
- estimating the business's value using multiple methods;
- running a detailed sensitivity analysis to assess the impact on value of changing forecast assumptions;
- performing scenario analysis to identify possible future strategic options; and
- estimating the potential net present value (NPV) and internal rate of return (IRR) of investing in the business.

Ultimately, valuations boil down to risk and return. What return would you require from investing in a particular business compared with other alternatives? The higher the perceived risk, the higher the required rate of return (and the lower the business's value).

Valuations are required for multiple purposes. They may be required for capital-raising purposes, mergers and acquisitions (M&A), or personal investing decisions. M&A is the favoured growth option of most large businesses. This book covers this important topic in Chapters 13 to 19. The intention is to provide an overview of all the key steps and issues to be addressed in M&A. Valuations and M&A are inextricably linked as a price needs to be determined in every deal.

Bloomberg estimated the value of global M&A deals concluded in 2014 to be over US$1,2 trillion (that's 12 zeros after 1,2!). It's a huge market and the evidence of value creation through M&A is somewhat damning. Various research studies have been performed on the value created for acquiring companies in M&A, and roughly a third are successful. The key reasons, in the authors' opinion, for failing to unlock perceived value through acquisitions and mergers are:

- Overpaying for acquisitions (making valuations critical);
- Insufficient attention paid to post-merger integration; and
- Misdirected or insufficient due diligence prior to acquisition.

The book may seem disjointed by covering valuations and then moving onto M&A, which is a topic worthy of an entire book on its own. In fact, various aspects of M&A could be expanded into separate books, such as due diligence, strategy and post-merger integration. The intention of this book is to provide a high-level overview of key M&A topics for undergraduate and postgraduate students. Hopefully, Chapters 13 through 20 will also be a useful reference guide to business executives and M&A practitioners.

Authors

DAVE THAYSER
Dave Thayser has spent the majority of his working life at Ernst & Young Transaction Advisory Services (EY TAS), Ernst & Young's Corporate Finance arm, where he was a director. He has retired from EY but now consults in his own right on M&A issues. He has lectured on M&A at Wits Business School and GIBS for the past fifteen years. His Corporate Finance experience includes due diligence reviews, financial performance assessment, valuations, transaction structuring and transaction implementation.

GREG BEECH
Greg is a CA(SA) and consults on mergers and acquisitions, strategy, and valuations. He has been in corporate finance and private equity for over 20 years, working at various investment banks and for himself.

Greg chairs the SAICA APC Examinations Committee (responsible for setting the final qualifying exam for CAs) and remains a member of the Part I Examinations Committee. He has been setting examination questions for SAICA since 1993 and chaired the Financial Management Examinations Committee from 1999 to 2014.

Greg regularly presents to corporate audiences on valuations, mergers and acquisitions, financial analysis, behavioural finance, due diligence, financial modelling, costing methodologies, finance for non-financial managers and financial strategy. He also teaches part-time at GIBS to MBA students in mergers and acquisitions. Greg has been presenting valuation seminars for SAICA on a national basis for the past five years.

Part 1

VALUATIONS

CHAPTER 1

Introduction to valuations

LEARNING OUTCOMES

Once you have worked through this chapter, you should be able to:

- Distinguish between the indicative fair value, bid price, offer price and actual transaction price of an asset
- Understand the relevance and importance of valuations in practice
- Recognise that valuations are not a precise science
- Understand the major valuation methods at a high level
- Link valuations to other areas of financial management such as financial analysis and risk and return

Introduction

The key objective of the valuation of any asset is to minimise error, and not to achieve a result that is 100 per cent correct. The latter would be a strategic accident as opposed to a stroke of genius.

This statement may seem negative, but the reality is that we do not know the value of an asset or business with absolute certainty at a specific moment. The value of a company may vary depending on who the buyer is and the buyer's views on the business's future prospects. Some argue that valuations are a science; others believe they are an art. In practice, they are a mix of the two.

The valuation of firms is a forward-looking exercise, as it involves forecasting cash flows and/or earnings and present-valuing them. Peter Drucker, a well-known author and academic, reportedly said that '... trying to predict the future is like trying to drive on a country road at night with no lights while looking out the back window ...'. We should heed this advice and be less confident in our financial forecasts – and, indeed, in the results of our valuation exercises.

All assets have a range of values: an *indicative fair value*, a *bid price* and, potentially, an *offer price*. The price at which the asset is actually sold is often referred to as the *transaction price*. Consider a share in a listed company, for example. We may value the share at R100.00 (indicative fair value) after performing a comprehensive analysis of historical results, the company's strengths and weaknesses, the opportunities and threats facing the company, publicly available financial forecasts and industry research. Some shareholders may be offering to sell at R102.00 a share (offer price), while potential buyers may be offering R95.00 (bid price). A share may have recently been sold at R98.00 (transaction price).

The range of potential values for a significant minority interest or a controlling stake in listed and private companies by an acquirer will unleash a range of different values. The sellers will seek to maximise the price per share, while buyers will attempt to pay as little as possible. Each party will perform its own valuation of the company to arrive at an indicative fair value. The bid and offer prices in these scenarios can vary significantly. The actual transaction price, if the deal happens, is often a result of protracted negotiations. This book attempts to provide comprehensive guidance to potential buyers and sellers of assets in deriving an indicative fair value for the asset in question. It alludes to negotiation tactics, but negotiation is a subject for a book of its own.

The main focus of this book is on valuing ordinary shareholders' interests in companies. In Chapter 9, we will deal with the challenges of valuing businesses in emerging markets, high-growth businesses and loss-making firms. This chapter will also highlight some issues in valuing financial services and property businesses. The valuation of debt instruments and options will be covered in Chapter 11.

The relevance of valuations in practice

In business, the ability to value an asset is a pervasive skill. At some point in your career you will be required to perform this task, or to review the results of a valuation. In valuations in practice, you may be required to:

- establish a bid or offer price for an asset, division, company or group of companies in a merger and acquisition transaction;
- derive a price per share for the purposes of a capital-raising exercise, be it a rights issue or initial public offering (IPO) by a listed company or a private company raising capital to expand;
- value individual listed companies for the purpose of making decisions about your personal investment portfolio;
- estimate the fair market value of assets to assess whether an impairment provision is required for financial reporting purposes;
- provide a starting point for private equity managers in their negotiations regarding the fair value of companies being acquired;
- provide a basis for hold, sell or buy recommendations in research reports issued by stockbrokers and research analysts;
- evaluate whether a listed company's share is undervalued or overvalued for the purposes of share buy-back decisions by the board of directors;
- determine a fair value for a property transaction;
- complete capital budgets and make project decisions; and/or
- evaluate the performance of employees and managers in determining whether value has been created in businesses, divisions or projects.

Share prices of listed companies are instantaneously available. The issue is whether these prices reflect the indicative fair value of companies. Behavioural economists are becoming increasingly sceptical about stock markets. Some allege that they are a collective hallucination of the investing public and that prices bear little resemblance to actual fair value. (The efficiency of stock markets will be discussed and explored in further detail in Chapter 8.) Lewis (2014) estimated that 65 per cent of all equity trades in public stock markets in the USA in 2008 were by high-frequency traders. That percentage fell to about 50 per cent in 2012 according to various media reports. However, it still represents a significant portion of total trading volumes. High-frequency trading involves sophisticated and rapid trading in shares by computers without human intervention. Market information is processed and trading is automated using algorithms and other quantitative tools. The indicative fair value of individual shares is irrelevant in this trading strategy – what is important is that shares are bought and sold rapidly for profit.

Prior to making any decision to buy or sell listed shares, you should perform your own research and valuation of companies. The ruling price may not reflect indicative fair value. We have seen many instances of exuberant behaviour in stock markets in recent decades. The stock market correction on 19 October 1987, in which the Dow Jones Industrial Average index dropped by over 22 per cent in one day, still baffles many academics and market commentators. The market correction in late 2008, purportedly in response to the overexposure of financial institutions to sub-prime mortgages and credit default swaps, is another example of market myopia. The 'dot com' bubble in the late 1990s, in which any company involved in the Internet was forecast to grow at unrealistic rates into infinity, was another example of over-exuberance. However, be warned that although stock markets may overreact in the short term, in the long term it is nigh impossible to outsmart the market.

The valuation of private companies, unlisted property, intangible assets and other assets is far more subjective than that of listed shares. There is less publicly available information about these assets and scant details of recent transaction prices. The specific challenges of valuing private companies will be covered in Chapter 6.

Historical stock market behaviour

The historical returns (Credit Suisse 2014) on equities and bonds on the USA, UK, Australian and South African stock markets over the period 1900 to 2013 are set out in Figure 1.1.

FIGURE 1.1 Real returns 1900–2013

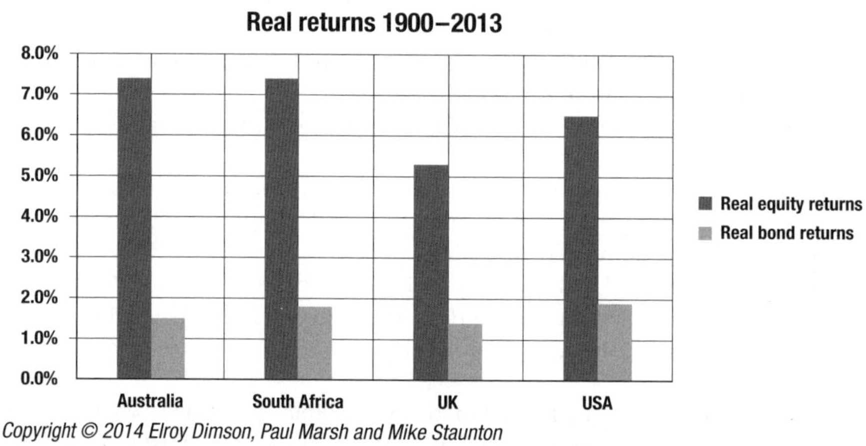

Source: Copyright © 2014 Elroy Dimson, Paul Marsh and Mike Staunton

Figure 1.1 shows that South Africa and Australia outperformed the major stock markets (UK and USA) over a considerable period of time, averaging a 7,4 per cent real return annually. The real return on bonds in South Africa was estimated to be 1,8 per cent over the 113-year period, lagging behind equity returns by some margin.

Historical equity returns are relevant if history is to repeat itself. The difference between equity returns and long-term bond returns is also relevant. (Refer to Chapter 2 for further discussion about market risk premiums.)

Stock markets are volatile and annual returns can vary significantly over time. You would have noticed this variability if you have invested in an index tracking fund in recent years.

Statistics can also cloud data interpretation - returns could be expressed as an average (arithmetic mean) or in compound annual growth terms (geometric mean), and these results could differ materially.

How is historical stock market data relevant to valuations? It is highly relevant, as we will see when we delve into discounted cash flow valuations and earnings-based valuations. Some of the key inputs into the discount rate used to present value forecast cash flows are derived from market data. Similarly, earnings multiples applied to sustainable profits are often derived from the stock market.

When investing in shares of listed and private companies, the average returns one could achieve by passively investing in the overall stock market are highly relevant. Figure 1.2 sets out the annual returns on the JSE over the period 1900 to 2013 (Firer & Staunton 2013).

FIGURE 1.2 Annual equity returns 1900–2006 – South Africa

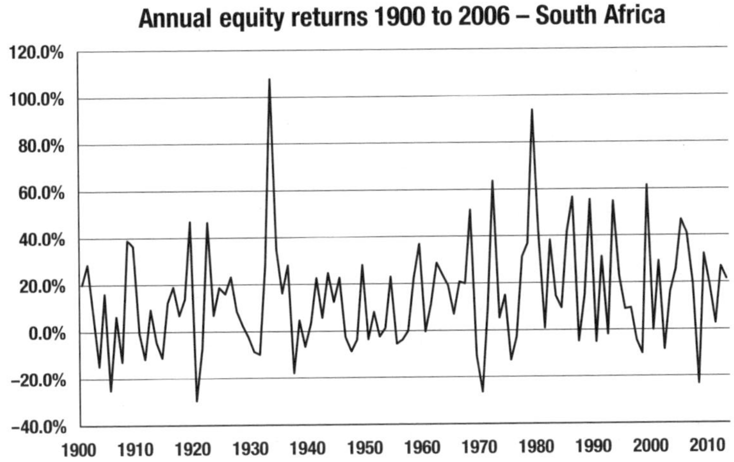

It is apparent that annual stock market returns in South Africa have been, and remain, highly volatile. In some years, the JSE All Share Index (ALSI) has risen by over 50 per cent and in other years it has declined by more than 20 per cent. Over the 115-year period from 1900 to 2013, the overall stock market in South Africa delivered an average annual return of 14,8 per cent in nominal terms (7,4 per cent after inflation, according to Credit Suisse). The geometric return was 12,5 per cent over this period, meaning that if our forefathers had invested R100 in the overall stock market in 1900, the portfolio would have been worth R79,7 million by the end of 2013. There would have been highs and lows during the millennium, but, if we remained steadfast, the returns would have been more than respectable.

When investing in any individual company, these historical returns are useful benchmarks. If we can achieve a 14,8 per cent average return by passively investing in the overall stock market, then we need to make a risk assessment when investing in a particular company. There may be occasions on which we are prepared to accept a lower return than the overall market. On other occasions, we may insist on a higher return on investment due to the high risk associated with investing in a particular company, such as a start-up venture.

Within a financial management context, valuations should not be seen in isolation. As illustrated above, valuations could be seen as a risk return exercise. Financial or ratio analysis is a useful tool when assessing whether forecast cash flows and profits are realistic.

Valuation techniques

There are four common valuation techniques used to value a business, namely:

- the discounted cash flow (DCF) method;
- the earnings-based method;
- the net asset value (NAV) method; and
- the market multiples method.

The discounted cash flow method

The discounted cash flow (DCF) method values the free cash flows forecast to be generated by a firm into infinity by an appropriate discount rate. This is arguably the most technically correct method available and is supported by mountains of theory. For the purposes of this method, profits and net asset value are irrelevant: all that matters is the ability of the business to generate cash.

The earnings-based method

The earnings-based method derives a value for a business by multiplying the expected sustainable profits of the business by an appropriate multiple. These multiples are obtained from stock market data and/or data from recent transactions. The most frequently used multiples are:

- the price earnings (PE) multiple;
- the earnings before interest and taxation (EBIT) multiple; and
- the earnings before interest, taxation, depreciation and amortisations (EBITDA) multiple.

We can determine what the current and historic earnings multiples of listed companies are by analysing stock market data and the companies' financial statements. For example, the PE multiple of a listed company is calculated as follows:

PE multiple = market capitalisation ÷ profit after tax

where

market capitalisation = number of shares in issue × ruling share price

We will cover earnings-based valuations in detail in Chapter 4. It can be argued that an earnings-based valuation is not a method, but is rather the result of a valuation – the stock market has already valued the business and the PE multiple is the result of this. Nevertheless, earnings multiples provide invaluable insights into how the market values particular businesses and industries; we ignore this collective wisdom at our own peril.

The net asset value method

The net asset value (NAV) method involves determining the fair value of assets and liabilities to estimate the net proceeds if the company was to dispose of them. The NAV method is often used where the firm's main business is the holding of assets such as property and investment holding companies. It is also used as a reasonability check on the results of other valuation methods.

The market multiples method

The market multiples method is often used as a rule of thumb when valuing businesses. Market multiples may be:

- price to book – equity value divided by NAV or shareholders' equity;
- revenue multiples – equity value divided by revenue; or
- industry-specific benchmarks – for example, equity value divided by number of subscribers of a cellular phone business.

Using market multiples as the primary valuation technique is fraught with danger. The current hype around social media companies is a case in point. Valuing Facebook or Twitter using a multiple of the number of their users may be interesting, but provides minimal value in determining the indicative value of the business. Valuing a social media business by blindly using a market multiple is likely to gloss over the fundamentals of the business and key value drivers going forward.

It is highly recommended that you use numerous methods when valuing a business to provide a range of potential values and to corroborate assumptions using each method. If the primary valuation method you select is the DCF method, then you should corroborate your findings by valuing the business on an earnings basis. Thereafter, check the valuation results against the NAV and market multiples.

Other valuation methods

Other valuation methods include the dividend discount method. This method was popular decades ago. This method values expected future dividends by an appropriate discount rate. Dividend yields (dividends expressed as a percentage of reported profit after tax) declined to an average of 2,1 per cent over the period 1990–2013 on the New York Stock Exchange and NASDAQ (Damodaran 2014). This technique is seldom used in practice any more as it often leads to a gross undervaluation of the business. The dividend discount method will be covered in more detail in Chapter 5.

The International Financial Reporting Standards (IFRS) Foundation published a comprehensive guide to valuing unlisted companies in December 2012, which was updated in February 2013. While the guide is useful, it contains terms that may be inconsistent with the approach followed in this book. IFRS refers to the earnings-based method as the market approach and the DCF method as the income approach. We suggest using the terminology in this book, as it reflects the terminology used in practice.

Links to other areas of financial management

Valuations are intrinsically linked to most aspects of financial management theory and should not be seen in isolation. The ability to analyse and interpret financial statements is fundamental to valuations. The concept of risk and return is implicit in the art of valuations. The time of value of money underpins the science of deriving a fair value of a business per the DCF method. Strategy, past and future, is embodied in the financial numbers. Sources of funding and capital structure impact on the discount rate to be used in valuing a business.

Valuations are arguably the most exciting aspect of financial management as they draw upon multiple disciplines and are both an art and a science. This book attempts to provide insights into the skills and techniques required to arrive at a tight range of indicative fair values for a business.

Structure of the book

In Part 1, Chapters 1 to 4 cover the basics of the DCF and earnings-based valuation methods. These chapters are intended to be suitable as reference material for undergraduate and postgraduate students either studying to be chartered accountants or pursuing a finance qualification. Certain sections in Chapters 5, 6 and 7 may also be useful for these readers' purposes.

Chapters 5 to 12 are aimed at valuation practitioners as source material for honing their practical valuation skills and/or assisting them in performing real-life valuations. These chapters should also be useful to academics and to postgraduate students pursuing their masters or doctoral degrees. Hopefully, these chapters will stimulate debate in a subject area that is fraught with misunderstandings and differing opinions.

Chapter 5 covers the NAV and dividend discount valuation methods. It also deals with market multiples, a technique often used in practice to justify the results of valuations or as a reasonability check.

Chapter 6 deals with the valuation of private companies. This is an area of mystery and conjecture in practice, given the limited market data to support discount rates and earnings multiples. There are certainly more private companies than listed companies in existence – hence, this chapter should be particularly useful to valuation practitioners. While there are many unanswered questions about the valuing of private companies, this chapter provides some practical insights.

Chapter 7 is worthy of a book of its own given the paucity of data on discounts to be used in valuing minority interests in companies (listed and unlisted), investment-holding companies and thinly traded listed company shares. The topic of control premiums will also be covered, with no apologies to investment bankers for debunking their commonly used practice to drive up bid prices.

Chapters 8 and 9 delve into the practical difficulties of valuing businesses given the growing criticism of financial theories such as the Efficient Markets Hypothesis and the Capital Asset Pricing Model (CAPM). They discuss the challenges of valuing businesses in their early development stages and/or businesses in high-growth stages. The book also highlights particular issues in valuing financial institutions and property companies.

Chapter 10 should be essential reading for valuation practitioners. It is often said that more time should be spent on sensitivity analysis than on any other part of the valuation process. We give real-life examples of sensitivity analyses to illustrate how you could move from a being a proficient practitioner to being a 'pain in the butt' in a negotiation process. Chapter 10 may also provide useful reading to both middle management and executives in business, whether in financial functions or otherwise.

Chapter 11 covers the valuation of debt instruments and options. It does so for the sake of completeness; we recommend the use of more technical reference sources in these specialised areas. Chapter 12 wraps up the valuations portion of this book and links this discipline to other areas such as delivering increasing value to shareholders.

Part 2, consisting of Chapters 13 to 20, moves from valuations into mergers and acquisitions (M&A). It covers critical issues such as using M&A as a growth strategy, pricing an M&A deal, managing risk by understanding the business you are buying, structuring the deal effectively, fairness opinions and the post-merger integration.

Conclusion

Ultimately, the objective of valuations is to minimise error. Numerous examples of valuation errors have been reported in the press in recent times: Hewlett-Packard's acquisition of Autonomy in 2011 for US$11 billion and its subsequent write-off of US8,8 billion of the acquisition price is an unfortunate example of possible over-exuberance in valuing a business. Tiger Brands announced in May 2014 that it had impaired its investment in Dangote Flour Mills, a Nigeria-based business, by R849 million. The original acquisition consideration for a 63,4 per cent interest in Dangote Flour Mills in September 2012 was R1,5 billion: a material adjustment within a short period.

Sometimes, 'unknown unknowns' occur, which valuations were unable to anticipate. More often than not, though, the 'errors' in valuations are attributable to inappropriate valuation techniques, over-optimistic forecasts and technical errors in valuation workings.

References

Credit Suisse Research Institute. (2014). *Credit Suisse Global Investment Returns Yearbook 2014.* Zurich: Credit Suisse AG.

Damodaran, A. (2014). Available at www.stern.nyu.edu/adamodar/pc/datasets. [Accessed October 2014]

Dimson, E., Marsh, P. & Staunton, M. (2002). *Triumph of the Optimists: 101 Years of Global Investment Returns.* Princeton: Princeton University Press.

Firer, C. & Staunton, M. (2002). 102 years of South African financial market history. *Investment Analysts Journal* 31(56): 57–65. Updated to 2013 courtesy of the FTSE Fact Sheet.

IFRS Foundation. (2013). *Measuring the fair value of unquoted equity instruments within the scope of IFRS 9 Financial Instruments.* London: IFRS Foundation.

Lewis, M. (2014). *Flash boys: A Wall Street revolt.* New York: W.W. Norton & Company.

CHAPTER 2

Discounted cash flow (DCF) valuations (no debt)

LEARNING OUTCOMES

Once you have worked through this chapter, you should be able to:

- Understand what is meant by free cash flow
- Determine the cost of equity (required rate of return) for a business
- Recognise some of the pitfalls of the free cash flow (FCF) valuation method
- Value a company that has no interest-bearing debt in its capital structure
- Recognise the need for ratio analysis to assess the reasonability of forecast cash flows

Introduction

DCF valuations are arguably the most technically sound approach to valuing a business. This approach is supported by convincing financial theory by theorists who have received Nobel prizes for their efforts in determining mechanisms of pricing assets. These laureates include Harry Markowitz, Merton Miller, William Sharpe and Franco Modigliani. This group was joined by Eugene Fama and Robert Shiller in 2013, an interesting choice of joint prizewinners given their diametrically opposed views on the behaviour of stock markets. Fama has been a proponent of the view that stock markets are efficient since the 1960s and is well known for his empirical research. Shiller, on the other hand, is a behavioural economist and has published widely on the volatility of stock markets and their over-exuberance at times.

DCF valuation methodology is widely used in practice by valuation practitioners including investment bankers, research analysts, in-house corporate finance teams, consulting firms and valuation experts. It is the pre-eminent method taught, globally, at most business schools and universities. As you will discover, the theory is appealing and logical. Unfortunately, its practical application challenges valuation practitioners at times. Certain empirical data contradicts the theory, as you will see later in this chapter. However, it is a very useful and comprehensive tool for attempting to determine the indicative fair value of a business.

DCF valuations simplified

DCF valuations present-value the forecast free cash flows into infinity at an appropriate discount rate back to today's money. An appropriate discount rate is generally determined using the Capital Asset Pricing Model (CAPM), which is described in further detail later in this chapter.

Free cash flows are defined as the net cash generated by a firm after investment in working capital, capital expenditures and paying taxes, but before any distributions to shareholders. Free cash flow, assuming the firm has no interest-bearing debt but has surplus cash on hand, can be determined as follows:

Earnings before interest, taxation, depreciation and amortisations (EBITDA)	xxxx
Non-cash items (movements in provisions etc.)	x
Taxation paid*	(xx)
Net change in working capital	(xx)
Capital expenditure (net)	(xxx)
Free cash flow	xxx
** Adjusted for the tax effect of interest income*	

CRITICAL THINKING

Interest income on surplus cash is ignored for the purposes of determining free cash flow as surplus cash is added at the end of the valuation to derive the equity value. This is accordance with financial theory. Practically, it is better to ignore interest income on surplus cash as the yield on cash may be very different from the required return (discount rate) used to present-value (PV) forecast cash flows. Also, we would be doublve counting if we discounted cash generated in perpetuity and included any interest income earned on these increasing cash balances.

The value of the firm or enterprise is attributable to equity shareholders, preference shareholders and financiers. Equity value is that portion of enterprise value attributable solely to equity shareholders. Depicting this as slices of a cake is an apt way of explaining it:

FIGURE 2.1 Equity and enterprise value

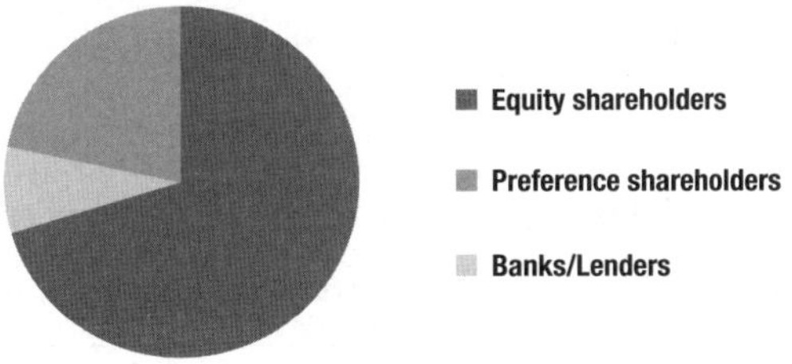

Source: Author's own construction

The entire circle in Figure 2.1 represents enterprise value (value of the firm), and the blue shaded area represents equity value (enterprise value less claims by other parties such as preference shareholders, banks, etc.). Equity value represents the portion of enterprise value to which ordinary shareholders are entitled.

If the company had no interest-bearing debt and had surplus cash on hand, enterprise and equity values would be determined as follows.

Enterprise value	xxx
Add surplus cash on hand	xx
Equity value	xxxx

For the remainder of this chapter we will focus on valuing companies that have no interest-bearing debt on their balance sheets. In Chapter 3 we will delve into how to value companies that use interest-bearing debt to fund a portion of their operations.

EXAMPLE 2.1

Let's assume the following for ABC Limited:

Surplus cash on hand – Year 0	R10 000 000
Cash flows – Year 0	**R000s**
EBITDA	50 000
Non-cash items (movements in provisions etc.)	1 500
Interest income – surplus cash on hand	5 000
Taxation paid	-14 280
Net change in working capital	-2 220
Capital expenditure (net)	-4 500
Dividends paid	-5 500
Net movement in cash	30 000
Other assumptions	
Annual growth in free cash flows from Year 1 onwards	5,0%
Income tax rate	28,0%
Required rate of return of shareholders (discount rate)	15,0%

We could build an Excel model extrapolating free cash flows into infinity based on the above assumptions. However, that would be inefficient as an algebraic formula (often referred to as Gordon's Growth Model) simplifies this, where cash flows are expected to grow at a constant rate in the future:

PV of future cash flows = cash flow Year 0 ÷ (discount rate – growth)

Before we use this formula for ABC Limited, we need to determine the free cash flow in Year 0.

	R000s
Net movement in cash	30 000
Dividends paid	5 500
Deduct interest income earned on surplus cash	-5 000
Tax paid on interest income	1 400
Free cash flow	31 900

We can now determine the enterprise and equity values of ABC Limited:

		R000s
Enterprise value	31 900 ÷ (15% – 5%) =	319 000
Surplus cash on hand – Year 0		10 000
Equity value		329 000

Free cash flow to firm versus free cash flow to equity

Finance literature refers to the free cash flow to firm (FCFF) method versus the free cash flow to equity (FCFE) methods. The differences between these methods are summarised in Table 2.1.

TABLE 2.1 The differences between the FCFF and FCFE methods

	FCFE method	FCFF method
Free cash flows to be discounted	Net cash generated + dividends – finance charges (after tax) – debt repayments + debt raised	Net cash generated + dividends + finance charges (after tax) + debt repayments – debt raised
Discount rate	Required rate of return (cost of equity)	Weighted average cost of capital (WACC)

The FCFF method values the business or enterprise as a whole and then allocates the result to equity shareholders and financiers. The FCFE method focuses on valuing equity shareholders' interests directly. The FCFF method is most commonly used in practice.

The WACC represents the blended discount rate, which weights the cost of equity and the cost of debt finance by their respective use in the firm to fund operations. We will explore the WACC in further detail in Chapter 3. For the remainder of this chapter, we will ignore the WACC and focus exclusively on companies that have no interest-bearing debt in their capital structures.

The theory behind DCFs

There is much conjecture about the originator(s) of the CAPM. Harry Markowitz is credited with being the forerunner of the model as he published articles in the 1950s and a book in 1959. His theory, in essence, was that, by carefully selecting a portfolio of various assets, it is possible to minimise risk for an expected rate of return. It is essentially about risk and return, and the benefits of diversification. Investing in a collection of assets should have a lower risk than investing in a single asset.

Markowitz's theory is seen in practice today through asset allocation strategies employed by fund managers and the emergence of the 'fund of funds' strategy in recent decades, for example, with multi-managers investing in numerous unit trusts.

Most financial literature credits William Sharpe and John Lintner for the birth of the CAPM in the early 1960s. Sharpe and Lintner purportedly built on Markowitz's portfolio theory and created a tool for estimating the cost of capital for firms and for evaluating portfolio performance. An article in 2003 by Craig French suggests that the CAPM was developed by John Treynor during the period 1958 to 1960. His research papers were distributed to well-known economists such as Lintner, Merton Miller and Franco Modigliani, who then took the model to the next level. Sharpe was apparently developing his models independently and concurrently, but these were only published in 1964. In 1962, the *Journal of Finance* rejected Sharpe's first attempt to publish an article on the CAPM, apparently due to the article's restrictive assumptions and the uninteresting nature of the topic. Little did they know that the CAPM would become the basis for most DCF valuations performed globally for the next 50-odd years.

The well-known formula embedded in CAPM, which is used for DCF valuations, is:

cost of equity = risk-free rate + (beta coefficient × market risk premium)

To summarise the CAPM theory as used in practice:

- Investors are able to invest in a risk-free asset and earn a return.
- Investors would require a premium to the risk-free rate when investing in equities (tradeable shares in companies) as an asset class (referred to as the market risk premium).
- The risk of investing in a single share can be measured by the sensitivity of the movement in the share price of that share in relation to the overall equity market movements – referred to as the beta coefficient of the share.
- The required rate of return (cost of equity) of equity shareholders can be determined by applying the formula set out above.

Simplistically, if the risk-free rate is 8 per cent and the market risk premium is 7 per cent in South Africa, then investing in the overall Johannesburg Stock Exchange (JSE) should yield a return of 15 per cent. The beta coefficient of the overall stock market is 1 – it is perfectly correlated to itself. If the beta coefficient of a particular listed company is 1.1, then the required rate of return for investing in that company would be:

15,7% [8% + (1.1 × 7%)]

CRITICAL THINKING

The CAPM has numerous limiting assumptions and many have criticised it over the years. We will deal with some of the empirical failings of the CAPM in Chapter 8. However, it remains a useful tool for estimating the discount rate to use in DCF valuations. Its simplicity could well be its strength.

Discount rates

The CAPM assumes that the rate of return required by shareholders is a risk/return trade-off. The higher the risk, the higher the rate of return required. If the overall JSE is expected to yield a 15 per cent nominal return per annum for the next 50 years, would you require a higher or lower return than 15 per cent from investing in the following industrial sectors?

1. The construction industry
2. The food retail industry
3. The pharmaceutical industry
4. The banking industry
5. The platinum-mining industry

The likely answers are as follows:

Industries in which you may expect a higher return than overall JSE
+ Construction industry
+ Banking industry
+ Platinum-mining industry
Industries in which you may expect a lower return than overall JSE
+ Food retail industry
+ Pharmaceutical industry

This is often a controversial exercise. Those in the banking sector, for example, may argue strongly that South Africa has a sound and robust banking infrastructure in place. After all, we survived the post-2007 global financial crisis relatively unscathed, except for the consequential impact on global demand for products and services. Many large financial institutions in the USA and UK were not as fortunate, and had to be bailed out. The bankruptcy of Lehman Brothers remains the largest bank failure in modern history.

Higher volatility of share price movements implies higher risk, according to the CAPM. Objectively, the ranking of industries in the table above is supported by empirical evidence of profit history over an extended period. Banks generally overperform in good times and underperform in recessions. The construction industry in South Africa regularly goes through boom and bust cycles. The platinum mining industry's fortunes are inextricably linked to global demand for automotive vehicles and jewellery.

Humans need food and medicine irrespective of the prevailing economic conditions – hence the lower expected volatility of the profits and cash flows in the food retail and pharmaceutical industries (presumably reflected in their less volatile share price movements compared to certain other industries).

CRITICAL THINKING

It is highly recommended in DCF valuations that you use judgement in determining an appropriate cost of equity. Blindly using market data over short periods of time may result in gross misvaluations of assets. Temporary spikes in financial markets may provide misleading inputs into valuations. In 1998, the contagion effect of the Asian financial crisis in 1997 and the Russian and Brazilian debt defaults resulted in abnormally high interest rates in South Africa. The prime overdraft rate shot up to 25,5 per cent and long-term government bond yields breached 17 per cent during late 1998. Using 17 per cent as a risk-free rate proxy would have resulted in a very low valuation of any company in South Africa at the time (the higher the discount rate, the lower the present value of future cash flows).

Risk-free rates

The risk-free rate represents an instrument that:
+ has no default risk; and
+ has no reinvestment risk.

No reinvestment risk implies that the yield on the risk-free instrument is certain and will not change.

Long-term government bond yields are widely used in practice as an estimate of the risk free rate. No risk-free assets exist, arguably, as there is always a chance that governments may default on debt repayments. However, in most First World economies that have a reasonable credit rating, this risk is negligible.

When selecting an appropriate government bond yield, you should choose individual bonds that are redeemable as far in the future as possible and that are actively traded. Reference details, redemption dates and turnover ratios of certain RSA government bonds are set out in Table 2.2 (National Treasury 2013), together with more recent quoted yields (RMB 2015).

TABLE 2.2 Reference details, redemption dates, turnover ratios and yields of some RSA government bonds

Bond reference	Redemption date(s)	Turnover ratio	Yields on 11 May 2015
R203	2017	18%	7,02%
R207	2020	19%	7,51%
R186	2025/2026/2027	30%	8,06%
R209	2036	22%	8,84%

Turnover ratio in Table 2.2 represents the trading volume in particular bonds over a 12-month period as a percentage of the outstanding bond amounts.

You will notice that bonds with the latest redemption dates have the highest yields. The spread of yields by redemption date is referred to as the yield curve and is usually upward-sloping. Free cash flows are discounted into infinity; hence, we should use a long-term risk-free rate to match the period of cash flows. It is recommended that you use the R209 yield as an estimate of the risk-free rate in South Africa presently, as this bond is actively traded and long-dated.

CRITICAL THINKING

PricewaterhouseCoopers performs surveys of valuation practitioners in Africa. The 2012 survey revealed that 28 per cent of respondents used either the R157 or the R203 bond yields as risk-free rate proxies, and 17 per cent used the R207 yield. With respect, 45 per cent of these practitioners are using rates that are inappropriate. The R157 was redeemed in 2014 and the R203 is due to be redeemed in 2017, which does not match the duration of the forecast free cash flows in valuation models. The difference between using the R209 yield of 8,84 per cent as per Table 2.1 and that of the R157 (6,63 per cent in May 2014) is likely to have a significant impact on the valuation result.

Market risk premium

The market risk premium represents the additional return that investors require from investing in equities as an asset class versus the risk-free rate. According to the finance theory embodied in the CAPM, this is a future expectation - which premium do investors require over the next 50 to 100 years over and above the current risk-free rate? It follows that this premium is either unknowable or subject to much conjecture.

In practice, historical differences between risk-free rates and actual stock market returns are analysed to derive an estimate of what investors may expect in the future. There are numerous studies of historical data in South Africa. The results of historical analysis will vary depending upon:

+ the time period analysed (past 20 years versus 100 years);
+ the risk-free asset proxy selected (short-term treasury bill yields versus long-dated government bond yields); and
+ whether the arithmetic or geometric average is used.

Dimson et al. (2003) performed an extensive analysis of the historical market risk premiums in countries with established stock markets over the period 1900 to 2002. According to their research of the South African financial markets over the period 1900 to 2002, equities outperformed long-term government bond yields by an average of 7,1 per cent.

The 7,1 per cent historical market risk premium for South Africa is corroborated by:

+ Credit Suisse's (2011) calculations in 2011 of 7,2 per cent; and
+ Damodaran's (2013) workings of 7,4 per cent.

Aswath Damodaran is a Professor of Finance at New York University's Leonard Stern School of Business. He is world renowned for his work on, and teachings of, valuations. Damodaran kindly makes available his workings on beta coefficients, risk-free rates, market risk premiums and other datasets on his website.

CRITICAL THINKING

A reasonability check on market risk premiums is to add the historical risk premium to the current risk-free rate. It is of great comfort if it is similar to the long-term average return on the JSE. If it is not, the basis of calculating the market risk premium and the current long-term government bond yields needs to be analysed in further depth.

For example, if the current yield on long-term bonds is 8,5 per cent and Dimson's historical market risk premium is 7,1 per cent, this translates into an average equity market return of 15,6 per cent. This is similar to the long-term average return on the JSE of 14,8 per cent per Dimson over a 102-year period.

Beta coefficients

Beta coefficients are estimated using regression analysis by comparing movements in individual share prices relative to movements in the overall stock market. The slope of the regression is the individual share's beta. Betas are the only unique component of the cost of equity for individual companies. The risk-free rate and market risk premium are identical for all companies being valued.

Higher volatility per the CAPM implies higher risk. A beta of 1.5 for a company implies that this company is riskier (or more volatile) than the overall stock market.

+ If the overall stock market rises by 10 per cent, the company's share price is predicted to increase by 15 per cent.
+ If the overall stock market declines by 20 per cent, the company's share price should decrease by 30 per cent.

There are numerous sources of beta coefficients available in South Africa, so you do not have to calculate these yourself. According to the PricewaterhouseCoopers 2012 survey, the most popular reference source for betas is Bloomberg, followed by Cadiz Financial Risk Services and McGregor BFA.

Table 2.3 sets out the betas of some JSE-listed companies, calculated relative to the JSE ALSI for the five-year period ending 30 June 2014 per BNP Paribas Cadiz Securities (2014).

TABLE 2.3 Betas of some JSE-listed companies to 30 June 2014

Company	Nature of business	Beta coefficient
Murray & Roberts	Construction	0.46
Shoprite	Food retail	0.22
Aspen	Pharmaceutical manufacturer and distributor	0.70
Standard Bank	Retail and investment bank	0.73
Anglo Platinum	Platinum mining	0.83

Do these beta coefficients make intuitive sense? They certainly conflict with our predictions earlier in the chapter! Murray & Roberts' beta seems far too low given the cyclical nature of the construction industry. Refer to Table 2.4 for these companies' betas relative to the FTSE/JSE Financial and Industrial Index (J250), as per BNP Paribas Cadiz Securities (2014).

TABLE 2.4 Beta coefficients relative to the FTSE/JSE Financial and Industrial Index (J250)

Company	Nature of business	Beta relative to J250
Murray & Roberts	Construction	0.78
Shoprite	Food retail	0.49
Aspen	Pharmaceutical manufacturer and distributor	0.94
Standard Bank	Retail and investment bank	0.98
Anglo Platinum	Platinum mining	N/A

The betas in Table 2.4 are perhaps more consistent with what we would expect. Perhaps the mining sector of the JSE reacts to different external factors from those to which industrial companies react? Beware of betas in valuations that you review as these could be calculated relative to the Financial and Industrial Index as opposed to the All Share Index, and yield very different results.

The results of beta coefficient calculations can vary depending on:

- the time period over which volatility is measured, for example one year, three years or five years;
- the frequency of measurement - daily, weekly or monthly share price movements; and
- the stock exchange index against which individual shares are benchmarked - All Share or Industrial index.

It is recommended that betas be calculated over a five-year period at least, and that weekly or monthly data is used. Movements over a shorter period (fewer than five years) may contain too much 'noise'. Weekly or monthly share price data is more useful as it eliminates non-trading bias (days on which there is little or no movement in share prices).

You can calculate your own betas, if you wish. This is hard work, but a worthwhile exercise if you do not have sufficient information about how betas are calculated by your chosen service provider. Two methods of calculating betas are illustrated below – monthly data over a 12-month period is used for illustrative purposes (you should use weekly data over a five-year period in practice):

TABLE 2.5 Calculating betas using monthly data over a 12-month period

		ALSI change	ABC Ltd share price change
Column A	***Column B***	***Column C***	***Column D***
Row 3	31 January 20X0	3,0%	2,0%
4	28 February 20X0	-1,2%	-0,8%
5	31 March 20X0	2,4%	1,5%
6	30 April 20X0	1,0%	0,8%
7	31 May 20X0	-1,5%	-1,1%
8	30 June 20X0	0,2%	0,2%
9	31 July 20X0	1,0%	0,7%
10	31 August 20X0	0,5%	0,4%
11	30 September 20X0	2,5%	2,2%
12	31 October 20X0	1,8%	1,6%
13	30 November 20X0	2,1%	1,9%
14	31 December 20X0	0,3%	0,1%
15			
16	Annual change	12,1%	9,5%
17			
18	Beta		0.74

Using Excel, you can calculate the beta coefficient using two different formulas:

$$(1) = \frac{COVAR(D3{:}\ D14;\ C3{:}\ C14)}{VARP(C3{:}C14)}$$

or

$$(2) = SLOPE\,(D3{:}\ D14;\ C3{:}\ C14)$$

Both formulas should yield the same result.

In the example in Table 2.5, ABC Limited's beta is 0.74, meaning that it is less volatile and risky than the overall JSE according to the results of the calculations.

It is worthwhile to check the results of beta calculations by using the R-squared function in Excel:

$$= RSQ(C3{:}\ C14;\ D3{:}\ D14)$$

The R-squared function result indicates how well the movements in the share price of a particular listed company fit into the overall stock market. In the above example, the R^2 formula yields a result of 0.97, which represents a near-perfect fit between the data sets (changes in the ALSI and ABC Limited's share price). Many argue that the R^2 result indicates how much of the individual share's risk is accounted for by overall market risk. For example, if the R^2 result is 10 per cent, then 90 per cent of the risk associated with the share is attributable to its unique characteristics and 10 per cent is attributable to overall market risk.

CRITICAL THINKING

Unfortunately, the empirical evidence regarding betas as a measure of risk for individual companies is damning. We will explore this in depth in Chapter 8. In performing valuations, we can overcome this issue as betas do not necessarily have such a profound impact on the end result. We can also use our discretion and common sense in estimating betas for the business being valued.

Why a pre-tax rate?

Many students and practitioners wonder why a pre-tax discount rate is used to discount post-tax free cash flows generated by the entity being valued. Some argue that capital gains tax (CGT) should be incorporated into the cost of equity when evaluating the potential purchase of shares in a company. This logic may appear to have merit. However, it is best to incorporate the potential tax consequences of investment and disposal decisions in a net present value (NPV) or internal rate of return (IRR) analysis rather than in the indicative valuation. Also, the business acquired may never be disposed of, making potential CGT consequences irrelevant.

The reasons for using a pre-tax cost of equity to discount free cash flows include the following:

+ Each investor has differing tax profiles – CGT rates vary for individuals (effective rate of 13,3 per cent), companies (18,6 per cent) and trusts (26,6 per cent). Certain entities, such as retirement funds and unit trusts, are exempt from CGT when buying and selling equity instruments. It follows that different investors will arrive at diverse valuations if taxation is incorporated into the discount rate.
+ The financial theory underlying the CAPM requires a pre-tax discount rate to be used.

The indicative value of the company being valued and the potential returns for the shareholder should always be distinguished. Consider the example that follows for an illustration of the suggested process of dealing with the tax consequences of potential acquisitions and disposals. Assume that XYZ Limited, an investment holding company, is seeking to acquire 51 per cent of Target (Pty) Limited:

TABLE 2.6 Dealing with the tax consequences of potential acquisitions and disposals

	20X0	20X1	20X2	20X3	20X4	20X5
Indicative fair value of 51% of Target (Pty) Ltd	-50 000					
Forecast dividends (after dividend tax)		2 500	2 625	2 750	2 900	3 030
Sale of equity stake at forecast fair value						88 000
CGT arising on sale of equity interest						-7 068
	-50 000	2 500	2 625	2 750	2 900	91 030
IRR (post-tax)	16,4%					
IRR (pre-tax)	18,0%					

To clarify, it is recommended that you perform DCF valuations using pre-tax rates in the cost of equity determination. The tax implications of investing should then be analysed later using NPV and IRR techniques, once you have established the indicative fair value of the asset in question.

CRITICAL THINKING

It is easy to lose sight of what we are attempting to do in valuing a business. Many practitioners get bogged down by the mechanics and technicalities of valuations – using the correct risk-free rate, market risk premium and betas. The CAPM provides us with the tools to estimate the overall expected return on equities as an asset class and then to adjust this for unique risk associated with the business being valued. Dimson et al. (2003) estimated the overall nominal long-term return on equities to be 14,8 per cent in South Africa. If history repeats itself, we should adjust this return for specific risks associated with investing in the firm we are valuing. By all means use published betas, but evaluate whether these make intuitive sense. If they don't, start delving into the detail and check them against other reputable sources of betas.

Free cash flows

We defined free cash flows at the start of the chapter as the net forecast movement in cash and cash equivalents after adjustment for interest income and distributions to shareholders. Let's illustrate the principles again with a more comprehensive example. The example does not follow accounting disclosure conventions for simplicity's sake: it is provided purely to illustrate valuation principles.

EXAMPLE 2.2

Hipotet Limited	Historical	Forecast →				
R000						
Statement of comprehensive income	**20X0**	**20X1**	**20X2**	**20X3**	**20X4**	**20X5**
Revenue	505 400	581 210	668 392	768 650	845 515	930 067
Cost of sales	-328 510	-371 974	-417 745	-480 406	-528 447	-581 292
Gross profit	176 890	209 236	250 647	288 244	317 068	348 775
Operating expenses	-101 080	-113 210	-126 795	-142 010	-153 371	-165 641
EBITDA	75 810	96 026	123 852	146 234	163 697	183 134
Depreciation	-8 500	-8 625	-8 672	-8 825	-9 083	-9 445
EBIT	67 310	87 401	115 180	137 408	154 614	173 689
Interest income	2 300	2 575	3 011	3 533	4 348	5 530
Profit before taxation	69 610	89 976	118 191	140 941	158 961	179 219
Income tax	-19 491	-25 193	-33 094	-39 464	-44 509	-50 181
Profit for the year	50 119	64 783	85 098	101 478	114 452	129 038

Statement of financial position	20X0	20X1	20X2	20X3	20X4	20X5
Plant and equipment	69 000	69 375	70 603	72 668	75 563	79 295
Current assets	207 628	225 282	258 202	298 431	340 599	389 517
Inventories	67 502	71 338	80 115	92 133	101 346	111 481
Trade receivables	96 926	103 503	119 029	136 883	150 571	165 628
Cash and cash equivalents	43 200	50 441	59 058	69 415	88 681	112 408
Total assets	276 628	294 657	328 805	371 098	416 162	468 812
Share capital	50 000	50 000	50 000	50 000	50 000	50 000
Retained profits	163 526	168 309	187 407	216 284	250 877	292 068
Total equity	213 526	218 309	237 407	266 284	300 877	342 068
Current liabilities	63 102	76 348	91 398	104 814	115 285	126 744
Trade payables	58 502	71 338	85 838	98 714	108 585	119 444
Provisions	4 600	5 010	5 560	6 100	6 700	7 300
Total equity and liabilities	276 628	294 656	328 805	371 098	416 162	468 812

Cash flow statements	20X0	20X1	20X2	20X3	20X4	20X5
Profit before taxation	69 610	89 976	118 191	140 941	158 961	179 219
Add back:						
Depreciation	8 500	8 625	8 672	8 825	9 083	9 445
Interest income	-2 300	-2 575	-3 011	-3 533	-4 348	-5 530
Movement in provisions	350	410	550	540	600	600
Working capital movements:						
Inventories		-3 836	-8 778	-12 017	-9 213	-10 135
Trade receivables		-6 577	-15 525	-17 854	-13 688	-15 057
Trade payables		12 836	14 500	12 876	9 871	10 859
Cash generated by operations	76 160	98 859	114 599	129 778	151 267	169 401
Interest income	2 300	2 575	3 011	3 533	4 348	5 530
Taxation paid	-19 491	-25 193	-33 094	-39 464	-44 509	-50 181
Net cash inflow from operating activities	58 969	76 241	84 517	93 847	111 106	124 750
Investment in plant and equipment	-8 200	-9 000	-9 900	-10 890	-11 979	-13 177
Distribution to shareholders	-50 000	-60 000	-66 000	-72 600	-79 860	-87 846
Net increase in cash and cash equivalents	769	7 241	8 617	10 357	19 267	23 727
Opening cash and cash equivalents	42 431	43 200	50 441	59 058	69 415	88 682
Cash and cash equivalents at year end	43 200	50 441	59 058	69 415	88 682	112 409

The first principle that needs to be established is whether the forecast cash flows are in nominal or real (net of forecast inflation) terms. The norm is for forecast cash flows and the cost of equity to be expressed in nominal terms. Whichever is selected, it is important that both the cash flows and discount rate are consistent.

The forecast period, in practice, varies from three to five years. It is preferable for the initial forecast period to be as long as possible; however, assumptions tend to be similar after Year 3. In certain industries, the forecast period is much longer. For example, mining and utility companies (e.g. Eskom) tend to forecast for 20 to 30 years.

Deriving free cash flows from forecasts is relatively simple. The net movement in forecast cash flows needs to be adjusted for interest income and distributions to shareholders in a company or venture that has no interest-bearing debt. The forecast free cash flows for Hipotet are set out below, assuming an income tax rate of 28 per cent.

Free cash flows	20X0	20X1	20X2	20X3	20X4	20X5
Net movement in cash	769	7 241	8 617	10 357	19 267	23 727
Add back interest income	-2 300	-2 575	-3 011	-3 533	-4 348	-5 530
Tax – interest income	644	721	843	989	1 217	1 548
Distributions to shareholders	50 000	60 000	66 000	72 600	79 860	87 846
Free cash flows	49 113	65 387	72 449	80 413	95 996	107 591

CRITICAL THINKING

Certain practitioners derive the forecast free cash flows by re-performing the cash flow statement, starting from EBIT or EBITDA. This wastes time as the same result is achieved by using the format above.

You should analyse how much of cash the business has is surplus to its operational requirements. For Hipotet, we have assumed that all cash on hand is surplus for trading purposes. This is not true for all businesses – for example, a retail operation needs cash in its tills to operate and a portion of cash on hand is therefore required for operational purposes. If a portion of cash is an operational asset, you will need to include this in your forecast movements of working capital.

Forecast cash flows should always be assessed for reasonableness by calculating relevant ratios and reviewing these. Ratios for Hipotet could include:

Ratios	20X0	20X1	20X2	20X3	20X4	20X5
Revenue growth	8,0%	15,0%	15,0%	15,0%	10,0%	10,0%
Gross profit margin	35,0%	36,0%	37,5%	37,5%	37,5%	37,5%
Increase in operating expenses	9,0%	12,0%	12,0%	12,0%	8,0%	8,0%
EBITDA/Revenue	15,0%	16,5%	18,5%	19,0%	19,4%	19,7%
EBIT/Revenue	13,3%	15,0%	17,2%	17,9%	18,3%	18,7%

Continued

Inventory days	75	70	70	70	70	70
Trade receivable days	70	65	65	65	65	65
Trade payable days	65	70	75	75	75	75
ROIC	28,5%	37,5%	46,5%	50,3%	52,5%	54,5%
ROE	23,5%	29,7%	35,8%	38,1%	38,0%	37,7%
Annual growth in free cash flows		33,1%	10,8%	11,0%	19,4%	12,1%
Compound annual growth in FCF 20X0–20X5						17,0%*

* Calculated as follows:

$$[\text{20X5 } \textit{free cash flow } (107\ 591) \div \text{20X0 } \textit{free cash flow } (49\ 113)]^{1/5} - 1$$

Ratio analysis is critical in valuations as it may reveal over-ambitious forecasts, a common occurrence in practice. Historic results generally reveal long-term trends that apply to the company and the industry. The most revealing ratios tend to be:

+ EBITDA/Revenue
+ Return on Invested Capital (ROIC)*
+ Compound annual growth in free cash flows.

ROIC = (EBIT – tax) ÷ (Total equity + debt – surplus cash)

The ROIC ratio is far more useful than return on equity (ROE) as it eliminates the impact of debt and cash on funding operations. A company using more debt than an equivalent business would have a superior ROE ratio. Using ROIC, the two companies would yield similar results.

Analysing Hipotet's forecast cash flows and resultant ratios, we could conclude that:

+ Profit forecasts could be unrealistic due to the EBITDA/Revenue ratio increasing from 15 per cent in 20X0 to 19,7 per cent in 20X5 – a significant improvement, which may not be achievable;
+ The ROIC ratio improves from 28,5 per cent in 20X0 to 54,5 per cent in 20X5, a massive jump and possibly not sustainable; and
+ The annual compound growth in free cash flows from 20X0 to 20X5 is 17 per cent per annum, an impressive result in South African terms, which may be ambitious. The underlying reasons for this need to be critically assessed.

Certain assets owned by a business may be more appropriately valued separately and cash flows from these assets excluded from forecast cash flows. Examples could include:

+ Investments in associate companies (in this case, exclude any dividend income from these investments); and
+ Property investments, where these are unrelated to core operations (exclude rental income and operating costs associated with these properties).

With regards to investments in associate and investment property, value the business excluding these assets and then add their fair value to the derived enterprise value at the end of the process.

Note that where groups have subsidiaries in foreign domiciles, it is recommended that these subsidiaries be valued separately and translated into rands at the valuation date. This is preferable to forecasting future exchange rates and including translation adjustments.

Some final advice on forecasting free cash flows:

- Exclude abnormal or non-recurring cash flows from your historical analysis. These may obscure trends in ratios.
- Consider the capital expenditure cycles of the business. It may transpire that investment in new plant and equipment is required every five, 10 or 15 years in order to sustain the current and forecast levels of operation.

Continuing value

In the Hipotet example, we forecast cash flows for five years. Given that we are attempting to discount cash flows into perpetuity, we need to forecast cash flows beyond 20X5. Generally, future cash flows reach a stage at which they grow at a constant rate into infinity. This may be due to the inability to forecast accurately beyond, say, five years, or due to forecasting fatigue.

It may transpire that you do not need to forecast in perpetuity – for example, if you are valuing a mine with a limited lifespan or a project with a clear end date. In that case, you do not need to estimate the continuing value of the business in question.

A formula to derive the present value of free cash flows growing at a constant rate in future is:

$$PV = \textit{Free cash flow Year}^n \times (1 + \textit{growth rate}) / (\textit{Discount rate} - \textit{Constant growth})$$

If we assume that Hipotet's cost of equity is 15 per cent and its free cash flows will grow by 5 per cent per annum into infinity after Year 20X5, the PV at the end of 20X5 of these cash flows will be:

$$107\ 591 \times (1 + 5\%) / (15\% - 5\%) = 1\ 129\ 705$$

However, we need to present-value these cash flows back to Year 20X0 (assuming this is the valuation date):

$$1\ 129\ 705 \times 1{,}15^{-5} = 561\ 663$$

The portion of the FCF valuation after the initial forecast period (20X1 to 20X5) is often referred to as the *terminal value* or *residual value* in practice. Terminal value has morbid connotations, and it is suggested that continuing value be used. Residual value is also acceptable.

Completing the valuation of Hipotet based on the above assumptions:

Hipotet FCF valuation	20X0	20X1	20X2	20X3	20X4	20X5
Assumptions:						
Cost of equity	15,0%					
Growth in perpetuity after 20X5	5,0%					
Free cash flows		65 387	72 449	80 413	95 996	107 591
Discount factor		0.870	0.756	0.658	0.572	0.497
Discounted FCF 20X1 to 20X5	272 891	56 858	54 782	52 873	54 886	53 492
Continuing value	561 663					
Enterprise value	834 554					
Cash on hand	43 200					
Equity value	877 754					

The above FCF valuation assumes that cash flows occur at the end of the period. Some argue that cash flows occur throughout the period and that perhaps free cash flows should be discounted assuming annual cash flows happen at the midway point in the period. This can be achieved by amending the discount factor to $(1 + i)^{-0,5}$ If we used this amended basis of discounting free cash flows for Hipotet, the enterprise value would be R938 162. Assuming that cash flows occur at the period end is obviously a conservative approach. Instead of discounting using $(1 + i)^{-0,5}$, $(1 + i)^{-1,5}$ etc., it is recommended that you analyse monthly cash flows of the company in question and future-value these to the period end.

This FCF valuation of Hipotet should be tested for reasonableness. We will cover this critcial analysis in further detail in Chapter 10.

The constant growth assumption often has a profound impact on the valuation result. Table 2.7 sets out differing constant growth assumptions for Hipotet:

TABLE 2.7: Constant growth assumptions for Hipotet

Constant growth assumed 20X5 →	Resultant equity value (rands)
3,0%	775 230
4,0%	821 833
5,0%	877 754
6,0%	946 107
7,0%	1 031 546
8,0%	1 141 395

The above growth rates are in nominal terms and appear low in a South African context. Inflation over the period 1900 to 2002 was estimated by Dimson et al. to be an average of

5,1 per cent. If history is to repeat itself, Hipotet's constant growth of 5 per cent assumed in our valuation means no real growth beyond 20X5. The reality is that few, if any, companies will grow by a higher rate than the country's GDP growth into infinity. In fact, many companies will have to reinvent themselves or become extinct as competitors and/or changing technology forces them to 'adapt or die'. Infinity is a long time, and the assumption of a constant growth rate is an uncomfortable one in practice.

CRITICAL THINKING

Can you think of any company or industry that you are 100 per cent certain will be around in 50 years' time?

To overcome the potential over-valuation of companies as a result of high constant growth rates in perpetuity, numerous approaches are adopted in practice:

+ After the initial forecast period (three, five or 10 years), assume that the company's free cash flows will grow at the expected country GDP growth rate; or
+ Forecast free cash flows for 15/20 years and then assume no residual value; or
+ Use the accounting NAV as an approximation of residual value at the end of the forecast period.

The issue of growth rates in perpetuity will be covered in more depth in Chapter 8. This is, and remains, a key practical issue in DCF valuations because continuing value generally represents a high proportion of total enterprise value.

CRITICAL THINKING

The estimation and determination of continuing value in practice is a moot point. To overcome this issue, it is suggested that you analyse the historical nominal and real growth rates in the industry in which the company operates. This may provide some insights into what a realistic growth rate could be going forward. In addition, test your valuation result for reasonableness through ratio analysis and calculating the implied earnings multiple of the FCF valuation result.

Merits and pitfalls of FCF valuations

The FCF valuation method is the most holistic and theoretically sound method available. Merits include the following:

+ It focuses on cash flows, which are less susceptible to manipulation than accounting earnings.
+ It takes a long-term view on the business.
+ It facilitates the identification of the key value drivers in the business.
+ It enables a comprehensive sensitivity analysis to be performed (refer to Chapter 10 for some practical examples).

The pitfalls associated with the FCF method include the following:

+ Beta coefficients are poor indicators of risk in practice.
+ The assumption regarding growth in free cash flows in perpetuity needs to be tempered in order to produce realistic valuation results; and
+ FCF methodology can be inappropriately applied in practice (a list of common errors is included at the end of Chapter 3).

In conclusion, valuations require vigilance in practice. Valuing a company without considering the veracity of the forecast cash flows and the inputs into the cost of equity can lead to significant errors. The CAPM provides a sound basis for determining the cost of equity. This and supporting theories have stood the test of time, having been used in practice for many decades. Hopefully, you will have gained some knowledge of the issues to look out for in practice. The ultimate test is whether you as the seller, buyer or advisor can reach a reasonable conclusion about value and the implied returns on investment. The objective is to minimise the valuation error as opposed to achieving a result that is 100 per cent correct. Only time will tell whether your conclusions were appropriate – if you were 100 per cent correct, it is likely to have been a strategic accident. If you were 90 to 95 per cent correct, or if the investment returns were higher than expected, it was a job well done!

EXAMPLE 2.3

This example is for illustrative purposes and the scenario is hypothetical. Any resemblance to a similar listed entity is coincidental and unintended.

FWC Limited is a listed South African retail pharmacy chain and currently has 85 stores open nationwide. Most of the stores also have in-store dispensaries. It focuses on the sale of personal care products (predominantly skincare and haircare), over-the-counter medication, nutritional supplements and vitamins, and small household appliances. The sale of snack products and beverages at till points also contributes towards profits. The dispensaries are an important drawcard – however, revenue and profits from this activity are not a significant contributor to the company. This largely due to government restrictions on dispensing fees for medicines.

FWC's historical profitability, balance sheets and cash flow statements, with relevant ratios, are summarised in the statements that follow.

Statements of comprehensive income ***Rmillions***	**20X0**	**20X1**	**20X2**	**20X3**	**20X4**
Revenue	899,0	1 071,4	1 241,7	1 477,1	1 689,3
Cost of sales	-611,3	-733,9	-854,3	-1 001,4	-1 152,1
Gross profit	287,7	337,5	387,4	475,7	537,2
Operating expenses	-210,0	-256,8	-295,0	-356,4	-412,6
Provisions	-0,2	-0,2	-0,4	0,0	-0,1
Share-based payments expense	-1,1	-1,2	-1,4	-1,1	-1,2
EBITDA	76,4	79,3	90,6	118,2	123,3
Depreciation	-16,8	-17,7	-18,6	-20,3	-22,3
EBIT	59,6	61,6	72,0	97,9	101,0
Interest income	1,9	2,0	2,6	3,1	3,5
Profit before tax	61,5	63,6	74,6	101,0	104,5
Taxation	-17,3	-17,8	-21,0	-28,1	-29,2
Profit for the year	44,2	45,8	53,6	72,9	75,3

Continued

Ratios					
Number of stores open at start of year	56,0	60,0	67,0	72,0	80,0
New stores opened	4,0	7,0	5,0	8,0	5,0
Number of stores at year end	60,0	67,0	72,0	80,0	85,0
Average number of stores during the year	58,0	64,0	69,0	76,0	82,0
Average revenue per store	15,5	16,7	18,0	19,4	20,6
Percentage credit sales	24,0%	26,0%	27,0%	24,0%	25,0%
Revenue growth	12,0%	19,2%	15,9%	19,0%	14,4%
Gross profit margin	32,0%	31,5%	31,2%	32,2%	31,8%
Operating expenses/Revenue	23,4%	24,0%	23,8%	24,1%	24,4%
Annual change in operating expenses	11,9%	22,3%	14,9%	20,8%	15,8%
Depreciation/Opening fixed assets		11,5%	12,2%	14,0%	15,0%
EBITDA/Revenue	8,5%	7,4%	7,3%	8,0%	7,3%
EBIT/Revenue	6,6%	5,7%	5,8%	6,6%	6,0%
Effective tax rate	28,1%	28,0%	28,2%	27,8%	27,9%

Statements of financial position *Rmillions*	**20X0**	**20X1**	**20X2**	**20X3**	**20X4**
Non-current assets	188,7	187,9	179,9	186,6	189,3
Property, plant and equipment	153,7	152,9	144,9	148,6	151,3
Intangible assets	35,0	35,0	35,0	38,0	38,0
Current assets	155,3	186,8	233,4	269,9	322,0
Inventories	98,8	124,7	149,8	178,3	208,3
Trade receivables	16,6	17,9	19,6	25,5	33,0
Cash and cash equivalents	39,9	44,2	64,0	66,1	80,7
Total assets	344,0	374,7	413,3	456,5	511,3
Stated capital	50,0	50,0	50,0	50,0	50,0
Share based payments reserve	11,9	13,1	14,5	15,6	16,8
Distributable reserves	154,4	163,7	174,8	192,7	208,0
Equity	216,3	226,8	239,3	258,3	274,8

Continued

Deferred tax liabilities	2,5	2,7	2,8	2,9	3,0
Current liabilities	125,2	145,2	171,2	195,3	233,5
Trade payables	120,6	140,7	166,2	189,3	227,3
Provisions	2,5	2,7	3,1	3,2	3,3
Tax payable	2,1	1,8	1,9	2,8	2,9
Total equity and liabilities	344,0	374,7	413,3	456,5	511,3
Check	*0,0*	*0,0*	*0,0*	*0,0*	*0,0*
Ratios					
Inventory days	59	62	64	65	66
Trade receivable days	28	23	21	26	29
Trade payables days	72	70	71	69	72
ROE	20,4%	20,2%	22,4%	28,2%	27,4%
ROIC	24,3%	24,3%	29,5%	36,8%	37,5%

Statements of cash flow ***Rmillions***	**20X0**	**20X1**	**20X2**	**20X3**	**20X4**
EBITDA	76,4	79,3	90,6	118,2	123,3
Movement in provisions	0,2	0,2	0,4	0,1	0,1
Share based payments	1,1	1,2	1,4	1,1	1,2
Interest income	1.9	2.0	2.6	3.1	3.5
Taxation	-16,0	-17,9	-20,8	-27,1	-29,0
Dividends	-35,0	-36,5	-42,5	-55,0	-60,0
Working capital movements					
Inventories	-19,8	-25,9	-25,1	-28,5	-30,0
Trade receivables	-1,2	-1,3	-1,7	-5,9	-7,5
Trade payables	18,8	20,1	25,5	23,1	38,0
Net cash generated from operations	26,4	21,2	30,4	29,1	39,6
Capital expenditure	-17,1	-16,9	-10,6	-24,0	-25,0
Intangible assets	0,0	0,0	0,0	-3,0	0,0
Net movement in cash and cash equivalents	9,3	4,3	19,8	2,1	14,6
Opening cash	30,6	39,9	44,2	64,0	66,1
Closing cash balance	39,9	44,2	64,0	66,1	80,7

The material risks facing FWC per their 20X4 annual report are as follows:

- There is a shortage of qualified pharmacists in South Africa, which could limit the company's growth and impact on operating margins.
- The over-indebtedness of consumers could impact on revenue growth.
- Potential regulatory changes regarding dispensing fees could impact on profit margins.
- Potential restrictions on granting new pharmacy licenses to encourage rural development could limit FWC's new store growth.
- Increasing competition from larger retail pharmacy groups could negatively affect revenue, profits and market share.

Management of FWC have prepared five-year forecasts for internal strategic and budgeting purposes. These are summarised below.

FWC Limited – five-year forecasts Statements of comprehensive income *Rmillions*	**20X5**	**20X6**	**20X7**	**20X8**	**20X9**
Revenue	1 928,8	2 181,7	2 352,7	2 470,4	2 593,9
Cost of sales	-1 311,6	-1 483,6	-1 599,9	-1 679,9	-1 763,8
Gross profit	617,2	698,2	752,9	790,5	830,0
Operating expenses	-474,5	-540,9	-573,4	-607,8	-644,2
Provisions	0,0	0,0	0,0	0,0	0,0
Share based payments expense	0,0	0,0	0,0	0,0	0,0
EBITDA	142,7	157,2	179,5	182,7	185,8
Depreciation	-22,7	-23,2	-23,6	-22,3	-21,3
EBIT	120,0	134,0	155,9	160,4	164,5
Interest income	4,2	4,8	5,9	7,4	8,9
Profit before tax	124,3	138,8	161,8	167,8	173,3
Taxation	-34,8	-38,9	-45,3	-47,0	-48,5
Profit for the year	89,5	100,0	116,5	120,8	124,8
Ratios					
Number of stores open at start of year	85,0	90,0	95,0	95,0	95,0
New stores opened	5,0	5,0	0,0	0,0	0,0
Number of stores at year end	90,0	95,0	95,0	95,0	95,0
Average number of stores during the year	87,5	92,5	95,0	95,0	95,0
Average revenue per store	22,0	23,6	24,8	26,0	27,3

Continued

Percentage credit sales	25,0%	25,0%	25,0%	25,0%	25,0%
Revenue growth	14,2%	13,1%	7,8%	5,0%	5,0%
Gross profit margin	32,0%	32,0%	32,0%	32,0%	32,0%
Operating expenses/Revenue	24,6%	24,8%	24,4%	24,6%	24,8%
Annual change in operating expenses	15,0%	14,0%	6,0%	6,0%	6,0%
Depreciation/Opening fixed assets					
EBITDA/Revenue	7,4%	7,2%	7,6%	7,4%	7,2%
EBIT/Revenue	6,2%	6,1%	6,6%	6,5%	6,3%
Effective tax rate	28,0%	28,0%	28,0%	28,0%	28,0%

FWC Limited – statements of financial position Rmillions	**20X5**	**20X6**	**20X7**	**20X8**	**20X9**
Non-current assets	192,6	195,4	186,8	180,2	175,4
Property, plant and equipment	154,6	157,4	148,8	142,2	137,4
Intangible assets	38,0	38,0	38,0	38,0	38,0
Current assets	361,4	412,0	466,8	513,1	559,1
Inventories	233,6	264,2	284,9	299,2	314,1
Trade receivables	39,6	44,8	48,3	50,8	53,3
Cash and cash equivalents	88,2	102,9	133,6	163,2	191,7
Total assets	554,0	607,4	653,6	693,3	734,5
Stated capital	50,0	50,0	50,0	50,0	50,0
Share based payments reserve	16,8	16,8	16,8	16,8	16,8
Distributable reserves	225,9	245,9	269,2	293,4	318,3
Equity	292,7	312,7	336,0	360,2	385,1
Deferred tax liabilities	3,0	3,0	3,0	3,0	3,0
Current liabilities	258,3	291,7	314,7	330,2	346,4
Trade payables	251,5	284,5	306,8	322,2	338,3
Provisions	3,3	3,3	3,3	3,3	3,3
Tax payable	3,5	3,9	4,5	4,7	4,9
Total equity and liabilities	554,0	607,4	653,6	693,3	734,5

Continued

Check	*0,0*	*0,0*	*0,0*	*0,0*	*0,0*
Ratios					
Inventory days	65	65	65	65	65
Trade receivable days	30	30	30	30	30
Trade payables days	70	70	70	70	70
ROE	30,6%	32,0%	34,7%	33,6%	32,4%
ROIC	42,3%	46,0%	55,5%	58,6%	61,2%

FWC Limited – statements of cash flow ***Rmillions***	**20X5**	**20X6**	**20X7**	**20X8**	**20X9**
EBITDA	142,7	157,2	179,5	182,7	185,8
Movement in provisions	0,0	0,0	0,0	0,0	0,0
Share-based payments	0,0	0,0	0,0	0,0	0,0
Interest income	4,2	4,8	5,9	7,4	8,9
Taxation	-34,2	-38,5	-44,7	-46,8	-48,4
Dividends	-71,6	-80,0	-93,2	-96,7	-99,8
Working capital movements					
Inventories	-25,3	-30,6	-20,7	-14,2	-15,0
Trade receivables	-6,6	-5,2	-3,5	-2,4	-2,5
Trade payables	24,2	33,0	22,3	15,3	16,1
Net cash generated from operations	33,5	40,7	45,6	45,3	45,1
Capital expenditure	-26,0	-26,0	-15,0	-15,8	-16,5
Intangible assets	0,0	0,0	0,0	0,0	0,0
Net movement in cash and cash equivalents	7,5	14,7	30,6	29,6	28,5
Opening cash	80,7	88,2	102,9	133,6	163,2
Closing cash balance	88,2	102,9	133,6	163,2	191,7
Net movement in cash	7,5	14,7	30,6	29,6	28,5
Interest income (after tax)	-3,0	-3,4	-4,3	-5,3	-6,4
Dividends paid	71,6	80,0	93,2	96,7	99,8
Free cash flow	76,0	91,3	119,6	120,9	122,0
Annual change in free cash flow		20,0%	31,0%	1,1%	0,9%

Conclusion

In this chapter, we looked at free cash flow and determining the cost of equity (required rate of return) for a business. We also explored some of the pitfalls of the free cash flow (FCF) valuation method, beta coefficients and continuing value, the process of valuing a company that has no interest-bearing debt in its capital structure, and the need to perform ratio analysis to assess the reasonability of forecast cash flows.

Questions

1. The enterprise value of a company represents:
   A. The value of the company to which commercial bankers lay claim
   B. The value of the company attributable to all stakeholders
   C. The value of equity shareholders' interests
2. When determining equity value:
   A. You add the market value of interest-bearing debt and subtract surplus cash on hand from enterprise value
   B. You discount free cash flows by the after tax cost of debt
   C. You determine enterprise value and then deduct interest-bearing debt and add surplus cash
3. The free cash flow to equity method:
   A. Discounts future cash flows after adding back dividends, interest income (after tax) and finance charges (after tax), and deducting net debt payments, by the cost of equity
   B. Discounts forecast net cash generated after adding back dividends, interest income (after tax), finance charges (after tax) and net repayments of interest-bearing debt
   C. Is the most commonly used DCF method in practice
4. When estimating the risk-free rate in South Africa, you should use:
   A. The R157 bond yield
   B. The R209 bond yield
   C. The current three-month government treasury bill rate
5. The market risk premium is the:
   A. Historic difference between the average annual return on the JSE and long-term government bond yields
   B. Correlation between long-term stock exchange returns and government bond yields
   C. The expected future higher returns from investing in equities as an asset class versus long-term government bonds
6. Beta coefficients represent:
   A. The slope of the line in a graph with annual stock exchange returns on the x-axis and long-term government bond yields on the y-axis
   B. The sensitivity of individual share price movements as compared to movements the overall stock exchange
   C. The degree of riskiness of investing in equities as an asset class

7. Historic beta coefficients:
   A. Provide unequivocal proof of the riskiness of individual companies
   B. Are calculated by comparing the average return of investing in a particular company versus the overall JSE
   C. Should be reviewed with caution as they may not accurately reflect the unique risk of investing in a particular company versus the overall stock market
8. Free cash flows of an enterprise represent:
   A. The annual change in the firm's net cash position
   B. The net cash generated annually by a company before dividend payments, interest income, finance charges and net debt repayments
   C. The pro forma EBIT of the firm after working capital changes and net investment in plant and equipment
9. Continuing value is the:
   A. Discounted free cash flows of an entity after the initial forecast period
   B. Entity's net asset value after the initial forecast period present-valued to today
   C. Estimated value of the entity in future
10. The estimated growth rate in free cash flows of the firm after the initial forecast period should:
   A. Be equivalent to the expected inflation rate into infinity
   B. Be the average growth rate in the firm's free cash flows over the past five years
   C. Not be higher than the estimated nominal growth rate in the country in which the firm operates

Task

Perform an indicative FCF valuation of FWC Limited at the end of 20X4, assuming the following:

+ Risk-free rate of 8,8 per cent
+ Market risk premium of 7,1 per cent
+ Beta coefficient of FWC of 0.8
+ Growth in free cash flows after 20X9 of 5,0 per cent per annum in perpetuity
+ Cash on hand at the end of 20X4 that is surplus to operational requirements of R75 million.

Suggested approach to valuing FWC Limited using the FCF method

1. Identify and analyse the key risks facing FWC.
2. Evaluate FWC's forecast strategy.
3. Calculate and review relevant historic and forecast financial ratios.
4. Benchmark FWC's key ratios against major competitors to identify any unrealistic forecasts and competitive advantages or disadvantages.
5. Perform FCF valuation using forecast information and estimated cost of equity.

6. Perform sensitivity analyses to identify the key value drivers going forward (refer to Chapter 10 for suggested techniques).
7. Test the valuation result for reasonableness by calculating the implied EBIT multiple, revenue multiple and price-to-book ratio (you will be given guidance in Chapters 4, 5 and 10 on how to perform these analyses).

FWC identified and disclosed certain key risks in their 20X4 annual report:
- The potential constraints on new store openings due to the lack of qualified pharmacists and the inability to obtain new pharmacy licenses
- The potential slowdown in revenue growth due to consumer indebtedness and competitor actions
- Further possible government intervention in restricting dispensing fees although dispensing revenue is not a material profit contributor.

There were some risks that were not disclosed:
- Rising costs (fuel, electricity and general inflationary pressure) in South Africa, which may not be recovered through price increases
- Exchange rate volatility, which could result in higher imported costs of medicines - will FWC be able to pass on these price increases?
- Labour strike action, which could result in the loss of trading days
- Business interruption due to natural disasters and/or IT system failure.

The assessment of risks is important for assessing whether the financial forecasts are reasonable and for identifying potential reasons for future underperformance.

FWC's forecast strategy is not known although it appears that revenue growth will be driven by new store openings.

Historic financial ratios have been calculated for you in the information disclosed. With regards to the period 20X0 to 20X4:
- Revenue growth has been driven by new store openings.
- Gross profit margins have been relatively stable.
- Operating expenses have been increasing at a higher rate than revenue growth, indicating an inability to pass on all cost increases to customers.
- The EBIT/revenue margin has declined from 6,6 per cent in 20X0 to 6,0 per cent in 20X4, a potentially concerning trend.
- Working capital management appears to be adequate, although inventory days have increased over the period.
- The ROIC ratio has been increasing over the five-year period. This is largely due to aggressive dividend payouts.

The assumptions underpinning the cash flow forecasts for the period 20X5 to 20X9 appear reasonable in comparison to the prior five years. The only ratio that may need further analysis is ROIC, which increased from 24,3 per cent in 20X0 to 61,2 per cent in 20X9. This is a significant enhancement and should be compared with major competitors and industry averages.

You would need to perform your own research on competitors - the Clicks Group and Dis-Chem are currently the two major competitors in South Africa. Clicks is listed, so you would be able to calculate ratios and analyse its financial information over the comparable period. Dis-Chem is unlisted, so you may not be able to obtain any useful information on its performance.

Indicative FCF valuation of FWC Limited at the end of 20X4

FWC Limited: Indicative FCF valuation	20X4	20X5	20X6	20X7	20X8	20X9
Assumptions						
Risk-free rate	8,8%					
Market risk premium	7,1%					
Beta coefficient	0.8					
Growth in perpetuity after 20X9	5,0%					
Surplus cash on hand 20X4	75,0					
Valuation workings	**20X4**	**20X5**	**20X6**	**20X7**	**20X8**	**20X9**
Cost of equity	14,48%					
Free cash flows 20X5 to 20X9		76,0	91,3	119,6	120,9	122,0
Discount factor		0,8735	0,7630	0,6665	0,5822	0,5086
Discounted free cash flows 20X5 to 20X9	348,2					
Continuing value	687,2					
Enterprise value*	1 035,4					
Surplus cash	75,0					
Equity value	1 110,4					

** Calculated as follows: [(122,0 × 1,05) ÷ (14,48% – 5%)] × 0,50857*

We will expand on the suggested sensitivity analysis to check the reasonableness of the FCF valuation at the end of Chapter 10.

References

BNP Paribas Cadiz Securities. (2014). *Equity Risk Service – Q2 2014*. Johannesburg: BNP Paribas Cadiz Securities.

Credit Suisse. (2011). Dimson, Elroy, Paul Marsh, and Mike Staunton, 2011b *Credit Suisse Global Investment Returns Yearbook 2011*. Zurich: Credit Suisse Research Institute.

Damodaran, A. (2013). www.pages.stern.nyu.edu/~adamodar/archived data/discount rate estimation/risk premiums for other markets/1/14 Accessed 12 May 2015].

Dimson, E., Marsh, P. & Staunton, M. (2002). Global evidence on the equity risk premium. *Journal of Applied Corporate Finance* 15(4): 27–38.

French, C.W. (2003). The Treynor Capital Asset Pricing Model. *Journal of Investment Management* 1(2): 60–72.

National Treasury. (2013). *Debt management report 2012/13*. Pretoria: National Treasury.

PriceWaterhouseCoopers. (2012). *An African perspective: Valuation methodology survey*. South Africa: PricewaterhouseCoopers.

RMB. (2015). http://www.rmb.co.za/GlobalMarkets/rates_historicalRates.asp?product=Bonds&instrument=R189&rateDisplay=R189. [Accessed 12 May 2015].

CHAPTER 3

DCF valuations (debt in capital structure)

LEARNING OUTCOMES

Once you have worked through this chapter, you should be able to:

- Understand the benefits of using debt as opposed to equity to fund operations
- Use two techniques for incorporating the benefits of debt into an FCF valuation
- Calculate the WACC
- Recognise the potential errors in using the WACC to value a business with debt
- Adjust the beta coefficient of a business for leverage and distinguish between levered and unlevered betas
- Understand and apply the APV method in practice
- Evaluate the optimal capital structure of a business

Introduction

Chapter 2 covered DCF valuations that assumed there was no debt on a company's balance sheet. The burning question is: What impact does the introduction of debt into the capital structure of businesses have on DCF valuations? This concept is widely misunderstood in practice. Many valuation practitioners simply calculate the weighted average cost of capital (WACC) and use this to discount forecast cash flows. This is the approach that is widely taught at universities and business schools, and students and practitioners seldom question the resultant valuation results. The cost of debt is generally lower than the cost of equity. Therefore, using an average of debt and equity in the capital structure often results in the WACC being lower than the cost of equity. The end result is that the value of businesses with debt in their capital structures is mostly higher than if they did not use interest-bearing debt to fund operations - the lower the discount rate, the higher the valuation result.

The financial theory underpinning the calculation and use of the WACC is sound: it is its application in practice that is problematic. In this chapter, we unpack the benefit of using debt to fund businesses and the resultant impact on company valuations. The common valuation errors associated with debt in a capital structure will also be analysed and discussed.

The benefits of debt in the capital structure

Using debt to fund the operations of a company, venture or project - instead of shareholder money - has numerous benefits. The key benefit to a company is that the interest payments associated with debt are deductible for income tax purposes (assuming the debt is used to fund income-generating pursuits per South African tax rules). This is often referred to as the tax shield – refer to Table 3.1 for an illustration of this.

TABLE 3.1 The tax shield

	Year 1	Year 2	Year 3
Total interest-bearing debt	100 000	100 000	100 000
Interest rate – debt	10,0%	10,0%	10,0%
Income tax rate	28,0%	28,0%	28,0%
Interest expense	-10 000	-10 000	-10 000
Tax deduction benefit	2 800	2 800	2 800
Net interest expense after tax	-7 200	-7 200	-7 200

The benefit of deducting interest expense (R2 800) is the tax shield. This means that the entity will pay R2 800 less tax due to the deductibility of interest for tax purposes than it would have with no debt in the capital structure.

There are many distracting arguments about using debt as opposed to equity to fund a company's operations. Claims that the cost of debt is generally cheaper than that of equity are true, but the source of the additional value created in this way is often misunderstood. The only source of new value for the company arising from the introduction of debt is the tax shield on interest, which introduces a new cash flow into the valuation calculation.

Similarly, the argument that using debt to fund operations instead of their own money leverages returns to shareholders has significant merit. The leverage effect refers to the fact that if shareholders elect to use a portion of debt to fund operations of the company, they have to invest less of their own capital and still benefit from owning 100 per cent of the equity. However, it is a mistake to believe that the underlying value of the company's operations is increased in this way. We should not confuse the benefits to shareholders with the benefits within the entity being valued. The primary benefit to the company is the tax shield. The source of funding is largely irrelevant to the company except for the cost of funding, the terms and conditions attached to funding, and the tax merits of each funding source.

The cost of debt funding is normally embodied in loan agreements and, hence, readily ascertainable. Ordinary shareholders may have expectations regarding their future returns but there is generally no legally binding obligation on the company to provide these returns. Shareholders will hopefully receive dividends and make a gain when they dispose of their shares at a later stage. Companies are not obliged to pay dividends and even if there is pressure from shareholders to do so, the board of directors has a fiduciary duty to ensure that solvency and liquidity requirements are adhered to.

Companies have limited control over the future proceeds that shareholders will receive when they sell their shares. Businesses need to focus on generating profits and cash flows. The resultant valuation of these is a matter for current and future shareholders to determine and negotiate.

The terms of loan agreements may include security for amounts advanced, debt covenants (financial ratios and contractual terms that need to be adhered to) and a limitation on certain corporate actions without prior approval of bankers. Ordinary shareholders have the right to appoint directors, who are expected to look after their interests and those of other stakeholders. Directors are no longer required just to protect shareholders' interests – they need to be cognizant of other stakeholders' rights, such as employees, trade unions and creditors. Companies also need to be responsible corporate citizens and consider the sustainability of the environment and engage with local communities.

The leverage benefit

The leverage benefits for shareholders can be illustrated using a simple example. Shareholders, banks or a combination of both could fund operations. Let's illustrate the impact on shareholder returns of differing funding structures using two scenarios.

The assumptions of Scenario A are as follows:

- A company needs R100 million of funding at the end of Year 0 to operate.
- Shareholders subscribed for 100 per cent of the shares in issue at the end of Year 0.
- Enterprise value at the end of Year 4 will be R200 million.
- Net cash flows generated will be R10 million per annum in Years 1 to 4 (no inflation).
- All net cash flow is available to be paid out as dividends.
- There is no dividend tax.
- The income tax rate is 28 per cent.
- Shareholders sell 100 per cent of their shares at the end of Year 4 to a third party.
- Shareholders would like a return of 15 per cent on their capital.
- There is no capital gains tax (CGT).

The returns for shareholders in Scenario A are illustrated in Table 3.2.

TABLE 3.2 Returns for Scenario A shareholders

Scenario A 100% equity funded	Year 0 R000	Year 1 R000	Year 2 R000	Year 3 R000	Year 4 R000
Initial investment	-100 000				
Dividends		10 000	10 000	10 000	10 000
Sale of equity (assume)					200 000
Net cash receipts	-100 000	10 000	10 000	10 000	210 000
IRR	26,9%				
NPV @ 15%	42 900				

Should the shareholders have elected to raise R50 million of debt and only inject R50 million of their own capital, their returns would differ. Assume that the assumptions for Scenario B are the same as those for Scenario A, except for the introduction of debt on the following terms:

- The loan bears interest at 10 per cent per annum, payable annually in arrears.
- The capital portion of the loan is repayable in a single bullet repayment at the end of Year 4.
- The interest is deductible for income tax purposes.

The returns for shareholders in Scenario B are set out in Table 3.3.

TABLE 3.3 Returns for Scenario B shareholders

Scenario B 50% equity funded	**Year 0 R000**	**Year 1 R000**	**Year 2 R000**	**Year 3 R000**	**Year 4 R000**
Company cash flows					
Cash flows before interest		10 000	10 000	10 000	10 000
Interest paid		-5 000	-5 000	-5 000	-5 000
Tax shield		1 400	1 400	1 400	1 400
Net cash flows		6 400	6 400	6 400	6 400
Shareholder cash flows					
Initial investment	-50 000				
Dividends		6 400	6 400	6 400	6 400
Sale of equity (assume)					150 000*
Net cash receipts	-50 000	6 400	6 400	6 400	156 400
IRR	40,7%				
NPV @ 15%	54 035				
** 200 000 – debt*					

The IRR and NPV are superior for shareholders in Scenario B. The question is, how much of this superior return is due to the leverage effect and how much is due to the tax shield?

- The company pays out R10 million annually, whether to shareholders or to the bank.
- In Scenario B, the company has an extra R1,4 million of cash flow annually due to the tax shield.
- In Scenario B, the shareholders invest significantly less of their own money upfront, which enhances their return. This is the leverage effect.

The NPV of Scenario B is 11 135 higher than in Scenario A, attributable to:

- the value of the tax shield of R3,997 million; and
- the leverage effect, which adds R7,138 million of value.

TABLE 3.4 Differential cash flows for Scenario A and Scenario B

	Year 0	**Year 1**	**Year 2**	**Year 3**	**Year 4**
Required rate of return (shareholders)	15,0%				
Leverage benefit for shareholders	50 000	-5 000	-5 000	-5 000	-55 000
Scenario A	-100 000	10 000	10 000	10 000	210 000
Scenario B	-50 000	5 000	5 000	5 000	155 000
NPV @ 15% rate of return	7 137,5				
Tax shield benefit	0	1 400	1 400	1 400	1 400
NPV @ 15% rate of return	3 997,0				

When valuing a business, the benefit that accrues to the business from introducing debt into the capital structure is the present value of the tax shield. The leverage effect accrues to the shareholders directly from their using other people's money to invest.

The leverage effect could accrue from shareholders' introducing debt into the business invested in or from raising debt instruments themselves. For example, if the shareholder was a corporate entity it could issue redeemable preference shares to fund its investment and benefit from the leverage effect. However, it will lose the tax shield benefits within the business being valued. Assume that the shareholders in the above example elected to raise R50 million of preference share funding in their own holding company on the following terms:

+ An annual preference dividend of 7,2 per cent* (10 per cent debt rate after tax), payable annually in arrears; and
+ Preference shares are redeemable at par value at the end of Year 4.

* Note that the after tax return for the lenders is 7,2 per cent per annum (assuming an effective corporate tax rate of 28 per cent) if they advance a loan bearing interest at 10 per cent per annum. If they invest via preference shares, their return is 7,2 per cent after tax, given our simplistic assumption that there is no dividend tax. In practice, investors in preference shares may require a higher return to cater for dividend tax (currently 15 per cent in South Africa).

The IRR of the shareholders' investment is illustrated in Table 3.5.

TABLE 3.5 The IRR for shareholders

Preference share funding obtained by shareholder	**Year 0**	**Year 1**	**Year 2**	**Year 3**	**Year 4**
Preference share coupon rate	7,2%				
Initial investment	-100 000				
Preference share issue	50 000				
Dividends paid		-3 600	-3 600	-3 600	-3 600
Dividends received		10 000	10 000	10 000	10 000
Sale of equity					200 000
Redemption of preference shares					-50 000
Net cash flows to shareholders	-50 000	6 400	6 400	6 400	156 400
IRR	40,7%				

The IRR for shareholders using preference shares to fund their investment is identical to that of Scenario B – the leverage effect.

While leverage enhances returns for shareholders, it does so by introducing the potentially higher financial risk associated with having external competing claims on capital.

The WACC

The tax shield benefit of introducing debt into the capital structure of a business can be incorporated in the valuation of the business in two ways:

- Adjusting the discount rate; or
- Present-valuing the tax shield.

In practice, the most common approach is to adjust the discount rate by calculating the WACC. The WACC is the blended cost of capital after taking into account the relative weightings of equity and debt in a company's capital structure. The formula used to estimate the WACC is:

WACC = (Ce x E/EV) + (Cd x D/EV)

Where:

Cd = after tax cost of debt

Ce = Cost of equity

D = market value of debt

E = equity value of company

EV = enterprise value of company

Some guidance when determining the WACC:
- Use long-term debt rates.
- Use debt rates on an after tax basis (if the interest rate is 10 per cent, deduct the effective tax rate from this, e.g. 10% × (1 – 28%) = 7,2%
- The weighting of debt and equity relative to enterprise value should be based on market values and not book values.
- Use a sustainable ratio of debt to enterprise value.

The long-term cost of debt is far more appropriate than short-term rates. The value of a business is based on its free cash flows into perpetuity in terms of the FCFF valuation method. Hence, it makes sense to use a sustainable debt rate into the future as opposed to, say, the bank overdraft rate. Many corporates do not have access to long-term (10+ years) finance from banks in the RSA to fund operations and there are not many actively traded corporate bonds locally. Certain of our larger listed entities actively raise longer-term debt capital offshore and locally. However, the vast majority of South African companies do not share this privilege. It follows that in many instances we have to estimate the long-term cost of debt for companies on the assumption that they could raise such finance.

The weightings should be based on market values and not book values. Damodaran (2012) emphasises this point, stating that '... every textbook is categorical that the weights in the cost of capital calculation be market value weights ...'.

It is common practice to use the entity's target capital structure to determine relative weights of debt/equity to enterprise value. This is certainly more practical than estimating future weightings, as debt levels often vary from year to year depending on the business life cycle. However, often these target capital structures bear little resemblance to reality. A review of cash flow forecasts in an FCFF valuation model may reveal that the business is expected to be cash generative and repay all debt within five years. Using a target debt to EV ratio of 30 per cent into infinity in those circumstances would be inappropriate, as it would artificially raise the enterprise value of the business.

The use of a target capital structure instead of actual weightings is widespread in practice. This is even used for businesses that have no debt and have no intention or need to raise debt in the foreseeable future. The argument used is that such companies could raise debt but have not, for whichever reason. The use of a target capital structure often results in inflated valuations of businesses. Let's illustrate with an example. Assume the following for a company:

- Free cash flow of R100 million in Year 0
- Annual growth in free cash flows from Year 1 onwards of 5 per cent
- Cost of equity of 15 per cent
- After tax cost of debt of 8 per cent
- No debt in the capital structure or surplus cash at end of Year 0.

Valuing the above business on a DCF basis would result in an equity value (and enterprise value) of R1 billion [R100 million ÷ (15% – 5%)].

If a target capital structure of 30 per cent debt and 70 per cent equity were to be assumed in the above example, the enterprise value and equity value of the business would change dramatically:

WACC = (15% x 70%) + (8% x 30%)
= 12,9%

Enterprise value = [R100 million ÷ (12,9% - 5%)]
= R1,265 billion

The equity value would also be deemed to be R1,265 billion, assuming the target capital structure above of 30 per cent debt to enterprise value. There is no actual debt on the balance sheet; hence, there is nothing to deduct from enterprise value to derive equity value. This seems too good to be true – the equity value has increased from R1 billion to R1,265 billion by simply assuming a target capital structure. That's a 26,5 per cent enhancement in value by simply making an assumption!

The assumption of a target capital structure becomes even more difficult to believe when its implications are considered. A target capital structure in the above example means that:

- the capital structure will remain constant into infinity – 30 per cent debt and 70 per cent equity;
- banks will keep lending money to the business irrespective of whether it needs it to fund growth (free cash flows are growing by 5 per cent per annum, therefore enterprise value will grow annually. Assumed debt will also need to grow by 5 per cent per annum to maintain a constant debt to enterprise value ratio); and
- the business will be able to employ increasing debt productively and maintain implicit return on capital ratios.

The use of a target capital structure in DCF valuations is not recommended in practice. It will, more often than not, artificially inflate valuation results.

The WACC unfortunately, is widely misunderstood, misapplied and abused in practice. Hearing investment bankers, company directors and financial alchemists state 'introduce debt onto the balance sheet as it will lower the cost of capital and increase company and/or underlying asset value' should leave finance academics with severe heartburn. If generating value was that easy, we would all be billionaires!

An iteration

Let's assume the following for a business to be valued:

+ Free cash flows of R10 million per annum in Year 0
+ No inflation
+ Cost of equity of 15 per cent
+ Growth in free cash flows from Year 1 of 5 per cent per annum in perpetuity
+ No dividend tax
+ No cash on hand or debt at the end of Year 0.

The enterprise and equity value of the above business would be R10 million ÷ (15% - 5%) = R100 million.

Retaining the assumptions for the above business, assume further that:

+ long-term debt of R50 million is introduced at the end of Year 0
+ R50 million raised is immediately paid out to shareholders
+ the long-term debt interest rate is 10 per cent
+ the income tax rate is 28 per cent
+ there is a constant debt to enterprise value ratio in perpetuity.

It may be apparent that we do not know the debt to enterprise value ratio at the start of the valuation - the enterprise value and equity value are the results of the valuation. So, we need to guess the debt to enterprise value and, hence, the equity value to EV ratio. If we guessed the ratio to be 50 per cent, the valuation results would be as follows:

TABLE 3.6 Valuation results with an estimated debt to EV ratio of 50 per cent

R000			**Guess**	
Free cash flow Year 0 before debt	10 000		Debt to EV	50,0%
Annual growth in free cash flows	5,0%		Equity to EV	50,0%
Cost of equity	15,0%		Resultant WACC	11,10%
Cost of long-term debt (pre tax)	10,0%			
Income tax rate	28,0%			
Market value debt end of Year 0	50 000			
Actual result		*Weighting*		
Debt value	50 000	30,5%		
Equity value	113 934	69,5%		
Enterprise value	163 934*	100,0%		
* 10 000 ÷ (11,1% – 5%) = 163 934				

So, our guess was clearly incorrect - we estimated debt to EV to be 50 per cent, but it is actually 30,5 per cent at the end of the valuation. The correct answer is set out below.

TABLE 3.7 Correct valuation results

Actual result	**Weighting**		**Guess**	
Debt value	50 000	35,97%	Debt to EV	35,97%
Equity value	89 000	64,03%	Equity to EV	64,03%
Enterprise value	139 000	100,00%		
			Resultant WACC	12,194%

It is relatively simple to derive the appropriate weightings using an Excel spreadsheet. This approach of ensuring that the estimated weightings are equivalent to the actual debt to EV weightings is seldom used in practice. The main reason is that it is simpler to use a target debt to EV ratio throughout the forecast period. In reality, the weightings vary from year to year as debt levels vary. The calculation of the WACC in each year becomes a tiresome task.

The enterprise value derived following the introduction of debt into the capital structure is astounding! Without debt, EV was R100 million. This increased to R139 million following the introduction of R50 million of debt. We should be extremely sceptical of the latter result. The value of the tax shield in Year 1 is R1,4 million [R50 million × 10% × 28%]. Discounting this benefit into perpetuity using the cost of equity:

$$\text{PV of tax shield using cost of equity} = \text{R1,4 million} \div (15\% - 5\%)$$

$$= \text{R14 million}$$

The R39 million enhancement in value per our original calculations (discounting free cash flows by WACC) does not make sense, given that the NPV of the tax shield is only R14 million. We will explore a more conservative technique later in this chapter – namely, the adjusted present value (APV) method, which yields far more realistic results.

The impact of leverage on cost of equity

The introduction of debt into the capital structure introduces higher financial risk for the entity. The cost of equity should increase as a result: higher risk = higher required returns. As you recall, the only unique element of the cost of equity for individual companies is the beta coefficient. Calculated betas of listed companies should reflect this risk if there is debt in capital structures. Levered betas reflect this higher risk. Unlevered betas represent the inherent volatility of the individual share price movements relative to the market prior to the introduction of debt into the capital structure.

Hence, if you are uncomfortable with the results of betas obtained or you are valuing a private company (no betas are available because their shares are not actively traded), you should estimate betas as follows:

- Obtain the average levered betas of similar listed companies.
- Unlever these betas to determine the risk associated with selected companies before the introduction of debt into the capital structure (unlevered betas are also referred to as asset betas).
- Re-lever betas for the capital structure of the entity being valued.

A commonly used formula in practice, named after Robert Hamada (Hamada 1972), for determining the unlevered beta of a listed company is:

$$B_u = B_l \div [1 + (1 - t)(D \div E)]$$

Where

B_u = unlevered beta

B_l = levered beta

t = income tax rate

D = market value of debt

E = equity value

Let's illustrate with an example. Assume that the following listed companies are similar to the company we are attempting to value. We can calculate the unlevered betas from levered betas:

TABLE 3.8 Unlevering betas

	A Ltd	B Ltd	C Ltd
Assumptions:			
Equity value	200 000	400 000	300 000
Market value of debt	100 000	100 000	30 000
Enterprise value	300 000	500 000	330 000
Levered beta	0.680	0.649	0.482
Income tax rate	28,0%	28,0%	28,0%
Debt/Equity value	50,0%	25,0%	10,0%
Results			
Unlevered beta	0.500	0.550	0.450

The unlevered beta of A Ltd would be derived as follows:

$$B_u = B_l \div [1 + (1 - t)(D \div E)]$$

$$= 0.680 \div [1 + (1 - 28\%)(100\,000 \div 200\,000)]$$
$$= 0.680 \div [1.36]$$
$$= 0.50$$

In A, B and C Ltd, the unlevered beta is lower than the levered beta, reflecting the increase in systematic risk for each company following the introduction of debt into the capital structure.

The average unlevered beta of the three listed companies above is 0.50. Let's use that to calculate the beta of the business we are valuing, using the assumptions below. Remember, calculating the WACC is an iteration. So, let's guess the debt to EV as 50 per cent and see the result. However, we now have two iterations – guess debt to EV, calculate the resulting levered beta and then calculate the WACC.

The assumptions for a private company being valued are as follows:

- Free cash flow Year 0 of 10 000
- Annual growth in free cash flows of 5 per cent from Year 1 onwards
- Risk free rate of 8,8 per cent
- Market risk premium of 7,1 per cent
- Unlevered beta of 0.50 for similar listed companies
- Income tax rate of 28 per cent
- Market value of debt at end of Year 0 of 50 000
- Debt bears interest at 10,0 per cent per annum
- Constant debt to enterprise value in perpetuity.

TABLE 3.9 Using an unlevered beta to value a business

Assumptions:				
Free cash flow Year 0 before debt	10 000		**Guess**	
Annual growth in cash flows from Year 1	5,0%		Debt to EV	50,0%
			Equity to EV	50,0%
Risk-free rate	8,8%		Debt to equity therefore	100,0%
Market risk premium	7,1%		Resultant levered beta	0.86
Unlevered beta	0.50		Resultant cost of equity	14,91%
			Resultant WACC	11,05%
Income tax rate	28,0%			
Market value of debt end of Year 0	50 000			
Interest rate – debt	10,0%			
Actual result:				
Debt	50 000	30,3%		
Equity value	115 207	69,7%		
Enterprise value	165 207	100,00%		

Let's go through the steps inherent in the above table slowly:

1. Estimate the debt to EV (50%).
2. Calculate the resultant equity value to EV (50%).
3. Calculate the resultant debt to equity values (50% ÷ 50% = 100%).
4. Calculate the levered beta.

$$= B_u \times [1 + (1 - 28\%)(100\%)]$$
$$= 0{,}50 \times 1{,}72$$
$$= 0{,}86$$

5. Calculate the resultant cost of equity.

$$= 8{,}8\% + (0{,}86 \times 7{,}1\%)$$
$$= 14{,}906\%$$

6. Calculate the resultant WACC.

 = (50% × 14,906%) + (50% × [10% × (1 – 28%])
 = 11,053%

7. Determine the enterprise value.

 = 10 000 ÷ (11,053% – 5%)
 = 165 207

8. Derive the equity value

 = 165 207 – 50 000
 = 115 207

Our guess of debt to equity proportion was yet again incorrect in Table 3.9. We keep doing the iteration (or using the Goal Seek function in Excel) until our guess is equivalent to the actual result. Refer to Table 3.10 for the correct result.

TABLE 3.10 Using an unlevered beta to value a business

Assumptions:				
Free cash flow Year 0 before debt	10 000		**Guess**	
Annual growth in cash flows from Year 1	5,0%		Debt to EV	32,53%
			Equity to EV	67,47%
Risk-free rate	8,8%		Debt to equity therefore	48,22%
Market risk premium	7,1%		Resultant levered beta	0.674
Unlevered beta	0.50		Resultant cost of equity	13,58%
			Resultant WACC	11,51%
Income tax rate	28,0%			
Market value of debt end of Year 0	50 000			
Interest rate – debt	10,0%			
Actual result:				
Debt	50 000	32,53%		
Equity value	103 701	67,47%		
Enterprise value	153 701	100,00%		

Did you notice how the cost of equity increased from 12,35 per cent without any leverage – 8,8% + (7,1% × 0,5) – to 13,58 per cent following the levering of the beta coefficient? This is solely due to the levering adjustment to beta from 0.50 to 0.674.

The WACC in practice

The WACC is widely used in practice and often based on a target capital structure. The financial theory is intuitive and appealing, but its practical application makes it almost impossible to apply. Consider these fundamental assumptions that are required for using the WACC in practice in accordance with the theory:

- The debt to enterprise value ratio needs to be consistent year on year in perpetuity; and
- Financial institutions need to keep lending money to the business to maintain these consistent debt levels.

CRITICAL THINKING

In addition to the above factors, we also need to consider the impact of additional debt raised on the free cash flow generation of the business. It may transpire that the business can use the additional capital to generate higher free cash flows, which then impacts on the end valuation result. The iterations become endless, and you are potentially faced with recalculating the WACC for each year in the forecast period.

The next time you review a valuation that contains WACC, ask the following uncomfortable questions:

1. Which rate did you use for long-term debt?
2. If the entity does not have 10 year+ borrowings on its balance sheet, how did you estimate the long-term debt rate?
3. Are the debt levels implicit in the cash flow forecasts consistent with the target capital structure assumed in calculating the WACC? In other words, is the actual debt divided by enterprise value equivalent to the target capital structure assumption?
4. Did you perform an iteration to determine the WACC?
5. Did you use a levered or unlevered beta?
6. Where did you obtain your betas?
7. What's your favourite colour? (Lighten the moment as things will start getting tense after question 3.)

The adjusted present value (APV) approach

The APV approach is simpler and less prone to error for valuing a business with varying debt levels in the future. The method essentially discounts the free cash flows of an entity using the cost of equity and then adds the present value of the tax shield. When estimating the value of the tax shield, it is preferable to use the cost of equity to discount these future benefits. Using the cost of debt in the PV calculation may result in an overstatement of the value of the tax shield – increasing the free cash flows by the tax shield and lowering the discount rate for the introduction of debt amounts could result in double-counting the benefit.

Let's illustrate this with some examples.

EXAMPLE 3.1

TABLE 3.11 B Ltd – equity value before introduction of debt

Free cash flow Year 0 before debt	20 000	Enterprise value	200 000
Annual growth in free cash flows	5,0%	Equity value	200 000
Risk-free rate	8,0%		
Market risk premium	7,0%		
Beta (unlevered)	1.00		
Cost of equity	15,0%		
Cost of long-term debt (pre-tax)	10,0%		
Income tax rate	28,0%		
Market value debt end of Year 0	0		

Enterprise value above is calculated as R20 000 ÷ (15% – 5%). Since there is no debt or cash on hand, enterprise value = equity value.

Now let's assume that B Ltd introduces R100 000 of debt at the end of Year 0 and the debt to enterprise value ratio is constant in perpetuity. Furthermore, let's assume that B Ltd can pay out the R100 000 raised to its shareholders as a capital distribution or dividend and still obtain a tax deduction on interest paid going forward:

TABLE 3.12 B Ltd – equity value after introduction of debt

Value enterprise then add present value of tax shield			
Free cash flow Year 0 before debt	20 000	**Enterprise value**	200 000
Annual growth in free cash flows	5,0%	Value of tax shield	28 000
		Less debt	-100 000
Risk-free rate	8,0%	**Equity value**	128 000
Market risk premium	7,0%		
Beta (unlevered)	1.00		
Cost of equity	15,0%		
Cost of long-term debt (pre-tax)	10,0%		
Income tax rate	28,0%		
Market value debt end of Year 0	100 000		

The calculations are as follows:

$$\text{Enterprise value} = 20\ 000 \div (15\% - 5\%) = 200\ 000$$

$$\text{Value of tax shield} = (100\ 000 \times 10\% \times 28\%) \div (15\% - 5\%)$$

According to the above calculations, the enterprise value of B Ltd, before allocating this value to shareholders and lenders, has increased from 200 000 to 228 000 (200 000 plus tax shield of 28 000), a 14 per cent uplift in value.

We could estimate the equity value using the Hamada formula. Here, we would calculate the levered beta and WACC, then present-value to the forecast free cash flow. Remember, this is an iteration. The solution is as follows:

TABLE 3.13 B Ltd – equity value after introduction of debt

Value enterprise at WACC			
Free cash flow Year 0 before debt	20 000	**Guess**	
Annual growth in free cash flows	5,0%	Debt	43,937%
		Equity	56,063%
Risk-free rate	8,0%		
Market risk premium	7,0%	Levered beta	1.564
Beta (unlevered)	1.00	WACC	13,79%
Cost of equity	15,0%	**Enterprise value**	227 600
Cost of long-term debt (pre-tax)	10,0%	Less debt	-100 000
Income tax rate	28,0%	**Equity value**	127 600
Market value debt end of Year 0	100 000		

The results obtained using the Hamada formula and the APV method are very similar, which is reassuring: they should be! The APV method present-values the increased cash flows to the business associated with the tax shield.

Calculating enterprise value using the WACC and adjusting for the higher financial risk per the Hamada method lowers the discount rate (WACC of 13,79% versus the cost of equity of 15%) and ignores the PV of the tax shield.

Fernandez (2002) lists various methods of calculating the present value of the tax shield. While these provide interesting topics for debates and mathematical gyrations, practitioners are advised to keep it simple. Use the cost of equity to present-value the tax shield – it suffices and allows you to PV varying interest payments over the forecast period. Using the WACC where debt levels are not constant in the future is impractical.

FCFE = FCFF?

In Chapter 2, we mentioned the FCFF and FCFE methods. In this chapter, we have adopted the preferred FCFF method. However, let's check if the results would be the same if we used the FCFE method for B Ltd.

TABLE 3.14 B Ltd – free cash flow to equity method

Free cash flow Year 0 before debt	20 000
Interest paid	-10 000
Tax effect	2 800
Free cash to equity	12 800
PV of free cash flow to equity in perpetuity	128 000*
**12 800 ÷ (15% – 5%)*	

The result is identical to that obtained through the APV method. However, using the FCFE method in practice is not recommended. The debt levels may vary from year to year, which could affect the outcome significantly. The simple Example 1 assumes constant debt to EV levels into the future, with no repayment of capital ever. This is clearly unrealistic.

The only difference between the APV and FCFE methods relates to the discounting of interest and debt capital repayments – the free cash flows are otherwise identical. To recap, the free cash flows to equity represent the free cash flows of the enterprise/firm (assuming no surplus cash but debt in the capital structure):

+ less debt capital repayments;
+ plus debt raised; and
+ less interest (after tax) payments.

EXAMPLE 3.2

Let's assume for C Ltd:

+ Cost of equity of 15,0 per cent
+ Debt balance of R500 000 at the end of Year 0
+ Debt bears interest at 10,0 per cent per annum, payable annually in arrears
+ Capital repayable in a single bullet repayment after five years
+ Income tax rate of 28,0 per cent.

TABLE 3.15 The APV and FCFE methods for C Ltd

C Ltd	**Year 0**	**Year 1**	**Year 2**	**Year 3**	**Year 4**	**Year 5**
Per APV method						
Debt	-500 000					
Tax shield		14 000	14 000	14 000	14 000	14 000
	-500 000	14 000	14 000	14 000	14 000	14 000
NPV @ 15,0%	-453 070					
Per FCFE method						
Capital repayment						-500 000
Interest paid		-50 000	-50 000	-50 000	-50 000	-50 000
Tax effect		14 000	14 000	14 000	14 000	14 000
Free cash flow impact	0	-36 000	-36 000	-36 000	-36 000	-536 000
NPV @ 15,0%	-369 266					

Both methods incorporate the present value of the tax shield. The distinguishing feature is the present value of interest and capital repayments relating to the debt. Present-valuing these per the FCFE method at 15 per cent equates to R416 196 (present-valuing the capital and interest payments before the tax implications of these) whereas the actual liability at the end of Year 0 is R500 000. This is due to interest and capital repayments being discounted at 15 per cent, whereas the inherent yield of the debt is 10 per cent. It strongly recommended, therefore, that the APV method rather than the FCFE method be used in practice.

Optimal capital structure

There is much debate in academic literature and in practice regarding the optimal capital structure of a firm. We know that introducing debt into the capital structure has benefits (the NPV of the tax shield). However, what is the 'cost' of the increased financial risk? The Hamada formula attempts to adjust the beta for the increased risk associated with higher gearing. Let's use that formula and evaluate the benefits versus potential higher return required by shareholders at varying debt levels.

Before we analyse a hypothetical example, it is important to note that in practice, debt interest rates increase as gearing levels of the firm increase. Credit rating agencies have formulas to assess the risk of default. They classify entities from AAA (lowest risk) to D (highest risk). In our example, we will estimate the interest rate charged at varying debt levels rather than apply rigorous credit analyses.

Let's use an example to illustrate the potential optimal mix of debt and equity in a capital structure.

EXAMPLE 3.3

Assume for D Limited:

- EBIT in Year 0 of R12 000
- Free cash flow Year 0 before debt of R10 000
- Annual growth in free cash flow from Year 1 onwards of 5 per cent
- Risk-free rate of 8,0 per cent
- Market risk premium of 7,0 per cent
- Unlevered beta for D Ltd of 1.0
- Income tax rate of 28,0 per cent
- Long-term borrowing rate of 9,25 per cent for D Ltd before the introduction of leverage.

As mentioned above, the interest rates on long-term borrowings have been estimated based on the degree of leverage in D Ltd for illustrative purposes. Levered betas have been calculated using the Hamada formula. There are three iterations in each debt level below. So, if you attempt this personally, be aware of the complexity.

TABLE 3.16 Debt/enterprise ratio, D Ltd

Debt/enterprise ratio (market values)	0%	10%	20%	30%	40%	50%
Cost of debt	9,25%	9,50%	11,00%	12,50%	14,50%	16,00%
Levered beta	1.00	1.08	1.18	1.31	1.48	1.72
Cost of equity	15,00%	15,56%	16,26%	17,16%	18,36%	20,04%
WACC	15,00%	14,69%	14,59%	14,71%	15,19%	15,78%
Interest cover	NA	10.6	5.2	3.5	2.8	2.4
Debt to equity (market values)	NA	11,1%	25,0%	42,9%	66,7%	100,0%
Market value of debt*	0	10 322	20 851	30 890	39 247	46 382
Equity value	100 000	92 898	83 403	72 076	58 870	46 382
Enterprise value	100 000	103 220	104 254	102 966	98 117	92 764

It is interesting to note that the enterprise value of D Ltd peaks at a 20 per cent debt to EV level (not to be confused with debt equity or debt to shareholder funds). Thereafter, enterprise value steadily declines. This is depicted in Figure 3.1.

FIGURE 3.1 Enterprise value versus leverage

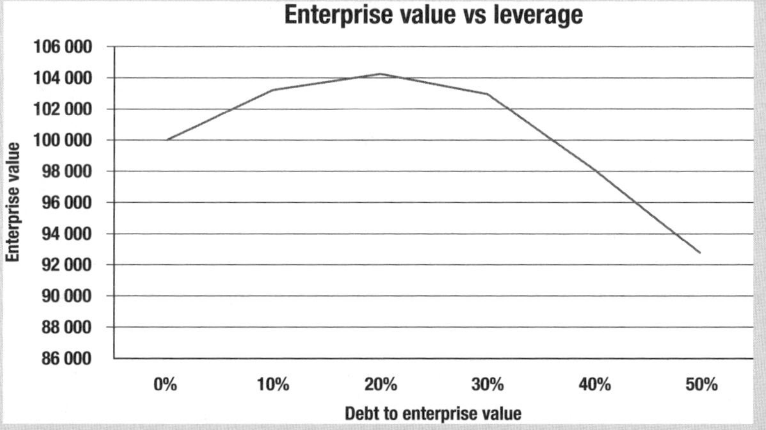

Figure 3.1 illustrates that determining the optimal capital structure is a theoretical debate. The enterprise value of D Ltd peaks at just under R105 000 at a 20 per cent debt to enterprise value (25 per cent debt to equity) from a base of R100 000. That's not a massive enhancement in value. In practice, the ability to raise debt will be more constrained by:

- banks and investors' appetite to advance loans to D Ltd;
- D Ltd's ability to deploy debt funding raised in projects/acquisitions/organic growth at a rate higher than the cost of capital; and
- management's assessment of risk.

Certain businesses can easily be geared. For example, utility companies such as Eskom should have reasonable forecasts of future electricity demand and be able to reassure investors of their ability to service debt. Other businesses, such as construction companies, should be more risk averse with regards to raising debt given the cyclicality in their industry and the cash flow investment required for new projects.

Common errors in DCF valuations in practice

You will have gathered that valuations are not an exact science and that they contain numerous areas in which you could unwittingly make errors. Forgive the repetition, but the objective of any valuation should be to minimise error.

Fernandez (2002) lists the most common errors in discounted cash flow valuations:

- Procedural/method errors
  - Calculating the WACC using book values instead of market values
  - Using a constant WACC when borrowing levels vary
  - Calculating the market risk premium and beta using historical data
  - Disparity between discount rates and expected inflation
  - Confusing the WACC and cost of equity

- Data errors
  - Illogical assumptions regarding future sales growth, margins and costs
  - Hypotheses on future profits contradicting the competitive analysis
  - Incorrect calculation of continuing value.

DID YOU KNOW?

The risk-free rate, market risk premium and beta are future predictions per the financial theory. Historical data is obtained and reviewed to assist us forecasting the CAPM inputs. Hence, the inputs are subject to much conjecture. Keep it simple and use estimates that make sense – simply ask whether you as an investor would be prepared to accept the rate of return implied by the resultant cost of equity. For example, would you be prepared to accept a required rate of return of 10 per cent in a South African context for investing in the construction industry?

In the author's opinion and practical experience, the most significant errors in FCF valuations are as follows:

- Growth in free cash flows in perpetuity beyond the initial forecast period is too high. Continuing value generally represents the largest part of enterprise value, and hence the growth rate in perpetuity is the first assumption that should be reviewed;
- Calculating the WACC based on the target capital structure when the cash flow forecasts, for example, indicate that the entity will be cash positive in five years' time;
- Calculating the WACC based on the book values of debt, equity and enterprise value;
- Overly ambitious cash flow forecasts; and
- Using inappropriate risk-free rates, market risk premiums and betas in the calculation of the cost of equity.

To illustrate this, let's consider a simple DCF valuation. We have dealt with the potential errors in the WACC, so the example is based on a business that is entirely equity funded:

- Risk-free rate of 8,0 per cent
- Market risk premium of 7,0 per cent
- Beta of 1.0
- Free cash flow in Year 0 of R10 000
- Growth in free cash flows in perpetuity of 5,0 per cent.

The enterprise and equity value of the above business is R100 000, calculated as follows:

$$10{,}000 \div ([8{,}0\% + (7{,}0\% \times 1.0)] - 5{,}0\%)$$

$$= 100\ 000$$

Figure 3.2 illustrates the impact of erroneous assumptions made on enterprise value, assuming that the initial assumptions were correct.

FIGURE 3.2 The impact of erroneous assumptions on enterprise value

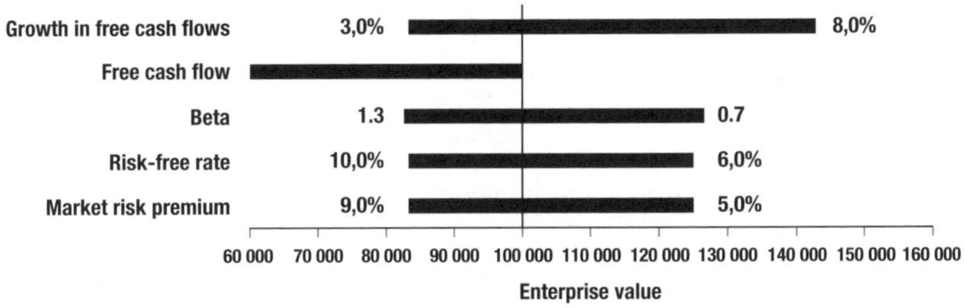

Conclusion

The introduction of debt into the capital structure of a firm enhances shareholder value, provided it is within reasonable levels of gearing for firms. However, the true source of this value enhancement is often misunderstood, miscalculated and grossly exaggerated. The firm and shareholders benefit due to the tax shield (deductibility of interest for income tax purposes). In addition, shareholders may benefit from the leverage effect (investing less of their own money by using external sources of finance such as debt). The tax shield impact can be incorporated into FCF valuations. The leverage effect cannot, since it occurs outside of the entity.

In this chapter, we introduced the concept of the WACC and the APV method of incorporating the tax benefits of debt into FCF valuations. The WACC is complicated to calculate and use if debt levels are anticipated to vary in the future. The APV method should be preferred as it is less likely to result in a valuation error and is relatively simple to apply in practice.

Questions

1. The key benefit of having debt on the balance sheet of a company is:
   - A. That it lowers WACC
   - B. The tax deductibility of interest paid
   - C. Is the leverage effect for the company.

2. Having debt on the balance sheet of a company is beneficial to its shareholders because of:
   A. The lower rate of return required by financiers than shareholders; or
   B. The leverage effect of not investing their own money to fund the entire operations of the company; or
   C. The limited dividend tax payable.
3. The calculation of the WACC is based on:
   A. The optimal capital structure; or
   B. Target debt to enterprise values; or
   C. The market values of debt and equity
4. The cost of debt for the purposes of calculating WACC is:
   A. The after tax cost of long-term debt that the entity could raise
   B. The current short-term borrowing rates of the firm
   C. Irrelevant.
5. Calculating the WACC involves:
   A. Weighting the market value of debt and the estimated equity value of the firm
   B. An iteration as the end valuation result is not known at the start
   C. Building complicated option pricing models.
6. The levered beta of a firm is:
   A. The beta coefficient of the firm assuming it is ungeared
   B. Also referred to as the asset beta
   C. The estimated future movements in the firm's share price, assuming it has debt on its balance sheet, as compared to the overall stock market
7. The target capital structure of an entity assumes:
   A. That interest will always be deductible for tax purposes
   B. A constant relationship between debt, equity and enterprise values
   C. That betas should be unlevered for valuation purposes.
8. The APV method:
   A. Discounts future free cash flows of the firm using the cost of equity and present-values the tax shield separately
   B. Discounts the expected dividends that shareholders may receive in the future
   C. Involves discounting forecast free cash flows by the WACC
9. The optimal capital structure of a firm is:
   A. That level of debt and equity funding for the firm that maximises enterprise value
   B. An estimate of the likely debt facilities that a firm can raise from its bankers
   C. A matter for the board of directors to debate
10. A common error in valuations in practice is to:
   A. Use the incorrect PV factors for discounting future cash flows
   B. Use the APV method to estimate the leverage effect for shareholders
   C. Use unrealistic growth rates to determine continuing value

References

Damodaran, A. (2012). *Investment valuation: Tools and techniques for determining the value of any asset.* New Jersey: John Wiley & Sons, Inc.

Hamada, R.S. (1972). The effect of the firm's capital structure on the systematic risk of common stocks. *The Journal of Finance* 27(2): 435–452.

Fernandez, P. (2002). *Valuation methods and shareholder value creation.* USA: Academic Press.

CHAPTER 4

Earnings-based valuations

LEARNING OUTCOMES

Once you have worked through this chapter, you should be able to:

+ Understand the merits and pitfalls of using the earnings-based method to value a listed company
+ Calculate EBIT, EBITA and EBITDA multiples
+ Know never to use a PE multiple in practice
+ Recognise the adjustments that may be required to determine sustainable earnings
+ Identify items that are better treated as assets or liabilities than as adjustments to earnings

Introduction

Earnings-based multiples are widely used in practice to value listed and private companies. This is perhaps due to their relative simplicity of calculation and the investing public's obsession with accounting earnings. The most common earnings-based multiples are summarised below:

PE multiple	equity value ÷ profit after tax
EBITDA multiple	enterprise value ÷ EBITDA
EBITA multiple	enterprise value ÷ earnings before interest, taxation and amortisation (EBITA)
EBIT multiple	enterprise value ÷ EBIT

Earnings-based multiples are obtained from stock market data and from recently concluded transactions. In a South African context, there is currently no database of earnings multiples of private-company merger and acquisition (M&A) transactions. Hence, earnings multiples are largely obtained from stock market transactions.

The earnings-based valuation method is arguably not a method but the results of stock market and recent M&A transactions. Earnings multiples represent the value at which willing buyers and sellers have transacted. There is no underlying financial theory supporting why a particular company should trade at, say, a 15 PE multiple versus a 12 multiple. Rather, it represents the collective consciousness of the stock market over a period of time. Stock markets can be overly exuberant at times, as alluded to in prior chapters. However, in the long run, their pricing of listed shares displays interesting insights and trends.

Earnings-based multiples may seem simplistic. It would appear that we need only obtain reliable data regarding long-term PE multiples and apply these to sustainable profit after tax to derive a reasonable valuation result. Unfortunately, in practice, this is easier said than done. PE multiples vary over time; we need to be discerning in identifying the 'outliers' and find a reasonable trend over a number of years. Accounting profits have become very complicated with a myriad of international financial reporting standards (IFRS), some of which seem to be illogical. Later in this chapter we will deal with particular challenges of adjusting reported profits for items that may be non-recurring or that distort annual profits.

A deficiency in the earnings-based method is that it largely ignores the working capital and infrastructure investment required to sustain or grow earnings. These do not materially impact on earnings in the short term except through higher finance charges and depreciation. The earnings-based method, however, provides invaluable insights into business valuations and should always be used in conjunction with DCF valuations.

Empirical evidence

The average PE multiples of the S&P 500 index (reflecting the largest 500 listed companies by market capitalisation on the New York and NASDAQ stock exchanges in the USA per Standard & Poor's) over the period 1960 to 2013 (Damodaran 2014) are set out in Figure 4.1.

FIGURE 4.1 S&P 500 average PE multiple

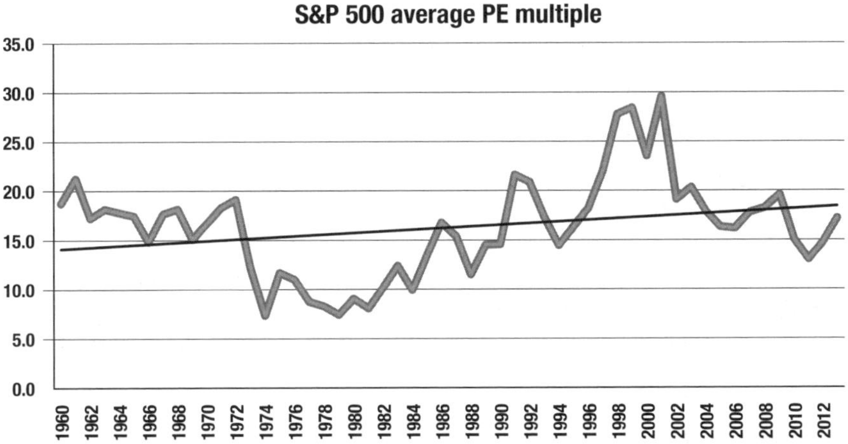

The average PE multiple over this 54-year period was 16,3. The average S&P 500 average PE multiple in 1973 and 1974 was significantly below the long-term average. The major global stock markets at the time, particularly the London Stock Exchange, perhaps overreacted to the poor prevailing economic conditions. The oil crisis, rising inflation and mining strikes in the UK provided a perfect backdrop for a sharp and sudden bear market. With hindsight, it is clear that the S&P 500 was undervalued at the time, but it takes immense bravery to invest while others are running for the hills. Apparently, a favourite joke at the time was:

> *What do you call a stockbroker?*
>
> *'Waiter.'*

The underlying causes of bear and bull markets on stock exchanges are subjects of much research and debate. There are usually some underlying economic causes for market corrections, although the reasons for sustained bull markets are difficult to fathom. Economists such as Robert Shiller simply attribute them to 'irrational exuberance'.

An important lesson, though, is to study and analyse overall stock market PE multiples relative to long-term averages. When the average PE multiple is significantly higher than the long-term average, it may be worth being overly cautious.

The JSE kindly supplied data on the JSE ALSI and Industrial Index (INDI) average PE multiples, albeit over a shorter period than the S&P 500 in Figure 4.1.

FIGURE 4.2 The JSE ALSI average PE multiple

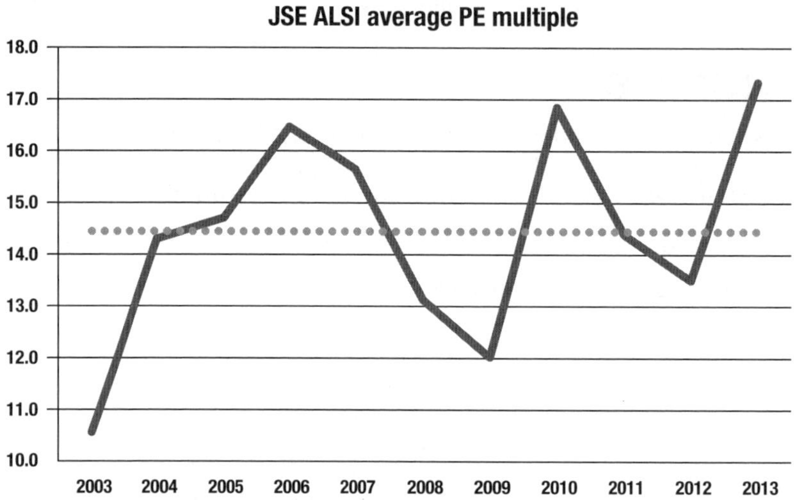

The average PE multiple over the 11-year period ended 2013 was 14.4. The market correction in late 2008 and during 2009 is well depicted in Figure 4.2. The rebound was swift in 2010. It is interesting to note that the average PE in 2003 was significantly lower than the historical average.

FIGURE 4.3 JSE INDI average PE multiple

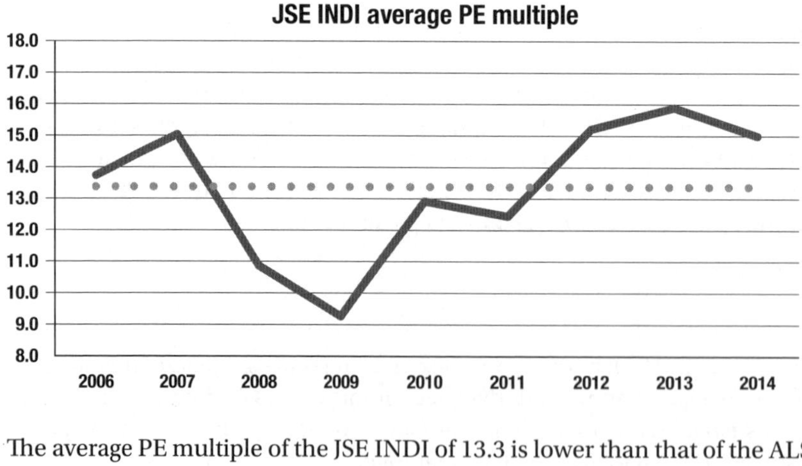

The average PE multiple of the JSE INDI of 13.3 is lower than that of the ALSI and generally seems less volatile.

PE versus EBITDA, EBITA and EBIT multiples

PE multiples should not be used in practice as they ignore the capital structure of the business being valued and inherently misprice surplus cash and debt in the business. The best way to illustrate this is through an example of a valuation of a private company.

EXAMPLE 4.1

Let's assume the following for XYZ (Pty) Ltd:

- Sustainable EBIT of R50 million per annum
- Current surplus cash on the balance sheet of R100 million, bearing interest at 5 per cent per annum
- Income tax rate of 28 per cent
- Appropriate PE multiple of 7.0 based on recent sale transactions of similar private companies (businesses similar in nature and size, except that the other private companies had no debt or surplus cash).

The typical attempt at valuing XYZ (Pty) Ltd may take the following form:

Typical approach	R000s
EBIT	50 000
Interest income	5 000
Profit before tax	55 000
Taxation	–15 400
Profit after taxation	39 600
Appropriate PE multiple	7.0
Resultant valuation of 100% of equity interest	277 200

Valuing 100 per cent of the ordinary shares in issue of XYZ (Pty) Ltd at R277,2 million would be a significant error. We should rather value the business excluding surplus cash and then add this to the valuation result. The recommended approach to valuing XYZ (Pty) Ltd is as follows:

Recommended approach	R000s
EBIT	50 000
Interest income	–
Profit before tax	50 000
Taxation	–14 000
Profit after taxation	36 000
Appropriate PE multiple	7.0
Valuation of 100% of the business excluding surplus cash	252 000
Add surplus cash	100 000
Resultant valuation of 100% of equity interests	352 000

The valuation difference is significant – selling shareholders receive 27 per cent or R74,8 million more should they value surplus cash separately.

The difference relates to the valuation of cash:

Differences	R000s
Interest income	5 000
Related taxation	–1 400
After-tax interest earnings	3 600
Valuation of interest income using a PE of 7.0	25 200
Actual value of surplus cash	100 000
Difference	74 800

The implicit after-tax yield of cash per the above example is 3,6 per cent – or, expressed differently, a PE multiple of 27.8 (the inverse of 3,6 per cent). Obviously, valuing actual surplus cash using a 7.0 PE multiple is a gross undervaluation. This mistake is made countless times daily on stock markets, which still refer more often to PE multiples than to other more technically accurate multiples such as EBIT, EBITA and EBITDA multiples.

Suppose XYZ (Pty) Ltd had R100 million of debt (bearing interest at 10 per cent per annum) instead of surplus cash in Example 1:

Differences	R000s
Finance charges	–10 000
Related taxation	2 800
After-tax finance charges	–7 200
Valuation of finance charges using a 7 PE	–50 400
Actual market value of debt	–100 000
Difference	49 600

The error is significant yet again – in the opposite direction, however. Valuing debt using a PE multiple is likely to result in a gross undervaluation of the liability – favourable to the selling shareholders, but an unfortunate error for the acquirer.

Hence, it is strongly recommended that you never use PE multiples in practice to avoid these errors. Rather use an EBIT, EBITA or EBITDA multiple.

Adjustments to accounting earnings

Financial reporting has become incredibly complex since the mid 1990s. The increasing number and complexity of IFRS statements requires valuation experts to be proficient from an accounting perspective or to have ready access to IFRS experts. Here, we cover the major accounting adjustments that require a closer examination and that may impact on the determination of sustainable earnings.

When valuing a particular business, it is highly recommended that you:

- review at least five years of the business's annual financial statements, or annual reports if it is a listed entity;
- perform a detailed analysis of historical financial ratios; and
- benchmark the business's performance against competitors, if this is possible.

Adjustments to historical profits may be required for:

- non-recurring items;
- accounting entries that have little or no impact on future profits; and
- items that may be best regarded as assets and liabilities rather than as annual adjustments to profits.

Identifying these items requires a detailed read-through of financial statements – not just the statements of financial position (balance sheet), comprehensive income (income statement) and cash flows, but the accompanying notes as well. Annual reports of listed companies often include very useful information in other sections such as the CEO's report and segmental/divisional financial analysis.

Non-recurring items could include:

- profit or loss on sale of assets;
- retrenchment costs;
- Competition Commission fines; and
- claims arising from litigation (damages awards or fines levied).

Accounting entries that could have little or no impact on the sustainable profits of a business for valuation purposes include:

- impairment of tangible and intangible assets (a more detailed discussion of these items follows later in this chapter); and
- revaluation of biological assets.

For example, forestry and forestry products companies generally have their own plantations, which they harvest periodically to produce wood products. These plantation assets are required to be revalued annually and have any fair value adjustments processed through the statement of comprehensive income. These fair value adjustments to biological assets should be ignored for the purposes of determining sustainable EBIT. The main business of forestry product companies is to invest in plantations and, subsequently, to harvest these to produce wood products. To recognise income from revaluing plantations that may only be harvested in five or 10 years' time makes little logical sense from a valuation perspective. If we valued this business using a DCF approach, these annual revaluations would be ignored since they are non-cash-flow items. Similarly, the annual sustainable profits from harvesting and producing wood products are the primary source of income, not the potential future value of planted trees.

Items that may be more appropriately regarded as assets and liabilities than as annual adjustments to profits include:

- income from associate companies;
- retirement funding obligations;
- revaluation of investment property; and
- fair value adjustments to financial instruments.

Associate companies are defined as investments in which the investor has significant influence but does not control. Equity interests of between 20 and 49 per cent are generally regarded as associate companies, provided the investor does not have the ability to control the voting rights in the entity.

The investor's annual share of the associate company's profits are recorded in the statement of comprehensive income. The valuation of the associate company for the purposes of the investor could be recorded in one of two ways:

- Include the investor's share of associate company profits in the company's sustainable earnings and multiply this by the investor's PE multiple; or
- Exclude the income from the associate company and value the investor's stake in this business separately.

The latter approach is recommended as the nature of the investor and associate company's business may be dissimilar and, therefore, have different earnings multiples. Also, a minority discount adjustment may be required to the value of the associate company (refer to Chapter 7 for more discussion about such discounts). Such a minority discount cannot be readily applied if income from associate companies is included in the sustainable profits of the investor.

Valuing the investment in an associate company separately is particularly relevant where the investment in the associate company is material to the overall valuation result. For example, Naspers' 33,8 per cent interest in 2015 in Tencent, a Chinese instant messaging and social networking business, represents a significant portion of its total market capitalisation. Tencent should rather be valued separately and Naspers' share thereof (after an appropriate minority discount) added to the value of Naspers' core business. Some may argue that Tencent is it's core business – however, Naspers does not have control over this venture and is subject to different business risks to its pay television and print businesses.

Investment properties may be carried at cost or revalued annually. Investment properties are, by definition, unrelated to a company's core business. Here, again, it is recommended that any fair value adjustments to investment properties be excluded in the determination of sustainable profit. The fair value of such investment property should rather be added to the company's enterprise value at the end of the valuation process.

Impairment of assets

The annual impairment testing of tangible and intangible assets absorbs significant time on the part of finance teams and auditors in practice. This is required for financial reporting purposes and any impairment provisions or reversals are processed through the statement of comprehensive income. From a valuation perspective, these exercises are irrelevant. The purpose of valuing a business is to determine the indicative fair value of the entity and not individual assets and liabilities.

Impairment provisions can be useful to executives. They provide the opportunity to decrease the value of goodwill, other intangible assets, and property, plant and equipment in tough times. When economic and trading conditions improve, certain financial ratios may appear to be better than reality. For example, ROE and ROIC ratios would certainly be lower than if assets had not been impaired.

It is recommended that impairments provisions and reversals be added back when determining sustainable EBIT. These items are non-recurring and are also unrelated to the business's profit generation.

Share-based payments

Accounting rules dictate that the expected value of share options in the hands of employees be amortised through the statement of comprehensive income. This intention is noble as it provides some indication of the 'cost' of retaining and incentivising employees. The accounting for share-based payments, however, is too uncertain to be useful for valuation purposes.

In a South African context, employee share incentive schemes tend to comprise share options. Employees are granted the right to acquire shares at a predetermined strike price in, say, three years' time. During the period between the option grant date and the vesting thereof (in which employees can exercise their rights if they elect to), there are usually other terms and conditions attached to being able to benefit from any uplift in the share price – for example:

- Employees need to be have been employed at the company throughout the period; and
- Employees may need to meet certain criteria in terms of workplace performance.

Put simplistically, the 'cost' to be amortised by the company is the difference between the expected future value per share at vesting date and the strike price. Future value is usually estimated using an option-pricing model (refer to Chapter 11 for further details about valuing options).

EXAMPLE 4.2

Let's illustrate this with an example.

Number of options granted to employees	1 000 000
Strike price	R10,00
Vesting period	3 years
Expected fair value per share at end of Year 3*	R16,00
Total share-based payment expense	R6 000 000
Amortisation in each of Year 1, 2 and 3	R2 000 000

* This is the estimated present value per share at the start of Year 1, including any dividends receivable over the three-year period.

The major difficulties of including share-based payment expenses in sustainable EBIT are as follows:

- The estimate of the fair value of the option is performed upon grant of the option. Subsequent changes in market conditions, such as share price movements, may materially affect the value of the option. These changes do not affect the amortisation amount as the entity is generally not allowed to change its estimate of the fair value of the option. Hence, the accounting charge may be materially different from the economic reality.
- Certain schemes have no cash flow impact on the entity – employees can elect to purchase shares from a share trust and sell these into the market.

The accounting for share-based payments is complicated. The terms and conditions of each scheme need to be analysed in detail and the economic impact on the entity ascertained. Factors that could affect the accounting treatment and expense from a valuation perspective include whether:

- options are cash or equity settled (the entity issues shares to settle the difference between the ruling share price and the strike price);
- options vest if there is a change in control of the entity;
- the employee has a choice about settlement (cash or equity) of the option arrangement;
- the entity provides loans to employees to acquire shares; and
- there are modifications to the terms and conditions of the share option scheme.

Given the complexity surrounding share-based payments and the risk that annual amortisation charges may not reflect economic reality, it is recommended that share-based payment expenses be reversed out of EBIT for valuation purposes. Rather estimate the liability associated with share option schemes at the valuation date and deduct this from enterprise value.

Share-based payments could be a material expense for businesses. Employees working at technology companies such as Google and Apple tend to receive a significant portion of their remuneration from option-type schemes. These companies use restricted stock units to incentivise and compensate employees. Employees receive a number of shares with no strike price, and are entitled to sell these after the vesting period, provided service conditions (e.g. that they were employed during the vesting period) and performance criteria (workplace performance) are met. This is an interesting variation on option-type schemes – should the share price decline, employees still benefit. In option-type schemes, these would be 'out of the money'.

Other suggestions: Sustainable EBIT

Accounting earnings are affected by estimates. Provisions for inventory obsolescence, bad debts, rebates due to suppliers and contingent claims are all subject to judgement and forecast. Annual charges through the statement of comprehensive income could vary materially. These changes can occasionally be detected through ratio analysis. It is worth devoting time and effort to identifying any unusual trends.

When a group has foreign subsidiaries that are material to the group's financial results, it is recommended that you value these entities in their functional currency then add the valuation result at the end of the valuation process. This approach is preferable to including annual translation differences in sustainable EBIT.

CASE STUDY **Let's analyse Shoprite**

Shoprite Holdings Ltd (Shoprite) is a leading food retailer in South Africa, one that has been expanding on the African continent over the decade 2005–2015. The company is listed on the JSE. Table 4.1 summarises selected financial information about Shoprite over the period 2010 to 2014.

TABLE 4.1 Shoprite financial information, 2010 to 2014

Shoprite June year-end	2010 Rm	2011 Rm	2012 Rm	2013 Rm	2014 Rm
Revenue	67 402	72 298	82 731	92 457	102 204
Cost of sales	–54 148	–57 624	–65 753	–73 156	–80 936
Gross profit	13 254	14 674	16 978	19 301	21 268
Other income	1 576	1 856	2 325	2 607	2 840
Operating expenses	–10 502	–11 609	–13 548	–15 180	–16 869

Continued

EBITDA	4 328	4 921	5 755	6 728	7 239
Depreciation and amortisations	–839	–934	–1 090	–1 336	–1 525
EBIT	3 489	3 987	4 665	5 392	5 714

Source: Shoprite annual reports

Exchange rate losses and items of a capital nature (impairments, profit/losses on sale of assets, etc.) have been excluded from the EBIT in Table 4.1.

A closer examination of the EBIT reveals that share-based payments were significant in financial years (FY) 2010, 2011 and 2012. In subsequent periods, these have declined to immaterial levels. Shoprite has a share option scheme in place and gains made by executives and employees are cash-settled – a group company pays the difference between the ruling share price on exercise and the strike price to scheme beneficiaries. The number of outstanding options at year-end and the average strike price is summarised in Table 4.2.

TABLE 4.2 Outstanding options and average strike price

Shoprite June year-end	**2010**	**2011**	**2012**	**2013**	**2014**
Number of shares entitled to be acquired by beneficiaries	13,40m	9,44m	5,21m	1,22m	1,04m
Average strike price	R6,22	R6,50	R28,02	R14,59	R8,73
Year-end share price (Bloomberg)	R83,40	R101,80	R150,67	R185,50	R154,00
Share-based payments expense* for the year	R278m	R257m	R276m	R79m	–R25m
Potential liability at year-end	R1 034m	R900m	R639m	R208m	R151m
* *Per income statement*					

Source: Shoprite annual reports

The average strike price per share was low in FY2010 and FY2011 compared to the ruling share price at year-end. This implies that share options were granted some time back and have not yet been exercised and/or the Shoprite share price has risen dramatically since the option grant dates. The low average strike price per share in FY2013 and FY2014 is attributable to unexercised options historically granted to a non-executive director (CH Wiese) of Shoprite, totalling one million shares at a strike price of R6,50.

The debate is whether we should reverse the share-based payments expenses in analysing historical EBIT and rather deduct the potential liability at the end of the valuation result. Given the volatility in share-based payment expenses, the latter is the preferred approach.

TABLE 4.3 Shoprite's gross profit and EBIT/revenue margins

Shoprite June year-end	**2010 Rm**	**2011 Rm**	**2012 Rm**	**2013 Rm**	**2014 Rm**
Reported EBIT	3 489	3 987	4 665	5 392	5 714
Share-based payments	278	257	276	79	–25
Adjusted EBIT	3 767	4 244	4 692	5 471	5 689

Continued

Revenue growth		7,3%	14,4%	11,8%	10,5%
Gross profit margin	19,7%	20,3%	20,5%	20,9%	20,8%
EBIT growth		12,7%	10,6%	16,6%	4,0%
EBIT/revenue	5,6%	5,9%	5,7%	5,9%	5,6%

Source: Shoprite annual reports

Shoprite's gross profit and EBIT/revenue margins were relatively stable over the period FY2010 to FY2014. The compound annual growth in revenue and adjusted EBIT remained identical at 10,9 per cent over the five-year period.

Let's analyse Shoprite's stock market rating.

TABLE 4.4 Shoprite's stock market rating

Shoprite June year-end	**2010 Rm**	**2011 Rm**	**2012 Rm**	**2013 Rm**	**2014 Rm**
Market capitalisation°	45 326	55 326	85 969	105 842	88 222
Cash and cash equivalents*	–2 219	–1 962	–7 939	–6 122	–8 161
Borrowings*	915	2 092	4 035	4 152	4 684
Enterprise value	44 022	55 456	82 065	103 872	84 745
EBIT multiples					
Historic	11.7	13.1	17.5	19.0	14.9
Forward	10.4	11.8	15.0	18.3	
° *Total number of ordinary shares × year end share price*					
* *Per statements of financial position*					

Source: Shoprite annual reports

Stock markets are forward-looking by nature. Investment analysts and asset managers tend to be more interested in next year's profits than last year's. Analysts' forecasts are often published and subject to much conjecture in the market. (Have you ever noticed, occasionally, that when a listed company reports growth in earnings its share price drops immediately after the announcement? This is often due to the company not meeting market expectations regarding earnings growth rather than the actual numbers reported.)

Shoprite's forward EBIT multiple in FY2013 was calculated as follows:

Enterprise value as FY2013 year-end ÷ FY2014 EBIT

= 103 872 ÷ 5 689

= 18.3

Empirical evidence shows that forward-looking multiples are more accurate predictors of value (Koller et al. 2005). This makes sense, as all valuations should be forward-looking, aiming to value future cash flows and earnings. It is worthwhile calculating implied forward EBIT, EBITA and EBITDA multiples when analysing multiples of listed entities. This generally gives a more discernable trend than analysing historical multiples.

Shoprite's forward EBIT multiples in FY2012 and FY2013 seem high. Remember that a company's EBIT multiple should be lower than its PE multiple, as EBIT precedes tax being deducted. Simplistically, assuming no surplus cash or debt in the capital structure of the overall JSE:

Average long-term PE multiple, say 15.0

Implied EBIT multiple 10.8 [15.0 × (1 – tax rate)] = 15.0 × 0.72

It could be argued that Shoprite's EBIT multiple has been high relative to the overall JSE. However, food retailers tend to have lower betas than the overall stock market – we buy food whether times are good or bad. Shoprite's beta at June 2014 was 0.22 (BNP Paribas Cadiz Securities 2014), however. This seems extraordinarily low.

There are a few complications in valuing Shoprite:

- How much of the cash and cash equivalents per the statements of financial position is surplus and how much is required for operations?
- Shoprite has a convertible bond in issue. How should we incorporate this into the valuation?
- Shoprite has non-convertible, non-participating no par value deferred shares in issue. How do we treat these for valuation purposes?

Shoprite requires cash in its till points to trade – customers may elect to pay in cash and need change. How much of its cash and cash equivalents at year-end is required for trading purposes and how much is surplus to operational requirements? Shoprite itself would know the answer to this question as it should have a record of physical cash on hand on any given trading day.

We could attempt to estimate the surplus cash on hand by dividing interest income for the year by a reasonable return on short-term cash deposits:

Shoprite	
Interest income per FY2014 statement of comprehensive income	R225m
Estimated short-term deposit rate	5,5%
Implied average cash on deposit	R4 090m
[R225m ÷ 5,5%]	
Reported cash at FY2014 year end	R8 161m
Surplus cash	–R4 090m
Cash required for trading	R4 071m

If our estimation of surplus cash is correct, R4 090 million would be added to enterprise value to derive equity value (or deducted from equity value to derive enterprise value).

Note that a useful ratio to calculate is to divide interest income by average cash balances during the year. In Shoprite's case in FY2014, this would amount to:

R225m ÷ [(R8 161m + R6 122m) ÷ 2] = 3,15%

The result of 3,15% is very low in the current South African context. Hence, we can deduce that the average surplus cash on deposit during FY2014 was significantly lower than ±R7,1 billion.

Convertible bonds

Shoprite issued R4,7 billion of convertible bonds in April and May 2012 on the following terms and conditions:

+ Bonds bear interest at a fixed rate of 6,5 per cent per annum payable semi-annually in arrears.
+ Unless not previously converted, redeemed or purchased and cancelled, the bonds will be redeemable at par on 3 April 2017.
+ Shoprite may redeem the bonds prior to April 2017 if the weighted average price of its ordinary shares is 130 per cent of the conversion price (R168,94) for 20 out of 30 consecutive trading days on the JSE.
+ Shoprite may purchase bonds from bondholders at any time.
+ Bondholders may convert their bonds into ordinary shares at a price of R168,94 at any stage until 10 days prior to 3 April 2017.
+ Bondholders may elect to have bonds redeemed in the event of a change in control of Shoprite.

The burning question is, how do we treat these convertible bonds from a valuation perspective?

+ Do we assume that bonds will be convertible into ordinary shares – a dilution of existing ordinary shareholders?
+ Do we assume that the bonds will be redeemed and hence deduct R4,7 billion from enterprise value?

Shoprite's share price has traded at above R168,94 since the bond issue. No bondholders have yet elected to convert their bonds into ordinary shares.

The financial accounting for the bonds in FY2014 was interesting:

Shoprite	FY2014
Fair value of bonds	R4 742m
Equity component	–R361m
Liability component at June 2014	R4 381m

The liability component was estimated using a market yield on debt of 8,9 per cent, and the balance was transferred to equity.

Let's analyse the results if we treat Shoprite's convertible bonds as either equity or debt, assuming an enterprise value of R85 billion and surplus cash of R4 billion:

TABLE 4.5 Shoprite's convertible bonds at June 2014

Convertible bonds at June 2014	Equity Rm	Debt Rm
Enterprise value	85 000	85 000
Surplus cash	4 000	4 000
Borrowings excluding bonds	–403	–403
Convertible bonds	–	–4 742
Equity value	88 597	83 855

Continued

Number of shares in issue	572 871 960	572 871 960
Conversion of bonds	27 820 522	–
Diluted number of shares	600 692 482	572 871 960
Equity value per share	R147,49	R146,38

Source: Shoprite annual reports

The difference between equity value per share in Table 4.4, assuming the bonds are debt or are converted into ordinary shares, is marginal. This is likely to remain the case given that the potential dilution in number of shares in issue is largely immaterial.

Deferred shares

Shoprite has 290,6 million non-convertible and non-participating deferred shares in issue, which are held by a non-executive director (C.H. Wiese). These shares are not entitled to dividends. However, they carry the same voting rights as ordinary shares. It follows that the deferred shares have 33,7 per cent of the total voting rights and their holder is able to block most material corporate actions (company decisions requiring a special resolution).

Shares with voting rights but no entitlement to dividends are unusual and pose serious challenges from a valuation perspective. Shoprite's deferred shares have no economic right to share in its profits. However, there may be some value attached to these shares due to negative control. Interestingly, when Brait made a takeover bid for Shoprite in 2006/2007, it attached no value to the deferred shares and indicated that these would be cancelled should its bid succeed.

Facebook and Google both have different classes of shares in issue. Facebook has class A and class B shares. Both have equal dividend rights but the class B shares have 10 votes per share (class A shares are entitled to one vote per share). These class B shares enable Mark Zuckerberg, the founder and CEO of Facebook, to control 61,6 per cent of the votes of the company with an economic interest of only 18,9 per cent as at February 2014 (Facebook 2014, proxy statement).

Google has three classes of shares in issue: class A, class B and class C. All classes of shares have equal rights to receive dividends. Class A shares are entitled to one vote per share, while class B shares have 10 votes per share. Google's founders, Larry Page and Sergey Brin, hold significant class B shares and control over 55 per cent of the votes of the company (Google 2014, proxy statement, March). Google then confused the stock markets even further by issuing class C shares in April 2014 - these shares are entitled to dividends but have no voting rights!

Voting shares generally trade at a slight premium to non-voting shares on the NYSE and NASDAQ. It is relatively simple to allocate equity value per share based on dividend rights. The difficulty lies in whether to allocate proportionately more value to shares with higher voting rights. Each situation needs to be assessed on its own merits and there are no general rules.

The link to DCF valuations

It would be ideal if the valuation result of applying an earnings-based method was equivalent to that using the DCF method. Unfortunately, in practice, the results are often very different. This is not surprising as the methods are fundamentally different:

- The DCF method present-values free cash flows for a significant period of time (infinity, actually) using a risk-adjusted cost of capital. Earnings-based methods tend to focus on sustainable profits over the next year or two, a much shorter time span than that of the DCF method.
- Free cash flows do not equal accounting profits – free cash flows are after working capital movements and investment in infrastructure to maintain and grow the business.
- Earnings multiples are derived from stock market and recent transaction data representing the collective consciousness of investors. There is little justification or theory underpinning why a particular industry sector should trade on a particular multiple. Stock markets do, however, provide important benchmarks in the long term, whereas in the short term they often overreact to prevailing sentiment.

It is recommended that both the DCF and earnings-based methods be used where possible to value a business. This provides corroborating evidence of an indicative fair value range. If the valuation results of the DCF and earnings-based methods are far apart, it indicates that assumptions in either method may be unrealistic. It's a very useful check.

Conclusion

Earnings-based methods are much simpler than DCF valuations to apply in practice. Earnings-based methods do, however, face the following issues:

- It is difficult to adjust for specific risks in the earnings multiple – this is possible but unscientific.
- They focus purely on profits, largely ignoring the impact of working capital movements and capital investment.
- Accounting profits can be massaged to an extent and certain accounting rules make little logical sense from a valuation perspective.
- It is difficult to value businesses undergoing rapid growth on an earnings basis.
- Rigorous sensitivity analysis is difficult to apply as the focus is on short-term profits as opposed to a more holistic approach in DCF valuations.

Calculating EBIT, EBITDA or EBITA multiples for listed companies requires a careful review of historical reported profits, debt and surplus cash balances. The historic and forward implied multiples should reveal long-term trends. While it is difficult to outsmart the market, should you discover that multiples are out of sync with history, there may be a buying opportunity or a warning that the share price is overvalued.

Applying the earnings-based method to private companies will be dealt with in Chapter 6. The shares in private companies are generally not traded on an active market. So, their multiples have to be deduced by analysing similar listed companies.

Questions

1. PE multiples are highly recommended in practice because they:
   - A. Represent the collective consciousness of stock markets
   - B. Fail to value debt and surplus cash correctly
   - C. Are easy to use

2. Sustainable earnings should be determined after:
   A. Including impairments of intangible and tangible assets
   B. Including income from associate companies
   C. Adjusting for non-recurring items
3. Share-based payment expenses in statements of comprehensive income are:
   A. An accurate reflection of the cost of retaining and incentivising employees
   B. Subject to estimation based on the expected future value of options granted to employees
   C. A major expense in most businesses
4. The EBIT multiple is calculated by:
   A. Dividing enterprise value by EBIT
   B. Dividing equity value by EBIT
   C. Dividing revenue by EBIT
5. A high EBIT multiple of a listed company reflects:
   A. Market expectation of high growth in EBIT for the next three years
   B. Market perception that the company's risk profile is lower than that of other listed companies generally
   C. Low surplus cash in the capital structure of the company
6. Stock markets tend to:
   A. Place more emphasis on historical profits than forecasts
   B. Be efficient at all times, absorbing all known information instantaneously
   C. Value companies based on forecast profits
7. In determining equity value, you should:
   A. Add debt and subtract surplus from enterprise value
   B. Add debt and deduct surplus cash from shareholders' equity in the statement of financial position
   C. Deduct debt and add surplus cash to enterprise value
8. The long-term average PE multiple of the JSE All Share Index is:
   A. Between 14 and 16
   B. Impossible to calculate
   C. Irrelevant for valuation purposes
9. The earnings-based method:
   A. Is suitable for valuing high-growth and start-up businesses
   B. Is based on extensive financial theory, for which academics have won Nobel prizes in economics
   C. Provides useful information about the collective consciousness of the stock market.
10. The EBIT multiples of listed construction companies:
   A. Should be higher than those of retail banks
   B. Should be lower than those of listed food retailers
   C. Are difficult to calculate because of the level of complexity in accounting for construction contracts

References

Damodaran, A. (2014). www.stern.nyu/adamdor/datasets. [Accessed 30 September 2014].

Bloomberg. (2014). www.bloomberg.com. [Accessed 8 October 2014].

Koller, T., Goedhart, M. & Wessels, D. (2005). *Valuation: Measuring and managing the value of companies.* Fourth edition. New Jersey: John Wiley & Sons.

BNP Paribas Cadiz Securities. (2014). *Equity Risk Service - Q2 2014.* Johannesburg: BNP Paribas Cadiz Securities.

Facebook. (2014). Investor relations. Available at investor.fb.com. [Accessed 9 October 2014].

Google. (2014). Investor relations. Available at investor.google.com. [Accessed 9 October 2014].

CHAPTER 5

Other valuation methods

LEARNING OUTCOMES

Once you have worked through this chapter, you should be able to:

+ Apply the dividend discount and adjusted net asset value (NAV) methods to value companies
+ Understand the deficiencies of using the dividend discount method in practice
+ Identify the potential adjustments to asset and liability values in financial statements in deriving the NAV of a business
+ Recognise that recent transaction multiples provide useful, but not conclusive, information to value a similar business
+ Use caution when using industry multiples as the primary valuation method

Introduction

Chapters 2 to 4 dealt with the primary valuation methods for determining an indicative fair value for a company or a business as a going concern. The DCF and earnings-based methods are the most commonly used in practice, and should be both be performed to corroborate each other's results. However, in certain circumstances other methods may be more appropriate or used as a reasonability check on valuation results.

The adjusted net asset value (NAV) method is often used to value shareholders' interests in investment holding companies or businesses in financial distress. The results of the adjusted NAV method are generally much lower than those of the DCF and earnings-based methods for going concerns that are profitable and undergoing growth. The adjusted NAV method can sometimes be a useful check on the valuation results of other methods.

The dividend discount method is a technique in which expected future dividends to be received are present-valued using the cost of equity. It is generally not used to value controlling interests as dividend payout ratios (dividends ÷ profit after tax) are low, and discounting future distributions will result in an abnormally low value. Average dividend payout ratios of S&P 500 companies over the period 2000 to 2014 (FactSet 2014) are illustrated in Figure 5.1.

Figure 5.1 shows that the average S&P 500 company distributes between 25 and 35 per cent of annual profits on average as dividends. The peaks in payout ratios in 2002 and 2009 may be attributable to lower corporate profits in those years, as opposed to changing dividend policies.

Other valuation methods used in practice include earnings multiples from recently concluded merger and acquisition transactions and industry multiples. The former provide interesting information but should be treated with some caution. Industry multiples provide benchmarks such as enterprise value against revenue and NAV, and industry-specific data – for example, the number of monthly active users in social media businesses.

FIGURE 5.1 Average dividend payout ratios of S&P 500 companies, 2000 to 2014

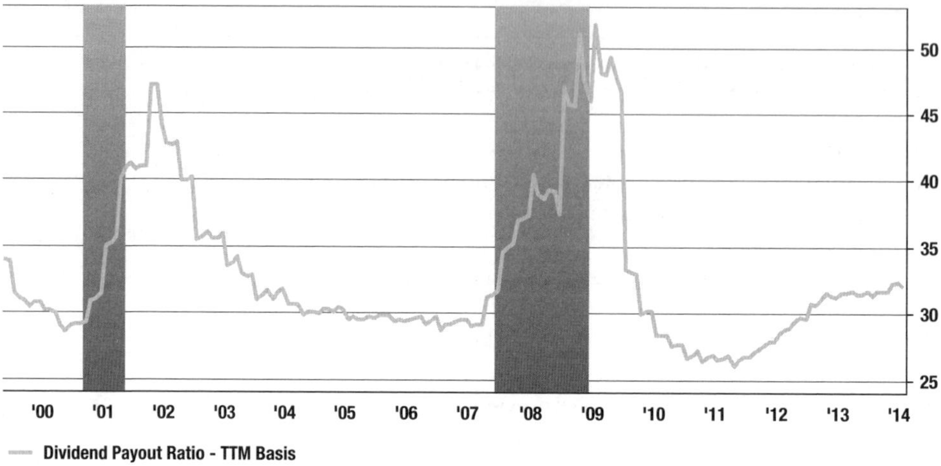

Source: FactSet Market Aggregates via FactSet

The adjusted NAV method

The adjusted NAV method estimates the fair value of assets and liabilities, thereby deriving the net asset value. The numbers reflected in statements of financial position provide a useful start to this process but the adjusted NAV method is more concerned with market values than with accounting conventions. In addition, certain assets and liabilities, such as intangible assets and contingent liabilities, may not be reflected in the financial statements.

Table 5.1 presents asset and liability values per financial statements that may require review and revision.

TABLE 5.1 Asset and liability values per financial statements that may require review and revision

Value	Description
Investment property, other land and buildings	If carried at cost, market value will need to be estimated.
Goodwill	Goodwill arose due to prior acquisitions and is unlikely to have any direct value.
Intangible assets	Capitalised software expenditure may not reflect its realisable value. The value of trademarks, patents and brands will also need to be assessed from a perspective of their potential sale.
Plant and equipment	The expected proceeds on selling these assets are more relevant than their value in use.
Inventories	Inventories are generally stated at cost less provisions for slow-moving or obsolete items. The estimated realisable value of inventories is far more relevant in the adjusted NAV method.

Continued

Trade receivables	The collectability of amounts outstanding from customers needs to be carefully assessed, particularly in a liquidation scenario. Customers may become tardier in paying amounts owed when a company is in financial distress.
Investments in associate companies	Underlying investee companies will need to be separately valued, particularly if they are unlisted entities.
Share-based payment reserves	The current difference between the average strike price of options granted and the ruling market price will need to be determined. The net result is likely to be different from the accounting provision. If options are to be equity-settled, the overall NAV result may need to be diluted.
Interest-bearing debt	The amounts outstanding may be different from what is reflected in the financial statements – for example, where debt instruments bear interest at rates different from prevailing market rates.
Provisions	Provisions for warranty claims, rebates and environmental rehabilitation may need to be re-assessed.

Certain intangible assets, such as internally developed brands and trademarks, will not be reflected in the financial statements. So, they will need to be valued on the premise that they could be sold to third parties. Contingent liabilities may also need to be estimated with regards to any litigation in progress or contractual disputes with customers and suppliers.

The adjusted NAV method is often used to value businesses that are in financial distress or already in liquidation. In these circumstances, the following factors could be relevant:

- The realisable value of assets may be lower than when the business was trading profitably. Potential buyers will perceive weakness on the part of the company or its appointed custodians and may not offer the best possible prices for assets.
- The costs of liquidation will need to be considered (liquidators' fees, legal fees and commissions arising on sale of assets).
- The costs of maintaining operations while assets are being disposed of and liabilities settled will also need to be considered.

The adjusted NAV method may be suitable for valuing loss-making businesses. The earnings-based and DCF methods will be difficult to apply in these circumstances, given the difficulties in forecasting future profits and cash flows.

The recognition of normal taxation, deferred taxation and withholding tax on dividends is a contentious issue in the adjusted NAV method. The approach adopted will depend on the circumstances. For businesses in liquidation or facing imminent liquidation, the taxation debate is less perplexing. The expected tax consequences - normal tax and capital gains tax (CGT) - of selling assets will need to be deducted in deriving enterprise NAV. Deferred tax assets and liabilities reflected in the statement of financial position can largely be ignored since the immediate tax consequences of disposing of assets and settling liabilities will be individually considered.

The recognition of potential income tax, CGT and dividend withholding tax is more complex in valuing going concerns. It could be argued that certain assets that a company owns, such as investment property and listed and unlisted investments, need not be sold. Instead, shares in the company itself can be disposed of instead of triggering CGT on the sale of underlying assets. The tax consequences of selling inventories at market value, writing off bad debts and settling outstanding claims may, however, need to be provided for in the valuation.

Investment holding companies can be valued using the adjusted NAV method. The main business of these companies, typically, is owning minority or majority stakes in other companies. The underlying investments will need to be separately valued in determining the NAV of the holding company.

DID YOU KNOW?

Listed investment holding companies generally trade at a discount to the intrinsic value of their underlying investments. This discount depends on the circumstances and could range between 10 and 25 per cent of the cumulative fair value of underlying assets. The inherent reasons for this discount could include:

- potential CGT consequences of selling underlying investments;
- potential discounts arising from selling minority stakes as opposed to controlling interests;
- potential downward pressure on share prices of underlying investments if the stock market becomes aware of the disposal intentions of the investment holding company; and/or
- the present value of future expenditure to operate the investment holding company (operating expenses, employee costs and incentive bonuses).

CASE STUDY LET'S VALUE PSG

PSG Group Limited (PSG) is an investment holding company listed on the JSE. Its major investments at the end of February 2014 were:

- a 28,3 per cent equity interest in Capitec Bank, a financial institution that focuses on the unsecured lending market in South Africa;
- a 57,1 per cent shareholding in Curro, a private schooling business; and
- a 64,7 per cent stake in PSG Konsult, a financial services and insurance brokerage and asset manager.

All three of the above companies are listed on the JSE, so their fair values can be estimated at any point in time by reference to ruling share prices. PSG estimated the fair value of its investments at 28 February 2014 to be as follows:

TABLE 5.2 Estimation of fair value of investments at 28 February 2014, PSG

February 2014	Shareholding	Investment fair value R millions	Implied 100% value R millions	Investee's historic PE multiple
Capitec	28,3%	5 989	21 163	10.4
Curro	57,1%	4 660	8 161	208.9
PSG Konsult	64,7%	4 004	6 189	23.3
Other investments		3 387		
Net asset value		18 040		

The investments in Capitec, Curro and PSG Konsult represented 81 per cent of PSG's total NAV at February 2014. Each underlying investment would need to be valued separately to assess whether its current share prices represent indicative fair values. Curro, in particular, seems to be trading at a very high earnings multiple. The stock market is obviously expecting enormous growth in earnings from Curro and, to a lesser extent, from PSG Konsult. Simply using prevailing share prices to value PSG could lead to a significant valuation error. Issues that need to be considered when valuing PSG's investment portfolio include:

- whether Capitec was undervalued at February 2014 given the negative sentiment towards unsecured lending institutions following the funding crisis at African Bank;
- whether Curro's current share price is overly exuberant;
- whether there is sufficient 'free float' of Curro and PSG Konsult shares. PSG owns significant stakes in these companies and there may not be sufficient shares traded in Curro and PSG Konsult to provide an accurate reflection of their indicative fair values; and
- whether a minority discount (see Chapter 7) should be applied to the value of Capitec.

PSG calculates and discloses its sum-of-the-parts (SOTP) value per share at each reporting period. This represents the net asset value derived (R18 billion, as per Table 5.2) divided by the number of shares in issue. The SOTP value per share at 28 February 2014 was estimated at R95,01 by PSG, while the closing share price at year-end was R89,02. The discount of 6,3 per cent between the prevailing share price and underlying net asset value per share is on the low end of the usual investment holding company discounts. There appears to be a strong correlation between historic SOTP and share price movements (PSG Group Limited 2014).

FIGURE 5.2 PSG share price versus SOTP value per share

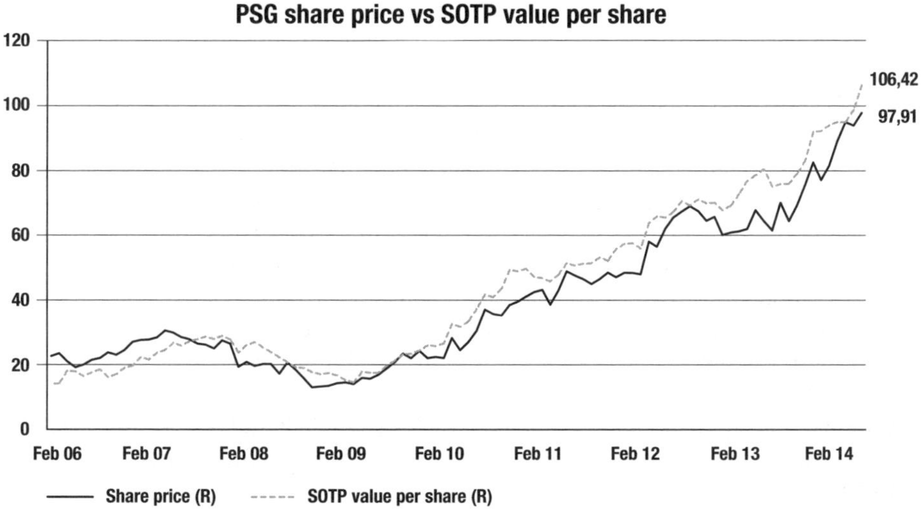

Source: PSG Group Limited (2014)

The dividend discount method

The dividend discount method present-values future dividends that shareholders expect to receive from underlying investee by the cost of equity. Let's illustrate this with an example.

EXAMPLE 5.1

Assume the following for CG Limited, a hypothetical company listed on the JSE:

- Profit after tax in Year 0 of R100 million
- Historical dividend payout ratio of 30 per cent
- No dividend tax
- Expected growth in profit after tax of 5 per cent in perpetuity
- Cost of equity of 15 per cent.

The valuation of 100 per cent of the shares in issue of CG:

- Dividend paid in Year 0 = R100m × 30% = R30m
- Discounted future dividends using Gordon's Growth Model

R30 million ÷ (15% – 5%) = R300 million

The valuation result for CG Limited using the dividend discount method appears very low. The implied PE multiple is 3.0 (R300 million equity value ÷ R100 million PAT). If 100 per cent of annual profits were paid out as dividends, the valuation result would have been R1 billion - R100m ÷ (15% - 5%).

Dividend payout ratios of S&P 500 listed companies vary between 25 and 35 per cent, as depicted in Figure 5.1. The dividend payout ratio of listed South African companies over the period 1973 to 2009 was 43,3 per cent (Vermeulen & Smit 2011). Discounting future expected dividends, which often represent less than 50 per cent of annual profits, is likely to result in undervaluing businesses. For this reason, the method should only be used in exceptional cases in practice. It could be appropriate when the dividend payout ratio is high and you are attempting to value a minority interest.

The practice of share buy-backs, as opposed to paying dividends, to return capital to shareholders also complicates the use of the method in practice. Share buy-backs may reduce amounts available for dividend payouts, or may replace these distributions to shareholders. Dividend policies of listed companies tend to be consistent unless exceptional circumstances occur. Share buy-backs, however, tend to be irregular occurrences depending on stock market conditions and the cash holdings of companies. Apple Inc. commenced a share buy-back programme in 2013 following pressure from shareholders to return some of its cash pile of US$121 billion at the end of 2012. Boards of directors may also elect to pursue a share buy-back programme if they perceive that the company's current share price is below its intrinsic fair value.

It could be argued that share buy-backs should be included as dividends for the purposes of the dividend discount method. The complication with doing this is that future share buybacks are difficult to predict.

Recent transaction prices

Recent earnings multiples paid in acquisition transactions of businesses similar to the one you are valuing provide useful information. These transactions need to be similar in size as well.

For example, if we are valuing a controlling interest in a listed company, recent transaction multiples need to be for changes in control of listed entities of similar size and nature of business. If a minority stake is to be acquired in a private company, we need to find market data on similar transactions.

In a South African context, there are no known databases of transaction multiples paid in private company transactions. It is therefore difficult to benchmark earnings multiples in unlisted deals in South Africa. It is possible to obtain data on listed company acquisitions, but these multiples need to be carefully analysed. The reported EBIT of listed entities acquired needs to be adjusted for non-recurring items; income and expenditure that may be better treated as assets and liabilities; and items that should simply be ignored. Refer to Chapter 4 for a detailed discussion about this.

You should therefore perform your own calculations for each relevant transaction to derive the implied EBIT or EBITDA multiple paid on acquisition. These multiples may need further analysis and adjustment prior to being applied to the situation at hand:

- Stock market cycles may influence average earnings multiples. In bear markets, multiples may be lower than average, and higher in upward cycles.
- The nature and size of the listed companies' businesses need to be similar to the entity being valued. If they are different, suitable adjustments need to be made to average earnings multiples paid.
- Expected future growth in revenue and profits is likely to influence acquirers to pay more for target companies than businesses with lower forecast growth.
- The financial ratios of companies acquired should be compared to the entity being valued. Useful ratios here could include EBIT/revenue, historical revenue and EBIT growth, and ROIC. Companies with more favourable ratios may attract higher transaction multiples on acquisition

Figure 5.3 shows the average EBITDA multiples (enterprise value ÷ EBITDA) of listed companies on the African continent (RisCura 2014). Note that these are based on share prices as opposed to concluded merger and acquisition transactions.

FIGURE 5.3 Listed EV/EBITDA multiples over time

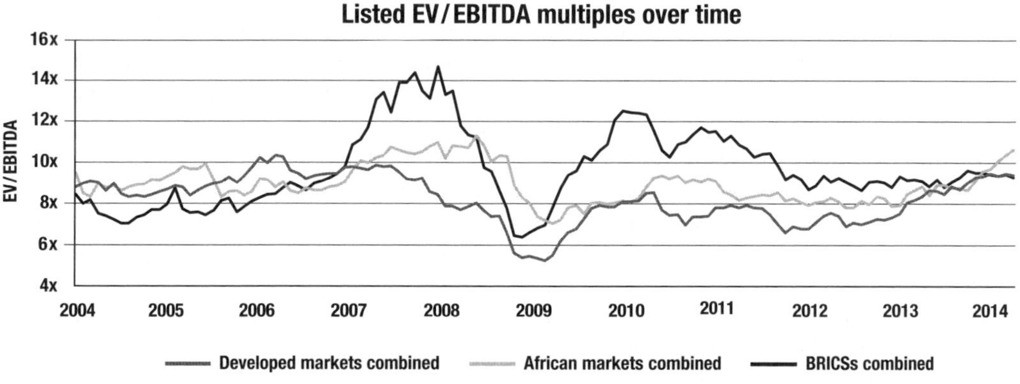

Source: RisCura (2014)

The average EBITDA multiple over the past 10 years, of approximately 9 times, is informative. These multiples are considerably higher than those paid in private equity deals (RisCura 2014). Refer to Figure 5.4 for average multiples paid by private equity firms over an eight-year period in Africa.

FIGURE 5.4 African EV/EBITDA multiples compared with US multiples

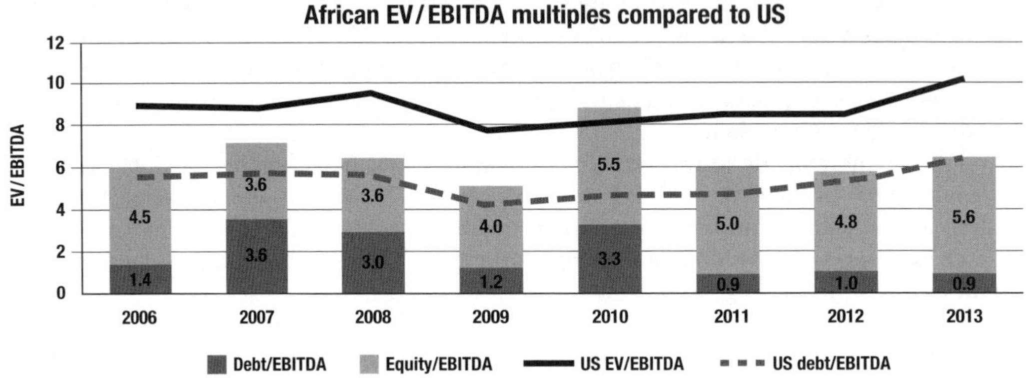

Source: RisCura (2014)

The average EBITDA multiple paid in private equity deals on the continent over the period 2006 to 2013 was 6.5 times, compared with the 10-year average listed company multiple of 8.8. This could reflect the potential discount between listed and private company multiples, specific risks identified in private equity deals and the ability to raise debt to finance acquisitions.

Average listed company earnings multiples per industry sector provide useful comparative data when valuing a specific listed company. However, it should be remembered that merger and acquisition (M&A) transactions rarely occur at ruling share prices. Generally, acquirers have to offer a premium to the prevailing share price to entice existing shareholders to sell their shares and to gain control of the entity. The investment banking industry refers to these premiums as control premiums. This practice will be critically analysed in Chapter 7.

The practical reality is that shareholders are unlikely to sell unless a premium is offered. Acquirers need to perform their own assessment of indicative fair value and may have to present-value expected synergies after the transaction to derive an acceptable offer price.

Recent transaction multiples are informative, but acquirers are strongly recommended not to use these multiples blindly to value a target company for the following reasons:

- Transaction multiples may include the PV of expected synergies that could inflate multiples. Also, expected synergies depend on individual circumstances and the mindset of the deal champions (who are likely to overestimate synergies to ensure that the deal happens).
- Multiples vary over time (refer to Figures 5.3 and 5.4). Acquirers should use long-term averages rather than prevailing multiples. In addition, implied forward multiples provide far more reliable data than historic multiples as stock markets tend to be forward-looking in nature.

Industry multiples

Assessing the valuation result by benchmarking it against comparable companies and/or industry averages is useful in practice. Useful ratios include the following:

Price to book ratio	market value of equity ÷ shareholders' equity per statement of financial position (or NAV per financial statements)
Revenue multiple	equity value ÷ revenue or enterprise value ÷ revenue
Enterprise value/number of customers	enterprise value ÷ number of active users or enterprise value ÷ number of subscribers

It is strongly recommended that you do not use these ratios and multiples as your primary valuation method, but rather as a reasonability check on the valuation result.

The price to book ratio is commonly used to assess the prevailing stock market valuations of, or bid prices for, financial services businesses. The price to book ratios of the major banks in South Africa over the period 2010 to 2013 are set out in Figure 5.5.

FIGURE 5.5 Price to book ratios of major South African banks

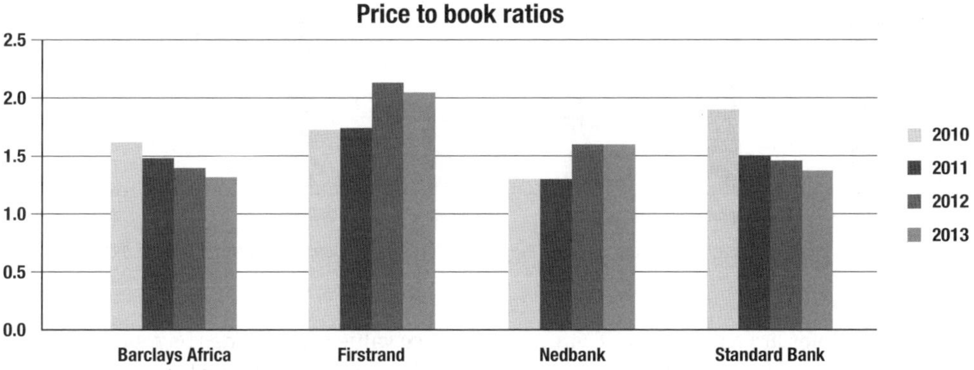

Source: Annual reports of each bank

The average price to book ratio for Barclays Africa and Nedbank was 1.5 times while Standard Bank averaged 1.6 times. These are remarkably similar over the period 2010 to 2013. The FirstRand Group's price to book averaged 1.9 over the period, indicating a higher market rating than the others.

The price to book ratio should not be used as the primary valuation method but rather as a reasonability check on the results of a retail and investment banking operation. In a South African context, it would appear that the ratio should be between 1.5 and 1.9 times, unless there are exceptional circumstances.

Revenue multiples and enterprise value ÷ average number of users is interesting, but arguably provides little insight into how to value businesses. Selected social media and online marketplace businesses listed on NASDAQ have been analysed to determine their industry multiples:

+ Facebook - needs no further introduction given its estimated 1.2 billion monthly active users
+ Groupon - operates online local marketplaces globally that connect merchants to potential customers and offer goods and services at discounted prices
+ LinkedIn - an online professional network enabling members to share information about their careers and discover knowledge and insights
+ TripAdvisor - an online travel company enabling consumers to book airline tickets, accommodation and restaurants
+ Twitter - a social messaging platform.

All of the above companies have December financial year-ends and derive the majority of their revenue from advertising. Figure 5.6 summarises their implied revenue multiples and enterprise values per active user.

FIGURE 5.6 Multiples at 31 December 2013

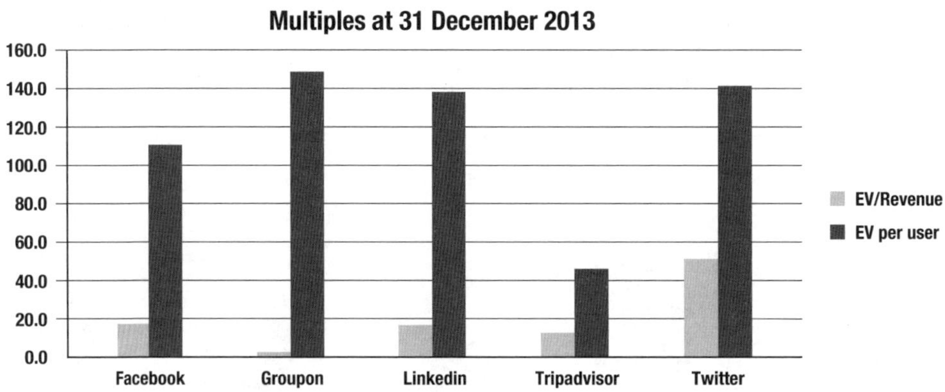

Source: Multiples were calculated based on financial data per the companies' 2013 annual reports and share price data was obtained from Yahoo.

The revenue multiples are astounding. Twitter's enterprise value is 51.2 times its reported revenue for the year ended 31 December 2013 despite incurring an operating loss of US$636 million. Even Facebook's multiples seem exuberant, with a 17.3 times revenue multiple and a historic EBIT multiple of 48.4 times.

It would be foolish to blindly value social media and mobile commerce businesses using revenue multiples or based on average enterprise values per active user. The stock markets may prove to be correct in placing high earnings multiples on these businesses however, spectacular earnings and cash flow growth is required over the next 5 years to return multiples to more realistic levels.

PEG ratios

A PEG ratio is calculated as current PE ratio ÷ expected growth in profit after tax for the next two or three years. It is used in practice to evaluate potentially overvalued or undervalued listed companies within specific industries, particularly those undergoing high growth. Comparing PEG ratios across industries is of little informational value.

EXAMPLE 5.2

Let's consider a hypothetical example of companies in the food retail sector.

	Current equity value R millions	Current PE ratio	Expected earnings growth* %	PEG ratio
FRA Limited	7 200	24.0	25	0.96
FRB Limited	3 600	18.0	15	1.20
FRC Limited	6 400	16.0	10	1.60
Average		19.3	16.7	1.25
* *One-year earnings forecasts*				

It is difficult to interpret the results of calculated PEG ratios. It is perhaps more meaningful to estimate forward PE ratios and analyse these – let's attempt this for the above companies.

	Equity value R million	Historic PAT R millions	Forecast PAT R millions	Forward PE multiple
FRA Limited	7 200	300	375	19.2
FRB Limited	3 600	200	230	15.7
FRC Limited	6 400	400	440	14.6
Average				16.5
* *One-year earnings forecasts*				

FRA Limited may appear overvalued relative to its peers. However, it could be facing less risk than FRB Limited and FRC Limited, or have higher long-term growth prospects. PE multiples reflect the stock market's perception of earnings growth, risk and future volatility.

Conclusion

The DCF and earnings-based valuation methods should be the primary tools used to value a business in practice, except for companies in financial distress and investment holding companies. The adjusted NAV method is a useful technique for estimating the expected proceeds from selling assets and settling liabilities of investment holding companies.

The dividend discount method has lost popularity in practice because it often underestimates companies' equity values. Dividend payout ratios are generally less than 50 per cent, resulting in dividends not reflecting the full expected present value of future profits and cash flows.

Industry multiples and PEG ratios provide interesting information about market expectations of future profit growth and equity valuations. However, these multiples and ratios should not be used as the primary valuation method, but rather as a reasonability check on valuation results.

Recent transaction multiples are informative about acquisition prices recently paid. These multiples are also a useful benchmark for evaluating a bid price for a business. However, using earnings multiples that acquirers have applied without applying them, in turn, to the scenario in question can compound the errors that others have made.

Questions

1. The dividend payout ratio represents:
   A. Dividends paid divided by the ruling share price
   B. Dividends declared and paid divided by profit after tax
   C. Dividends divided by EBITDA
2. The average dividend payout ratio of South African listed companies:
   A. Averaged 43,3 per cent over the period 1973 to 2009
   B. Should be adjusted to include share buy-backs
   C. Is increasing as companies recognise the folly of holding onto surplus cash
3. The values of assets and liabilities in statements of financial position:
   A. Are an accurate reflection of their market values
   B. Exclude the deferred tax consequences of realising assets and settling liabilities
   C. Need to be adjusted to reflect the expected proceeds from selling assets
4. The adjusted NAV method is:
   A. Suitable for valuing profitable, growing businesses
   B. Best used to value a business in financial distress
   C. Outdated and no longer used in practice
5. The dividend discount method should:
   A. Produce a valuation result similar to the DCF and earnings-based methods
   B. Present-value expected future dividends in perpetuity
   C. Provide a reasonability check on the adjusted NAV method
6. The dividend discount method:
   A. Is best used to value a controlling interest in a company
   B. Is the only valuation technique that should be used as it reflects the expected future cash return to shareholders
   C. Is likely to produce a valuation result lower than that of the DCF method
7. Recent transaction multiples paid:
   A. Reflect the acquisition prices paid divided by EBITDA, EBIT or PAT
   B. Are not useful in evaluating the indicative fair value of unlisted companies
   C. Are generally constant over an extended period of time
8. Revenue multiples:
   A. Are the preferred method of valuing social media businesses
   B. Provide limited information on the true value of a business
   C. Provide a useful reasonability check on business valuations
9. The price to book ratio is:
   A. A useful check on the market value of retail banking businesses
   B. Indicative of the capital intensity of an industry
   C. Calculated by dividing enterprise value by revenue

10. PEG ratios:

A. Provide an indication in practice of whether a business is overvalued or undervalued

B. Are calculated by dividing enterprise value by PAT

C. Should be treated with extreme caution in analysing future profit growth

References

FactSet. (2014). *Dividend Quarterly September 2014*. Available at www.factset.com/websitefiles/PDFs/dividend. [Accessed 24 October 2014].

PSG Group Limited. (2014). *Annual report for the year ended 28 February 2014*. Stellenbosch: PSG Group Limited.

RisCura. (2014). *Bright Africa: A guide to equity investing on the continent*. Cape Town: RisCura.

Vermeulen, M. & Smit, E. v.d. M. (2011). Dividend payout and future earnings growth: A South African study. *South African Journal of Business Management* 42(4): 33–46.

Yahoo. (2014). finance.yahoo.com. [Accessed 30 October 2014].

CHAPTER 6

Private company valuations

LEARNING OUTCOMES

Once you have worked through this chapter, you should be able to:

- Understand the reasons for the private company discount (PCD)
- Estimate the PCD in practice
- Recognise the challenges of valuing private companies
- Use practical tips to value private businesses

Introduction

Valuing private companies presents various challenges. Their shares are not actively traded on a stock market, so we do not have access to prevailing EBIT or EBITDA multiples; nor can we determine their historic beta coefficients. This data is critical to the earnings-based and DCF valuation methods respectively. It follows that valuing a private company is a difficult task and that our estimate of indicative fair value may be subjective.

In a South African context, there are no known databases of private company multiples paid in recent transactions per industry. Even if there were, we would need to adjust these multiples for differences in size, growth and specific risks between the company being valued and the industry average.

We could obtain earnings multiples and betas of similar listed companies. However, it is unlikely that these would be directly comparable. There is a limited number of listed companies on the JSE - approximately 400 companies at last count. It is highly unlikely that we will find a listed company similar in nature of business and size of operations to the private company we are attempting to value. Industry multiples and betas over a period of time could be useful. However, these need to be adjusted for specific risks and for the illiquidity of private company shares.

There has been debate in academic literature for decades about the illiquidity discount to be applied to private companies. Shares in listed companies can readily be bought and sold, while the process of trading in private companies can take up to 24 months to conclude. Mergers and acquisitions will be covered in later chapters. However, the common steps in concluding an acquisition of a minority or majority interest in a private company could include:

- initial discussions between the acquirer and target company management and shareholders;
- the exchange of operational and financial information;
- valuation of the target company;
- structuring the deal (funding of acquisition consideration and taxation issues);
- negotiating the acquisition price and other key terms;
- recording the key terms in a memorandum of understanding;
- drafting of comprehensive legal agreements to give effect to the acquisition, such as sale of shares/business, service and restraint of trade, and shareholders' agreements;
- negotiation of, and agreement on, the terms of legal agreements;
- performance of a due diligence investigation;

- preparation and lodging of submissions to the Competition Commission;
- notifying trade unions and creditors about the acquisition;
- getting approval of the deal by the boards of directors and shareholders of both the acquirer and target company; and
- transaction closing (fulfilment of conditions precedent and acquisition price settlement).

The above process is lengthy; in the author's opinion, it takes, on average, between nine and 12 months to complete in private company transactions. The length of the process introduces significant uncertainty and risk regarding disposing of shares in a private company. Market conditions may change, the potential acquirer may undergo a change of heart and external influences (government intervention, regulatory changes or strike action) could scupper a potential deal.

The private company discount

The private company discount (PCD) represents the discount in earnings multiples (PE, EBIT and/or EBITDA multiples) between a private and listed company that is similar in nature of business. The discount incorporates both illiquidity and differences in size, risks and growth prospects. The common techniques for estimating the PCD include researching restricted stock and pre-IPO pricing discounts, and recent transaction multiples paid for similar private companies.

Restricted stock studies

Restricted stock consists of shares issued by a listed company that cannot be traded on a stock exchange but can be sold privately. Restricted stock is occasionally used to part-settle an acquisition consideration and often used in share incentive schemes in the USA. Restricted stock is also issued as part of private placements in order to raise capital for early-stage businesses or those urgently requiring capital. These securities are regarded as restricted because they are not registered with the Securities and Exchange Commission (SEC) and are generally only marketable on stock exchanges after a period of six months or one year – and, even then, in limited quantities.

DID YOU KNOW? ?

Technology businesses such as Apple, Google and Facebook issue significant quantities of restricted stock to attract and retain employees. These shares are generally subject to vesting conditions such as period of service and performance in the workplace.

The average discount between the price at which restricted stock is issued and the ruling market price of unrestricted shares at the time has been the subject of numerous research studies since the 1960s. The average discount, according to these studies, has varied from 22 per cent to 35 per cent (Koeplin 2000). The most widely quoted study is that performed by William Silber (1991), which reported an average discount of 33,75 per cent. However, Silber's findings need to be treated with extreme caution:

- The number of restricted stock issues covered was 69 private placement transactions between 1981 and 1988, arguably too small a sample to be extrapolated to all restricted stock issues.

- The average discounts in the study were widely dispersed, the highest being 84 per cent and the lowest being a premium of 12,7 per cent.
- Discounts increased dramatically where issuers were smaller companies reporting losses.

FMV Opinions Inc. (2014) has analysed private placements of unregistered stock by listed companies in the USA from 1980 to 2013. The average discount for 754 transactions analysed was 21,1 per cent. The average discount, however, varied significantly (from 4,2 per cent to 43,3 per cent) depending on the net asset value of issuers and profit margins. In fact, most of the companies analysed were reporting operating losses at the time of issuing restricted stock. Unfortunately, the results of the FMV study may not provide reliable data for the purposes of estimating the PCD for the following reasons:

- The SEC rules regarding the initial holding period for restricted shares (the period during which shares may not be traded on a stock exchange) changed during the period of the survey. Prior to 1997, the initial holding period was three years, but this was subsequently reduced to two years in 1997 and six months in 2008. The median discount calculated by FMV declined to 12,1 per cent after the initial holding period was reduced to six months.
- The majority of issuers were not profitable when issuing restricted shares - which, in itself, could explain discounts. In any event, rights issues are generally at a discount to prevailing share prices to entice shareholders to subscribe for new shares. This could well apply to restricted stock issues.
- In the author's opinion, restricted stock studies provide limited relevant evidence for the extent of private company discounts.

Pre-IPO pricing

The pricing of stock transactions prior to successful initial public offerings (IPOs) may provide useful data on the liquidity discount between private and listed companies. Emory (2014) performed an analysis of stock prices occurring within five months of companies successfully listing to the subsequent IPO price over the period 1980 to 2000 in the USA. The study covered 543 transactions and reported an average discount of 46 per cent between shares issued pre-listing and the IPO price. Of the 543 transactions, 282 were sales of shares and 261 were option transactions.

Koeplin et al. (2000) were critical of the earlier Emory research, claiming that:

- the majority of share issues in the study were between 'insiders' and thus not at arm's length; and
- that most of the transactions were for restricted options, and not issues for cash.

The average discount of 46 per cent reported by Emory seems implausible. Why would existing shareholders permit third parties to subscribe for new shares at such discounts when an IPO was imminent? Option transactions can certainly be ignored since these are not at arm's length and are more related to employee incentivisation.

Transaction multiples

Studies of recent EBIT and EBITDA multiples paid for private versus listed companies provides more compelling evidence of the potential PCD. Empirical research performed by Koeplin et al. (2000) and De Franco et al. (2007) provides interesting insights.

Koeplin, Sarin and Shapiro (2000) analysed 84 transactions in the USA and 108 deals in foreign markets between 1984 and 1988. Private company transactions were first selected and then similar listed company transactions were matched to these based on industry, size of business and date of acquisition. The EBIT and EBITDA multiples paid for private companies were then compared to listed equivalents. The results of their research indicated a discount between listed and private company EBIT multiples paid of between 28 and 44 per cent.

The De Franco et al. (2007) study was more extensive than the Koeplin research, covering 2 249 listed company and 673 private company controlling interest transactions in the USA over the period 1995 to 2004. The private company data was obtained from Pratt's Stats Private Transaction Database. The results of their research are enlightening.

TABLE 6.1 De Franco et al.'s private and listed company transactions research results

De Franco, Gavious, Jin and Richardson	Private companies	Listed companies	Difference
Average EBITDA multiples	7.41	11.11	-33,3%
EV*/Revenue	0.73	1.09	-32,8%
** Enterprise value*			

Source: Pratt's Stats Private Transaction Database; De Franco et al. (2007)

The average EBITDA multiples in the De Franco study were more diverse than those of the Koeplin research, and the average discount was approximately 33 per cent. The listed companies were significantly larger than the private companies, with an average enterprise value of US$1,5 billion versus US$49 million for the latter.

Private equity

Private equity investors provide debt and equity funding to private companies in exchange for equity interests in businesses. These investors seek a premium return to the overall stock market given the illiquidity of shares in private companies and specific risks associated with investing in private companies. Hurdle rates vary from 20 to 30 per cent but it should be noted that a portion of this return is generated from leverage.

The IRRs sought by private equity investors are interesting, but not directly relevant to the private company discount. What could be more pertinent is the entry EBITDA multiples paid by private equity investors compared with the overall stock market. Figure 6.1 contains the average EBITDA multiples paid in African private equity deals over the period 2006 to 2013 together with the average EBITDA multiple on African stock markets over the comparable period. Data was obtained from RisCura (2014).

FIGURE 6.1 EBITDA multiples – African markets

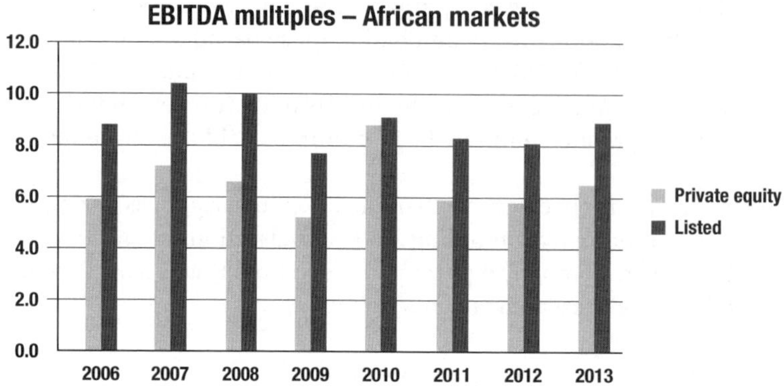

Source: RisCura (2014)

The average discount between EBITDA multiples paid by private equity investors compared with implied average stock market multiples is 27,2 per cent over the period 2006 to 2013. Arguably, the discount should be greater since acquirers of significant equity interests in listed companies would generally pay more than the prevailing share price.

The average EBITDA paid by private equity investors in Africa averaged 6.5 times over the period 2006 to 2013 compared with the average EBITDA multiple on stock exchanges of 8.9 times. The average multiple in 2010 paid for private companies was significantly higher than in other years due to a number of large transactions concluded on the continent.

Some conclusions about the private company discount

The empirical evidence regarding the private company discount is not definitive. The most convincing research was performed by De Franco et al., which indicated that an average discount of 33 per cent would be appropriate. Ultimately, the return required by investors is a matter of personal preference. Investing in private companies is more risky than a passive investment in the overall stock exchange given the lack of diversification, the illiquidity of unlisted shares and specific risks associated with individual companies. The author's personal view is that a premium of 5 to 10 per cent above the expected return in equities as an asset class is appropriate for the above-mentioned factors. Hence, if we expected the long-term return on the JSE ALSI to be 15 per cent, the required return from investing in a private company could range between 20 and 25 per cent.

The average EBITDA multiples paid by private equity investors in Africa was approximately 27 per cent lower than listed multiples over the period 2006 to 2013. This corroborates the De Franco findings and is intuitively appealing.

Factors that could affect the extent of the private company discount used in practice include:

- the size of the business – larger companies would attract less of a discount than small private companies;
- the nature of the assets held by the private company – if assets themselves are highly liquid, the discount could be minimal;

- specific risks such as over-reliance on key personnel, concentration risks involving customers and suppliers, and competitive positioning; and
- plans to list the business – if listing is imminent, the discount should potentially be lower.

Challenges of valuing private companies

Shareholders are often involved in managing private companies, which can lead to an intermingling of personal and professional affairs. For example, salaries paid to shareholders/managers may not be market-related. Also, personal expenditure may be paid through the business. The detailed management accounts of the business being valued need to be carefully reviewed to identify any adjustments required to future profits and cash flows.

Private company shareholders often lease land and buildings owned by them to their operating company. Premises rentals could be more related to mortgage bond repayments than going market rates for similar properties.

Private companies are unlikely to adopt the same level of corporate governance as listed companies. It follows that accounting practices and internal controls may not be up to the standard of larger listed entities. Accounting policies and estimates need to be carefully scrutinised to identify any potential adjustments required for valuation purposes, such as:

- depreciation of property, plant and equipment;
- provisions for bad debts and inventory obsolescence;
- accrual for expenditure incurred but not yet paid; and
- provisions for warranty claims, etc.

Private companies do not disclose their annual financial results to the investing public. Hence, it is difficult to benchmark a private company's historical financial performance against its peers. Similar listed companies could be analysed. However, these are likely to be larger and more diversified entities, making direct comparison difficult.

Shareholders in private companies often provide loans to the company to fund its operations. These entrepreneurs often ask how their loans should be treated in a valuation – does the value of their loan accounts increase the valuation of their shareholding interests? The equity value of the business (enterprise value less external debt plus surplus cash) should generally first be allocated to shareholder loans and thereafter to their relative shareholding interests.

DCF valuations

We cannot obtain a beta directly for private companies. So, we need to:

- research betas of similar companies and/or industry sectors;
- unlever these betas for the gearing levels of listed entities and estimate the unlevered beta (refer to Chapter 3 for the Hamada formula for doing this); and
- review unlevered betas for reasonableness. If betas seem too high or too low, we should perform our own evaluation of a reasonable risk adjustment to the market risk premium.

Having determined an appropriate cost of equity for the private company being valued, the remainder of the DCF valuation is identical to that for listed companies, except for the PCD.

The issue is whether to adjust the cost of equity for the illiquidity of private companies' shares and other risk adjustments or whether to apply this discount at the end of the valuation.

EXAMPLE 6.1

Let's consider an example to illustrate the issue.

Assume the following for Mink (Pty) Ltd:

- A risk-free rate of 8,0 per cent
- A market risk premium of 7,0 per cent
- An industry beta (unlevered) of 0.9
- Free cash flow in Year 0 of R50 million
- Annual growth in free cash flows from Year 1 onwards of 5 per cent
- No debt or surplus cash in the capital structure
- A PCD of 25 per cent.

Mink (Pty) Ltd	
Cost of equity adjusted	
Cost of equity [8.0% + (0.9 × 7.0)] =	14,300%
PCD adjustment	3,575%
Adjusted cost of equity	17,875%
Equity value [R50m ÷ (17,875% – 5%)] =	R388.4m
Adjustment at end of valuation	
Cost of equity (as per above)	14,3%
DCF value [R50m ÷ (14,3% – 5%)] =	R537,6m
PCD discount (25%)	-R134,4m
Adjusted equity value	R403,2m

You will notice that the end results for adjusting the cost of equity by the PCD and adjusting the DCF value at the end of the valuation are not identical. Mathematically, the results are likely to be different using the different approaches. Adjusting the equity value at the end of the valuation process is preferable – however, the quantum of the discount appears large expressed in Rand millions. Adjusting the cost of equity is a subtler way of amending the value of the private company for illiquidity and specific risks.

Earnings-based valuations

The process of valuing a private company is similar to that of listed entities in that we need to review historical EBIT and adjust for non-recurring items and items better reflected as assets and liabilities (refer to Chapter 4 for further details about these adjustments). We would then need to forecast sustainable EBIT.

Thereafter, we need to identify similar listed companies and determine their historic and forward EBIT multiples. This should be done by analysing these companies' reported EBIT and adjusting for non-recurring items and items better reflected as assets and liabilities. Stock markets are forward-looking and we are likely to obtain more useful data from implied forward EBIT multiples of listed companies. Refer to Table 6.2 for an example.

TABLE 6.2 Determining implied forward EBIT multiples

Nik Limited	20X0	20X1	20X2
Number of shares in issue (000s)	100 000	100 000	100 000
Year end share price	R50.00	R65.00	R75.00
Equity value at year end (R000s)	500 000	650 000	750 000
Adjusted EBIT (R000s)	45 000	60 000	72 500
Equity value (R000s)	500 000	650 000	750 000
Debt (R000s)	100 000	125 000	100 000
Enterprise value (R000s)	600 000	725 000	850 000
EBIT multiples			
Historic	13.3	12.1	11.7
Forward	10.0	10.0	?

In Table 6.2, implied forward EBIT multiples are determined by dividing enterprise value by EBIT achieved in the subsequent year – for example, 20X0 enterprise value (R600 million) divided by 20X1 EBIT (R60 million). The trends in these implied forward multiples tend to be more consistent than those of historic EBIT multiples. So, for Nik Limited in Table 6.2, the forward EBIT multiples are 10.0 whereas the historic multiples seem to be declining.

The issue arising is whether to adjust EBIT multiples for the PCD at the start or end of the valuation.

EXAMPLE 6.2

Let's illustrate with an example.

Assume the following for Mink (Pty) Ltd:

- A sustainable EBIT of R35 million forecast for 20X2
- Nik Limited is similar in nature of business to Mink (Pty) Ltd
- Forecast debt at 20X2 of R50 million
- A PCD of 30 per cent appropriate for illiquidity and specific risks.

Let's value Mink (Pty) Ltd using both approaches.

TABLE 6.3 Valuing Mink (Pty) Ltd using both approaches

Mink (Pty) Ltd	
EBIT multiple adjusted for PCD	
Forward EBIT multiple of Nik Ltd	10.0
PCD adjustment	-3.0
Appropriate EBIT multiple for Mink (Pty) Ltd	7.0
Forecast EBIT 20X2 (R000s)	35 000
EBIT multiple	7.0
Enterprise value (R000s)	245 000
Less debt 20X2	-50 000
Equity value (R000s)	195 000
Enterprise value adjusted at end	
Forecast EBIT 20X2 (R000s)	35 000
EBIT multiple of Nik Ltd	10.0
Enterprise value (R000s)	350 000
Less PCD (30%)	-105 000
	245 000
Less debt 20X2	-45 000
Equity value (R000s)	195 000

Adjusting the EBIT multiple for Nik (Pty) Ltd in valuing the business appears less severe than making the PCD adjustment at the end of the valuation. The end result, however, is identical.

Conclusion

The discount to be applied in valuing private companies compared with that of similar listed companies is subject to much conjecture. Valuation textbooks often cite a global average discount of 20 to 30 per cent without any empirical evidence to support this. Results of restricted stock studies and pre-IPO discounts are often quoted as evidence of the potential discount. However, this research is of limited use in practice. Companies generally issue restricted stock at an early stage in their life cycles or when they are unprofitable. The discounts applicable in these scenarios should not be extrapolated to all private company transactions.

Studies of share issues before successful IPOs as compared with the listing price provide unreliable evidence of the PCD. Most of these share issues are to insiders, such as existing shareholders and executives.

The most compelling evidence of the extent of the PCD derives from the analysis of actual EBIT and EBITDA multiples paid in private company transactions as compared to listed company deals. The empirical evidence indicates that private company multiples are 28 to 33 per cent lower than those of listed companies. The extent of the PCD is a matter of professional judgement in practice. Specific circumstances and risks need to be evaluated, and this is then incorporated into the cost of equity (DCF valuations) and lower multiples in earnings-based valuations.

Questions

1. Private companies generally trade at lower earnings multiples than listed entities because:
   - A. Of the illiquidity of private company shares
   - B. Private companies are generally smaller than listed companies
   - C. Of the illiquidity and specific risks associated with private businesses
2. Restricted stock represents:
   - A. Shares issued by listed companies in the USA that are not registered with the SEC
   - B. Share options granted to employees
   - C. Illiquid shares in publicly traded companies
3. The private company discount is:
   - A. On average 20 to 30 per cent globally
   - B. The discount applied to private company valuations due to illiquidity and specific risks
   - C. Best estimated through pre-IPO studies
4. The PCD should be incorporated in valuations by:
   - A. Adjusting the EBIT multiples of comparable listed companies
   - B. Deducting the value of debt from enterprise value
   - C. Decreasing the cost of equity and the WACC used to value private companies
5. Private companies are:
   - A. Easier to value than listed companies because they are often smaller
   - B. Less likely to apply scientific accounting policies
   - C. Likely to have transactions with connected parties that require adjustment in the valuation

References

De Franco, G., Gavious, I., Jin, J. & Richardson, G.D. (2007). *The private company discount and earnings quality*. Working Paper, University of Toronto, April 2007.

Emory. (2014). www.emoryco.com/valuation-studies.shtml. [Accessed 6 November 2014].

FMV Opinions Inc. (2014). *Determining discounts for lack of marketability: A companion guide to the FMV Restricted Stock Study 2014*

Koeplin, J., Sarin, A. & Shapiro, A.C. (2000). The private company discount. *Journal of Applied Corporate Finance* 12(4): 94–101, Winter 2000.

RisCura. (2014). *Bright Africa: A guide to equity investing on the continent*. Cape Town: RisCura.

Silber, W. (1991). Discounts on restricted stock: The impact of illiquidity on stock prices. *Financial Analysts Journal* 47(4): 60–64, July/August 1991.

CHAPTER 7
Discounts and premiums

LEARNING OUTCOMES

Once you have worked through this chapter, you should be able to:
+ Understand that control premiums in practice are not paid for control but for expected synergies after the deal
+ Understand the concept of small cap premiums and why these may or may not be appropriate in a valuation of a 'smaller' entity
+ Understand that a discount to intrinsic fair value may be appropriate when valuing a minority shareholding in a company
+ Have insight into why listed investment holding companies often trade at a discount to their net asset values

Introduction

Valuation practitioners often apply a variety of discounts and premiums at the end of a valuation process to encapsulate issues relating to control, or lack thereof, and the illiquidity of shares. While these issues need to be addressed in the valuation process, their mechanics and application are often questionable.

Control premiums

Acquiring control of an entity versus a passive minority interest has many benefits. Shareholder(s) with control are able to exercise a strong influence over the management of the entity and its strategic direction. A minority shareholder is unable to do so but could exert negative control if the stake held is 25 per cent or higher. In a South African context, any major corporate decision requires a special resolution, which means that 75 per cent or more of the shareholders present and voting at a shareholders' meeting need to approve the resolution. Major corporate decisions could include:

+ a material acquisition;
+ a scheme of arrangement between a company and its shareholders, which is the most common method of implementing a sale of control of a listed entity;
+ a disposal of the business as a going concern;
+ an issue of shares;
+ the granting of share options to directors;
+ a share buy-back; and
+ amendments to the company's Memorandum of Incorporation (MOI).

It follows that a shareholder who owns 75 per cent or more of a company can exercise effective control over the entity. A minority shareholder owning less than 25 per cent is powerless to influence major corporate decisions. The Companies Act (section 163) does, however, provide protection for minorities where the majority has acted in a manner that is oppressive and unfairly prejudicial. The applicant, in terms of section 163, can be a shareholder (minority or majority) or a director, and can seek relief from the Courts.

The question is, how much more is control worth than owning a minority shareholding? The answer depends on the specific circumstances, including the contents of the MOI. Shareholders' agreements could also regulate decision-making among shareholders by, for example, providing for unanimous consent on key decisions and/or entrenching the rights of minorities to appoint directors.

Interestingly, the Companies Act requires only an ordinary resolution (a 50,1 per cent shareholder vote in favour of resolution) to appoint and remove directors. The board of directors of a listed entity carries tremendous responsibility and power. It is only when issues become acrimonious that shareholders tend to intervene. This applies equally to the power of control. Minority and majority shareholders share proportionately in the economic benefits (dividends and share price appreciation) of being a shareholder. Control is useful but uneventful in well-run, successful companies. The benefit of control becomes apparent when a business underperforms and requires a change in directors and/or executive management.

The term 'control premium' is widely used in merger and acquisition transactions and refers to the difference between the takeover offer price and the average share price during the preceding four-week period. Occasionally, it also refers to the average share price for the three months before the takeover bid. The arguments for a control premium to be paid include the following:

+ Daily share prices reflect the amounts paid for small parcels of shares, which do not reflect the price that would be paid if a controlling interest was disposed of or acquired; and
+ The benefit of control is the ability to determine the strategic direction of the business, appoint the directors, influence dividend decisions and make important corporate decisions such as acquisitions and disposals.

Research studies indicate that bids for controlling interests in listed companies are generally 20 to 30 per cent higher than the short-term average share price prior to the takeover bid. This is conveniently referred to as the control premium. It would be nonsensical to apply this premium on a mechanical basis. Acquirers should perform their own valuations of target companies as opposed to blindly accepting prevailing share prices as indicative fair prices. Stock markets are notoriously volatile and – as some, such as Robert Shiller, would argue – 'overly exuberant'.

Acquirers performing their own valuations of listed target companies will value 100 per cent of the shares in issue. To add a control premium to a valuation of 100 per cent of the target would be verging on insanity. The reality is that acquirers generally have to bid at higher than prevailing share prices of targets, but this is more to do with securing the takeover than the value of control. Existing shareholders of target companies are unlikely to accept offers at ruling share prices and would require a premium to be enticed to sell. Acquirers should therefore seek targets that are undervalued and/or whose performance can be improved after the acquisition.

Perceived synergies post-acquisition are important in merger and acquisition transactions for two reasons. Firstly, acquirers need to unlock synergies to justify bid prices. The most common synergies are higher revenues and/or cost savings. Secondly, acquirers seek to achieve a higher return on investment than that implied in the purchase price. Achieving synergies post-acquisition would assist in enhancing shareholder returns.

Hanouna, Sarin and Shapiro (2001) studied 1 725 controlling interest transactions in the USA and 2 348 on international stock exchanges over the period 1986 to 2000. Their research indicated a median control premium of approximately 30 per cent in the USA. The results of their study annually over the period are depicted in Figure 7.1.

FIGURE 7.1 USA control premiums, 1986–2000

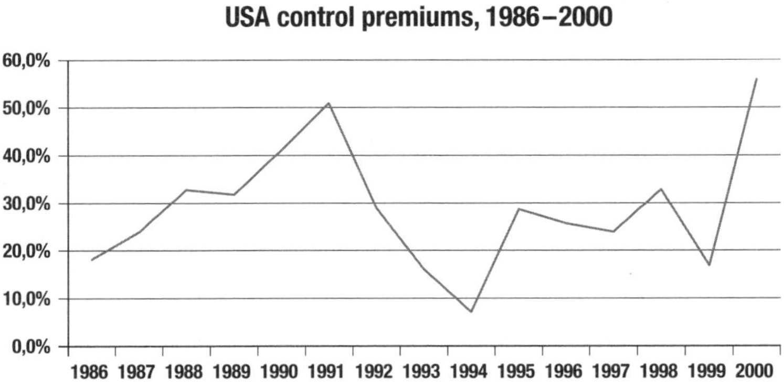

Source: Hanouna et al. (2001)

The average control premium paid according the Hanouna, Sarin and Shapiro study indicates an inconsistent trend. The highest average control premium was 55,9 per cent in 2000, at the height of the dot com bubble, and the lowest was 7,2 per cent in 1994.

Various databases available to subscribers provide information on control premiums. However, if you agree with the contention that premiums paid are sentiment-driven and largely based on perceived synergy benefits post-acquisition, then these databases may be of little relevance.

The premium paid by Woolworths in its acquisition of David Jones in 2014 is analysed at the end of this chapter, along with whether this premium was for control or for forecast synergies.

Small stock premiums

The average annual returns of 'small' listed companies versus 'large' listed companies on USA stock markets has been the subject of various research studies. Those by Banz (1981) and Fama and French (1992) (refer to www.etf.com) are often quoted in academic research and by fund managers. Professor Ken French continues to maintain a database of the performance of portfolios of various sizes (refer to mba.tuck.dartmouth.edu/pages/faculty/ken.french/data_library.html). ETF.com published an interesting summary of these in 2013, based on data from the Center for Research in Security Prices at the University of Chicago.

TABLE 7.1 Portfolio performance by size

	1963–1990	1991–2012	1927–2012
Compound annual return			
Large caps	10,2%	9,3%	9,6%
Small caps	12,3%	12,4%	11,5%
Difference	2,1%	3,1%	1,9%
Average annual return			
Large caps	11,3%	11,1%	11,5%
Small caps	15,6%	14,9%	15,6%
Difference	4,3%	3,8%	4,1%

Source: www.etf.com

Small caps were defined as the bottom half of all listed companies on USA stock markets and large caps as the top half. The compound annual growth in small caps was consistently higher than that of larger listed entities in all three time periods. The difference in average annual returns was even greater.

The fact that smaller listed companies outperformed larger entities should not be surprising. Intuitively, investing in smaller companies should be riskier and, hence, returns should be higher.

The PWC survey (PricewaterhouseCoopers 2012) revealed that the majority of its respondents apply a small cap premium (SCP) when valuing smaller businesses. The most common method is to add the SCP to the cost of equity derived using CAPM. A closer inspection of the survey results reveals that this is a not a material adjustment for most businesses as the average SCP for companies valued at more than R2 million is 1,0 per cent.

Arguably, the SCP is embedded in beta coefficients of listed companies. If this is the case, adding a small stock premium when valuing a smaller listed entity could be double counting. Furthermore, the private company discount used in valuations may already incorporate specific risk factors such as smaller size.

The differential returns generated by small versus large listed companies will vary depending on:

- the definition of 'small' versus 'large' – 'small' could be defined as the bottom half, quartile or decile of listed companies and this could have a significant impact on historical returns. Similarly, 'large' could be defined as the top decile or quartile;
- whether we compare compound annual growth versus arithmetic averages over time; and
- the time period covered – the past 20, 50 or 100 years?

Caution should be exercised prior to including an SCP in valuing a business. We should avoid double counting by adding an SCP when valuing a small listed company. The beta coefficient and implied EBIT or EBITDA multiples of such a listed entity should theoretically take cognisance of the specific risks facing the business, including its size.

When valuing a private company, we should also exercise caution in adding an SCP. The private company discount used should therefore exclude adjustments for its smaller size relative to its listed counterparts. This is difficult to estimate in practice given that the PCD, discussed in Chapter 6, includes illiquidity, size and specific risks in the implied discount.

The question is, how do we adjust for the SCP when valuing a private company?

- Do we adjust the market risk premium or do we add the SCP to the derived cost of equity?
- Do we adjust the EBIT multiple used or do we discount the valuation result?

EXAMPLE 7.1

Let's illustrate this with an example of a mythical private company:

- Risk-free rate of 8,0 per cent
- Market risk premium of 7,0 per cent
- Beta of 1.2
- Small cap premium of 3,0 per cent
- Free cash flow in Year 0 of R50 million
- Annual growth in free cash flows of 5,0 per cent
- EBIT in Year 0 of R75 million
- Appropriate EBIT multiple of 6.0
- No surplus cash or debt.

TABLE 7.2 DCF valuation

DCF valuation	
a. Adjust market risk premium	
Cost of equity	
8,0% + [1.2 × (7,0% + 3,0%)] =	20,0%
Enterprise value	
R50m ÷ (20,0% – 5,0%) =	R333,3m
b. Adjust cost of equity at end	
Cost of equity	
8,0% + (1.2 × 7,0%) =	16,4%
Add SCP	3,0%
	19,4%
Enterprise value	
R50m ÷ (19,4% – 5,0%) =	R347,2m

The enterprise values derived in Table 7.2 using the two different approaches are similar. The latter approach is most commonly used in practice. The market risk premium should probably be adjusted by analysing the annual returns of small caps against the historical risk-free rate to derive an adjusted small cap market risk premium. This task is fraught with potential errors so it is suggested that the SCP rather be added to the cost of equity if you choose to include this in your valuation.

Adjusting an earnings-based valuation for the SCP is more difficult than in a DCF valuation. Let's attempt two different approaches for the above example.

TABLE 7.3 Earnings-based valuation

Earnings-based valuation	
a. Adjust EBIT multiple	
Expected small cap return	18,0%*
Expected overall market return	15,0%°
** Calculated as overall market return + 3%*	
° Calculated as risk-free rate + market risk premium	

Continued

Difference [(18% – 15%) ÷ 15%] =	20%
Appropriate EBIT multiple	6.0
Small cap adjustment (20%)	-1.2
Adjusted EBIT multiple	4.8
Enterprise value	R360,0m
b. Adjust valuation result	
Enterprise value [R75m × 6.0] =	R450,0m
Less small cap adjustment (20%)	-R90,0m
Adjusted enterprise value	R360,0m

The approach in (a) in Table 7.2 is subtler and should probably be favoured. The important principle is that the expected return from investing in equities as an asset class should be compared to expected small cap returns and that the EBIT multiple should be adjusted by this differential.

In Example 1, we were valuing a private company. Presumably, we would have identified similar listed entities and calculated their EBIT multiples over time and then adjusted for illiquidity, specific risks and size. Including an SCP may be difficult in these circumstances as the PCD inherently includes adjustments for size.

Marketability discounts

Discounts for illiquidity of shares were covered in Chapter 6 with regards to private companies. We would not generally apply a liquidity discount for listed companies since their shares are readily tradable on stock exchanges. However, we should be aware of listed companies whose shares are not actively traded because of a limited free float of shares. For example, if a listed company's shares are 90 per cent held by two anchor investors, the 'free float' of shares would only be 10 per cent of total shares in issue. There may not be sufficient shares that are actively traded and the company's share price should be treated with caution. It may not reflect the price payable by willing buyers and sellers since there is a scarcity of shares available to buy and sell.

Thinly traded listed shares can often be identified by their calculated betas. Abnormally low betas or negative betas may indicate that shares are not actively traded and share prices movements are unrelated to external market influences. A review of the published betas by BNP Paribas (2014) reveals numerous JSE industrial listed companies (excluding property companies) with negative betas as measured at September 2014 (see Table 7.4).

TABLE 7.4 Published betas

Published betas	September 2014	Published betas	September 2014
Banks		**Industrial engineering**	
Finbond	-0.08	Austro	-0.26
Beverages		Master Drilling	-0.26
Awethu Breweries	-1.25	Mine Restoration	-0.84
Chemicals		PSV	-0.06
Delta EMD	-0.06	**Industrial metals**	
Spanjaard	-0.62	BSI	-0.26
Equity investment		**Personal goods**	
Brimstone	-0.10	Imbalie	-0.94
Sabvest	-0.13	**Software and computer services**	
Trematon	-0.08	Compu Clearing	-0.10
Food producers		Convergenet	-0.63
AH-Vest	-0.46	Datacentrix	-0.15
Financial services		**Support services**	
Transaction Capital	-0.15	Metrofile	-0.04
London Finance	-0.28	Kelly	-0.06
Prescient	-0.08	Marshall Monteagle	-0.92
Global Asset Management	-1.98	Morvest	-0.09
Vunani	-0.29	Primeserv	-0.73
Efficient Group	-0.72	CSG	-0.11
General retailers		Torre	-2.14
Cashbuild	-0.06	RG Smart	-0.85
Nictus	-0.32	**Technology and hardware**	
Rex Trueform	-0.37	Poynting	-1.07
Verimark	-1.18		
African and Overseas	-0.80		

It is interesting that all of the listed companies in Table 7.4 are smaller listed companies, categorised as 'small caps', 'fledgling' or AltX companies by the JSE. It is concerning that 37 listed industrial companies had negative betas in September 2014, given the total population of 204 listed companies in the large cap, mid cap, small cap, fledgling and AltX categories excluding property and mining. We could not use negative betas in valuing these smaller listed companies as doing so would produce bizarre results. Nor could we use their EBIT multiples in valuing private companies without carefully analysing derived multiples as their share prices may not be reflective of indicative fair value.

Minority discounts: Listed companies

The minority discount is occasionally treated as the inverse of the control premium in practice. Given the author's reservations about the calculation and application of control premiums in practice, as highlighted earlier in the chapter, inverting such premiums to derive a minority discount would be inappropriate.

It is recommended that, in practice, a business is valued based on acquiring a 100 per cent interest in it. No control premium is appropriate in these circumstances. However, a discount to the indicative fair value may be warranted if the stake being acquired is a minority interest. This discount would be attributed to the absence of control and the potential discount on subsequent selling of the stake. The extent of this discount is a matter for debate. There is limited, if any, empirical evidence of what the minority discount is in practice.

The Hanouna study (2001) included an analysis of 1 675 minority interest transactions on USA stock markets over the period 1986 to 2000. These transactions involved the acquisition of 5 per cent or more of the listed company shares but resulted in the acquirer owning less than a 30 per cent shareholding interest post-acquisition. Figure 7.2 summarises the average premiums paid over the prevailing share prices.

FIGURE 7.2 USA minority premiums 1986–2000

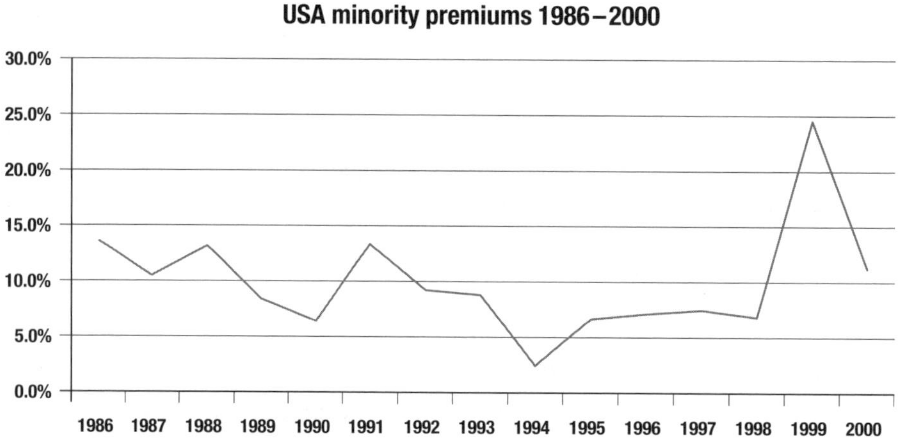

Source: Hanouna et al. (2001)

The average premium paid relative to the average share prices over the preceding four-week periods was 10,0 per cent. This may provide evidence of a minority premium as opposed to a discount. However, this would be an inappropriate conclusion since the minority discount should be the difference between what was paid and what would have been paid for a controlling stake. The prevailing share price may be relevant or irrelevant for these purposes.

A minority interest is defined as a non-controlling interest and could vary from 0,1 per cent to 49,9 per cent. The aforementioned percentages refer to voting control as opposed to the right to receive dividends (refer to Chapter 4 for discussion of voting and non-voting shares in practice).

The potential minority discount arising on selling shares in a listed entity will depend on the circumstances. Table 7.5 sets out various possibilities.

TABLE 7.5 Potential outcomes of shareholding blocks sold in listed companies

Shareholding blocks sold in listed companies	Potential outcomes
0,01% to 4,99%	Likely to be at prevailing bid and offer prices.
5,0% to 9,9%	Likely to be at a discount to prevailing bid and offer prices as the market becomes aware of selling pressure – typical supply and demand features. Or it could be a block trade – refer to the next row in this table. The acquirer will need to notify the company of beneficial interest acquired of 5,0% or more in terms of section 122(3) of the Companies Act, and the company will need to report this via SENS in terms of paragraph 3.83 of the JSE Listings Requirements. Transactions resulting in the acquirer obtaining 10% or more, and every 5% thereafter, also need to be notified.
10,0% to 25,0%	Likely to be a block trade of shares between a willing buyer and seller. These trades are entered into off the market and subsequently recorded on the JSE trading platform. The price will be negotiated between parties and could be higher or lower than the prevailing share price, depending on circumstances.
25,1% to 49,9%	Likely to be at a premium to the prevailing share price. Owning more than 25% will enable the acquirer to veto any major corporate decision.

Note that the transaction prices above may or may not reflect indicative fair value. There is transparency in share prices of listed companies and this will 'anchor' initial negotiations around price. Acquirers and sellers of shares in listed companies need to perform their own valuation of companies and then compare their results with prevailing share prices.

DID YOU KNOW?

Solomon Lew, a wealthy Australian businessman, frustrated Woolworths from acquiring 100 per cent of Country Road, a listed Australian retailer, for over 17 years. Lew reportedly owned over 10 per cent of the shares in issue of Country Road and could effectively block Woolworths from increasing its stake from 88 per cent to 100 per cent, thereby taking full control of Country Road. When Lew became aware of Woolworths' bid for David Jones, another listed Australian retailer, he bought shares in the open market, attempting to breach the 10 per cent shareholding mark. Whatever his intentions, it certainly unlocked value for his shareholding in Country Road. Woolworths offered A$17,00 a share to all remaining shareholders in Country Road in mid 2014, subject to the successful acquisition of David Jones. Country Road's share price was around A$5,00 in early February 2014, so the A$17,00 bid was a massive premium to the share price earlier in the year. Lew accepted Woolworths' offer for his Country Road shares and reportedly declined to vote at the David Jones shareholders meeting. Woolworths concluded its 100 per cent acquisition of David Jones in July 2014.

An interesting feature of the South African Companies Act, 2008, is the appraisal rights available to minority shareholders. Section 164 provides that minority shareholders are entitled to demand that the company buys its shares at fair value in certain circumstances. If the company amends its MOI or enters into a fundamental transaction (disposal of the business as a going concern, takeover or merger transaction, or enters into a scheme of arrangement), minorities may demand that the company acquires all of its shares, provided:

- they gave the company written notice of their objection ahead of the scheduled shareholders' meeting; and
- they voted against the resolution at the meeting.

Section 164 provides minorities in listed and private companies with a useful exit strategy if they wish to realise value or fundamentally disagree with the strategy of the majority shareholders. Their objection need not be justified or reasonable.

The circumstances that could potentially trigger minorities' appraisal rights are all decisions that require a special resolution (75 per cent or more of shareholders present and voting at a duly convened shareholders' meeting). Arguably, minorities owning 25 per cent of the shares in issue could exercise their rights and force the company to acquire their shares.

Takeover bids in South Africa now often have a condition precedent relating to appraisal rights, such as no more than 5 per cent of ordinary shareholders will exercise their rights in terms of section 164 of the Companies Act.

The difference between the premiums paid for controlling interests and minority shareholdings in the Hanouna et al. study (2001) are interesting. Figure 7.3 presents a graph of these differences over the period 1986 to 2000.

FIGURE 7.3 Implied minority discount 1986–2000

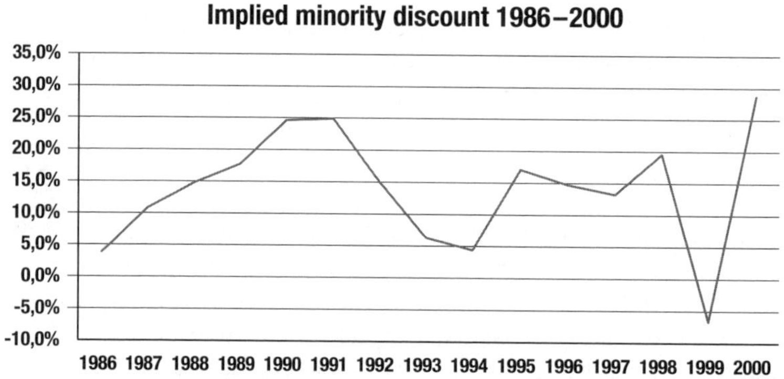

Source: Hanouna et al. (2001)

Figure 7.3 was based on the data from the Hanouna study after making the following assumptions:

- An assumed average share price for all companies in the research of $100;
- A calculated average price paid based on control premiums for the year. For example, if the average control premium paid was 18,4 per cent, then the assumed purchase price was $118,20;
- A calculated average price paid for a minority interest based on premiums or discounts paid during the year. For example, if the average minority premium paid was 13,6 per cent during the period, the assumed purchase price was $113,60; and
- The implied minority discount being the difference between $118,20 and $113,60, or 3,9 per cent.

The average implied minority discount was 14,0 per cent over the period 1986 to 2000. However, the average discount paid for minority interests versus controlling stakes was volatile and varied between a premium of 6,6 per cent in 1999 and a discount of 28,6 per cent in 2000. This data is of interest but should not be assumed to be indicative of the minority discount to be applied in all circumstances. Empirical research would be required of the average implied EBIT or EBITDA multiples paid for controlling interests versus that paid for minority interests over an extended period.

Minority discounts: Private companies

The transferability of shares in a private company is governed by the MOI and, if applicable, the shareholders' agreement. A common provision relates to pre-emptive rights - shareholders may not sell to third parties without first offering shares to existing shareholders. The MOI may also provide for:

- tag alongs - minorities are forced to sell their shares if majority shareholders sell out;
- come alongs - majority shareholders can force minority shareholders to procure that third parties acquire their shares too if minorities sell their shares. So, for example, if a minority shareholder was selling a 30 per cent interest, a majority shareholder holding 70 per cent could force the minority shareholder to procure a bid for 100 per cent of the company even though they only intended selling their 30 per cent interest; and
- put options - shareholders may be deemed to have offered their shares to other shareholders in certain circumstances such as resignation as employees, upon death or retirement, upon insolvency, or if they commit fraudulent acts.

Shareholders' agreements often provide guidance regarding the determination of fair value of shares upon sale by shareholders. The agreements may specify that if shares to be sold are minority interests, this should be ignored for the purposes of the valuation and no minority interest discount should be applied.

The acquisition of a majority interest in a private company, particularly stakes of higher than 75 per cent, provides more control of the future direction of the business and may make the majority interest easier to dispose of subsequently. Minority interests are likely to be less valuable than controlling interests given the absence of control and the illiquidity of private company shares. Table 7.6 provides some guidance about factors to consider when acquiring interests of different percentages in a private company.

TABLE 7.6 Potential outcomes of interests acquired in private companies

Shareholding interests acquired in private companies	Potential outcomes
0,1% to 10,0%	Unlikely to be able to exercise any influence over the company's affairs and potentially difficult to sell the stake later, given the limited marketability of the shares. Would apply a substantial discount to the indicative fair value of the company when acquiring an insignificant minority interest.
10,1% to 25,0%	Similar to the above, except the extent of the minority/ marketability discount may be lower.

Continued

25,1% to 34,9%	Minority discount still relevant – however, intuitively lower than for stakes under 25% acquired.
35,0% to 49,9%	Able to veto any major corporate decisions, so this stake is valuable in protecting own interests. Acquisition of 35% or more triggers a compulsory offer to remaining shareholders in terms of the Companies Act and Takeover Regulation Panel rules. Hence, caution should be exercised not to inadvertently trigger the acquisition of a controlling interest. Assuming this is not the case, the minority discount is still applicable, but to a lesser extent than for a 20% interest.

Table 7.6 is vague about the extent of the minority discount to be applied in different circumstances. This is deliberate given the lack of empirical evidence about minority discounts in practice. The minority discount is also inextricably linked to the illiquidity of private company shares. The discount for lack of control only becomes important for poorly managed businesses or where majority shareholders are acting in an unfair and prejudicial manner towards minorities. The lack of marketability of minority stakes in private companies is always relevant.

The PWC survey (PricewaterhouseCoopers 2012) revealed that respondents applied the following discounts for minority interests:

TABLE 7.7 Discounts for minority interests, PWC survey

Size of interest	1–24%	25–49%
Average 2012	18%	14%
Average 2010	22%	15%
Average 2007	20%	16%

Source: PricewaterhouseCoopers (2012)

It would appear that the average minority discount for shareholding blocks of under 25 per cent acquired is 20 per cent, and 15 per cent for minority interests above that. The survey results are interesting but by no means based on empirical evidence. The survey is based on valuation practitioners' answers to questions such as, 'Which minority discount do you apply ...?' as opposed to analysing actual earnings multiples paid in acquisitions of minority stakes versus controlling interests.

In Chapter 6, we discussed the extent of the private company discount, which varied between 20 and 33 per cent based on various empirical studies. Adding a minority discount of, say, 20 per cent on top of this would result in an overall significant discount to indicative fair value.

The minority discount to be applied in practice will depend on:

- the size of the business being valued – the discount should probably be lower for larger companies;
- the dividend policy of the company – if dividends payout ratio is high, future forecast dividends could be present-valued at the cost of equity; and
- the intention to list – if there are plans to list the company within the next six to 12 months, the minority discount could be lower.

Investment holding companies

In Chapter 5, we covered the suggested valuation approach for investment holding companies. We recommended valuing each underlying investment separately and aggregating it to determine the overall net asset value, after deducting liabilities. Listed investment holding companies generally trade at a discount to NAV. To illustrate, the NAV per share of three South African listed investment companies (Brimstone, PSG Group and Reinet) was compared to their year-end share prices over a five-year period. NAV per share numbers were obtained from their published annual reports over the period 2010 to 2014 for Reinet and PSG, and 2009 to 2013 for Brimstone. The results are summarised in Figure 7.4.

FIGURE 7.4 Average discount to NAV 2009/10 to 2013/14

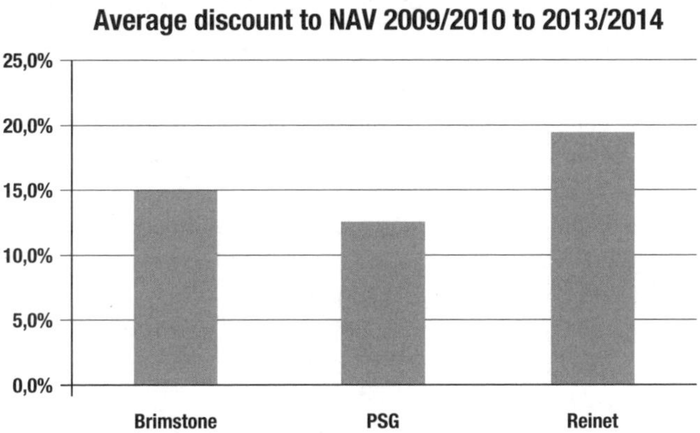

Source: Published annual reports – Reinert, Brimstone and PSG

Reinet had the largest average discount to NAV at 19,4 per cent over the period, while PSG had the lowest at 12,6 per cent. Reinet has various investments but its stake in British American Tobacco (BAT) represented over 80 per cent of its NAV during 2010 to 2014. Interestingly, BAT has been the largest listed company on the JSE for many years. Reinet's shareholding in BAT at March 2014 was 3,9 per cent.

DID YOU KNOW?

'Reinet' may seem to be an interesting name for an investment company, being Spanish for 'Queen'. However, the investment company's name may be more closely related to the town of Graaff-Reinet in the Eastern Cape, where Anton Rupert grew up. Anton's son Johann is the chairman of Reinet.

PSG's interests in three listed companies (Capitec, Curro and PSG Konsult) also contributed over 80 per cent of its sum of the parts valuation at February 2014. PSG had controlling interests in both Curro and PSG Konsult in 2014 and a 28,3 per cent interest in Capitec.

Brimstone is black-controlled and -managed investment company with a 5,0 per cent interest in Life Healthcare and a 16,8 per cent stake in Oceana, among others. These two listed investments contributed over 70 per cent of Brimstone's intrinsic NAV at December 2013.

The question is, why do listed investment holding companies trade at a discount to NAV? Reinet, PSG and Brimstone's major investments are in listed companies, whose values are readily determinable. Potential reasons for discounts include:

- minority discounts applied to underlying investments;
- the potential CGT consequences of realising investments in the future;
- potential illiquidity consequences – investors can buy underlying listed portfolio investments directly, whereas investing in holding companies leaves the subsequent disposal decisions in the hands of the investment holding companies' directors; and
- the future operating costs of managing the investment portfolio.

CASE STUDY Why would you invest in Reinet, the PSG Group and Brimstone instead of directly acquiring underlying listed investments?

Listed investment holding companies registered in South Africa may be tax inefficient in that the subsequent disposal of underlying investments would trigger CGT. The effective CGT rate for South African companies is 18,6 per cent of the capital gain on realisation of investments. This is a significant cost, which could be avoided if shareholdings were held directly by individual shareholders rather than through investment holding companies.

Reinet is a Luxembourg-registered company with a primary listing on the Luxembourg Stock Exchange and a secondary listing on the JSE. Reinet's domicile may be due to Luxembourg's lower corporate tax rates (income tax, CGT and dividend withholding taxes).

PSG has a long-standing track record of investing in fledgling businesses and partnering these through growth phases. These investment opportunities would not be directly available to the investing public, except through acquiring PSG shares.

Brimstone is an investment company that seeks to be a black economic empowerment (BEE) partner to medium and large South African companies. This focus unlocks opportunities that may not be available to the investing public and that provide an opportunity for individual and institutional investors to participate indirectly in BEE deals.

Earlier in the chapter, we discussed the potential minority discounts for listed investments. The subsequent realisation by Reinet, Brimstone and the PSG Group of their minority stakes in other listed companies could be at prevailing share prices, or at discounts or premiums thereto. It is difficult to predict the outcomes of these potential realisations. However, the management teams of Reinet, Brimstone and PSG are highly experienced businesspeople who would seek to maximise exit proceeds. It would be surprising if they sold minority stakes at lower than prevailing share prices.

It is difficult to establish the management and operational costs of Brimstone and PSG of managing their underlying investment portfolios. Both groups have controlling interests in certain underlying investments and these are consolidated for financial reporting purposes. Hence, it is not apparent from their annual reports which operating costs are attributable to their subsidiaries and which are related to their head office costs. It would be interesting to obtain this information and benchmark as a percentage of the intrinsic NAV annually.

Reinet's activities are managed by a general partner, Reinet Investments Manager SA (the Investment Advisor), a company registered in Luxembourg. This structure is similar to a private equity fund where the fund manager is paid annually to manage the portfolio and performance fees for exceeding benchmark returns. Reinet pays the Investment Advisor an annual management fee of approximately 1,0 per cent of the NAV of Reinet for its expertise and efforts in managing the investment portfolio. In addition, Reinet reimburses certain of the Investment Manager's operational expenses annually.

Reinet also pays the Investment Advisor a performance fee equivalent to 10 per cent of the cumulative total shareholder return annually. Simplistically, total shareholder return is defined as the increase in Reinet's share price annually together with any distributions to shareholders during the year. These management and performance fees are material and could explain the larger discount to NAV applied by the stock market when valuing Reinet.

As mentioned previously, Reinet's major investment is its 3,9 per cent interest in BAT. It follows that any increase in Reinet's underlying NAV and, presumably, share price would be directly attributable to the increase in BAT's share price. It seems generous to incentivise the Investment Advisor based on external influences rather than on its active management of the remaining investment portfolio.

CASE STUDY Woolworths' acquisition of David Jones

Woolworths Holdings Limited (Woolworths), the JSE-listed retail group, announced on 9 April 2014 that it had reached agreement with David Jones to acquire 100 per cent of the shares in issue of the listed Australian department store business for A$4,00 a share. The bid price was at a premium of 25,4 per cent to the closing share price of David Jones on 8 April 2014. This premium would typically be attributed to the fact that the David Jones share price reflected prices paid for small parcels of shares and did not include the value of control. We discussed and dispelled this myth earlier in the chapter. The reality is that Woolworths had to offer more than the ruling share price to entice David Jones shareholders to sell their shares to Woolworths. The question is whether the David Jones share price on 8 April 2014 of A$3,19 undervalued the company or whether Woolworths was building expected synergies post-acquisition into the purchase price.

David Jones's profits had been declining since its year ended July 2011. Its revenue and EBIT performance is set out in Table 7.8.

TABLE 7.8 Revenue and EBIT performance, David Jones

David Jones A$ millions Year end July	2011	2012	2013	2014*
Revenue	1 961,7	1 867,8	1 845,0	1 918,8
EBIT	246.5	154.3	149.0	135.4
EBIT/Revenue	12,6%	8,3%	8,1%	7,1%

Continued

Annual change in:				
Revenue	-4,5%	-4,8%	-1,2%	4,0%
EBIT	-1,1%	-37,4%	-3,4%	-9,1%
* Broker consensus				

Source: David Jones Scheme booklet 2014

David Jones had 38 stores open and trading in financial year 2013 (FY2013) in Australia. Product ranges included clothing, footwear and accessories, homeware, electrical, furniture and food. The group had an estimated 10 per cent market share in the Australian department store market, positioning itself as a premium price and quality operator. Revenue and EBIT declined over the period FY2010 to FY2013 due to soft retail conditions and increasing competition from international retailers such as Zara, Topshop and The Gap.

EBIT in FY2014 was expected to decline further after American Express halved its profit-sharing arrangement with David Jones during the year. American Express (Amex) operates the David Jones store card and extends credit to cardholders. Financial services EBIT (effectively the profit share received from Amex) represented 33,2 per cent of total EBIT in FY2013. The renegotiation of the Amex agreement could potentially have reduced financial services EBIT from A$50 million in FY2013 to A$24 million in FY2014.

Table 7.9 summarises the implied EBIT multiples of David Jones based on its year-end share prices and information from its annual reports.

TABLE 7.9 Implied EBIT multiples, David Jones

David Jones A$ millions Year end July	**2011**	**2012**	**2013**
Year-end share price	A$3,00	A$2,44	A$2,82
	A$ millions	**A$ millions**	**A$ millions**
Enterprise value	1 562	1 290	1 509
EBIT	247	154	149
Implied EBIT multiples			
Historic	6.8	9.1	11.4
Forward	10.3	10.9	11.1*
* Based on broker consensus			

Grant Samuel & Associates, the independent experts to David Jones, analysed international and Australian retail category specialists' EBIT multiples in 2014. The median 2014 EBIT multiple for international department store retailers was calculated to be 11.0 times, while the Australian listed retailers were trading on a median EBIT multiple of 11.6 times.

TABLE 7.10 High-level valuation assumptions, David Jones

	A$ millions
Forecast EBIT FY2014	135
EBIT multiple	11.0
Enterprise value – 100% of David Jones	1 485
Woolworths takeover bid price	2 150
Expected synergies	665

Source: Author's calculations, based on Grant Samuels' 11.0 EBIT multiple disclosed in the David Jones Scheme Booklet

It would appear that a reasonable valuation of 100 per cent of David Jones in April 2014 would have been A$1,49 billion based on its EBIT multiples over the past three years and international EBIT multiples. Woolworths bid A$2,15 billion and probably factored various synergies post-acquisition into its bid price for David Jones. Woolworths was transparent about expected synergies after the deal and disclosed an estimated A$130 million per annum of synergy benefits during FY2015 to FY2017. The source of expected synergies included:

- increasing private label sales from 3,5 per cent of sales to 20 per cent per annum;
- growth of Country Road (owned by Woolworths) brands within David Jones stores;
- improved margins through group sourcing; and
- optimising the David Jones real estate portfolio.

The expected synergies would significantly add to David Jones' EBIT over the period FY2015 to FY2017. The issue arising is whether Woolworths should have disclosed the extent of these synergies to the market and incorporated these into its bid price. The reality is that Woolworths needed to bid more than A$3,20 a share to secure control and probably had to include a significant portion of these future synergies to convince its shareholders to approve the deal. The debate in any merger and acquisition deal is whether the acquirer should pay the departing shareholders for benefits it will deliver post-acquisition.

Conclusion

Acquirers and their advisers often use control premiums to justify paying higher prices than the prevailing share price of the target firm. However, it is recommended that control premiums be ignored in practice to avoid overpaying for acquisition targets. Acquirers should perform their own valuations of 100 per cent of target companies rather than use the current share price and add a control premium. The reality is that bid prices will need to be higher than prevailing share prices to entice the target company shareholders to sell. The process of arriving at bid prices needs to be more rigorous than simply adding a control premium to current share prices.

It may be appropriate to apply a minority discount to the valuation of 100 per cent of the shares in issue of a company. Minority shareholders are unable to control the destiny of companies and this absence of control should be reflected in acquisition prices. Generally, the absence of control is not a major issue in well-managed and successful businesses. However, the power to enforce changes when the business is not performing is valuable. Minorities do not have this power, so their shareholding interests should trade at a discount to the value of controlling stakes. The extent of the discount is a matter of much conjecture in academic textbooks. An analysis of various research studies indicates that a discount of between 15 and 20 per cent would not be inappropriate for the lack of control. However, this discount needs to be assessed in each situation rather than being applied blindly as an average discount.

Any discounts deemed necessary in a valuation should be applied to enterprise value and not equity value. The value of surplus cash should then be added to enterprise value and interest debt should be deducted from enterprise value. To apply a discount to surplus cash and debt is inappropriate.

Questions

1. A control premium:
   - A. Represents the premium to be paid to the prevailing share price for the ability to control the company
   - B. Is redundant where 100 per cent of the target company is valued by the potential acquirer;
   - C. Of approximately 25 per cent should be paid in all circumstances
2. Small stock premiums represent:
   - A. The outperformance of smaller listed companies' share price increases as compared to larger listed shares over time
   - B. The discount that should applied when valuing a smaller entity
   - C. Evidence that stock markets are efficient
3. The minority discount:
   - A. Represents the discount that should be applied to the ruling share price of companies for acquiring a minority interest
   - B. Should, on average, be 5 per cent
   - C. Represents the discount that should be applied to a 100 per cent valuation of a company when only acquiring a minority stake
4. The discount applied to the indicative fair value of listed companies in the acquisition of minority interests:
   - A. Will vary depending on the size of the minority stake acquired
   - B. Will depend on prevailing market sentiment
   - C. Represents the inverse of the control premium payable
5. Investment holding companies' share prices are generally lower than their net asset values per share because:
   - A. The stock market does not trust the ability of investment companies to unlock value
   - B. Of, inter alia, the present value of expected future operating costs of investment holding companies
   - C. Of scepticism about share prices in general

References

BNP Paribas Cadiz Securities (2014). *The Equity Risk Service September 2014.* Johannesburg: BNP Paribas Cadiz Securities.

David Jones Scheme Booklet registered with ASIC, dated 23 May 2014.

Swedroe, L. (2013). Has the small-cap premium disappeared? Available at http://www.etf.com/sections/etf-strategist-corner/20051-has-the-small-cap-premium-disappeared.html?nopaging=1. [Last accessed 13 November 2014].

Hanouna, P., Sarin, A. & Shapiro, A.C. (2001). *Value of corporate control: Some international evidence.* USC Working Paper Series.

PriceWaterhouseCoopers. (2012). *An African perspective: Valuation methodology survey.* South Africa: PricewaterhouseCoopers.

CHAPTER 8

Challenging issues in DCF valuations

LEARNING OUTCOMES

Once you have worked through this chapter, you should be able to:

- Understand that stock markets occasionally overreact in the short term but are rarely 'wrong' in the long term
- Gain insights into the empirical failings of CAPM in practice
- Be wary of blindly using calculated betas without applying own judgement
- Use techniques to improve your estimates of continuing value in DCF valuations

Introduction

Chapters 2 and 3 covered the basics of DCF valuations and Chapter 4 provided some insights into earnings-based valuations. These chapters are predicated on the assumption that stock markets are efficient and provide invaluable inputs for our valuation models. Beta coefficients are obtained from market data, and this information is an important input in determining the cost of equity. Earnings multiples reflect the stock market's assessment of the value of individual shares and are used to value listed and private companies. Stock market behaviour over the past 30 years has provided many examples where the collective consciousness of investors may have overreacted to information and events. In this chapter we will examine and debate the efficiency of stock markets. The implications are serious – if stock markets are not efficient most of the time, then we may have to disregard betas and earnings multiples.

Hardened valuation practitioners should acknowledge that although the underlying CAPM theory is intuitively appealing and intellectually robust, its real-world application is often problematic. Beta coefficients obtained from credible sources are often counterintuitive or appear incorrect. This chapter will highlight some interesting empirical research on betas and provide some insights into overcoming potential issues in practice.

DCF valuations are based on forecasting free cash flows into infinity. The process of estimating the cash flow generation ability of a business for the next 20 or 30 years should be terrifying. It is impossible to know what will transpire next year, let alone in 20 years' time. Yet our valuations models are based on estimating cash flows for long periods of time. We will examine the practical difficulties in determining continuing value in practice and provide some pointers on how to minimise the error.

Efficient stock markets?

The efficient markets hypothesis (EMH) or theory is widely attributed to Eugene Fama, the Nobel laureate. Fama defined an efficient market as one in which share prices fully reflect all known information at any point in time (Fama 1970). His theory built upon prior work by Bachelier in 1900 and by Samuelson and Mandelbrot in the 1960s. EMH essentially proposes that future share price movements will be random and unpredictable. Stock markets will absorb new information and incorporate these into share prices. Since we cannot predict the future, these future movements will be unknowable until they occur.

It is often debated in academic circles whether EMH implies that stock markets accurately value individual shares given that all known information about these entities is already absorbed in share prices. Behavioural finance proponents such as Robert Shiller argue that stock markets are often driven by psychological factors and emotions, so markets tend to be inefficient at times. Others would argue that EMH does not imply that perfect valuations are performed by stock markets, but rather that future movements are random in nature.

EMH would, however, imply that we should invest our savings in the overall market as by definition our chances of outperforming the market by stock picking is at best a 50:50 endeavour.

A chart of historical stock market movements on the JSE over the period 1900 to 2006 was included in Chapter 1. This data (Firer and Staunton 2002) was updated to 2013 courtesy of the FTSE Fact Sheet and Statistics SA. Figure 8.1 shows the annual movements in the JSE ALSI and inflation data over the period 1964 to 2013.

FIGURE 8.1 JSE ALSI and inflation data 1964–2013

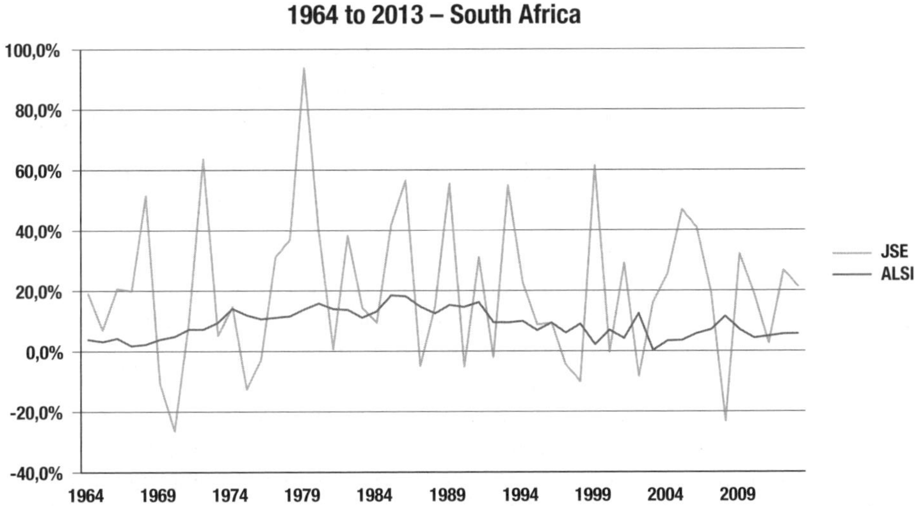

The South African stock market has been volatile over the past 50 years. The market corrections in 1970 and 2008 are visually obvious in Figure 8.1. It would appear that each correction followed a period of steep increases in the overall market.

The stock market 'crash' on 19 October 1987 is widely remembered:

> *Fama's efficient-market theory was instantly called into question. How could the market be 'right' one day, then suffer a 23 per cent collapse on virtually no new information the next day, then be fine the day after? (Patterson 2010)*

Jackwerth and Rubinstein offered incontrovertible proof that 19 October 1987 was statistically impossible: '...even if one were to have lived through the entire 20 billion year life of the universe and experienced this 20 billion times (20 billion big bangs), that such a decline could have happened even once in this period is a virtual impossibility...' (Patterson 2010). The reality is that it did happen – the probability of an event occurring is between 0 and 100 per cent, but hindsight is an exact science.

Some have argued that the 1987 stock market crash was not unexpected given certain events leading up to October of that year. Various minor events may have contributed to a lack of confidence in the equity markets. The long-term treasury bond yields increased by 1,5 per cent in the two months prior to the crash and various announcements by government officials caused some consternation in the market. There was talk of the introduction of a merger tax and a weakening of the US dollar. With hindsight, these factors should not have precipitated a 23 per cent correction. Nothing changed fundamentally during October 1987 and the markets did overreact. Warren Buffett reportedly stated that ' the fact that people are full of greed, fear and folly is predictable. The sequence is not predictable...' (Buffett & Clark 2006).

The 'bubbles' of 1999 and 2007 are recent examples of potential stock market mispricing of trends. The lofty valuations of Internet-based businesses and high-technology companies in the late 1990s could not be supported by economic fundamentals. The implied growth rates in their profits and cash flows would have required an expansion of the global economy that was unrealistic. Alternatively, these high-tech businesses would have needed to usurp most conventional businesses.

The credit 'bubble' that spectacularly burst in late 2008 was another example of mispricing in markets. With hindsight, housing price growth in the USA and certain European countries was unsustainable, as was the credit extension to consumers. The question is, how could efficient stock markets allow such mispricing? Shiller (2013) has interesting observations on bubbles:

> *Bubbles are not, in my mind, about craziness of investors. They are rather about how investors are buffeted en masse from one superficially plausible theory about conventional valuation to another...*

The current hype around social media valuations is concerning. The current market valuations of Facebook, Twitter, LinkedIn and Groupon would require significant earnings and cash flow growth to provide a reasonable long-term return for investors. The author is praying that we do not encounter another bubble so soon after 2008.

In Chapter 1 we referred to high-frequency trading and estimated that 50 per cent of all trades on the NYSE happen via these automated platforms. The CEO of the JSE, Nicky Newton-King, was quoted in the Business Day on 24 October 2014 as saying that high-frequency trading now accounts for 20 per cent of total trading volumes on the JSE. She hoped that this would increase in future as the JSE's co-location centre gave these traders faster access to market information. High-frequency trading is certainly good for trading volumes and JSE revenues – however, its impact on company valuations is unknown.

It is not known how much of trading volumes are accounted for by what could be termed mechanical investors. Koller (2010) estimates that 35 to 40 per cent of institutional equity is held by such investors. Mechanical investors include index funds that accumulate shares in an attempt to replicate the performance of the overall stock market or selected indices. Other investors that acquire shares with little regard to their underlying intrinsic values may include quants.

Quants trade in financial markets (equities, currencies, bonds, derivatives, commodities etc.) based on highly complicated mathematical models attempting to predict patterns. The intrinsic value of financial assets is generally irrelevant in quant trading; what is more important is predicting the movement in prices correctly. Patterson (2010) attributes the start of quant trading to Ed Thorp in the 1960s in the USA. It is interesting that two famous Nobel laureates, Myron Scholes and Robert Merton, founded and operated a hedge fund called Long-Term Capital Management (LTCM) in the 1990s. Scholes is famous for his contribution to option pricing (refer to Chapter 11 for a discussion of Black–Scholes option pricing model) while Merton has made various contributions to financial theory and asset pricing. LTCM operated on the principles of quant trading and was spectacularly successful during the period 1994 to early 1998. According to Patterson (2010), LTCM had a short position in US Treasury bonds in August 1998. The Russian government defaulted on its bonds in mid-August 1998, causing chaos in global financial markets. Investors behaved in a predictable manner by selling of risky assets such as emerging market shares and bonds and shifted into US Treasury bonds. The yield spread moved contrary to what LTCM had expected and forced it to exit its positions. Unfortunately, pricing in the financial markets did not adhere to theoretical behaviour as liquidity dried up. The Federal Reserve Bank of New York subsequently organised a bailout of LTCM through a consortium of banks taking control of the hedge fund and recapitalising it with an estimated US$3,6 billion.

The discussion above of high-frequency trading, mechanical investing, quants and hedge funds is relevant to valuations. There may be times in financial markets when government bond yields, share prices and currency movements are out of line with historical trends. Simply using market data without applying common sense will result in valuation errors at times. An example of this would have been in 1998 in South Africa. The yields on 10-year government bonds increased dramatically during the year, arguably in response to the Russian government default referred to earlier, to a peak of 20,7 per cent (source: South African Reserve Bank). If we had mechanically used the South African government bond yields in late 1998 as a risk-free proxy in our DCF valuations, we would have grossly undervalued most business. A review of historical bond yields in South Africa would have revealed that 1998 was an exception and there were abnormal factors influencing the market. Perhaps the best strategy in 1998 would have been to avoid performing company valuations or to have aggressively purchased potentially undervalued listed company shares?

The current hype around social media businesses may also prove to be unsustainable. Simply using earnings yields and revenue multiples of listed companies such as Facebook, Twitter and Groupon to value emerging private social media businesses is likely to result in significant error. We should rather resort to fundamental analysis to determine the future cash flow generation ability of the business being valued and present-value it using a reasonable discount rate. We will discuss the challenges of valuing high-growth businesses in Chapter 9.

Stock markets are prone to overreaction at times. This may be due to psychological factors according to behavioural finance proponents and/or it may be due to Buffett's reference to greed and fear. However, you should be warned that stock markets do tend to provide clear long-term patterns that are of great use in valuations. Burton Malkiel, author of the book *A random walk down Wall Street* (Malkiel 2003), concluded:

> *As long as stock markets exist, the collective judgment of investors will sometimes make mistakes. Undoubtedly, some market participants are demonstrably less than rational. As a result, pricing irregularities and even predictable patterns in stock returns can appear over time and even persist for short periods. Moreover, the market cannot be*

perfectly efficient, or there would be no incentive for professionals to uncover information that gets so quickly reflected in market prices ... But I suspect that the end result will not be an abandonment of the belief of many in the profession that the stock market is remarkably efficient in its utilization of information. Periods such as 1999 where 'bubbles' seem to have existed, at least in certain sectors of the market, are fortunately the exception rather than the rule. Moreover, whatever patterns or irrationalities in the pricing of individual stocks that have been discovered in a search of historical experience are unlikely to persist and will not provide investors with a method to obtain extraordinary returns ...

Wise words indeed, although the author doubts that Warren Buffett would agree. If he did, there would be no continuing reason for Berkshire Hathaway to exist or an explanation for its historical success in beating the return of the S&P 500 most years.

Beta coefficients

In Chapters 2 and 3 we covered betas. This data is the only unique input in determining the cost of equity per the CAPM. The risk-free rate and market risk premium should theoretically be identical whether we are valuing Apple Inc. or a small private company in the USA. Beta coefficients represent the volatility of individual share price movements versus the overall stock market.

The beta coefficients of certain listed JSE companies published by BNP Paribas (BNP Paribas Cadiz Securities 2014) may appear contentious. This is not the fault of BNP Paribas, whose service the author has used for years and whose calculations are performed by highly talented mathematicians, but rather a reflection on stock price movements. The betas calculated by BNP Paribas are based on five-year data after rigorous analysis. Table 8.1 sets out some industry betas that should be challenged before being used in practice.

TABLE 8.1 Industry betas

Betas relative to JSE ALSI	September 2014
Construction and materials	0.57
Industrial engineering	0.45
Food producers	0.39
Food and drug retailers	0.37
Banks	0.84

Source: BNP Paribas Cadiz Securities (2014)

Applying intuition and common sense, it would be expected that construction businesses would have a higher beta than the overall JSE. The period 2004 to 2013 provided clear evidence of the volatility of performance of listed construction companies in South Africa. The period leading up to the Soccer World Cup in 2010 in South Africa provided a stimulus to the industry. The global financial crisis in 2008 and the South African government's limited investment in infrastructure since 2009 have resulted in a slowdown in construction activity. It is unsurprising that the revenue and profits of listed construction businesses have been volatile over the period 2008 to 2013. Figure 8.2 depicts the movement of the JSE ALSI versus the Construction Index during this period (PWC 2013).

FIGURE 8.2 Movement of the JSE ALSI versus the Construction Index, 2008–2013

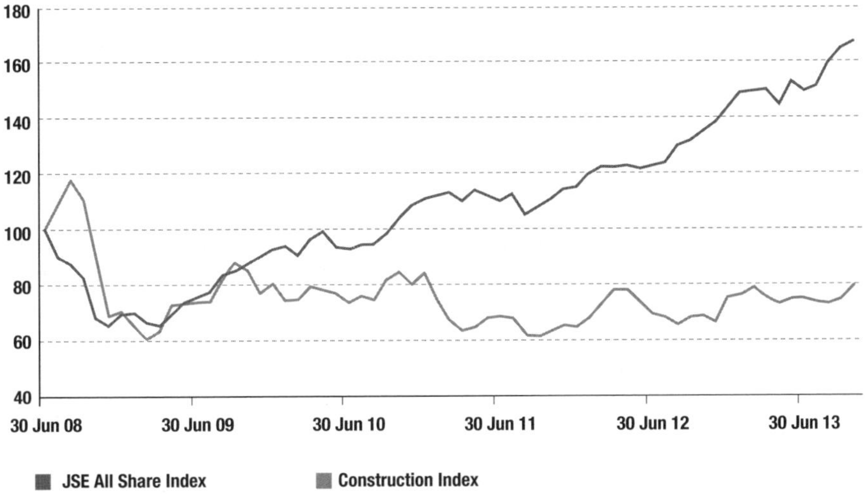

It is clear that the construction sector has lagged behind the overall stock market in recovering from the global financial crisis. In fact, the Construction Index in June 2013 is lower than it was in 2008. From a beta perspective, the construction industry is expected to be more volatile than the overall stock market. Hence, the betas of construction companies should arguably be higher than 1.0. But the data in Table 8.1 indicates that listed construction groups have betas of 0.57?

It could be argued that the profits and cash flows generated by industrial engineering businesses, food producers and banks would be more volatile than the overall stock market. This is not a reflection on their business models, but rather a reality of external forces that impact on their profitability. South African banks escaped the global financial crisis of 2008 relatively unscathed. That is testament to their robust business models and, perhaps, their conservativeness. However, analysing their historical profit performance, it is no surprise that they overperform in good times and struggle to maintain these profit levels when economic growth slows.

Food producers often struggle to cope with external forces such as fluctuating commodity prices and competition from imports. Analysing the profit performance of chicken producers reveals high volatility. Intuitively, the share price performance of listed food producers should be more volatile than the overall stock market. Yet, the beta data indicates that this was not the case per Table 8.1?

Food and drug retailers will continue to sell their products in good and tough economic conditions. Their cash flow generation and profit performance should be less volatile than that of other industry sectors. The data in Table 8.1 indicating a beta of less than 1.0 is unsurprising yet the question arising is whether the sector beta of 0.37 is, perhaps, too low?

Assuming a risk-free rate of 8,5 per cent and a market risk premium of 7,0 per cent in South Africa, the sector betas in Table 8.1 would translate into the following costs of equity:

TABLE 8.2 Estimated costs of equity of industry sectors

Estimated cost of equity per industry sector	September 2014
Construction and materials	12,5%
Industrial engineering	11,7%
Food producers	11,2%
Food and drug retailers	11,1%
Banks	14,4%

Source: Author's own calculations

Based on the risk-free rate and market risk premium assumptions above, this translates into an overall cost of equity (before the beta adjustment) of 15,5 per cent. This is in line with the long-term returns on the JSE over the past 100 years. The costs of equity per industry sector in Table 8.2 may, however, be too low?

A comparison of the beta coefficients of the industry indices per BNP Paribas (BNP Paribas Cadiz Securities 2014) and the JSE Financial and Industrial Index is revealing.

TABLE 8.3 Beta coefficients of industry indices

Betas at September 2014	JSE ALSI	JSE Financial and Industrial Index
Construction and materials	0.57	0.75
Industrial engineering	0.45	0.35
Food producers	0.39	0.54
Food and drug retailers	0.37	0.59
Banks	0.84	1.08

Source: BNP Paribas Cadiz Securities (2014)

The betas of the construction and materials, banks, and food and drug retailers sectors increase when benchmarked against the Financial and Industrial Index in Table 8.3. The banking sector beta is line with the author's expectations. The construction and materials beta is much lower than expected.

The industrial engineering sector beta, however, defies logic. Listed companies in this sector supply the following, among others:

- Materials handling equipment;
- Air and gas handling equipment;
- Bearings and seals;
- Power transmission equipment;
- Tools and fasteners;
- Agricultural equipment; and
- Diesel engines.

The industrial engineering sector's fortunes should be highly correlated with activities in the general industrial market, agriculture and mining. A beta of 0.45 relative to the JSE ALSI and 0.35 to the Financial and Industrial Index seems very low.

The interim conclusion when analysing betas of listed companies in certain JSE sectors is that these appear incorrect. The scenario worsens when we analyse individual listed companies' betas and discover that many have negative betas - refer to Chapter 7 for a list of financial and industrial companies at September 2014 that display this attribute.

The JSE may have features that other major stock markets do not have, namely that:

+ the top 20 listed companies by market capitalisation represent a significant proportion of the total value of all listed companies on the JSE;
+ certain of the top 10 listed companies - such as BAT, SAB, Glencore, Naspers, Billiton, Richemont and MTN - have significant interests outside South Africa; and
+ the overall JSE is heavily weighted towards mining and commodity-based businesses and financial services companies.

Table 8.4 sets out the market capitalisation of the largest 20 listed companies on the JSE at the end of November 2014 (Sharenet) and their betas at September 2014 (BNP Paribas).

TABLE 8.4 Market capitalisation and betas of the largest 20 companies listed on the JSE, 2014

		Market capitalisation Rbillions	Beta
1	British American Tobacco	1 318	0.36
2	SABMiller	1 022	0.85
3	Glencore Xstrata	740	#
4	Naspers	599	1.55
5	BHP Billiton	560	1.71
6	Compagnie Richemont	539	1.36
7	MTN	403	0.67
8	Anglo American	322	1.66
9	Sasol	301	1.03
10	FirstRand	280	1.03
11	Standard Bank	220	0.75
12	Vodacom	198	0.62
13	Aspen	183	0.66
14	Old Mutual	170	0.89
15	Sanlam	159	0.85
16	Barclays Africa	151	0.93
17	Steinhoff	146	1.27
18	Remgro	122	0.82
19	Nedbank	121	0.74
20	Anglo American Platinum	100	0.92
		7 654	
	Overall JSE*	11 680	
	** Source: www.jse.co.za* *# Recently listed*		

It is interesting to note that the top five listed companies on the JSE represent approximately 36 per cent of the total market capitalisation of the JSE in November 2014 and the top 20 listed companies contribute 66 per cent of the overall market value.

There is nothing startling about the betas of the top 20 JSE-listed companies in Table 8.4 except that Anglo American Platinum and BAT's seem a bit a low. These betas would need to be unlevered to determine the unlevered (or asset) betas of individual companies. Refer to Chapter 3 for the Hamada formula for unlevering and levering betas.

The above-mentioned features of the JSE may result in a disconnect between the share price movements of medium-sized and smaller listed companies versus the overall stock market. Factors influencing the share prices of the top 20 listed companies may not be the same as those affecting smaller listed entities, for example:

- commodity price movements;
- consumer demand for products and services in countries besides South Africa; and
- exchange rate movements.

Before we provide some practical tips on using betas in practice, let's examine some empirical research on betas.

Empirical research on betas

Various studies have been performed on historical betas that provide damning evidence of this technique as a risk measure. Certain research indicates that betas are far too volatile, while other research indicates an unexpected risk-return trade-off.

Fama and French (2004) calculated betas for every listed share on the NYSE over the period 1928 to 2003 and the NASDAQ from 1972 to 2003. The returns on these shares were then computed for the subsequent 12 months. The results were summarised as follows:

> *Confirming earlier evidence, the relation between beta and average returns for the ten portfolios is much flatter than the Sharp-Lintner CAPM predicts. The returns on the low beta portfolios are too high, and the returns on the high beta portfolios are too low. For example, the predicted return on the portfolio with the lowest beta is 8.3 per cent per year; the actual return is 11.1 per cent. The predicted return on the portfolio with the highest beta is 16.8 per cent; the actual return is 13.7 per cent ...*

Fama and French (2004) then proceed to make some profound statements in their article:

> *... If betas do not suffice to explain expected returns, the market portfolio is not efficient, and CAPM is dead in its tracks ...*
>
> *... But in the late 1970's, research begins to uncover variables like size, various price ratios and momentum that add to the explanation of average returns provided by beta. The problems are serious enough to invalidate most applications of CAPM ...*
>
> *... We continue to teach the CAPM as an introduction to the fundamental concepts of portfolio theory and asset pricing ... but warn students that despite its seductive simplicity, the CAPM's empirical problems probably invalidate its use in applications ...*

The empirical research performed by Fama and French and their publicised statements are not encouraging. Particularly since Fama is the pioneer of the efficient markets hypothesis!

Ward and Muller (2012) performed a study of the 160 largest listed shares on the JSE over the period 1986 to 2011. They constructed five different portfolios based on beta ranking. Their findings were enlightening:

> *... the portfolio with the highest beta shares exhibits an annualised return of 7.1% over the 25 year period. The portfolio with the lowest ranked betas exhibits an annualised return of 21.6% pa, significantly exceeding the 15.8% pa return of the J203 (ALSI) index ...*
>
> *...In contradiction to the CAPM, we find a monotonic, inverse relationship between beta and returns. Our results support the findings of Fama and French (1992, 2004), Montier (2007), van Rensburg and Robertson (2003) and Struggnell, Gilbert and Kruger (2011). We also observe that although this relationship was evident for the first 15 years of our analysis, the inverse effect appears to have been 'washed out' and is not evident after 2004, indicating no association between beta and returns in the last seven years ...*
>
> *... These findings have profound implications for the theory and use of single parameter Capital Asset Pricing Model, effectively rendering it redundant ...*

Fernandez (2004) also performed some interesting research into betas. His research analysed the betas for 3 813 companies listed on the NYSE and NASDAQ over the period 1 December 2001 to 31 January 2002 on the following basis:

- Betas were calculated on each day for the two-month period based on monthly share price data over the preceding five years; and
- Individual share price movements were compared to the S&P 500 index.

For example, Fernandez calculated the beta of Coca-Cola on 1 December 2001 based on its monthly share price over the period 1 December 1996 to 1 December 2001 relative to movements in the S&P 500 index over the same period. He then recalculated the beta of Coca-Cola on 2 December 2001 using the monthly share price movement over the preceding 60 months. This was repeated every day over the two-month period ending on 31 January 2002.

The results of Fernandez's research revealed the minimum and maximum betas for the following well-known companies:

TABLE 8.5 Betas of selected listed companies, December 2001 and January 2002

Betas of selected listed companies December 2001 and January 2002	Minimum beta	Maximum beta
AT&T	0.14	0.44
Coca-Cola	0.32	0.61
Exxon Mobil	0.24	0.58
Hewlett-Packard	0.39	0.68
McDonald's	0.30	0.49
Microsoft	0.52	0.66
Phillip Morris	–0.07	0.25
Wal-Mart	0.46	0.67
Procter & Gamble	–0.02	0.45

Source: Fernandez (2004)

Needless to say, the results were astonishing. How could the beta of certain large listed companies vary so much on each of the 62 days between 1 December 2001 and 31 January 2002? Perhaps it could be plausible if Wal-Mart's beta changed from 0.46 to 0.67 over a number of years or decades. However, for Wal-Mart's calculated beta to vary between 0.46 and 0.67 over a two-month period seems unrealistic.

Fernandez (2004) concluded that 'we have shown that, in general, it is an enormous error to use historical beta as a proxy for the expected beta ... industry betas are unstable too ...'.

Fernandez (2004) further contends that:

> *a model that works well individually for a number of people may not work for all of the people together. For the CAPM, this means that although the CAPM may be a valid model for each investor, it is not valid for the market as a whole, because investors do not have the same return and risk expectations for all shares. The prices are a statement of expected cash flows discounted at a rate that includes the expected market risk premium and the expected beta. Different investors have different cash flow expectations and different future risk expectations ... one could only talk of a market risk premium if all investors had the same expectations ...*

Fama (2004) concurs that the cost of capital is forward-looking. This provides us with a useful strategy for overcoming the damning research into betas. We can analyse historic betas but ultimately we each need to make our own assessment of expected risk and return. Our required rate of return when investing in a specific company is unique and defensible since we need not justify it to anyone else.

Continuing value

As discussed in Chapter 2, continuing value represents the net present value in free cash flows after the initial forecast period. So, for example, when valuing a specific company, we may only have cash flow forecasts for the next five years. From Year 6 onwards, we would typically assume a constant growth rate in perpetuity and present-value these to Year 0 using the following formula:

PV = ([Free cash flow Year 5 × (1 + growth rate)] ÷ (Cost of equity – growth rate))
× PV factor Year 5

Alternatively, we could use Excel to calculate this for us. Let's illustrate with an example.

EXAMPLE 8.1

Assume the following:

+ Initial forecast period Year 1 to 5;
+ Free cash flow in Year 5 of R100 million;
+ Cost of equity of 15,0 per cent; and
+ Growth in free cash flow from Year 6 onwards of 5 per cent.

	A	B
1	Cost of equity	15,0%
2	Growth rate	5,0%

Continued

3	Net rate	= (1 + B1) ÷ (1 + B2) – 1
4	Period (years)	200
5	Free cash flow Year 5	100
6	PV factor Year 5	$(1 + B1)^{-5}$
7		
8	Continuing value	= PV (B3, B4, –B5 × (1 + B2), 0, 0) × B6 ÷ (1 + B2)
		= 522,0

In practice, continuing value often represents a significant portion of the overall enterprise value derived due to the initial forecast period being relatively short. We are able to dissect continuing value into different periods to assess where the bulk of continuing value accrues. We can use Excel to calculate this for us by changing the forecast period. We use the inputs per the above example but we change the forecast period to say the next 10 years:

	A	B
1	Cost of equity	15,0%
2	Growth rate	5,0%
3	Net rate	= (1 + B1) ÷ (1 + B2) – 1
4	Period (years)	10
5	Free cash flow Year 5	100
6	PV factor Year 5	$(1 + B1)^{-5}$
7		
8	Continuing value	= PV (B3, B4, –B5 × (1 + B2), 0, 0) × B6
		= 311,8

We use Excel to keep changing the forecast period and deduct the cumulative prior results. Table 8.6 illustrates the results.

TABLE 8.6 Results – changing the forecast period and deducting cumulative prior results

	Total PV Rmillions	Differential PV Rmillions
Year 6 to Year 15	311,8	311,8
Year 6 to Year 25	437,4	125,6
Year 6 to Year 35	488,0	50,6
Year 6 to Year 45	508,3	20,3
Year 6 to Year 55	516,5	8,2
Year 6 to Year 100	522,0	5,8
		522,0

Interpreting the results from Table 8.6:
- R311,8 million of continuing value is derived from Years 6 to 15;
- R125.6 million of total continuing value is derived from Years 16 to 25; and
- R84,6 million of total continuing value is derived from Year 26 onwards.

The analysis of continuing value per period in Example 1 is useful, but also illustrates that we should attempt to forecast as far out as possible in our initial forecast period. This reduces the percentage that continuing value represents of total enterprise value.

The difficulty with estimating continuing value is that we do not know whether the business being valued will exist in 30 years' time. If it does, we do not know if its existing operating margins will remain intact and what investment is required to support this growth in profits and cash flows.

Change is inevitable in business. The difficult part is anticipating or adapting to change. There are numerous examples of large companies that once dominated a market, only later to find that their entire business was under threat. Kodak is a classic example of this, having once dominated the camera market but subsequently being liquidated. Kodak reportedly invented the digital camera but failed to react to this threat until it was too late. Similarly, Nokia was once the largest global manufacturer and supplier of cellphones, but failed to react timeously to the threat posed by Apple and Samsung.

Most businesses face threats from competition, changing technology and/or the introduction or amendment of laws and regulations. Very few companies today can confidently predict that they will be in existence in 25 years' time. If they do manage to survive, it is highly likely that most will need to adapt to survive and prosper. DCF valuations are based on cash flow forecasts into infinity although the majority of value is derived from net present-valuing cash flows for the next 30 years.

Valuations happen at a point in time and we should attempt to forecast future cash flows based on what we know at this juncture. The key to producing reasonable results is to interrogate the forecast information and analyse resultant ratios. We will deal with financial analysis in Chapter 10, but for now, note that there are certain ratios that can tell us whether forecasts are too aggressive or conservative. They are:
- EBITDA/Revenue;
- EBIT/Revenue;
- growth in EBIT versus growth in revenue; and
- ROIC.

There tend to be clear historic trends within industries of the above ratios. If the forecast information produces ever-increasing EBIT/Revenue and/or ROIC ratios, then the underlying assumptions need to be scrutinised. Common errors tend to be:
- projecting revenue growth without the concomitant operating expense growth and/or investment in infrastructure;
- assuming gross margin improvement without regard to competitors' potential actions; and
- underestimating future capital expenditure required to maintain operations (at some stage, the infrastructure required to generate cash flows may need to be replaced completely).

Practical tips for producing a reasonable estimate of continuing value

As mentioned in Chapter 2, various techniques are used in practice to minimise overestimating continuing value. These include:

- estimating growth in free cash flows after the initial forecast period to be at country GDP growth;
- not calculating continuing value but forecasting and present-valuing free cash flows for the next 15 or 20 years instead;
- using net asset value at the end of the initial forecast period as a proxy for continuing value; or
- estimating continuing value by performing an earnings-based valuation at the end of the forecast period and discounting this back to today.

Unfortunately, many of the above suggestions are inherently flawed. Country GDP growth is generally quoted in real terms, so expected inflation needs to be added to this. For example, if country GDP growth of 2 per cent is expected and inflation is forecast to be 5,0 per cent, the nominal GDP growth is 7,0 per cent. Using a 7,0 per cent growth in perpetuity may still produce a result that is unrealistic.

Forecasting free cash flows for the next 20 years and then assuming zero value for the business may produce a low valuation result. This DCF value should be benchmarked against realistic earnings-based valuations to test its reasonableness.

Using the NAV at the end of the initial forecast period has no basis in finance theory. This is essentially a 'plug' to produce a reasonable result. The NAV after, say, 10 years may include surplus cash on the statement of financial position, an asset that has already been included in our DCF valuation. In addition, following the DCF approach and then changing this to the NAV method for the remaining expected useful life of the business is inconsistent.

Estimating continuing value by assuming that it is equivalent to EBIT in, say, Year 5 multiplied by a reasonable EBIT multiple is likely to overestimate the value of the business. Yet again, the valuation methodology is inconsistent. If you are following the DCF approach, then pursue this to fruition. If not, use the earnings-based method.

Let's illustrate this with a simple example.

EXAMPLE 8.2

Assume for a hypothetical business:

- The PV of forecast free cash flows forecast for Year 1 to Year 10 is R147 million using a cost of equity of 16,0 per cent;
- Free cash flow in Year 10 is forecast to be R44 million and to grow by 5,0 per cent per annum in perpetuity;
- The NAV at end of Year 10 is forecast to be R228 million, excluding surplus cash;
- An EBIT in Year 0 of R37 million growing to R77 million in Year 10; and
- An EBIT multiple of 9.0 times is the long-term trend for the business.

The detailed assumptions for the above business are included as an appendix to this chapter should you wish to review the veracity of the above assumptions or perform your own valuation.

Using different assumptions to estimate continuing value produces interesting, but not unexpected, results:

TABLE 8.7 Different methods of estimating continuing value

Differing methods of estimating continuing value	NPV of continuing value Rmillions	Resultant enterprise value Rmillions	Continuing value as a % of enterprise value
NAV at end of Year 10	52	199	26%
Growth in perpetuity of 5,0%	96	243	40%
Growth in perpetuity of 8,0%	136	283	48%
EBIT multiple of 9.0 at end of Year 10	157	304	52%

Using NAV as a continuing value estimate provides the most conservative estimate, while applying an EBIT multiple produces the highest result in Example 2.

The suggested approach to estimating continuing value is:

1. Analyse the historic financial performance of the business being valued. The past five years is informative; however, a longer period may be required to detect long-term trends. Adjust historic cash flows for non-recurring items and establish the trends in cash generation.
2. Forecast free cash flows for the next 10 or 15 years. Review these forecasts in detail to ensure that future ratios are in line with historic and industry trends.
3. After the 10- or 15-year forecast period, assume inflationary-type growth in free cash flows.
4. Perform sensitivity analysis by assuming differing growth rates and assessing the impact on enterprise value derived.
5. Perform an earnings-based valuation and compare this result to that obtained using the DCF method.

Conclusion

Stock markets are remarkably efficient in the long term, tending to revert to the mean. However, on occasion, markets overreact to information that may impact on future performance of listed companies. There have been various 'bubbles' over the past 50 years, periods where stock market valuations have increased in the short term only to be followed by corrections thereafter.

The implications for valuations include:

+ Be wary of using calculated betas without first applying common sense and your own judgement about expected future returns; and
+ Analyse long-term trends in EBIT multiples, preferably forward-looking multiples, to derive reasonable metrics for earnings-based valuations.

Continuing value often represents a significant portion of total enterprise value. Be wary of 'plugs' to reduce the continuing value derived to reasonable levels. Rather increase the initial forecast period to 10 years or more and use inflationary increases in free cash flows thereafter. Compare the DCF result to an earnings-based method and run extensive sensitivity analyses to attempt to minimise the potential error in asset pricing.

References

BNP Paribas Cadiz Securities. (2014). *Equity Risk Service: September 2014.* Johannesburg: BNP Paribas Cadiz Securities.

Buffett, M. & Clark, D. (2006). *The Tao of Warren Buffett: Warren Buffet's words of wisdom*. New York: Scribner.

Fama, E. (1970). Efficient capital markets: A review of theory and empirical work. *Journal of Finance* 25(2): 383–417.

Fama, E. & French, K. (2004). The Capital Asset Pricing Model: Theory and evidence. *Journal of Economic Perspectives* 18(3): 25–46.

Fernandez, P. (2004). Are calculated betas worth for anything? IESE Business School, University of Navarra, Madrid, Spain.

Firer, C. & Staunton, M. (2002). 102 years of South African financial market history. *Investment Analysts Journal* 31(56), as updated to 2013 courtesy of the FTSE Fact Sheet.

Koller, T., Goedhart, M. & Wessels, D. (2010). *Valuation: Measuring and Managing the Value of Companies*. (Fifth edition). New Jersey: John Wiley & Sons Inc.

Malkiel, B. (2003). The efficient markets hypothesis and its critics. *Journal of Economic Perspectives* 17(1): 59–82.

Patterson, S. (2010). *The Quants: The Maths geniuses who brought down Wall Street.* London: Random House Business Books.

PricewaterhouseCoopers. (2013). *Highlighting trends in the South African construction industry*. December 2013. Johannesburg: PricewaterhouseCoopers.

Sharenet. (2014). www.sharenet.co.za. [Accessed 30 November 2014].

Shiller, R.J. (2013). Speculative asset prices (Nobel Prize Lecture). Yale University.

Ward, M. & Muller, C. (2012). Empirical testing of the CAPM on the JSE. *Investments Analysts Journal* 76: 1–12.

Appendix

Continuing value example

	Year 0	Year 1	Year 2	Year 3	Year 4	Year 5	Year 6	Year 7	Year 8	Year 9	Year 10
Assumptions											
Revenue growth		15,0%	10,0%	8,0%	8,0%	8,0%	5,0%	5,0%	5,0%	5,0%	5,0%
EBITDA margin	25,0%	25,0%	25,0%	25,0%	25,0%	25,0%	25,0%	25,0%	25,0%	25,0%	25,0%
Depreciation/average P&E	20,0%	20,0%	20,0%	20,0%	20,0%	20,0%	20,0%	20,0%	20,0%	20,0%	20,0%
Interest on cash deposits	5,0%	5,0%	5,0%	5,0%	5,0%	5,0%	5,0%	5,0%	5,0%	5,0%	5,0%
Taxation rate	28,0%	28,0%	28,0%	28,0%	28,0%	28,0%	28,0%	28,0%	28,0%	28,0%	28,0%
Annual change in capex		20,0%	10,0%	8,0%	8,0%	5,0%	5,0%	5,0%	5,0%	5,0%	5,0%
Net working capital/Revenue	25,0%	25,0%	25,0%	25,0%	25,0%	25,0%	25,0%	25,0%	25,0%	25,0%	25,0%
Dividends/PAT	50,0%	50,0%	50,0%	50,0%	50,0%	50,0%	50,0%	50,0%	50,0%	50,0%	50,0%
Rmillions											
Revenue	200	230	253	273	295	319	335	351	369	387	407
EBITDA	50	58	63	68	74	80	84	88	92	97	102
Depreciation	-13	-15	-16	-17	-18	-19	-20	-21	-22	-23	-25
EBIT	37	42	47	52	56	61	64	67	70	73	77
Interest income	1	2	2	2	3	3	4	5	6	7	7
Profit before tax	38	44	49	54	59	64	68	72	76	80	84
Taxation	-11	-12	-14	-15	-16	-18	-19	-20	-21	-22	-24
PAT	27	31	35	39	42	46	49	52	54	58	61
Annual change in EBIT		14,1%	12,1%	8,9%	8,7%	8,6%	4,8%	4,8%	4,8%	4,9%	4,9%
EBIT/Revenue	18,5%	18,4%	18,7%	18,9%	19,0%	19,1%	19,0%	19,0%	19,0%	19,0%	18,9%
Abridged balance sheet											
Plant and equipment	75	78	82	86	92	97	102	108	114	120	126
Net working capital	50	58	63	68	74	80	84	88	92	97	102
Cash resources	28	33	41	51	61	73	88	104	121	139	158
Shareholders' equity	153	168	186	206	227	250	274	300	327	356	386
Forecast cash flows											
EBITDA	50	58	63	68	74	80	84	88	92	97	102
Taxation	-11	-12	-14	-15	-16	-18	-19	-20	-21	-22	-24
Interest income	1	2	2	2	3	3	4	5	6	7	7
Change in net working capital	-6	-7	-6	-5	-5	-6	-4	-4	-4	-5	-5
Capital expenditure	-15	-18	-20	-21	-23	-24	-25	-27	-28	-29	-31
Dividends paid	-14	-16	-18	-19	-21	-23	-24	-26	-27	-29	-30

Continued

Net movement in cash	6	6	8	10	10	12	15	16	17	18	19
Opening cash balance	22	28	33	41	51	61	73	88	104	121	139
Closing cash balance	28	33	41	51	61	73	88	104	121	139	158
ROE (average equity)	18,5%	19,6%	20,0%	19,8%	19,6%	19,4%	18,6%	18,0%	17,4%	16,9%	16,4%
ROIC (average invested capital)		23,4%	24,3%	24,8%	25,2%	25,6%	25,3%	25,2%	25,1%	25,0%	24,9%
Net movement in cash	6	6	8	10	10	12	15	16	17	18	19
Interest income	-1	-2	-2	-2	-3	-3	-4	-5	-6	-7	-7
Tax effect	0	0	1	1	1	1	1	1	2	2	2
Dividends paid	14	16	18	19	21	23	24	26	27	29	30
Free cash flow	19	20	24	27	30	32	36	38	40	42	44
Annual change in free cash flow		*8,2%*	*21,2%*	*12,2%*	*7,6%*	*10,0%*	*11,9%*	*5,1%*	*5,1%*	*5,1%*	*5,0%*

Cost of equity	16,0%
Growth in perpetuity	5,0%
PV factor Year 10	0,227

PV of free cash flows Year 1 to 10	147
Continuing value	96
Enterprise value	243
Cash resources	28
Equity value	270

Alternative Continuing Values:		***% of total***
NAV at end of Year 10	52	26,0%
EBIT multiple of 9.0	157	51,7%
Growth in perpetuity of 8,0%	136	48,1%
Growth in perpetuity of 5,0%	96	39,5%

CHAPTER 9

Valuation challenges in certain businesses

LEARNING OUTCOMES

Once you have worked through this chapter, you should be able to:

+ Appreciate some of the challenges in valuing a businesses in Africa
+ Use techniques to minimise the error in valuing high-growth businesses
+ Understand the approach to valuing a retail bank and other financial services companies
+ Gain some insights into property valuations

Introduction

Chapters 2 through 8 provided insights into valuation techniques and highlighted issues in practically applying methodologies. In addition to these issues, there are certain types of businesses that provide further challenges in arriving at a reasonable estimate of intrinsic value. High-growth businesses are tough to value given the difficulty in estimating future revenue. Such businesses could be undergoing rapid growth due to the disruptive nature of their products and services. Alternatively, these businesses could be start-up in nature. We will discuss the challenges in performing valuations of high-growth businesses and provide recommendations to minimise the valuation error. It is inevitable that the valuation result will be inaccurate; the key is to minimise the error in our favour.

Valuing businesses located in certain African countries is often a difficult assignment. Challenges include:

+ insufficient or unreliable financial market data (earnings multiples, betas, long-term government bond yields, historic market risk premiums etc.);
+ a lack of comparable listed companies against which to benchmark financial performance;
+ restrictions on repatriating funds out of countries;
+ government interventions in certain industries;
+ differing financial reporting standards; and
+ limited market research on the size of industries and expected future demand.

Certain South African groups, such as SABMiller and MTN, have had enormous success expanding through acquisition and organically on the African continent. Other groups have been spectacularly unsuccessful. Telkom's US$410 million acquisition of Multi-Links in Nigeria over the period 2007 to 2009 proved to be value-destructive. Media reports suggested that Telkom had not performed adequate due diligence on the Nigerian market and that the underlying Multi-Links network technology had a limited lifespan. After funding the business for a number of years, Telkom disposed of 100 per cent of Multi-Links for US$10 million in 2011.

Tiger Brands acquired a 63 per cent shareholding in Dangote Flour Mills for approximately R1,5 billion in 2012. Its stated intention was to grow the milling business by leveraging its expertise in managing similar businesses in South Africa. Within two years of the acquisition Tiger Brands made an impairment provision of R849 million against its investment in Dangote. The reasons for the value erosion in the Dangote deal reportedly included failure to identify that the market was oversupplied and underestimating the difficulty in turning the business around (*Business Day* 2014).

Valuing financial services companies and property businesses is challenging too. These issues are covered later in the chapter.

High-growth businesses

It is extremely difficult to use the earnings-based valuation method to value high-growth businesses. Earnings multiples are generally more appropriate for stable-growth businesses. The difficulty is forecasting when the period of high growth will stabilise and what maintainable profits will be thereafter. Let's illustrate with a simple example. Assume for a mythical private company:

- A 20X0 loss of R10 million;
- A forecast EBIT of R5 million in 20X1, increasing to R100 million in 20X5;
- Stable EBIT growth of 5,0 per cent per annum after 20X5 expected; and
- No directly comparable listed companies, but an industry-average EBIT multiple of 10.0 times.

If we were valuing the above business in 20X0, we would face the following challenges:

- Are we convinced that the business will generate profits in 20X1 and beyond?
- What are the drivers of future profitability?
- Do we value the business in 20X5 using a 10.0 EBIT multiple? If so, which discount rate do we use to present-value the result to 20X0?
- What are the probabilities that the business will generate R100 million of EBIT in 20X5?
- What discount should we apply for the fact that the business is unlisted and for specific risk factors?

The purpose of the valuation may inform the end result. If the above business intended to list on a stock exchange to raise capital, it may need to delay this until it had a profit history. If the current shareholders were seeking to raise capital privately, the valuation may be based on future profitability. New investors may inject capital but base their ultimate shareholding on the average EBIT generated in, say, 20X1 through 20X3.

If the above business were being sold, the reasons for selling would need to be explored. The sensible option would seem to be to delay selling until 20X3 or later. If the potential acquirer was that intent on acquiring the business, a DCF valuation may produce a more accurate estimate of intrinsic value.

An approach to valuing Facebook

It seems strange to describe what Facebook does given its global reach of over 1,3 billion monthly active users (MAUs) in 2014. In case you are not one of those 1,3 billion people, Facebook is a social media platform that allows its users to share information with friends. The service is presently free to its users, an important behavioural aspect. The behaviour of users towards Facebook Inc. would be fundamentally different if they had to pay for the use of the platform. Arguably, the number of users would decline significantly if they had to pay even a minimal monthly fee. Secondly, users may not be that willing to allow Facebook to use their data for their revenue purposes.

Facebook listed on the NASDAQ in May 2012 amid much hype about its future growth prospects. Its IPO pricing was at US$38 per share but it subsequently declined to below US$20 a share in August 2012. Facebook's share price recovered in late 2013 and exceeded US$77 at the end of November 2014.

Facebook derives the vast majority of its revenue from advertising. Marketers pay for placing adverts on Facebook's platform and for specific targeting of users based on their location, age, gender and specific interests.

Facebook's growth in revenue and profitability has been rapid over the period 2009 to 2013. Table 9.1 summarises pertinent financial information.

TABLE 9.1 Facebook Inc., financial information

Facebook Inc. December year-end	2010 US$millions	2011 US$millions	2012 US$millions	2013 US$millions
Average MAUs	518	734	951	1 142
Revenue	1 974	3 711	5 089	7 872
EBIT	1 032	1 756	538	2 804
EBIT excluding share-based payments	1 052	1 973	2 100	3 710
Revenue growth	154,1%	88,0%	37,1%	54,7%
EBIT/Revenue	52,3%	47,3%	10,6%	35,6%
EBIT margin excluding share-based payments	53,3%	53,2%	41,3%	47,1%

Source: Facebook annual reports

Facebook's EBIT in the year ending 31 December 2012 (FY2012) declined largely due to US$1,5 billion of share-based compensation costs being recognised during the year of its listing.

A valuation of Facebook will not be attempted – it would be too embarrassing, subsequently, to view the extent of the error in print! However, the recommended approach to performing a valuation of Facebook would be as follows:

- Estimate the growth in advertising revenue for the next 10 years, largely driven by growth (or decline) of MAUs and average advertising revenue per user. The growth in MAUs is unlikely to be significant given the current quantum of users, which represents a significant portion of global smartphone holders and those with computer access. Facebook's entry into the Chinese market would have to be assumed to be on permanent hold.
- The resultant advertising revenue would need to be assessed for reasonability in relation to the global advertising market and the digital portion thereof. The overall global advertising market is not expected to grow by significantly more than population growth – however, digital advertising may grow at the expense of other media. Facebook's resultant share of the digital market would need to be checked for reasonability. It is unlikely that competitors (new and existing) such as Google would allow Facebook unfettered growth and may attempt to restrict its market share.

- Estimate the operating costs and infrastructure investment that will be required to support the forecast growth in Facebook's revenue.

The total global advertising market was estimated to be worth US$473 billion in 2013, of which digital advertising represented US$125 billion (McKinsey 2013). Digital advertising includes advertising on search engines such as Google, advertising on social media sites such as Facebook and Twitter, e-mail and text messages sent to consumers, and online video advertising on sites such as YouTube. Television remains the dominant advertising category globally, with an approximate market share of 39 per cent in 2013. Digital advertising is the next largest category. According to McKinsey's forecasts, television advertising is set to retain its market share over the period 2014 to 2017 while digital advertising is forecast to increase to 34 per cent by 2017. The increase in digital advertising is likely to occur at the expense of radio, newspapers and magazine advertising.

Facebook's revenue has been growing rapidly over the past five years as advertisers have allocated more adspend to social media sites. Based on year-to-date results, Facebook reported advertising revenue of US$11.5 billion in the year ended December 2014, a 64,5 per cent increase on 2013. Facebook's future revenue growth is unknown but if revenue grows by a compound 20 per cent per annum in 2015, 2016 and 2017, revenue could be ±US$18 billion in FY2017. Is this forecast growth realistic?

TABLE 9.2 The global digital advertising market

Global digital advertising market	2013 US$billions	2017 US$billions
Total global market*	125	212
Less China (PWC 2013)	-14	-27
Google's share (say, 40%)	-50	-85
Available market for other participants	61	100
Facebook's share	7,9	18,0
As a % of estimated market size for other participants	13,0%	18,0%
* *McKinsey (2013)*		

Table 9.2 assumes that the average US$ versus Chinese Yuan Renminbi exchange rate was 6,12 in 2013 and this is expected to remain stable until 2017. The 2013 data and forecast for 2017 for the Chinese market were obtained from PWC (PricewaterhouseCoopers 2013a). In addition, it is assumed that Google's market share of total global digital advertising remains at 40 per cent for the period 2014 to 2017, despite it lacking a presence in China.

It is difficult to predict what Facebook's market share of the global digital advertising industry is going to be in 2017 and beyond. However, its growth is likely to be constrained by not participating in the Chinese market and competition from Google.

Facebook's EBIT margin in FY2013 was 35,6 per cent, or 47,1 per cent excluding share-based payments. Google's EBIT margins were high but steadily declined to 27,4 per cent in 2013 (source: www.google.com).

TABLE 9.3 Google Inc., December year-end

Google Inc. December year-end	2010 US$billions	2011 US$billions	2012 US$billions	2013 US$billions
Excludes Motorola results				
Revenue	29,3	37,9	46,0	55,5
EBIT	10,4	12,2	13,3	15,2
EBIT excluding share-based payments	11,8	14,2	16,0	18,5
Revenue growth	24,0%	29,3%	21,5%	20,6%
EBIT/Revenue	35,4%	32,3%	28,9%	27,4%
EBIT margin excluding share-based payments	40,1%	37,5%	34,6%	33,3%

Source: www.google.com

Facebook is unlikely to be able to maintain EBIT margins (before share-based payments) of above 50 per cent in the short or medium term. Facebook's chief financial officer, Dave Wehner, reportedly announced (Reuters 29 October 2014) that the company's expenses are likely to increase in FY2015 by between 55 and 75 per cent. This is not surprising, given the high revenue growth experienced in recent years and the need to invest in improving user and advertiser experiences on Facebook's social media platform.

Table 9.4 summarises Google's historic enterprise value and implied EBIT multiples.

TABLE 9.4 Google's historic enterprise value and implied EBIT multiples

Google Inc. December year-end	2010	2011	2012	2013
Year-end share price	$593,38	$645,26	$706,68	$1 119,58
	US$billions	**US$billions**	**US$billions**	**US$billions**
Equity value	173,3	209,6	233,2	376,0
Cash	-35,0	-44,6	-48,1	-58,7
Debt	3,5	4,2	5,5	5,2
Enterprise value	141,8	169,2	190,6	322,5
EBIT (continuing operations)	10,4	11,7	12,8	15,2
EBIT multiple	13,6	14,5	14,9	21,2

Google's share price increased significantly in 2013, following the trends of other listed digital advertising businesses. The historical EBIT multiples prior to 2013 were in a tight band between 13.5 and 15.0. The stock market is perhaps expecting higher growth in earnings going forward or has rerated Google based on multiples for similar businesses. Long-term, a more realistic multiple of 14.0 may be prudent once the high-growth period is over.

Performing a rudimentary, high-level valuation of Facebook based on the following assumptions:

- High-growth period 2015 to 2017;
- Forecast revenue (advertising plus other) in 2017 of US$20 billion;
- EBIT margin of 35 per cent in FY2017;
- EBIT multiple of 14.0 times in 2017; and
- Long-term required rate of return of 10,0 per cent by shareholders.

TABLE 9.5 Valuing Facebook Inc.

Facebook Inc.	US$ billions
FY2017 EBIT [US$20,0bn × 35%]	7,0
Enterprise value [US$7,0bn × 14.0]	98,0
Present valued to 2014 at 10,0% per annum	73,6

This valuation is significantly below Facebook's market capitalisation of US$217 billion in December 2014 (Yahoo Finance 2014). The issue arising is whether the above forecast EBIT is too conservative or whether the stock market will rerate Facebook prior to 2017 to more realistic levels? The EBIT multiple of 14.0 times used above is more than reasonable for high-technology businesses in the USA after a high-growth phase.

DID YOU KNOW?

Here are some practical tips for valuing high-growth businesses.

- Build a comprehensive DCF valuation, including key assumptions.
- Forecast key assumptions for next 10 years and derive free cash flows.
- Estimate continuing value after 10 years based on realistic growth in free cash flows in perpetuity.
- Discount forecast free cash flows and continuing value using a reasonable cost of equity.
- Perform extensive sensitivity analysis by changing key assumptions and reviewing the impact on the valuation result.
- Research the key variables – in Facebook's case, these would be growth in the digital advertising market, Facebook's estimated market share, key drivers in digital advertising and expected Facebook operating costs.
- Calculate and review key financial ratios implicit in the forecast free cash flows, for example EBIT/Revenue and ROIC. These ratios will tend to stabilise in most industries over time. Hence, ensure that ratios for business being valued are reasonable in the long term.
- Establish a range of potential enterprise values for the business.
- Reverse-engineer the result – which EBIT is required in 10 years to provide a reasonable valuation then, and how much is that worth today?
- Perform an IRR analysis of the investment today based on likely EBIT and expected exit proceeds in 10 years' time – if potential IRR is less than 15 per cent in South African terms or 10 per cent in US dollars, then reassess your assumptions.

In Chapter 10 we will illustrate a detailed sensitivity analysis on a rudimentary Facebook valuation and on the FWC Limited valuation performed at the end of Chapter 2.

African businesses

The methodology of performing DCF valuations for companies in African territories is identical to that in any developed economy. However, many African countries do not have:

- well-established stock exchanges – and, even if they do, there may not be an adequate number of listed entities;
- 20- or 30-year government bonds issued in local currency that are actively traded; or
- stable exchange rates relative to the US dollar.

The above factors make it very difficult to perform DCF valuations on the continent. Following the CAPM, we would need to estimate the country's risk-free rate and market risk premiums before applying specific risk adjustments through beta coefficients to derive companies' cost of equity. African countries do not have risk-free rates given the perception of potential default on government bonds. Most countries do not have 50-year data on movements of the overall equity market movements relative to long-term government bond yields. It follows that estimating market risk premiums and the overall cost of equity per African country is a difficult task indeed. Beta coefficients derived also lack robustness and provide limited empirical data on individual companies' volatility and risk.

South Africa is an exception to the rule on the continent as it has a well-established stock exchange and rich data on historic bond yields. It follows that we can estimate risk-free rates, the market risk premium and beta coefficients. As discussed in Chapter 2, the estimated market risk premium in South Africa currently ranges between 7,0 and 7,4 per cent. Long-term (20 years plus) government bond yields were trading at between 8,0 and 8,5 per cent during 2014. Hence, the overall cost of equity in South Africa is about 15,0 to 16,0 per cent, which is consistent with long-term returns on the JSE over the past 50 to 100 years. The problems in estimating betas in South Africa were covered in Chapter 8, and we need to be vigilant to ensure that we derive a reasonable estimate of individual company risk.

The PWC survey in 2012 posed some interesting questions regarding valuing businesses in Africa. The respondents indicated, inter alia, that they:

- obtain earnings multiples for similar companies in developed countries and then apply a discount to that for the particular African business being valued; and
- derive risk-free rates and market risk premiums by applying a country risk premium to these obtained in developed economies.

Risk-free rates

It is difficult to obtain risk-free proxies in most African countries as they do not have established bond markets with sufficient trade in long-term (20-year-plus) instruments. Risk-free rates could be estimated by using USA 20-year bond yields (assume 2,5 per cent) and adding default spread rates obtained from rating agencies. Table 9.6 shows estimated default risk spreads in January 2014 (Damodaran 2014):

TABLE 9.6 Estimated default risk spreads, January 2014

Estimating risk-free rates in Africa	Default risk spread	Plus USA 20-year bond yields (+2,5%)
Angola	3,60%	6,10%
Botswana	0,85%	3,35%
Cameroon	5,50%	8,00%
Democratic Republic of Congo	6,50%	9,00%
Ghana	4,50%	7,00%
Kenya	4,50%	7,00%
Mozambique	4,50%	7,00%
Nigeria	3,60%	6,10%
South Africa	1,60%	4,10%
Zambia	4,50%	7,00%

The rates in Table 9.6 are in US dollar terms, however, and either need to be converted into local currency or the forecast free cash flows need to be in US dollars. It should be noted that US long-term treasury bond yields have been very low post 2012 compared to prior decades. The average 20-year US treasury bond yield was approximately 8,0 per cent in 1995 and steadily declined to about 2,5 per cent in late 2014. There is much conjecture in the media regarding whether current long yields are sustainable or due for an increase.

The South African long-term bond yield of 4,1 per cent in US dollar terms according to Table 9.6 is much lower than market rates in 2014. The rates become more reasonable when adding expected inflation differentials between individual African countries and US inflation rates.

TABLE 9.7 Estimating risk-free rates in Africa

Estimating risk-free rates in Africa	USA 20-year bond yield + default spread	Inflation differential*	Adjusted risk-free rate in local currency
Angola	6,10%	7,8%	13,9%
Botswana	3,35%	4,6%	8,0%
Ghana	7,00%	10,2%	17,2%
Kenya	7,00%	4,2%	11,2%
Mozambique	7,00%	2,8%	9,8%
Nigeria	6,10%	7,0%	13,1%
South Africa	4,10%	4,2%	8,3%
Zambia	7,00%	5,6%	12,6%

** 2013 inflation data per country obtained from African Economic Outlook (2014) less average inflation in the USA of 1,5 per cent in 2013*

The adjusted rates set out in Table 9.7 seem more realistic, particularly in local currencies. The 8,3 per cent derived for South Africa is a reasonable reflection of market yields in 2013 and 2014.

Market risk premiums and beta coefficients

Market risk premiums are more difficult to determine given the lack of historical data about relative long-term bond yields versus overall equity market movements in African countries. As mentioned above, empirical data indicates that the market risk premium in South Africa is between 7,0 and 7,4 per cent. In other African countries, we need to use professional judgement to derive a reasonable market risk premium.

Koller et al. (2010) recommend using the estimated global market risk premium of between 4,5 and 5,5 per cent. With respect, this may be too low in an African context. Dimson (2002) estimated South Africa's market risk premium to be 7,1 per cent. Using a market risk premium of lower than this would yield an overall country cost of equity that may be too low for South Africa. Arguably, other African countries' market risk premiums should be equivalent to, or higher than, that of South Africa?

Credit Suisse (2014) estimated that the annualised real returns on global equity markets was 3,4 per cent higher than bonds over the period 1900 to 2013. Perhaps adding the inflation differential per African country relative to, say, the USA to this 3,4 per cent real market risk premium could yield a sensible result?

TABLE 9.8 Estimating market risk premiums in Africa

Estimating market risk premiums in Africa	Global real market risk premium	Inflation differential*	Estimated country market risk premium
Angola	3,4%	7,8%	11,2%
Botswana	3,4%	4,6%	8,0%
Ghana	3,4%	10,2%	13,6%
Kenya	3,4%	4,2%	7,6%
Mozambique	3,4%	2,8%	6,2%
Nigeria	3,4%	7,0%	10,4%
South Africa	3,4%	4,2%	7,6%
Zambia	3,4%	5,6%	9,0%

The result for South Africa in Table 9.7 is similar to that suggested by Dimson. Assuming that the above market risk premiums are reasonable, the overall nominal expected return from equities per African country are summarised in Table 9.8.

TABLE 9.8 Overall cost of equity per selected African countries

Overall cost of equity per selected African countries	Estimated risk-free rate	Estimated country market risk premium	Estimated overall cost of equity
Angola	13,9%	11,2%	25,1%
Botswana	8,0%	8,0%	16,0%
Ghana	17,2%	13,6%	30,8%

Continued

Kenya	11,2%	7,6%	18,8%
Mozambique	9,8%	6,2%	16,0%
Nigeria	13,1%	10,4%	23,5%
South Africa	8,3%	7,6%	15,9%
Zambia	12,6%	9,0%	21,6%

It should be emphasised that the estimated country costs of equity in Table 9.8 are in nominal terms and already incorporate country risks (exchange volatility, political instability, etc.). The results appear reasonable for South Africa, Botswana, Mozambique and Kenya. The implied costs of equity for Ghana, Angola and Nigeria seem high, but that may reflect the inherent risks of investing in businesses in those countries.

In DCF valuations, the market risk premium and beta coefficient used are future expectations of required returns and perceived risks. These are individual choices, so each investor should make his or her own assessment in the circumstances. There is some guidance about historical equity returns and betas – however, this needs to be applied after applying professional judgement. Ultimately, the question arising when investing in each African country is, what return on investment do you require to compensate for country risks? In South Africa, expecting an overall return on equities of between 14,0 and 16,0 per cent is not unreasonable, given historic returns and current risk-free rates. Perhaps returns in most other African countries need to be higher to compensate for potentially higher risks associated with investing there?

Whether to forecast free cash flows and earnings in local currencies or US dollars is a vexing issue. Each particular business needs to be assessed based on its unique characteristics. For example, an oil production facility in Nigeria needs to be assessed on whether its revenues and costs are US-dollar denominated or not. The sale of crude oil is likely to be dependent on ruling commodity prices and US dollar exchange rates. Operating costs could be a combination of US dollar and Naira-based costs. In Chapter 10, we will discuss sensitivity analysis tools for assessing the impact of various key assumptions on valuation results. For an oil well in Nigeria, detailed sensitivity of the impact of crude oil prices and exchange rate fluctuations on free cash flows and profits would need to be assessed.

Country risk premiums

Certain practitioners use estimated country risk premiums to adjust USA or UK costs of equity. Simplistically, the country risk premium represents the higher return required over USA or UK equity returns for investing in countries perceived to be more risky. Country risk premiums are often estimated by:

- analysing country default risk spreads obtained from global credit rating agencies; or
- using credit default spreads from trading in sovereign credit default swaps (CDSs).

CDSs were widely used prior to the global financial crisis in late 2008 to hedge against the potential default of collateralised debt obligations. Many investment banks also traded in these instruments, hoping to gain from movements in default spreads. CDSs are similarly used by investors in sovereign debt (government bonds, etc.) to hedge against the event of default or restructuring of debt obligations. The default spreads per country provide some indication of the perceived credit risk.

Country default risk spreads, obtained either from credit rating agencies or CDS instruments, are an emotive topic. Speculation about downgrading South Africa's country risk rating provokes much debate in the local media. The impact of the South African government's credit rating has an impact on its traded bond yields and the market yields required when raising further debt. The knock on impact on South African banks and large corporates' credit ratings is also a business reality.

Country risk premiums are generally incorporated into estimating individual emerging market companies' costs of equity in two different ways:

- Adding country risk premium to the cost of equity derived in local currency; or
- Adding country risk premiums to USA market risk premiums and adjusting for beta.

Let's illustrate this with a South African example.

EXAMPLE 9.1

Assume for a listed South African company:

- a 20-year South African government bond yield of 8,0 per cent;
- a USA market risk premium of 5,5 per cent;
- a South African country risk premium of 1,6 per cent; and
- a beta coefficient of the South African company of 0.80.

Approach A	
Risk-free rate + (beta × USA market risk premium) + country risk premium = 8,0% + (0,80 × 5,5%) + 1,6% =	14,0%
Approach B	
Risk-free rate + [beta × (USA market risk premium + country risk premium)] = 8,0% + [0.80 × (5,5% + 1,6%)] =	13,7%

In a South African context, we have reliable data on historic market risk premiums, so the above approaches are redundant. However, in other African countries, they may provide useful estimates. It is recommended that you triangulate your cost of equity calculations by performing the various suggested calculations.

Earnings multiples

There may be insufficient evidence for EBIT or EBITDA multiples in particular African countries, given the paucity of listed entities in these countries, or thinly traded shares. The PWC survey (PricewaterhouseCoopers 2012) revealed that valuation practitioners sometimes obtain earnings multiples from developed countries and then apply a discount to these for specific African businesses. This is largely unscientific and caution should be exercised. For example, retail industries may be fundamentally different in Nigeria to those in New York. Woolworths, the iconic South African food and clothing retailer, discovered that trading in Nigeria was difficult due to complex supply chain structures and high import duties. Food and clothing retailers' margins in Nigeria may be fundamentally different from those in First World territories, so they attract different EBIT multiples. Using global average EBIT multiples, even after adjustment for country and company risks, may be inappropriate.

In Chapter 6, we examined average EBITDA multiples in Africa per the Riscura report. The average EBITDA multiples of listed African companies was 8.9 times over the period 2006 to 2013. The average EBITDA multiple paid by private equity investors over that period was 6.5 times on the continent. Figure 9.1 summarises the average annual EBITDA multiples paid in global merger and acquisition transactions over the period 2007 to 2013 per American Appraisal (2013). The overall average, albeit over a short period of time, was 9.4 times.

FIGURE 9.1 Average global M&A EBITDA multiples

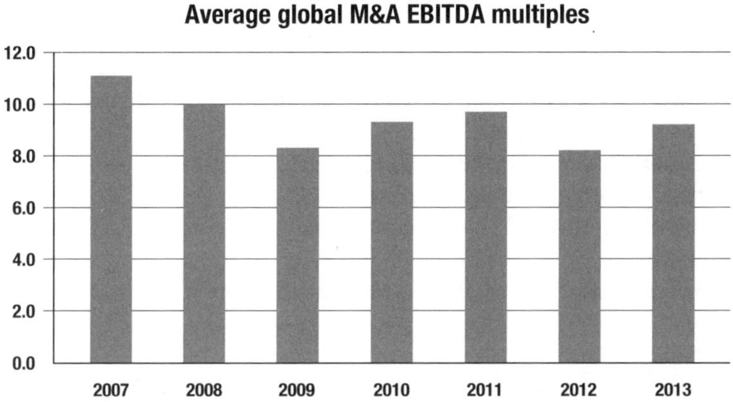

Koller et al. (2010) argue strongly that the long-term sustainable PE multiple on stock exchanges in the USA is about 15.0 times. There have been numerous periods during which the US stock markets have moved out of the aforementioned range, but ultimately they revert to the mean.

Assuming that, on average, US-listed companies have no debt or surplus cash on their balance sheets (surplus cash nets off debt) and an income tax rate of 35 per cent, a long-term PE multiple of 15.0 would translate into a EBIT multiple of 9.75 times. EBITDA multiples would be lower - however, it is difficult to make a simplistic assumption about average depreciation charges by listed companies.

When assessing average EBIT or EBITDA multiples in African countries, these worldwide benchmarks are relevant. The issue arising is how much to discount the overall EBIT multiple on the NYSE and/or JSE for specific country risks. Thereafter, adjustments need to be made for company-specific risks and potential marketability discounts for private companies.

The nature of the business being valued in Africa would profoundly impact on risk assessment and the earnings multiples applied. For example, alcoholic beverage manufacturers and cellphone networks may be easier to value given that demand for these products and services can be estimated with more confidence than IT services, for example.

A final warning about valuing businesses in Africa: review the quality of financial reporting in detail to ensure that it complies with global accounting standards and is subject to external audit by reputable firms.

Due diligence is critical

Due diligence will be covered in further detail in Chapter 14. However, when valuing an African business, particular care needs to be exercised. Donald Rumsfeld, the controversial former US Secretary of Defence, reportedly stated that:

There are known knowns. These are things that we know we know. There are known unknowns. That is to say, there are things that we know we don't know. But there are also unknown unknowns. There are things we don't know we don't know ...

The challenge in due diligence investigations is to ensure that we research the basics and attempt to uncover the unknowns. Human behaviour is such that we suffer from various cognitive biases. The behavioural financiers refer to certain of these, such as confirmation bias and overconfidence. Confirmation bias refers to the tendency to seek information to support our views rather than to refute them. Due diligence investigations are critical to confirm what we know but also to seek evidence to the contrary. Such information could have a material impact on the valuations we perform.

The destruction of value following acquisitions on the African continent by South African corporates seem to have followed common themes:

- Inadequate research into the markets served by target companies;
- Underestimating the difficulties in penetrating new markets;
- Sub-standard due diligence investigations before the acquisition;
- Investing in redundant technology;
- Reliance, in good faith, on governments to invest in suitable infrastructure to support business operations;
- Cultural and language barriers;
- Imposing South African practices on local management teams instead of embracing diversity;
- Ignoring potential regulatory changes and government intervention in certain industries;
- Failure to recognise supply chain difficulties; and
- Overpaying for businesses based on high expected growth that failed to materialise.

It may be worth compiling a checklist of lessons learnt by other South African and global businesses when concluding acquisitions on the continent, including valuation errors made prior to pursuing acquisition opportunities.

Investigation is also required into country risks such as over-dependence on commodities for economic growth. Countries such as Nigeria and Angola derive a significant portion of their GDP from oil revenues and any volatility in crude oil prices may have a consequential impact on country economic conditions. Lower oil production and revenue due to depressed crude oil prices could have wide-ranging effects on the economy as a whole and, ultimately, on consumer spending.

Financial services companies

We will deal with valuing retail banks in this chapter and highlight some approaches to valuing investment banks and asset management businesses. Retail banks referred to are those that have banking licences and operate under the auspices of the South African Reserve Bank (SARB). These banks are able to accept deposits from the public and lend monies to consumers, corporates and public sector businesses.

Banks in South Africa are subject to various regulations. The Banks Act (1990) provides for the regulation and supervision of banks in South Africa. The National Credit Act provides protection for consumers accepting credit from banks and any other business extending credit. Banks, in particular, are expected to act with diligence prior to extending credit and not to lend money to consumers who are unable to repay amounts owing. Retail banks are also required to comply with Basel III, which provides international guidance on capital adequacy and liquidity requirements.

Hence, banks are required to comply with various pieces of legislation as well as be subject to supervision by the SARB. This is unsurprising given that banks are the most highly leveraged businesses around and accept deposits from the public. It would be untenable for banks to collapse regularly and for the man in the street to lose money entrusted to banks. South African banks held up incredibly well through the global financial crisis and European debt crisis over the period 2008 to 2012. Unfortunately, African Bank Investments Limited (ABIL) went into curatorship in 2014, providing a shock to the fiscal system. This was one of the few blips on the radar of South African banking history.

The principles in valuing a retail bank are similar to any other business, except for the following:

- Lending money is their core business, so interest income forms part of their free cash flows;
- Deposits and advances are the working capital of banks and need to be included in forecast free cash flows; and
- Regulations such as capital adequacy requirements need to be complied with and solvency and liquidity is critical.

Some of the daily challenges of banks include:

- Being vigilant in advancing credit to consumers and companies - credit checks need to be performed as well as their own investigation into affordability (**credit risk**);
- Matching the duration of advances to deposits - banks should, for example, attempt to fund mortgage advances with long-term deposits rather than through 30-day notice deposits (**liquidity risk**); and
- Ensuring that interest rate movements and currency risks are adequately managed and hedged (**market risk**).

Banking is a complicated business and the majority of operating costs tend to be fixed in nature. Significant investment in infrastructure (physical, systems and people) is required to operate this type of financial services business. Banks generally perform well in good economic conditions, producing higher profit growth than most other industries. Profit growth slows and often declines during recession conditions and when consumers are either overly indebted or constrain spending.

Simplistically, banks lend money at a 'small' margin. For example, they lend R10 000 at an interest rate of 10,0 per cent whilst borrowing at an average of, say, 6,0 per cent. The failure to recover the full R10 000 owed has significant impact on relative profitability: the margin was R400 per annum (before operating costs), yet this could translate into a loss of R10 000 if the amount is not recovered.

CASE STUDY Let's attempt to analyse capitec

Capitec Bank Holdings Limited (Capitec) is a registered bank that focuses on unsecured lending to consumers. Compound annual growth in operating profit has been spectacular over the past 10 years. The group has ventured where most of the major retail banks have been cautious to tread. Capitec dominates the unsecured lending niche, particularly after the problems experienced by ABIL.

Capitec's profitability over the years ended February 2012, 2013 and 2014 is summarised in Table 9.9.

TABLE 9.9 Capitec, income statements 2012, 2013 and 2014

Capitec – income statements ***Rmillions***	**2012**	**2013**	**2014**
Interest income			
Interest on average advances	4 126	6 737	8 857
Interest on interest bearing cash/investments	220	348	577
Interest expense	-1 022	-1 663	-2 133
Net interest income	3 324	5 422	7 301
Loan fee income	1 657	1 496	1 307
Loan fee expense	-186	-343	-466
Transaction fee income	1 360	2 101	2 786
Transaction fee expense	-524	-752	-860
Net fee income	2 307	2 502	2 768
Net impairment charge	-1 604	-2 659	-3 976
Other income	39	29	1
Banking operating expenses	-2 486	-2 994	-3 242
Non-banking expenses	-22	-22	-19
Operating profit before tax	1 557	2 277	2 833
Normal income tax	-616	-710	-801
STC	-34	-29	0
Deferred tax	186	66	6
Profit for the year	1 094	1 604	2 037

Source: Capitec annual reports

Capitec's income streams include interest earned on advances and own cash, origination and administration fees on advances, and transaction fees charged. Banks disclose net interest income and net fee income to provide some insights into their profit generation. In FY2014, 27,5 per cent of Capitec's net income was generated from fee income as opposed to lending margin.

Capitec does not separately disclose interest income from advances but rather lumps this into overall interest income earned. The interest income generated from own cash balances and investments in treasury bills is estimated in Table 9.9 – the aggregate of this income plus interest on advances agrees to their annual reports. This was estimated to reverse engineer the average interest charged on loans and advances. Refer to Table 9.10 for some historical income statement ratios.

TABLE 9.10 Capitec – historical income statement ratios

Capitec – income statements	2012	2013	2014
Key ratios			
Interest income/average assets			
Interest on average advances	28,1%	27,5%	27,5%
Interest on interest-bearing cash/investments	6,0%	6,0%	6,0%
Interest expense/average deposits	7,3%	7,1%	6,6%
Loan fee income/average loans and advances	11,3%	6,1%	4,1%
Transaction fees/average loans and advances	9,3%	8,6%	8,7%
Loan fee expense/loan fees	11,2%	22,9%	35,7%
Transaction fee expense/transaction fees	38,5%	35,8%	30,8%
Net impairment charge/gross loans and advances	8,7%	8,7%	11,8%
Depreciation and amortisation/opening assets	42,4%	40,4%	39,0%
Cost to income	44,2%	37,8%	32,2%
Annual change in banking operating expenses	37,2%	20,4%	8,3%
Growth in operating profit	65,6%	46,2%	24,4%
Effective tax rate	39,6%	31,2%	28,3%
Dividend cover	3.2	3.3	2.8

Source: Author's own ratio calculations based on Capitec annual reports

The average interest rate on advances over the period FY2012 to FY2014 was estimated to be between 27,5 and 28,1 per cent. These interest rates are significantly higher than the prevailing prime overdraft interest rate in South Africa over this period (8,50 to 9,25 per cent). The high interest rates charged by Capitec are reflective of the higher risk associated with unsecured lending. However, the sustainability of these interest rates needs to be questioned both from the perspective of unsecured lenders and consumer affordability. Net impairment charges are also high, varying between 8,7 and 11,8 per cent of gross advances over the period – this certainly reduces net lending margins to more respectable levels.

Capitec's cost to income ratio should be the envy of most major banks. This ratio is calculated as:

Banking operating costs ÷ (Net interest income + net fee income)

The major retail banks in South Africa, namely Standard Bank, FNB, Barclays (Absa) and Nedbank, strive to reduce the cost to income ratio to below 60 per cent. This is generally not achieved.

Capitec's profitability is hence much higher than that of most retail banks – lending margins and fee income are high, while operating costs are tightly controlled.

TABLE 9.11 Capitec – balance sheets

Capitec – balance sheets *Rmillions*	**2012**	**2013**	**2014**
Cash and cash equivalents			
Interest-bearing	3 260	5 106	7 333
Non-interest-bearing	1 292	2 038	2 333
Investments at fair value	1 199	2 023	4 759
Loans and advances	16 863	27 935	30 053
Inventory	42	0	0
Other receivables	58	127	220
Derivative financial assets	0	14	203
Current income tax	62	0	23
Property, plant and equipment	543	698	855
Intangible assets	69	136	201
Deferred tax assets	234	271	212
Total assets	23 622	38 347	46 191
Loans and deposits	17 692	29 000	35 449
Provisions	25	28	11
Other liabilities	501	571	622
Share appreciation rights	217	188	127
Current income tax	1	46	0
Total liabilities	18 436	29 834	36 209
Share capital	2 926	5 331	5 513
Cash flow hedge reserve	-2	-16	81
Retained earnings	2 002	2 939	4 130
	4 926	8 254	9 723
Preference share capital	259	259	259
Total equity	5 185	8 513	9 982
Capital adequacy	39%	41%	39%
ROE (average equity balances)	25,3%	23,4%	22,0%

Source: Capitec annual reports

Capitec needs some cash in its branches and ATMs to service its customers. This is reflected in non-interest-bearing cash balances in Table 9.11, together with mandatory reserve deposits with the SARB. The Reserve Bank requires all banks to deposit a small portion of customer advances with it as a reserving and prudency requirement.

Investments in the above balance sheets mainly represent investment in short-term treasury bills.

Capitec's balance sheets are relatively simple. Deposits are accepted from customers and corporate clients, and these are then advanced to clients. There is a slight maturity mismatch between advances and deposits – the vast majority of advances are 12 months or longer in duration whilst most of its deposits mature within three months. It follows that in a worst-case scenario, depositors could insist on the return of their monies while Capitec would have to wait for over 12 months to receive capital owing from its customers. The benefit of having short-term deposits is that these attract lower interest rates and can be advanced at approximately 28 per cent to customers. In practice, Capitec would carefully manage the maturity mismatch and should have contingency plans to cater for exceptional circumstances.

The capital adequacy ratio is calculated in terms of the Basel III guidelines. Capitec categorises its advances and investments and applies risk weightings to these:

- Investments in South African government treasury bills and bonds are regarded as risk-free;
- Loans and advances to other banks have risk weightings of between 20 and 50 per cent, depending on their maturity (longer-dated loans attract a 50 per cent weighting); and
- Issuing loans to consumers attracts a 75 per cent risk weighting, and impaired loans a 100 per cent weighting.

The capital adequacy is then simplistically determined as follows:

shareholders' equity ÷ risk-weighted advances, loans and investments

The minimum capital adequacy ratio for South African banks is 9,5 per cent although the SARB can increase this at its discretion by a further 2,5 per cent. The Basel III rules are complicated and we will avoid them for the purposes of this chapter. However, if the bank being valued is close to these liquidity and capital adequacy ratios, it will require more detailed research and, possibly, expert advice. Capitec's capital adequacy far exceeds the minimum benchmark, with the ratio being 39 per cent in FY2014. Regulatory capital adequacy rules will certainly not be a constraint to growth in the short term for Capitec.

Capitec's ROE ratio is healthy compared with that of other major banks – 22,0 per cent in FY2014 based on average equity balances versus the South African average of 15,9 per cent (PricewaterhouseCoopers 2013b).

The challenge in performing DCF valuations on banks is to determine free cash flow. Refer to Table 9.12 for a summary of Capitec's audited cash flow statements for FY2012 to FY2014.

TABLE 9.12 Capitec – cash flow statements

Capitec – cash flow statements ***Rmillions***	**2012**	**2013**	**2014**
Operating profit	1 557	2 277	2 833
Adjustments:			
Fair value adjustments on financial assets	-12	0	19
Loan impairment charges	701	1 178	914
Depreciation and amortisation	174	247	325
Movements in provisions	11	3	-17
Share-based employee costs	74	-20	-53
Profit/loss on disposal of assets	4	0	0
Receivables at fair value	5	0	0

Continued

Loans and advances	-7 492	-12 249	-3 032
Inventory	-11	12	0
Other receivables	-14	-83	-92
Deposits	7 242	11 308	6 369
Trade and other payables	169	79	76
Income taxes paid	-603	-578	-830
Cash flow from operating activities	1 803	2 174	6 510
Property, plant and equipment	-314	-350	-407
Intangible assets	-66	-118	-141
Investments	-198	-1 527	-2 053
Derivative financial assets	0	0	0
Dividends paid	-338	-487	-718
Preference share issued	0	0	0
Ordinary shares issued	1 008	2 404	182
Settlement of employee share options	-186	-207	-149
Net movement in cash and cash equivalents	1 709	1 889	3 224
Opening balance	2 842	4 550	6 440
Closing balance	4 550	6 440	9 664

Source: Capitec annual reports

Some observations:

- Capitec's core business is to lend money, so interest income is part of its free cash flow, as is interest paid on deposits;
- Ordinary shares issued in FY2012 and FY2013 cannot be excluded for the purpose of determining free cash flows as the bank clearly needed additional capital to continue growing and shareholders were asked to support this;
- Dividends paid should be added back to net movements in cash to estimate free cash flows – distributions to shareholders are added back to determine free cash flows to equity (FCFE) or to the firm. We generally value banks on a FCFE basis; and
- We could exclude future expected employee share option scheme cash flows from free cash flows and value this liability separately at the valuation date, as covered in Chapter 4.

Interest-bearing or 'surplus' cash could arguably be valued separately in a DCF valuation as we would usually do for non-banking businesses. We then exclude interest income from this asset in determining free cash flows and rather add the surplus cash to enterprise value at the valuation date. However, banks are required to manage their liquidity and this will require retaining some cash to cover unexpected liquidity events. The general rule for a bank is to rather treat all interest income as free cash flow unless it is clear that the bank is grossly overcapitalised. In Capitec's case, all cash will be treated as working capital given the maturity mismatch between advances and deposits. Also, the current uncertainties regarding unsecured lending in South Africa and the potential for another ABIL saga would suggest that all cash is required for continued operations.

Investment banks

Investment banks focus on servicing corporate customers rather than consumers. These financial services businesses also provide M&A and debt advisory services to clients. The majority of global investment banks partake in proprietary trading in equities, debt instruments, derivatives and currencies. Some invest in private equity transactions off their own balance sheets and/or manage third-party private equity and hedge funds.

The principles applied in valuing retail banks would apply equally to investment banks' loan and advance activities. The difficulty lies in valuing their non-banking operations, such as proprietary trading and investing, and their advisory businesses. Net income from these activities tends to be very volatile and difficult to predict. Some tips:

- Analyse overall historical profits to identify any trends;
- Analyse the composition of net income – if the majority of profits are derived from proprietary trading and advisory activities, our challenge would be greater;
- Value any underlying private equity investments separately and add this to the valuation result;
- Value lending activities separately and add them to the overall valuation result; and
- Benchmark ROE achieved against industry averages – if ROE fluctuates widely, it may indicate volatility of trading activities.

As discussed in Chapter 5, banks are often valued using a price-to-book ratio. This could be a useful check to ensure that you do not overpay for an investment bank or overvalue for your personal investing purposes.

Asset management businesses

Asset management businesses manage third-party money by investing in listed shares, debt instruments, property and/or private equity. The investment management businesses could be structured through:

- **Unit trusts** – individuals, companies and pension funds can invest in unit trusts which, in turn, invest in various asset classes;
- **Multi-managers** – these operators pool funds and invest in a variety of different unit trusts and private equity funds, and/or outsource investment management to other asset managers;
- **Institutional mandates** – the management of pension and provident funds, medical aids, corporate financial institutions and public sector funds according to specific investment mandates;
- **Retirement products** – retirement annuities, living annuities and endowments products offered to individuals;
- **High-net-worth products and services** – private banks and boutique asset managers offering specialised investment advice and asset management services to high net worth individuals and family trusts; and
- **Structured products** – index tracking funds and products where downside risk is hedged.

The asset management industry is filled with complexity in terms of investment products and industry jargon. Simplistically, the industry invests and manages other peoples' money according to specific investment mandates. For example, a unit trust may offer high equity exposure for individuals with a long investment horizon (e.g. young people). Alternatively, a unit trust could be focused on individuals wishing to maximise income potential (e.g. older people) through investing in fixed income (debt instruments) and high dividend yield listed shares.

Ultimately, asset managers provide investment management expertise and charge a fee for services rendered. Fees are based on the value of assets managed and vary depending on the service provided. Unit trust fees are transparent and fully disclosed. The management of institutional money is subject to negotiated fees, of which some could be fees for performance in beating certain benchmarks.

Asset management businesses generally do not pose any major valuation challenge. The key inputs into the valuation model will be:

- Assets under management and expected future inflows/outflows;
- Expected market movements in assets managed – the return we think they will obtain by investing in certain asset classes;
- Investment management fees earned that are generally based on the value and type of asset managed; and
- Forecast operating costs.

The long-term returns on equities, government bonds, cash and property are relatively stable. Annual movements in prices of these assets may be volatile but, in the long term, these returns tend to revert to the mean and be reasonably predictable. The key challenge in valuing asset managers is to forecast inflows and outflows of assets over time. Individual ('retail') investors tend to be loyal to specific unit trusts and/or asset managers because of relationships with their investment advisers. Institutional money, however, tends to be very fickle. Large institutions can switch their money from asset manager to asset manager at short notice, and these outflows are difficult to predict. Future changes in the quantum of assets managed have a profound impact on future income streams (net fees earned).

Asset management businesses are often valued based on a percentage of assets under management. The percentage will vary depending on the type of service offered and whether assets are retail or institutional. Asset managers focusing on managing unit trusts for retail investors will attract a higher value than those managing large pension funds' money. Multi-managers will be valued at less than unit trusts themselves. As discussed in Chapter 5, these types of industry benchmarks, such as valuing asset managers based on assets under management, are useful checks but should not replace DCF and earnings-based valuations.

Property companies

Property is generally regarded as a less risky asset class than equities. Hence, the required return from property investments may be lower than investing in listed shares or private companies. The principles of valuation discussed apply equally to property. The DCF method is highly relevant and should be performed for each potential property acquisition. Earnings multiples such as EBIT or EBITDA are not generally used to value property but rather rental yields are referred to.

EXAMPLE 9.2

Let's use an example to illustrate rental yields.

Annual rental income	6 000
Operating costs	-900
Net income	5 100
Property value	50 000
Rental (gross) yield (6 000 ÷ 50 000) =	12,0%
Net rental yield (5 100 ÷ 50 000) =	10,2%

Properties are often purchased and sold based on prevailing rental yields. These yields will vary depending on the property location and nature of the asset. Shopping centres in densely populated areas will tend to attract lower yields, whereas industrial properties in outlying areas often have much higher yields. Ultimately, yields will reflect a risk-return relationship – rental income perceived as more stable and reasonable capital growth in properties will translate into higher values (lower yields).

Property is a specialised asset and expert advice should always be sought prior to investing. Experts' knowledge of market-related rentals, selling prices per square metre, future developments in the area and the condition of land and buildings provide invaluable insights.

Reported yields that properties are sold at may provide misleading information. For example, hearing that a large office park in Sandton, Johannesburg has been sold at an 8,0 per cent net rental yield may seem low compared with what can be obtained from investing in the overall JSE and in government bonds. However, these yields can be misleading as they do not incorporate expected future capital growth in properties, a key value driver in property investment.

Banks are generally prepared to lend against property and investors are able to enhance their returns through leverage. This may obscure the overall expected return from investing and caution should be exercised. As discussed in Chapter 3, leverage can significantly enhance shareholder returns but has limited impact on the value of the underlying asset. These benefits accrue to shareholders/investors and including this in the indicative fair value of property will diminish returns for investors.

Let's illustrate some of these principles with an example. Assume for an investor (a property holding company) seeking to acquire an office building that is fully occupied:

- A negotiated selling price R50 million;
- Gross annual rental income of R6 million paid by tenants;
- An agreed annual rental escalation for the next five years of 5,0 per cent per annum;
- Operating costs as a percentage of rental income of 15,0 per cent;
- An income tax rate of 28 per cent;
- Funding of the acquisition price through investors' own cash of R20 million and a bank loan of R30 million;
- Bank loan terms – 9,0 per cent interest per annum, 10-year repayment period and annual payments in arrears; and
- Expected annual capital growth of land and buildings of 5,0 per cent.

The repayments to the bank will be as follows:

TABLE 9.13 Repayments to the bank

	Year 1	Year 2	Year 3	Year 4	Year 5
Debt repayment	-4 675	-4 675	-4 675	-4 675	-4 675
Interest	-2 700	-2 522	-2 329	-2 117	-1 887
Capital	-1 975	-2 152	-2 346	-2 557	-2 787
Debt balance	28 025	25 873	23 527	20 970	18 183

The investor's annual cash flows associated with acquiring the property (and assuming that the property is disposed of in five years' time) will be as follows:

TABLE 9.14 Investor cash flows

Investor cash flows	Year 0	Year 1	Year 2	Year 3	Year 4	Year 5
Rental income		6 000	6 300	6 615	6 946	7 293
Operating costs		-900	-945	-992	-1 042	-1 094
Debt repayments		-4 675	-4 675	-4 675	-4 675	-4 675
Taxation		-672	-793	-922	-1 060	-1 207
Operating cash flows		-247	-113	26	169	317
Initial investment	-20 000					
Sale of land and buildings						63 814
Settlement of debt						-18 183
Net cash flows	-20 000	-247	-113	26	169	45 949
IRR	17,88%					

The investment appears lucrative – which it is, given the lower risk associated with property. The gross rental yield is 12,0 per cent and the net yield is 10,2 per cent per annum (refer to the box at the beginning of this example for these calculations). The yield seems reasonable yet the potential IRR is much higher. The question arising is, how much of the expected return is due to the property return and how is much is due to leverage? The property return can be determined by analysing what IRR the investor would receive if the land and buildings were acquired using 100 per cent of own resources to acquire it.

TABLE 9.15 100 per cent cash acquisition

100% cash acquisition	Year 0	Year 1	Year 2	Year 3	Year 4	Year 5
Initial investment	-50 000					
Sale of land and buildings						63 814
Rental income		6 000	6 300	6 615	6 946	7 293
Operating costs		-900	-945	-992	-1 042	-1 094
Taxation		-1 428	-1 499	-1 574	-1 653	-1 736
Net cash flows	-50 000	3 672	3 856	4 048	4 251	68 277
IRR	12,34%					

Table 9.15 indicates that the return from investing in the property is 12.34% per annum. The after tax return from net rental income provides an annual return of 7.34% [3,672 ÷ 50,000]. The capital growth per annum provides an additional 5.0% per annum, resulting in an overall return of 12.34% annually.

In practice, the net yield at which properties are acquired does not imply that this is the only return an investor will receive. Expected capital growth in the underlying property value enhances these returns, often significantly.

The leverage effect further enhances the return on the property from 12,34 per cent to 17,88 per cent. This effect is better illustrated through an NPV analysis. Assume that the investor above seeks a 12,0 per cent return from property investments generally and this return is pre-tax in his hands - that is, before capital gains tax. The NPV of investing in the property using 100 per cent of own cash to invest is R677,689 - insert the cash flows per the above table into an Excel spreadsheet or financial calculator and you should derive this answer.

The NPV of the investment, assuming it is partially bank-financed, improves to a remarkable R5,88 million at a 12,0 per cent required annual return. This difference in NPV (R5,2 million) is due to the leverage effect. The differential cash flows between 100% cash investment and raising a R30 million of bank loan are set out in Table 9.16.

TABLE 9.16 Differential cash flows

Differential cash flows	Year 0	Year 1	Year 2	Year 3	Year 4	Year 5
Initial investment	30 000					
Debt repayments		-4 675	-4 675	-4 675	-4 675	-22 857
Lower taxation paid		756	706	652	593	528
Net cash flows	30 000	-3 919	-3 968	-4 023	-4 082	-22 329
NPV	5 211					
Leverage effect	2 832					
Tax shield	2 379					

In the above example, the investor's returns have been enhanced from a positive NPV of R0.68 million to R5.89 million through:

- Using a bank loan to fund the acquisition (R2,83 million benefit) partially, instead of your own money; and
- Being able to deduct interest expense for income tax purposes (R2,38 million benefit) - referred to as the 'tax shield'.

These examples hopefully illustrate some of the basics of investing in property. The expected return from investing in property should generally be lower than on equities as an asset class. However, the expected return is a matter for each individual investor to decide and will often be influenced by the prevailing market values of property. Property investments can be significantly enhanced through leverage. However, caution should be exercised not to over-gear properties and to not pay the seller for these benefits.

Conclusion

Valuing high-growth businesses, companies operating in Africa, financial services and property businesses poses challenges. It is important to recognise that the fundamental principles of valuation apply no matter how unique or complicated the business is.

References

African Economic Outlook. (2014). www.africaneconomicoutlook.org. [Last accessed 16 December 2014].

American Appraisal. (2014). *Global M&A Valuation Outlook 2014*. Milwaukee: American Appraisal.

Business Day. (2014). Tiger Brands wary of African assets after Nigerian misadventure. 22 May 2014.

Credit Suisse. (2014). *Global Investment Returns Yearbook 2014*. Zurich: Credit Suisse Research Institute.

Damodaran, A. (2014). www.stern.nyu/adamdor/datasets. [Last accessed 16 December 2014].

Dimson, E., Marsh P. & Staunton, M. (2002). Global evidence of the equity risk premium. *Journal of Applied Corporate Finance* 15(4): 27–38.

Koller, T., Goedhart, M. & Wessels, D. (2010). *Valuation: Measuring and managing the value of companies*. (Fifth edition). New Jersey: John Wiley & Sons Inc.

McKinsey & Company. (2013). *Global Media Report 2013*. New York: McKinsey & Company.

PriceWaterhouseCoopers. (2012). *An African perspective: Valuation methodology survey*. Johannesburg: PricewaterhouseCoopers.

PriceWaterhouseCoopers. (2013a). *PWC Entertainment and Media Outlook 2013*. London: PricewaterhouseCoopers.

PricewaterhouseCoopers. (2013b). *PWC analysis of major banks' results for the reporting period 30 June 2013*. Johannesburg: PricewaterhouseCoopers.

www.finance.yahoo.com. [Last accessed 15 December 2014].

CHAPTER 10

Reasonability checks and sensitivity analysis

LEARNING OUTCOMES

Once you have worked through this chapter, you should be able to:

+ Understand the importance of ratio analysis to review the reasonability of forecast financial information
+ Recognise that sensitivity analysis is a critical part of the valuation process
+ Gain high-level insights into scenario analysis

Introduction

The result of a valuation is largely dependent on the underlying assumptions made regarding future cash flows and profits. This is particularly relevant in DCF valuations where the key inputs in the valuation model will have a profound impact on the end result. It's a classic case of 'garbage in, garbage out'. There are three recommended techniques for ensuring that the underlying assumptions in a valuation model are realistic. Firstly, ratio analysis should be performed to assess whether the forecast financial information is realistic in comparison with prior years and industry benchmarks. Secondly, detailed sensitivity analysis should be performed to examine the impact of changing assumptions on the valuation result. Thirdly, scenario analysis should be attempted to consider the impact of different strategic options on the value of the business.

It is recommended, in practice, that more time is spent on sensitivity and scenario analysis than on compiling and building the primary valuation model. This analysis will highlight the key value drivers in the business and provide guidance as to which further research and investigation is required. For example, if, in a retail business, the valuation result is insensitive to future capital expenditure but highly sensitive to gross profit margins, we would spend the majority of our time researching the latter. The outputs of sensitivity and scenario analysis also provide critical information for negotiation purposes.

Ratio analysis

The ratios to be calculated will largely depend on the industry in which the company operates. Relevant ratios for a construction business will be different to those of a bank or food retail business, for example. However, two key ratios, which are informative irrespective of the industry, are:

+ EBIT/Revenue or EBITDA/Revenue; and
+ ROIC.

The historic trends in industries tend to reveal consistent EBIT/Revenue and ROIC ratios. It is uncanny how these historic ratios converge into relatively tight bands. They also reflect the inherent characteristics of the industry. The EBIT margin in the food retail industry tends to be low, reflecting the lower gross margins associated with selling basic foodstuff. In Chapter 4 we examined Shoprite's EBIT margin over the period 2010 to 2014 – it varied between 5,6 and 5,9 per cent, a relatively tight range.

There is limited publicly available data on EBIT margins per industry in South Africa. Damodaran (2015) publishes this USA data annually. Table 10.1 shows some industry EBITDA margins.

TABLE 10.1 Industry EBITDA margins

Industry	EBITDA/Revenue
Beverages (soft)	21,8%
Broadcasting	28,7%
Construction supplies	12,6%
Drugs (pharmaceutical)	32,8%
Oil and gas (production and exploration)	45,0%
Paper/forestry products	12,2%
Retail (grocery and food)	4,7%
Telecoms (wireless)	18,9%

We would need to analyse the above industry EBITDA margins over a 10-year period at least to derive the low, high and average margins. This would be informative for benchmarking purposes.

EBITDA margins should be calculated and analysed from two perspectives:

- What are the historic and forecast EBITDA margins for the business being valued?
- How do EBITDA margins compare with industry averages?

Margins may fluctuate over time depending on prevailing economic conditions. However, these tend to revert to the mean. It is highly unlikely that EBITDA margins will constantly increase over time. There may be periods in which margins improve following cost-cutting exercises. However, costs often increase in subsequent periods. Costs generally do not decrease permanently in practice without a change in business processes.

Ratios in isolation are often misleading. It is more useful to analyse ratios in relation to each other, for example:

- Revenue growth versus operating cost increases;
- Revenue growth versus capital expenditure; and
- Revenue growth versus working capital ratios (inventory days, trade receivable days and trade payable days).

ROIC is another ratio that is particularly useful in checking the reasonability of forecast information. This ratio tends to be relatively stable over time, reflecting the profitability margins and capital intensity of individual industries. In Chapter 2, we explained the calculation of this ratio. In essence, ROIC is similar to ROE, but ignores the capital structure of the business.

ROIC = (EBIT – tax) ÷ (total shareholders' equity + debt – surplus cash)

McKinsey performed research on ROICs per industry in the USA over the period 1965 to 2007 (Koller 2010). Their findings included:
- The average ROIC for non-financial companies was about 10 per cent, and was relatively constant throughout the period; and
- ROICs vary by industry but not necessarily by company size.

The implied ROIC ratios calculated based on forecast financial information in valuation models provide a useful reasonability check. If ROIC ratios are constantly increasing over the next five to 10 years, this should be interrogated. Reasons could include:
- unrealistic forecast EBIT margins;
- insufficient capital investment to support forecast growth; and/or
- aggressive forecast dividend payouts to shareholders.

ROE ratios are also useful and should be calculated in conjunction with ROIC ratios. However, ROE can be 'managed' in the short term to display a flattering result. Let's illustrate this with an example.

EXAMPLE 10.1

Assume:
- an EBIT of R150 million;
- no interest-bearing debt or surplus cash;
- shareholders' equity of R800 million; and
- an income tax rate of 28 per cent.

Based on the above assumptions:

	Rmillions
EBIT	150
Tax	-42
PAT	108
Shareholders' equity	800
ROE	13,5%
ROIC	13,5%

If we further assume that R200 million of debt is raised (at an interest rate of 8,0 per cent), this amount is used to buy shares back and interest on the loan is tax-deductible, the ROE ratio will change:

	Rmillions
EBIT	150,0
Interest expense	-16,0
Profit before tax	134,0
Tax	-37,5
PAT	96,5
Shareholders' equity	600
Debt	200
ROE	16,1%
ROIC	13,5%

In this example, the ROIC remains constant but the ROE improves from 13,5 to 16,1 per cent. It follows in practice that companies can improve their ROE ratio by raising debt, pursuing aggressive dividend payout policies and using share buybacks. It is more difficult to improve ROIC through financial engineering, so this ratio is preferred for analysis purposes.

Sensitivity analysis

Sensitivity analysis is critical for identifying the key value drivers in a business and providing guidance as to where to focus in valuing a business. Sensitivity analysis involves changing key assumptions in the valuation model and analysing the impact on the end result. The analysis could be performed by changing one or more variables.

The structure of a valuation model is crucial for ensuring that sensitivity analysis can be performed. The key inputs in the model need to be separate from the resultant income statements, balance sheets and cash flow statements. Let's illustrate this with the valuation example from the end of Chapter 2, namely FWC Limited.

EXAMPLE 10.2

FWC is a retail pharmacy chain and the key assumptions driving forecast profits and cash flows in 20X5 are listed here:

Key assumptions 20X5	
New stores opened	5,0
Growth in revenue per store	7,0%

Continued

Gross profit margin	32,0%
Annual change in operating costs	15,0%
Depreciation/opening fixed assets	15,0%
% credit sales	25,0%
Inventory days	65
Trade receivable days	30
Trade payable days	70
Interest on cash balances	5,0%
Effective tax rate	28,0%
Capital expenditure per new store	5.2

There should be no assumptions included in the resultant income statements, balance sheets and cash flow statements. For example, operating cost increases should be based on the key assumptions rather than included in the operating cost cell in the spreadsheet.

Simplistically, we assumed in Chapter 2 that FWC would grow through opening new stores in 20X5 and 20X6 and focus, thereafter, on increasing revenue per store. The key assumptions in 20X7 (base case) together with the low- and high-road scenarios are as follows:

20X7 onwards	Low	Base	High
New stores opened	0	0	0
Growth in revenue per store	2,0%	6,0%	10,0%
Gross profit margin	30,0%	32,0%	35,0%
Annual change in operating costs	8,0%	6,0%	4,0%
Depreciation/opening fixed assets	20,0%	15,0%	12,5%
% credit sales	30,0%	25,0%	20,0%
Inventory days	80	65	50
Trade receivable days	40	30	20
Trade payable days	50	70	90
Maintenance capital expenditure	25.0	15.0	10.0

The issue arising is which of the above assumptions have the most profound impact on the valuation result. We do not know this until we perform the sensitivity analysis. You can purchase a useful Excel add-in from Treeplan (www.treeplan.com), which automates the sensitivity analysis. This tool performed a sensitivity analysis on the FWC discounted cash flow valuation model in Figure 10.1.

FIGURE 10.1 Sensitivity analysis, FWC Limited

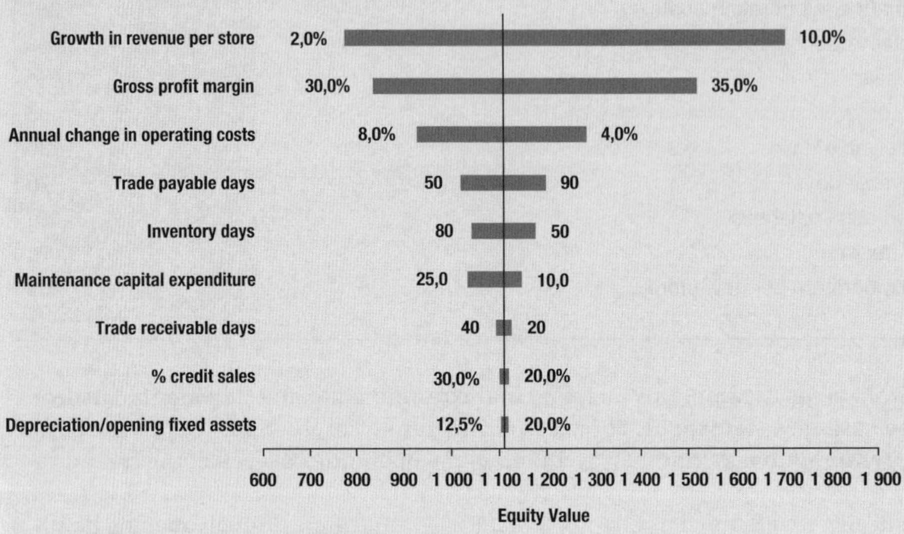

The above analysis is informative; its results are surprising, given that gross profit margins are generally the most critical value driver in retail businesses. The sensitivity analysis in Figure 10.1 reveals that revenue growth within existing stores is the key assumption in the model. The focus in valuing FWC, from a buyer or seller's perspective, should be on revenue growth and gross profit margins. The other assumptions can be reviewed later. Some do not warrant much attention – for example, percentage credit sales and trade receivable days. These assumptions need to be reasonable, but have limited impact on the valuation result.

The majority of time in valuing FWC should be spent in reviewing detailed trends and forecasts of revenue growth and gross profit margins by product category. As much detail as possible should be obtained about these assumptions.

There are always surprises in sensitivity analyses. Assumptions that would seem, intuitively, to be important are sometimes irrelevant to the end result.

Capitec analysis

In Chapter 9 we examined Capitec Bank, a South African registered bank focusing on unsecured lending to consumers. To illustrate sensitivity analysis, various assumptions have been made about Capitec's future operating activities. It should be emphasised that these assumptions are the author's, and that they will be incorrect.

TABLE 10.2 Capitec Bank

Capitec Bank	FY2015	FY2016	FY2017 onwards
Growth in loans and advances (gross)	8,0%	8,0%	7,0%
Interest income/average advances	27,5%	27,5%	27,5%
Interest on interest-bearing cash/investments	6,0%	6,0%	6,0%
Net impairment charge/gross loans and advances	10,5%	9,5%	9,5%
Impairment provision/gross loans and advances	11,0%	10,0%	9,5%
Growth in deposits	7,0%	7,0%	7,0%
Interest expense/average loans and deposits	6,5%	6,5%	6,5%
Loan fee income/average loans and advances	3,5%	3,5%	3,5%
Transaction fees/average loans and advances	8,5%	8,5%	8,5%
Loan fee expense/loan fees	35,0%	35,0%	35,0%
Transaction fee expense/transaction fees	30,0%	30,0%	30,0%
Annual change in banking operating expenses	15,0%	8,0%	8,0%
Effective tax rate	28,0%	28,0%	28,0%
Depreciation/opening assets	40,0%	40,0%	35,0%
Non-interest bearing cash/loans & advances	8,0%	8,0%	8,0%
Net change in investments	5,0%	5,0%	7,0%
Other receivables/net fee income	8,0%	8,0%	8,0%
Capital expenditure (Rmillions)	320	350	375
Other liabilities/Banking operating expenses	19,0%	19,0%	19,0%
Dividend cover	3.0	2.8	2.5
Risk-weighted assets/Banking assets	60,0%	60,0%	60,0%
Growth in perpetuity	–	–	7,0%

For the purposes of valuing Capitec at June 2014, a cost of capital of 17,0 per cent and growth in perpetuity of 7,0 per cent from FY2017 onwards was assumed. The equity value derived based on the above assumptions was R27,3 billion. The implied historic PE multiple is 13.4 and a price-to-book ratio of 2.7 times.

The resultant income statements, balance sheets and cash flow statements based on the assumptions in Table 10.2 are summarised In Table 10.3, 10.4 and 10.5 for completeness's sake.

TABLE 10.3 Income statements

Income statements *Rmillions*	**2015**	**2016**	**2017**
Interest income			
Interest on average advances	9 635	10 406	11 185
Interest on interest-bearing cash/investments	783	882	979
Interest expense	-2 385	-2 552	-2 730
Net interest income	8 033	8 737	9 434
Loan fee income	1 226	1 324	1 423
Loan fee expense	-429	-464	-498
Transaction fee income	2 978	3 216	3 457
Transaction fee expense	-893	-965	-1 037
Net fee income	2 882	3 112	3 345
Net impairment charge	-3 820	-3 733	-3 994
Other income	0	0	0
Banking operating expenses	-3 728	-4 026	-4 348
Non-banking expenses	0	0	0
Operating profit before tax	3 367	4 090	4 436
Normal income tax	-943	-1 145	-1 242
STC	0	0	0
Deferred tax	0	0	0
Profit for the year	2 424	2 945	3 194
Key ratios			
Interest income/average assets			
Interest on average advances	27,5%	27,5%	27,5%
Interest on interest-bearing cash/investments	6,0%	6,0%	6,0%
Interest expense/average loans and deposits	6,5%	6,5%	6,5%

Continued

Loan fee income/average loans and advances	3,5%	3,5%	3,5%
Transaction fees/average loans and advances	8,5%	8,5%	8,5%
Loan fee expense/loan fees	35,0%	35,0%	35,0%
Transaction fee expense/transaction fees	30,0%	30,0%	30,0%
Net impairment charge/gross loans and advances	10,5%	9,5%	9,5%
Depreciation and amortisation/opening assets	40,0%	40,0%	35,0%
Cost to income	34,2%	34,0%	34,0%
Annual change in banking operating expenses	15.0%	8.0%	8.0%
Growth in operating profit	18.9%	21.5%	8.5%

TABLE 10.4 Balance sheets

Balance sheets ***Rmillions***	**2015**	**2016**	**2017**
Cash and cash equivalents			
Interest bearing	9 008	10 154	11 634
Non-interest-bearing	2 591	2 829	3 044
Investments at fair value	4 997	5 247	5 614
Loans and advances	32 383	35 366	38 052
Inventory	0	0	0
Other receivables	231	249	268
Derivative financial assets	0	0	0
Current income tax	0	0	0
Property, plant and equipment	753	721	773
Intangible assets	201	201	201
Deferred tax assets	212	212	212
Total assets	50 375	54 980	59 798
Loans and deposits	37 930	40 585	43 426
Provisions	11	11	11
Other liabilities	708	765	826
Share appreciation rights	127	127	127
Current income tax	0	0	0
Total liabilities	38 777	41 488	44 390

Continued

Share capital	5 513	5 513	5 513
Cash flow hedge reserve	81	81	81
Retained earnings	5 746	7 639	9 555
	11 339	13 232	15 149
Preference share capital	259	259	259
Total equity	11 598	13 491	15 408
Check	0	0	0

TABLE 10.5 Cash flow statements

Cash flow statements *Rmillions*	**2015**	**2016**	**2017**
Operating profit	3 367	4 090	4 436
Adjustments:			
Fair value adjustments on financial assets	2	0	0
Loan impairment charges	365	-73	65
Depreciation and amortisation	423	382	323
Movements in provisions	0	0	0
Share-based employee costs	0	0	0
Profit/loss on disposal of assets	0	0	0
Receivables at fair value	0	0	0
Loans and advances	-2 695	-2 911	-2 751
Inventory	0	0	0
Other receivables	-11	-18	-19
Deposits	2 481	2 655	2 841
Trade and other payables	86	57	61
Income taxes paid	-920	-1 145	-1 242
Cash flow from operating activities	3 098	3 036	3 715
Property, plant and equipment	-320	-350	-375
Intangible assets	0	0	0
Investments	-238	-250	-367
Derivative financial assets	203	0	0
Dividends paid	-808	-1 052	-1 278
Preference share issued	0	0	0
Ordinary shares issued	0	0	0
Settlement of employee share options	0	0	0

Continued

Net movement in cash and cash equivalents	1 935	1 384	1 695
Opening balance	9 664	11 599	12 983
Closing balance	11 599	12 983	14 678
Net movement in cash	1 935	1 384	1 695
Dividends paid	808	1 052	1 278
Preference share issued	0	0	0
Ordinary shares issued	0	0	0
Settlement of employee share options	0	0	0
Free cash flow	2 743	2 436	2 972
Annual change in free cash flow	-29,8%	-11,2%	22,0%

Without access to Capitec management and detailed research into the unsecured lending market, the above forecasts are conjecture. However, the principle being illustrated is to identify the key value drivers in Capitec's business in order to fine-tune the valuation.

The following simplistic assumptions were made regarding FY2017 onwards:

TABLE 10.6 Capitec Bank, assumptions for FY2017 onwards

FY2017 onwards	Low	Base	High
Growth in loans and advances (gross)	6,0%	7,0%	10,0%
Interest income/average advances	25,0%	27,5%	28,5%
Interest on interest-bearing cash/investments	5,0%	6,0%	7,0%
Net impairment charge/gross loans and advances	11,0%	9,5%	8,5%
Impairment provision/gross loans and advances	12,0%	9,5%	8,0%
Growth in deposits	5,0%	7,0%	8,0%
Interest expense/average loans and deposits	9,0%	6,5%	6,0%
Loan fee income/average loans and advances	2,5%	3,5%	4,0%
Transaction fees/average loans and advances	6,0%	8,5%	9,5%
Loan fee expense/loan fees	45,0%	35,0%	30,0%
Transaction fee expense/transaction fees	40,0%	30,0%	25,0%
Annual change in banking operating expenses	10,0%	8,0%	7,0%
Effective tax rate	29,0%	28,0%	27,0%
Depreciation/opening assets	40,0%	35,0%	30,0%
Non-interest bearing cash/loans and advances	10,0%	8,0%	7,0%
Net change in investments	6,0%	7,0%	8,0%
Other receivables/net fee income	9,0%	8,0%	7,0%
Capital expenditure	420	375	350
Other liabilities/Banking operating expenses	15,0%	19,0%	22,0%

Continued

Dividend cover	2,0	2,5	3,0
Risk weighted assets/Banking assets	70,0%	60,0%	50,0%
Growth in perpetuity	5,0%	7,0%	8,0%

The results of the sensitivity analysis performed on FY2017 onwards are illustrated in Figure 10.2.

FIGURE 10.2 Sensitivity analysis, Capitec Bank

Capitec's equity value is sensitive to various factors, including growth in deposits, loans and advances, average interest earned and paid, impairment charges, and transaction fees. It is unusual to have so many key assumptions affecting the end valuation. Usually, two or three key factors have a profound impact on the value of a business – refer to the FWC sensitivity analysis in Figure 10.1. Capitec's business model is such that there are numerous factors, which would have to be thoroughly researched prior to forming an opinion on value.

It is also important to consider the interrelationships between key assumptions. Sensitivity analysis should be performed considering changing multiple variables simultaneously.

Key issues to research in Capitec's case would be:

+ the size and risks facing the unsecured lending market;
+ whether interest charged on loan advances is sustainable;
+ continued access to deposits;

- transaction fees charged; and
- potential future impairment charges.

The growth in perpetuity assumed will generally also have a significant impact on the valuation, as will the cost of equity used. Sensitivity analysis should be performed using different betas to assess the impact on the end result.

Scenario analysis

Most businesses face various strategic options. Scenario analysis involves summarising options going forward and encapsulating these into financial forecasts. An excellent example of scenario analysis and the potential impact on the valuation result was the Grant Samuel valuation report to David Jones' shareholders in May 2014. Woolworths Holdings acquired 100 per cent of David Jones, the Australian department store group, during 2014 for A$2,15 billion. Grant Samuels was appointed by the David Jones' shareholders as the independent expert to advise on whether the deal was in the shareholders' best interests.

The Grant Samuels report contained a scenario analysis, excerpts which are set out in Table 10.7 (David Jones 2014).

TABLE 10.7 David Jones – DCF scenarios

Scenario	Description
Scenario A	Future Strategic Direction Plan is fully implemented and achieves its objectives (e.g. gross margin increases to 40%, cost savings are achieved, new full-scale and 'village format' stores are opened). 'Like-for-like' sales growth, fixed operating expense growth and terminal growth rate are 2,5%.
Scenario B	Scenario A except that gross margin only increases to 39.0% by FY2017 (rather than 40%).
Scenario C	Scenario A except that fixed costs increase by 3,5% per annum (rather than 2,5%).
Scenario D	Scenario A except that three new full-scale stores (Sunshine Plaza, Eastland and Pacific Fair) are not opened. Capital expenditure for these stores is excluded.
Scenario E	Scenario A except that no new 'village format' stores are opened. Capital expenditure for these stores is excluded.
Scenario F	Scenario A except that 'like-for-like' sales growth is 4,0% per annum, fixed cost growth is 3,5% per annum and terminal growth is 4,0%.
Scenario G	Scenario A except that 'like-for-like' sales growth is 1,0%, fixed cost growth is 2,5% and terminal growth is nil.
Scenario H	Scenario A except that David Jones enters into a sale and leaseback of its freehold properties at a yield in the range of 6–6,5%. Rental expense for these stores is $40 million in FY2014, increasing by assumed fixed cost growth (2,5%).

Woolworths' stated intention was to unlock various synergies after the acquisition of David Jones. These included increasing private label apparel sales and cross-selling Country Road merchandise through David Jones stores. These synergies were included in the Grant Samuels valuation report, evidenced by the increased gross margin from 37,5 per cent historically to 40,0 per cent in Table 10.7's Scenario A.

The NPV results based on the above scenarios were published by Grant Samuels.

FIGURE 10.3 David Jones – NPV outcomes (at 10,0 to 11,0 per cent)

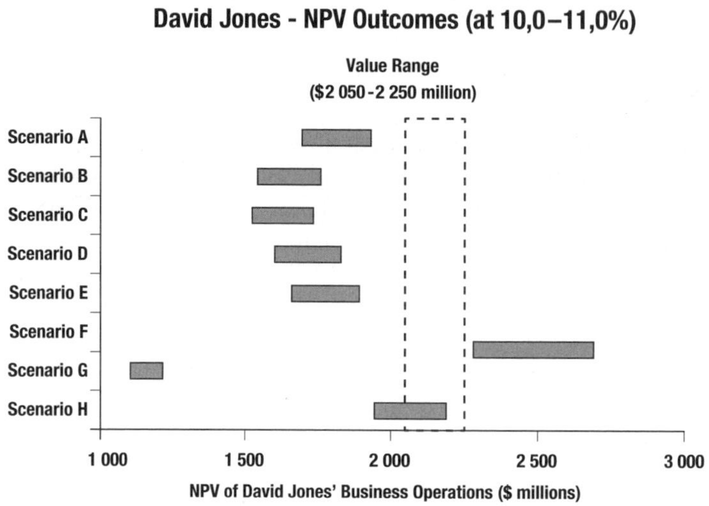

Source: David Jones (2014: 60)

It is interesting that only two scenarios in Figure 10.3 produced NPVs within or above the Woolworths bid price (A$2,15 billion). This would suggest that Woolworths' bid was fully priced or various synergies were not disclosed to the investing public.

Conclusion

The valuation result is highly dependent on the underlying assumptions regarding the business' operations in future. Ratio analysis, sensitivity analysis and scenario analysis are invaluable techniques and tools for assisting in evaluating the reasonability of forecasts. Ratios, particularly the EBITDA margin and ROIC ratios, will highlight if forecasts are too conservative or optimistic. Sensitivity analysis will highlight the key value drivers in the business and facilitate focus on the key assumptions in valuation models. Scenario analysis is useful for providing insights into the financial effects of pursuing various strategic options.

References

Damodaran, A. (2015). www.stern.nyu/adamdor/datasets. [Last accessed 13 January 2015].

David Jones Scheme Booklet registered with ASIC, dated 23 May 2014.

Koller, T., Goedhart, M. & Wessels, D. (2010). *Valuation: Measuring and Managing the Value of Companies.* (Fifth edition). New Jersey: John Wiley & Sons Inc.

CHAPTER 11

Valuing debt instruments and options

LEARNING OUTCOMES

Once you have worked through this chapter, you should be able to:

- Comprehend how to value debt instruments in practice using Excel
- Recognise that valuing preference shares is similar to the principles applicable to debt instruments
- Gain some insights into how to use preference shares for structuring purposes
- Create an Excel model to value options using the Black-Scholes model

Introduction

Valuing debt instruments is generally simpler than valuing equity interests. The market value of debt represents the present value of future interest receipts (also referred to as coupon payments) and the capital redemption. You should use the prevailing market yield for similar debt instruments to present-value future cash flows associated with the debt instrument. There is more certainty regarding future cash flows from debt instruments than from owning shares in a business – assuming that the debt issuer does not face bankruptcy.

Valuing preference shares is similar to valuing debt instruments as they generally have the same characteristics. Preference shares often pay fixed periodic dividends and there may be a specified redemption date for the capital portion. Preference shares, however, can have varying terms with regards to dividends, profit participation and redemption. In some cases, preference shares also have voting rights.

Options with regards to financial assets (equity shares, currencies, debt instruments etc.) provide the option holder with the right to sell or buy the underlying financial asset at a specified price at some stage in the future. The option to acquire a financial asset is commonly referred to as a call option, and the right to sell a put option. Option holders generally have to pay an option premium to acquire the option. Downside risk for option holders is usually limited to the option premium. If the underlying asset price is unfavourable, option holders will not exercise their rights to acquire or sell.

Let's illustrate this with an example.

EXAMPLE 11.1

Assume:

- You have the right to acquire 1 000 shares of HBG Limited, a listed company, at any stage in the next six months, at R100 a share;
- The total option premium is R2 500; and
- The current share price of HBG Limited is R80.

If the share price of HBG is R120 in six months' time, you would obviously exercise the option and make a profit of R20 a share (or R20 000). However, your net profit would be after deducting the option premium of R2 500 and the 'interest' cost on the option premium.

If you held a put option on the HBG Limited shares, you would be hoping that the underlying share price would decline over the six-month period. This would be favourable as you could exercise the option and sell the underlying shares at a higher price than the prevailing market price.

The valuation of options is complex and highly technical. This chapter will provide an overview of an option-pricing model that you could use in practice.

Debt instruments

Debt instruments could include a term loan, debenture, corporate bond or a mezzanine loan. The South African corporate bond market is underdeveloped compared to major First World countries such as the USA and UK. There is not much trade in corporate bonds, except those issued by parastatals such as Eskom and larger listed companies. Some South African companies raise debt in offshore markets where there are more active markets. However, these loans introduce currency risk as they are denominated in foreign currencies.

Debt instruments generally have specified interest rates, which could be fixed or variable. The latter would be linked to movements in the prime overdraft rate or the Johannesburg Interbank Agreed Rate (JIBAR). The interest rate of the debt instrument would not necessarily be the market rate as the credit rating of the borrower may change and market interest rates vary over time.

Let's illustrate the valuation of a corporate bond with a simple example.

EXAMPLE 11.2

Assume:

- a R500 million bond issued on 1 January 20X1;
- a fixed interest rate of 9,0 per cent per annum, payable annually in arrears;
- that redemption of the bond is due on 31 December 20X6; and
- a current market yield of 9,5 per cent.

The fair value of the above corporate bond on 1 January 20X3 would be as shown in Table 11.1:

TABLE 11.1 Fair value of corporate bond, 1 January 20X3

	20X3	20X4	20X5	20X6
31 December ...	**Rmillions**	**Rmillions**	**Rmillions**	**Rmillions**
Interest income	45,0	45,0	45,0	45,0
Capital redemption				500,0
Net cash flows	45,0	45,0	45,0	545,0
PV at 1 January 20X3	492,0			

The current fair value of the corporate bond is below its issued value of R500 million. This is due to the current market yield on the bond being higher than its fixed interest rate of 9,0 per cent. If the current yield was equivalent to the interest rate paid, its fair value would be R500 million (issue and redemption value).

Debt instruments can be issued at a discount or premium to face value, and can be redeemed at a discount or premium.

Government and corporate bonds often pay interest quarterly or biannually. Valuing these instruments or deriving their yield to maturity (YTM) requires knowledge of financial formulas to determine effective interest rates and present-value future receipts for periods less than a year. Excel has a built-in formula that makes these calculations simple.

Let's illustrate this with an example.

EXAMPLE 11.3

Assume for a corporate bond:

+ an issue value and redemption value of R1 600;
+ interest of 8,0 per cent paid biannually on 30 June and 31 December each year;
+ that the bond is redeemable on 30 June 2017; and
+ a market price of R1 550 on 19 January 2015.

To determine the YTM on 19 January 2015, we could use the XIRR function in Excel.

TABLE 11.2 Using the XIRR function to determine the YTM

A	B	C
1	19 January 2015	-1,550
2	30 June 2015	64.0
3	31 December 2015	64.0
4	30 June 2016	64.0
5	31 December 2016	64.0
6	30 June 2017	1,664.0
7		
8	YTM	9.89%
9		

Excel is able to calculate the YTM with varying dates based on future interest payments and capital redemption proceeds. However, dates need to be inserted into Excel cells in a recognisable format.

Should you wish to calculate the price to be paid on 19 January 2015 for the above corporate bond in order to achieve a 10,0 per cent YTM, you can use Excel's Goal Seek function.

TABLE 11.3 Excel's Goal Seek function

Goal Seek	
Set cell	C8
To value	10.0%
By changing cell	C1
OK	Cancel

The result of using the Goal Seek function above should yield a purchase price of R1 546,64 on 19 January 2015.

Valuing bonds and debentures is relatively simple, thanks to spreadsheet tools available. We do not have to be mathematical geniuses to perform these calculations. Complexity is introduced when these debt instruments have characteristics of equity and debt.

Convertible debt instruments

Debentures and corporate bonds are occasionally issued with conversion rights. The terms of these debt instruments can be complex and include:

- the right of debt instrument holders to convert debt into equity at a specified price on or before a future date; and/or
- the right of the issuer to redeem debt instruments early or prior to debt instrument holders having the opportunity to convert them into ordinary shares.

In Chapter 4, we analysed Shoprite's convertible bonds and how to treat these from Shoprite's perspective in a valuation of the company's ordinary shares. However, how do we value convertible bonds from the perspective of the purchaser of these instruments?

In essence, we need to value the debt component separately and then use option-pricing methodology to derive the 'equity' value. This can be deduced for actively traded convertible bonds. Let's illustrate this through an example.

EXAMPLE 11.4

Assume:

- a convertible bond trading at R1 707,10 on 1 January 2015;
- annual coupon payments of 10,0 per cent payable on 30 June and 31 December annually;
- a YTM for the corporate bond of 10,0 per cent; and
- redemption at face value of R1 600,00 on 30 June 2017 or convertible into ordinary shares based on a price of R80.00 per share on 30 June 2017.

Using the XIRR and Goal Seek functions in Excel, we can value the debt portion of the above convertible bond.

TABLE 11.4 Using the XIRR and Goal Seek functions to value the debt portion of a convertible bond

A	B	C
1	1 January 2015	-1,607.10
2	30 June 2015	80.00
3	31 December 2015	80.00
4	30 June 2016	80.00
5	31 December 2016	80.00
6	30 June 2017	1,680.00
7		
8	XIRR	10.0%
9		

It follows that the debt portion of the convertible bond is R1 607,10 and the 'equity' portion is therefore R100.00 on 1 January 2015 (R1 707,10 trading price less the debt portion of R1 607,10). The market has determined the option value of the convertible bond for us. This implies that on 30 June 2017, the bondholders are likely to convert into ordinary shares rather than requiring redemption of the bonds because the ordinary share price is forecast to be higher than R80.00 per share. Bondholders essentially have the option to receive a cash redemption of R1 600,00 or to receive 20 ordinary shares at R80.00 per share on 30 June 2017. The valuation of the option component will be covered later in this chapter.

Preference shares

The valuation of preference shares is similar to that of debt instruments. Preference shares generally pay a fixed dividend periodically and often have a specified redemption date. The difference in a South African context is that dividends are not subject to income tax, so preference dividend yields tend to be lower than yields on debt instruments. Dividends are, however, currently subject to dividends tax at a rate of 15,0 per cent in the hands of preference shareholders.

Let's assume that PDO Limited wishes to raise R100 million in debt finance for five years and is undecided about whether to issue redeemable preference shares or debentures. The interest rate on debentures would be 10,0 per cent per annum payable annually in arrears, and redemption would be in a single bullet payment of R100 million in five years' time. The question is, which dividend yield would PDO Limited have to offer corporate subscribers for preference shares to ensure that their after-tax return was identical to holding debentures? (Assume a corporate income tax rate of 28,0 per cent.)

The after-tax yield on debentures would be 7,2 per cent (10,0 per cent less income tax of 28,0 per cent). The preference share dividend yield would need to be 8,47 per cent to place corporate preference shareholders in the identical after-tax position to holding debentures.

TABLE 11.5 Debenture versus preference share yields

Debenture	20X0	20X1	20X2	20X3	20X4	20X5
Capital	-100,0					100,0
Interest		10,0	10,0	10,0	10,0	10,0
Income tax		-2,8	-2,8	-2,8	-2,8	-2,8
	-100,0	7,2	7,2	7,2	7,2	107,2
IRR	7,2%					
Preference share						
Capital	-100,0					100,00
Dividends		8,47	8,47	8,47	8,47	8,47
Dividend tax		-1,27	-1,27	-1,27	-1,27	-1,27
	-100,0	7,20	7,20	7,20	7,20	107,20
IRR	7,2%					

Preference shares rank ahead of ordinary shareholders with regards to capital redemption. Their other rights can be structured according to circumstances. Corporate financiers can use preference shares to structure numerous rights such as:

+ the right to receive annual dividends based on company profitability;
+ the right to vote at shareholders' meetings; and
+ the right to veto certain material company and shareholder decisions.

In Chapter 4, we discussed Shoprite's deferred shares in issue, which provide their holder the right to vote at ordinary shareholder meetings but have no dividend participation rights. Preference shares can be structured on a similar basis to entrench holders' control or negative control. They can also be structured to provide profit participation. The valuation of preference shares becomes complicated in circumstances where these shares have attributes of ordinary shares, such as enhanced dividend rights and voting power.

Valuing options

Options tend to be either European or American by nature. A European option entitles the holder to exercise the option on the expiration date. An American option permits the holder to exercise the option at any time prior to, or on, the expiration date. Option-pricing models generally assume that the underlying option is a European option.

Call options on ordinary shares are 'in the money' if the share price increases above the exercise or strike price. The converse applies to put options – if the share price declines below the strike price, these options become valuable. Let's illustrate this with an example.

EXAMPLE 11.5

Assume:

+ that the strike price for a call option is R20.00 a share;
+ that the option holder has the right to acquire 10 000 options on 31 January 20X5;
+ an option premium of R10 000 paid;
+ that the ruling share price on 31 January 20X5 is R25,00 a share; and
+ that the option holder exercises the option on 31 January 20X5 and subsequently sells the shares for R25,00 each.

Call option	**Rands**
Sale of shares	250 000
Option premium paid	-10 000
Exercise of option	-200 000
Profit	40 000

To make a profit on a put option, the share price needs to decline below the strike price. Assume the above, except that it is a put option and the share price on 31 January 20X5 is R16,00.

Put option	Rands
Sale of shares	200 000
Option premium paid	-10 000
Exercise of option	-160 000
Profit	30 000

Valuing options is mathematically complicated. There are two commonly used option-pricing models used in practice: the binomial model and the Black–Scholes model. The latter is the most popular. The originators of the Black–Scholes model were Myron Scholes and Fischer Black. Scholes received a Nobel Prize for his pioneering work in 1997.

The objective of option-pricing models is to estimate the expected 'profit' of existing options or to price these when selling them (determining a reasonable option premium). The Black–Scholes model for valuing options will be described in this chapter. It is unnecessary to explain its derivation since we can use Excel to input the formula and apply it to particular circumstances.

The Black–Scholes model relies on five inputs to estimate option value:

1. Current share price (P)
2. Strike price per share (S)
3. Time to maturity of the option (t)
4. Risk-free rate (Rf)
5. Share price volatility (V).

The time to maturity of the option is expressed in years. If the option is exercisable in 18 months' time, the input is expressed as 1.5.

The share price volatility is measured by estimating the annual standard deviation in the underlying share price. Historical movements will provide some guidance as to potential future share price movements and their standard deviation. However, volatility is an estimate over the remaining duration of the option.

The risk-free rate can be estimated by analysing current yields on government bonds with a similar lifespan to that of the option. Hence, if the time to maturity for the option being valued is two years, a risk-free rate proxy would be a treasury bill or government bond due to be redeemed in two years' time.

For the sake of completeness, the Black–Scholes formula is set out below.

$$\text{Formula 1 ('F1')} = \frac{\ln\left(P \div S\right) + \left(Rf + \dfrac{V^2}{2}\right) \times t}{V\sqrt{t}}$$

$$\text{Formula 2 ('F2')} = F1 - V\sqrt{t}$$

$$\text{Formula 3 ('F3')} = \textit{Normal distribution } F1$$

$$\text{Formula 4 ('F4')} = \textit{Normal distribution } F2$$

The **value of a call option** would be determined as:

$$= (P \times F3) - [(S \times e^{(Rf \times t)}) \times F4]$$

The value 'e' in the call option formula above is a natural logarithm with a value of 2,71828182845904.

The **value of a put option** is determined as follows:

$$= (Call\ option\ price - P) + (S \times e^{(-Rf \times t)})$$

Calculating the value of a call or put option manually is not advised. Rather use Excel! Let's illustrate this with an example.

EXAMPLE 11.6

Assume for an option:

- a current share price of R10,00;
- a strike price of R12,00;
- a risk-free rate of 6,5 per cent;
- a time to maturity of three years; and
- volatility of 30 per cent.

The question is, how much would a call and put option be worth today based on these assumptions? We can use Excel to calculate this for us, saving us much time and effort. We can also run a sensitivity analysis on the option value results.

TABLE 11.6 Calculating the call and put option value

A	B	C
1	Current price	10.00
2	Strike price	12.00
3	Risk-free rate	6.5%
4	Time to maturity	3.0
5	Volatility	30%
6		
7	**F1**	$= [LN(C1 \div C2) + (C3 + (C5^2 \div 2) \times t)] \div (C5 \times \sqrt{C4})$
8	**F2**	$= C7 - (\sqrt{C4} \times C5)$
9	**F3**	= *NORMSDIST*(C7)
10	**F4**	= *NORMSDIST*(C8)
11		
12	**Call option value**	= (C1 × C9) – (C2 × *EXP*(–C3 × C4) × C10)
13	**Put option value**	= (C12 – C1) + (C2 × *EXP*(–C3 × C4))
14		

The results you should obtain using the Excel formulae in Figure 11.4 is R2,10 for the call option and R1,97 for the put option.

The value of an option can be split into its intrinsic value and the time value of money. Interpreting the Black–Scholes results above in a very simplistic manner:

	Call option	Put option
Estimated share price in three years' time	R14,54	-R9,61
Strike price	-R12,00	R12,00
Profit	R2,54	R2,39
PV to today at risk-free rate	R2,10	R1,97
Implied CAGR in share price	13,3%	-1,3%

Option valuation experts would baulk at the above analysis. However, it illustrates what the share price would need to be to deliver the option value (PV of expected profit) in today's money. The holder of a call option would need the share price to be R14,54 on the option expiry date (three years' time) and the present value of this gain today would be R2,10. Similarly, the holder of a put option would need the share price to decline from its present R10,00 per share to R9,61 in three years' time to unlock the gain of R1,97 in today's money.

Sensitivity analysis is very useful in examining the impact of differing assumptions on option value. The assumptions in valuing the above call option have been varied to assess the impact on option value.

TABLE 11.7 Varied assumptions to assess the impact on option value

Assumptions	Low	Base	High
Current price	R10,00	R10,00	R10,00
Strike price	R10,00	R12,00	R15,00
Risk free rate	5,5%	6,5%	7,5%
Time to maturity	4,0	3,0	2,0
Volatility	10,0%	30,0%	50,0%

Performing sensitivity analysis reveals the following impact on the call option value:

FIGURE 11.1 Sensitivity analysis showing impact on call option value

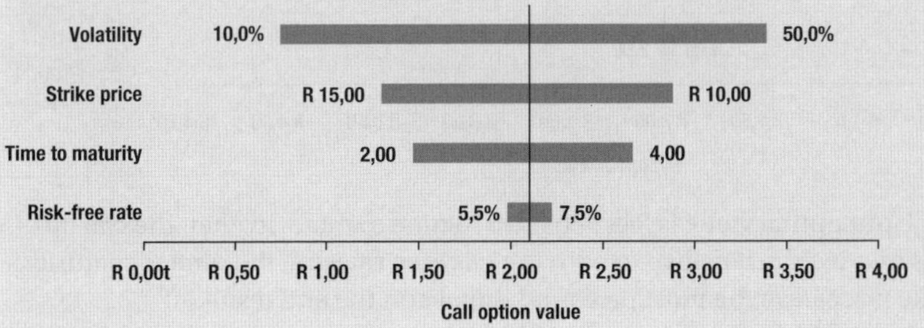

It is apparent that the assumption regarding volatility has the most profound impact on the call option value. The strike price would obviously affect the call option value – the lower the strike price, the more valuable the option.

The longer the time to maturity, the more valuable the call option. This is due to the present value of the strike price being lower in four years time' than two years hence. Also, the more time to expiry, the greater the chance of the share price escalating.

The sensitivity analysis in Figure 11.1 assumes that one assumption is amended and the remainder of the assumptions remain constant. This is probably unrealistic since the assumptions about strike price, volatility and time to maturity may be interrelated in practice. Running a two-variable sensitivity analysis provides some more insights.

FIGURE 11.2 A two-variable sensitivity analysis

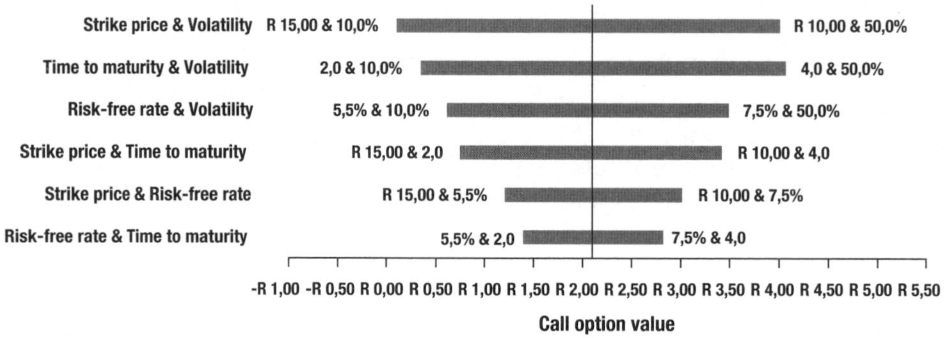

Volatility remains the key input into the model. The option value, before consideration of any option premium payable, can obviously not be below zero. The Figure 11.2 indicates that the call option could vary in value between R0,10 and R4,07, a wide range in the circumstances.

A sensitivity analysis was performed on the put option value based on the low-road, base-case and high-road scenarios as assumed for the call option in Figure 11.2.

FIGURE 11.3 Sensitivity analysis performed on the put option value based on the low-road, base-case and high-road scenarios

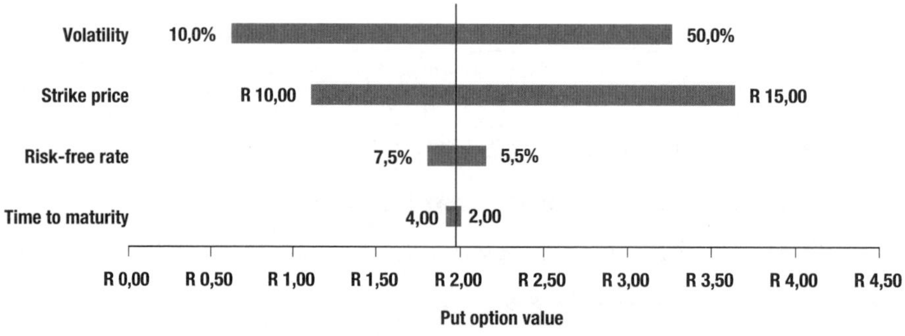

It is interesting that the put option value is less sensitive to time to maturity than the call option. The put option is relatively insensitive to both the risk-free rate and the time to maturity. Volatility and the strike price have the most profound impact on the end result.

The Black-Scholes model is commonly used in practice to value share incentive schemes for financial reporting purposes. It is also used by traders in commodities, equity shares, debt securities and foreign currencies to estimate the value of options with regards to these assets.

It is not recommended that you blindly believe the outputs of option pricing models. In addition to running the Black–Scholes model, you should perform your own sensitivity analysis regarding the potential future value of the option. Let's illustrate this with an example of a call option.

EXAMPLE 11.7

Assume:

- a current share price of R10,00;
- a strike price of R11,00;
- estimated compound annual growth in the share price of 10,0 per cent;
- no option premium payable;
- a time to maturity of 2,0 years; and
- a risk-free rate of 6,5 per cent.

The expected profit arising from this call option would be:

	Call option
Estimated share price in two years' time	R12,10
Strike price	-R11,00
Profit	R1,10
PV to today at risk free rate	R0,97

We can run a simple sensitivity analysis on the assumptions without using the Black–Scholes model, assuming the following:

TABLE 11.8 Simple sensitivity analysis

	Low	Base	High
Current price	R10,00	R10,00	R10,00
Strike price	R10,00	R12,00	R15,00
CAGR in share price	0,0%	10,0%	20,0%
Time to maturity (years)	1,0	2,0	3,0
Risk-free rate	5,0%	6,5%	7,5%

FIGURE 11.4 PV of call option profit

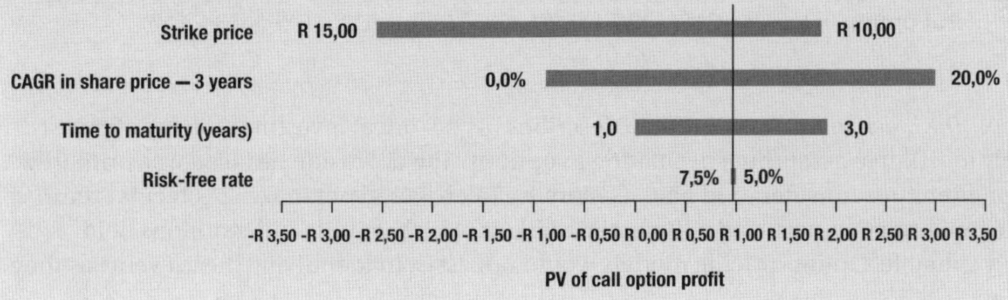

The present value of the call option profit in the base case per the above example is R0,97. The sensitivity analysis in Figure 11.8 is difficult to interpret. Perhaps it is more useful to analyse which assumptions (strike price, CAGR in share price and time to maturity) would result in zero profit or R2,00 profit using the Goal Seek function in Excel. The analysis has been performed for you, and its results are as follows:

Assumption required to yield profit of ...	**R0,00**	**R2,00**
Strike price	R12,10	R9,83
CAGR in share price – three years	4,9%	15,2%
Time to maturity (years)	1,0	3,1

It follows that a strike price of R9,83, CAGR in share price of 15,2 per cent or time to maturity of 3,1 years would yield a profit of R2,00 in today's money in this scenario.

Some practitioners adjust the Black–Scholes model for expected future dividend yields. Option holders do not receive dividends until they actually own shares, so it is irrelevant from this perspective. However, some believe that the future share price is affected by expected dividend yields. This has been the subject of many doctoral theses; the empirical research is not convincing either way. However, should you concur that dividend yields do impact on share prices, the Black–Scholes model can be adjusted in an Excel spreadsheet as follows:

TABLE 11.9 Adjusting the Black–Scholes model in Excel

A	B	C
1	Current price	10.00
2	Strike price	12.00
3	Risk free rate	6.5%
4	Time to maturity	3.0
5	Volatility	30%
6	Dividend yield	4.0%
7	**F1**	$= [LN((C1 \times EXP(-C6 \times C4)) \div C2) + (C3 + (C5^2 \div 2) \times t)] \div (C5 \times \sqrt{C4})$
8	**F2**	$= C7 - (\sqrt{C4} \times C5)$
9	**F3**	= *NORMSDIST*(C7)
10	**F4**	= *NORMSDIST*(C8)
11		
12	**Call option value**	= (C1 × *EXP*(–C6 × C4) × C9) – (C2 × *EXP*(–C3 × C4) × C10)
13	**Put option value**	= (C12 – (C1 × *EXP*(–C6 × C6))) + (C2 × *EXP*(–C3 × C4))
14		

In his book *The black swan*, Nassim Taleb describes his historical investing strategy of investing largely in risk-free assets but speculating in options. The downside he faced was primarily the option premium consideration paid. Generally, Taleb would not make spectacular returns until a major correction occurred in financial markets, which would render options held incredibly valuable. Option-pricing models would not assist in identifying these events as they are outliers.

Conclusion

Debt instruments and preference shares are relatively easy to value, assuming they do not have characteristics of equity instruments such as the right to share in profits and vote at shareholder meetings. The valuation principles were covered in this chapter and tips for using Excel to automate this were outlined.

Option valuation is mathematically complicated. Fortunately, we are able to use Excel to input the Black–Scholes model and can readily obtain call and put option values. The outputs of the option-pricing model are highly sensitive to certain assumptions, mainly assumed volatility. It is suggested that the results of option-pricing models not be accepted as fact - rather perform your own sensitivity analysis on the results.

CHAPTER 12

Concluding thoughts on valuations

LEARNING OUTCOMES

Once you have worked through this chapter, you should be able to:

- List common errors in DCF valuations in practice
- Spot potential errors in earnings-based valuations
- Question whether to include the benefit of synergies post-acquisition in bid prices
- Recognise the importance of IRR and NPV analysis in reviewing the attractiveness of potential acquisitions

Introduction

Chapters 1 through 11 have covered most aspects of valuing a business, together with practical tips in performing these valuations. The common theme has been that we are unlikely to derive a 100 per cent correct indicative value at a point in time. This may seem negative, but is the practical reality. Almost all valuations are forward-looking, attempting to forecast future earnings and free cash flows. We know the inherent limitations in forecasts - we are unable to predict the future. The aim in performing valuations is to minimise the error in our favour. If we are seeking to buy a business, our objective is to not overpay. If we are the seller of a business, the aim is to maximise our sale proceeds.

Hopefully the previous chapters have alerted you to ensure that valuation models are technically accurate. It can be tragic in practice to make a technical error such as using an inappropriate risk-free rate or blindly using published betas. We are able to value any business at a point in time without making too many errors. This pursuit requires an intimate knowledge of valuation theory, common sense and the use of multiple methods to triangulate the valuation result.

In concluding valuations, there are some issues that need repeating and others that need to be touched on. Issues such as whether we should use the cost of capital for the entity being acquired in a DCF valuation or the acquirer's cost of capital will be covered. Common errors in DCF and earnings-based valuations will be highlighted as a practical reference tool. The subsequent chapters will cover mergers and acquisitions. However, it is worth discussing the impact of potential synergies post-acquisition on the bid price for businesses.

The valuation of a business to be acquired provides critical information in the formulation of an offer price by the acquirer. This analysis needs to be completed by analysing the potential return on investment for the acquirer. This chapter will illustrate how IRR analysis could be useful in these circumstances.

There is often confusion between a company's ROIC or ROE and its cost of capital. Some attempt to find a relationship between the internal return on assets and capital, and the cost of capital. We will discuss this concept in closing.

DCF valuations: Which cost of equity?

A question occasionally asked is whether we should use the acquirer or target company's cost of capital in valuing the business to be acquired on a DCF basis. It is strongly recommended that the target company's cost of capital be used. Each business has its own unique strengths and weaknesses, systematic risk and growth prospects. These should be encapsulated into the valuation performed. Using the acquirer's cost of capital is unlikely to reflect these characteristics of the business being acquired. The acquirer and target company may operate in the same industry but could be very different with regards to size of operations, unique selling proposition, risks faced etc. Where the acquirer and the target company operate in different industries, the use of the target company's cost of capital is even more compelling.

The above principle applies equally to an earnings-based valuation. When valuing a business to be acquired, use appropriate EBIT or EBITDA multiples for that business rather than the acquirer's earnings multiple(s). The latter may undervalue or overvalue the target company. In practice, acquirers aim to purchase businesses using a lower earnings multiple than theirs. This is often referred to as the earnings accretion play: listed companies attempt to buy businesses at an earnings multiple lower than the one on which they are trading. The hope in these circumstances is that the stock market will re-rate the target company's earnings at a higher multiple than that paid and deliver value for existing shareholders. Let's illustrate this with an example.

EXAMPLE 12.1

Assume for the Acquirer (a listed company):

- an EBIT of R500 million in 20X0;
- no debt on its balance sheet at 20X0 but surplus cash of R1,4 billion at that date; and
- an enterprise value of R5,0 billion at end of 20X0 (implied historic EBIT multiple of 10.0 times) and an equity value of R6,4 billion (R5,0 billion plus surplus cash of R1,4 billion).

Assume further that the Acquirer purchased 100 per cent of the shares in the Target Company for R1,4 billion based on a 20X0 EBIT of R200 million, and settled the purchase price in cash. If the stock market believed that R1,4 billion was a fair price to pay for the Target Company, the Acquirer's market capitalisation would be R6,4 billion (R5,0 billion before acquisition plus R1,4 billion paid for Target Company) immediately post-acquisition. Many groups believe that the stock market will re-rate the acquired company's earnings and their earnings multiple – in the above example, placing a value of 10.0 times EBIT on the Target Company. Refer to Table 12.1 for the difference between the two scenarios.

TABLE 12.1 Two scenarios for re-rating a company's value

	Pre-acquisition	Post-acquisition	Difference
Assuming stock market does not re-rate Target Company's value			
Acquirer's equity value	R6,4 billion	R5,0 billion	-R1,4 billion
Target Company value	-	R1,4 billion	R1,4 billion
	R6,4 billion	R6,4 billion	-

Continued

Assuming stock market does re-rate Target Company's value			
Acquirer's market capitalisation	R6,4 billion	R5,0 billion	-R1,4 billion
Target Company value	-	R2,0 billion	R2,0 billion
	R5,0 billion	R7,0 billion	R0,6 billion

If the stock market placed a value of R2,0 billion on the Target Company instead of the R1,4 billion cash paid, the Acquirer's shareholders would be in for a windfall of R0,6 billion. This would seem like an excellent merger and acquisition strategy – if it happened in practice. However, be warned that the stock market is not that benevolent. Koller (2011) warns:

> *We sometimes hear that when a high P/E company buys a low P/E company, the earnings of the low P/E company get rerated at the high P/E of the higher company. If the growth, ROIC and cash flows of the combined company don't change, why would the market revalue the target company's earnings? In addition to bad logic, the rerating idea has no empirical support ...*

The issue of which cost of capital to use is also relevant when valuing a company with divisions or subsidiaries operating in different industries. Here again, the individual divisions and/or subsidiaries should be valued separately using earnings multiples and costs of capital appropriate for them. These should reflect the systematic risk associated with the different businesses and/or divisions. An example of this would be AECI Limited, which is listed on the JSE. AECI manufactures and distributes explosives and speciality chemicals but also has a substantial property portfolio. The explosives and chemicals divisions should be separately valued from the property division and the results aggregated.

Another example of a group in which underlying subsidiaries and divisions may need to be separately valued due to the differing nature of operations is Steinhoff International Holdings Limited (Steinhoff). The group owns furniture and household goods retail businesses in Europe, South Africa and the Pacific Rim, logistics businesses in Europe and South Africa, automotive retail operations in South Africa, a 45 per cent interest in KAP Industrial Holdings Limited (a JSE-listed diversified logistics and industrial manufacturing group) and extensive properties. The international retail operations would have different costs of capital to the South African businesses and should be valued separately. The logistics business, although inextricably linked to the retail operations, has different risks and opportunities. KAP would also need to be valued on a stand-alone basis given its diversified operations, from forestry products to chemical manufacturing. A minority discount should then be applied to the 100 per cent valuation of KAP, given Steinhoff's lack of control over this listed company.

Steinhoff's announced acquisition of 92,3 per cent of Pepkor, an unlisted apparel retailer, for R62,8 billion in November 2014 will further complicate the group valuation. This acquisition is one of the largest in South African corporate history and it will be interesting to monitor the value unlocked from this deal.

Common valuation errors: The DCF method

In the author's experience and opinion, the following are common errors in DCF valuations:

- Overly optimistic cash flow forecasts for the next five or 10 years that assume unsustainable growth in operating margins. Also, forecast growth is not supported by adequate investment in working capital and/or capital expenditure;
- Basing continuing value on growth in free cash flows that is significantly higher than nominal country GDP growth;
- Errors in calculating the WACC (using book values instead of market values or failing to perform the necessary iteration to determine the WACC);
- Basing the WACC on a target capital structure that is not supported by cash flow forecasts – for example, assuming debt in the capital structure when the business being valued has surplus cash at the valuation date;
- Using published betas blindly without the application of common sense;
- Using inappropriate risk-free rates and market risk premiums; and
- Failing to apply the necessary discounts for lack of marketability and minority interests at the end of the valuation.

Let's illustrate the potential for error in a DCF valuation model.

EXAMPLE 12.2

Assume for a business being valued:

- a risk-free rate of 8,0 per cent;
- a market risk premium of 7,1 per cent;
- a beta coefficient of 1.0;
- debt to enterprise value of 0 per cent;
- after-tax cost of debt of 7,5 per cent
- a 20X0 free cash flow of R100 million;
- growth in free cash flows of 15,0 per cent per annum from 20X1 to 20X5; and
- growth in perpetuity of 5,0 per cent.

The cost of equity (and the WACC) to be applied per above example is 15,1 per cent. The resultant enterprise value is R1,534 billion at 20X0, a calculation that Table 12.2 shows.

TABLE 12.2 The enterprise value calculation, Rbillion

	20X0	20X1	20X2	20X3	20X4	20X5
Free cash flow	100	115	132	152	175	201
NPV of free cash flows 20X1–20X5	499					
Continuing value	1 035					
Enterprise value	1 534					

Let's illustrate the impact on the valuation result by making erroneous assumptions such as those in Table 12.3.

TABLE 12.3 Erroneous assumptions and the valuation result

	Low	Base	High
Risk-free rate	10,0%	8,0%	6,0%
Market risk premium	9,0%	7,1%	5,0%
Beta coefficient	1.4	1.0	0.6
Debt to enterprise value	0,0%	0,0%	25,0%
20X0 free cash flow	90,0	100,0	110,0
Growth in free cash flows 20X1 to 20X5	5,0%	15,0%	25,0%
Growth in perpetuity	2,0%	5,0%	8,0%
After-tax cost of debt	9,0%	7,5%	5,5%

The impact of the errors in Table 12.3 is depicted in Figure 12.1.

FIGURE 12.1 The impact of erroneous assumptions on the valuation result

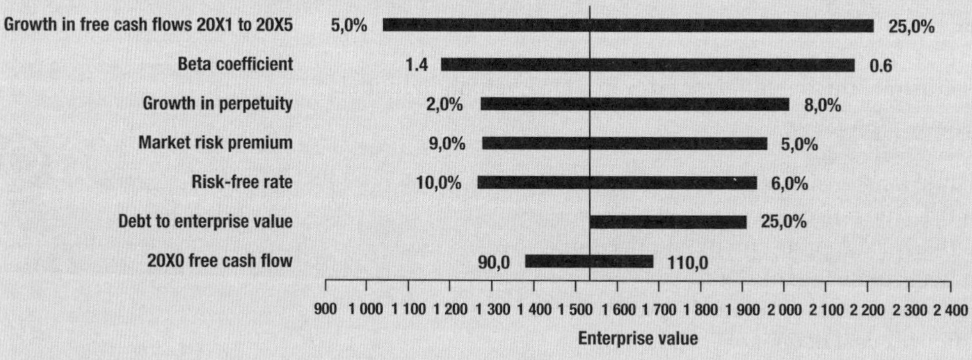

It is unsurprising that two of the top three most sensitive assumptions relate to the free cash flow forecasts. The valuation result is most sensitive to the growth in free cash flows forecast over the initial five-year period. It follows that in practice we should pay particular attention to the forecast financial information before concerning ourselves with the discount rate used to present-value these.

The above valuation result is sensitive to most assumptions. The above chart is a single-factor sensitivity analysis – enterprise value changes based on changing a single assumption at a time. The impact of multiple errors should also be of concern. If we had used an incorrect risk-free rate (say, 6 per cent), a market risk premium of 5 per cent instead of 7,1 per cent and a beta of 0.60 rather than 1.00, the valuation result would have been R4,02 billion – a 162 per cent increase on the initial valuation of R1,534 billion!

We discussed the impact of assuming a target capital structure in Chapter 3. If we had incorrectly assumed a 25 per cent debt to enterprise value in this scenario and an after-tax cost of debt of 5,0 per cent instead of 7,5 per cent, the valuation result would have increased by R541 million.

The DCF valuation results should always be checked for reasonability by determining the implied earnings multiple – enterprise value per DCF method divided by historic and/or forecast EBIT. If an error was made in the key assumptions underlying the DCF valuation, this should be highlighted by the earnings multiples. In the scenario in Example 2, if the implied historic EBIT multiple was 25.0 times yet the industry average was 8.0 times, this probably indicates that some of the DCF assumptions were far too optimistic or incorrect.

Common valuation errors: The earnings-based method

Earnings-based valuations are equally prone to error, although the extent of these errors is unlikely to be as severe as for DCF valuations. Common errors encountered in practice by the author include:

+ Using PE multiples without adjusting for capital structure (refer Chapter 4 for detailed examples of this);
+ Failure to analyse historic earnings for non-recurring items in estimating sustainable profits going forward;
+ Including items in historic and forecast EBIT that should be ignored for valuation purposes such as impairments, share-based payments and fair value adjustments to financial instruments; and
+ Failure to analyse long-term EBIT and/or EBITDA multiples for the company being valued and the industry in which it operates – in other words, using prevailing earnings multiples without checking against long-term trends.

Let's illustrate the extent of potential errors using an example.

EXAMPLE 12.3

Assume for a company being valued:

+ a reported EBIT 20X0 of R100 million;
+ non-recurring profit included in 20X0 EBIT of R30 million;
+ an impairment charge of R20 million included in 20X0 EBIT;
+ surplus cash on hand of R200 million at 20X0;
+ interest rate on cash deposits of 6,0 per cent;
+ an income tax rate of 28 per cent;
+ non-recurring profit subject to taxation and impairment charge not deductible for tax purposes; and
+ PE multiple for business excluding surplus cash or debt of 12.0 times.

Valuing the business by applying a PE multiple to after-tax profits without adjusting for interest income, non-recurring items and impairments would result in the following equity value:

TABLE 12.4 Erroneous valuation

Erroneous valuation	20X0
EBIT	100,00
Interest income (200,0 × 6%)	12,00
Profit before tax	112,00

Continued

Taxation [(112 + 20) × 28%]	-36,96
Profit after tax	75,0
Equity value (75,0 × 12)	900,48

Adjusting for non-recurring items and impairment charge, and valuing surplus cash separately, would result in the following more appropriate equity value:

TABLE 12.5 Appropriate valuation

Appropriate valuation	**20X0**
EBIT	100,0
Adjust: Non-recurring items	-30,0
Adjust: Impairment charge	20,0
Profit before tax	90,0
Taxation (90 × 28%)	-25,2
Profit after tax	64,8
Enterprise value (64,8 × 12)	777,6
Add surplus cash	200,0
Equity value	977,6

The valuation error in Table 12.4 is R77.12 million or -7,9 per cent, an error but perhaps not as dramatic as could be encountered in a DCF valuation. It is a significant amount of money in any event! The reasons for the error are summarised in Table 12.6.

TABLE 12.6 Valuation error reasons

Reasons for the valuation error	**20X0**
Interest income	12,00
Taxation	-3,36
After tax interest income	8,64
Cash valued at 12 PE (8.64 × 12)	103,68
Actual value of surplus cash	200,00
Valuation error – surplus cash	-96,32
Impairment charge	-20,00
Impact on valuation at 12 PE	-240,00

Continued

Non-recurring items	30,00
Taxation	-8,40
	21,60
Valuation error: Non-recurring profit	259,20
Cumulative errors	
Surplus cash	-96,32
Impairment charge	-240,00
Non-recurring items	259,20
	77,12

The overall valuation error in this example could have been more severe if there were no non-recurring items in 20X0.

Valuing synergies

In most acquisitions or mergers, the acquirer seeks to unlock synergies post the deal. These synergies generally relate to improving revenue or reducing costs. Synergies will be covered in more detail in Chapter 16. Briefly, revenue synergies include:

- improving channels to market;
- faster market penetration;
- improving service or product offering;
- increasing product/service pricing through higher value-add; and
- access to funding to fuel growth.

Cost synergies could involve improving systems and processes, reducing headcount, consolidating infrastructure and sharing best practices between two businesses post-acquisition.

The issue arising is whether to include the financial benefits of potential synergies in the acquisition price. Ideally, the acquirer should not pay the departing shareholders for the benefits to be introduced after the merger or acquisition. In reality, bid prices need to be enticing enough to induce the target company shareholders to accept the offer to sell their shares. It follows that acquirers often have to build the expected synergies into the bid price. In Chapter 10 we referred to Woolworths' acquisition of David Jones in 2014. It was evident from reviewing the David Jones circular to its shareholders that a significant portion of the perceived synergies after the acquisition was built into Woolworths' offer price.

Unfortunately, empirical research indicates that revenue synergies are often overestimated. Cost synergies do generally materialise. Caution should be exercised in practice in estimating synergies and including these in the indicative valuation of the target company. Figure 12.2 highlights what may happen in mergers and acquisitions.

FIGURE 12.2 Bid prices

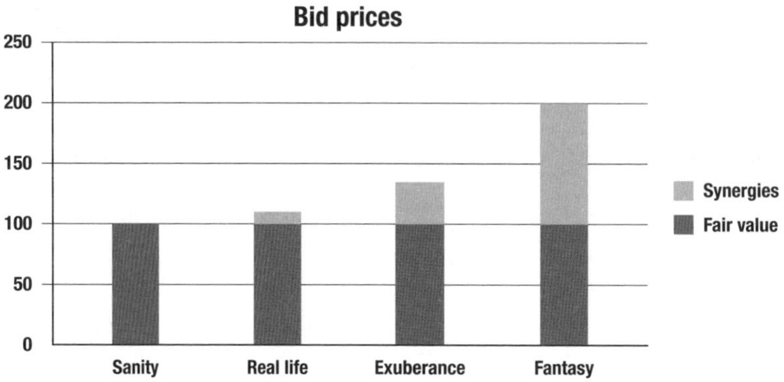

IRR and NPV analysis

Performing a valuation of a business is critical to deriving a reasonable offer price for acquisition purposes. However, the ultimate test is the potential IRR and NPV for the acquirer. Let's illustrate this with an example.

EXAMPLE 12.4

Assume:

- the target company has been valued at R600 million using the DCF and earnings-based methods;
- the acquirer is paying cash to acquire 100 per cent of the target company for R600 million at the end of 20X0;
- the target company reported an EBIT of R100 million in 20X0;
- the target company's EBIT is forecast to grow by 10 per cent per annum for the next five years;
- the target company declared a dividend of R35 million in 20X0 and expects to continue paying annual dividends, growing by 10 per cent per annum;
- the acquirer estimates that it could sell 100 per cent of the target company based on an EBIT multiple of 6.0 at the end of 20X5; and
- the acquirer's cost of capital and required rate of return on investments is 15 per cent.

The potential IRR and NPV of the investment in the target company is set out in Table 12.7.

TABLE 12.7 Potential IRR and NPV

Rmillions	20X0	20X1	20X2	20X3	20X4	20X5
Initial investment	-600,0					
Dividends received		38,5	42,4	46,6	51,2	56,4
Sale of investment						966,3
	-600,0	38,5	42,4	46,6	51,2	1,022,7
IRR	16,4%					
NPV	33,9					

The proposed acquisition meets the acquirer's criterion of generating an IRR of higher than 15 per cent and the investment is expected to result in a positive NPV. The acquirer would certainly want to generate a return of much higher than 15 per cent, but it meets the minimum hurdle rate. If the potential IRR on investment was 8 per cent, the deal is unlikely to be approved by the acquirer's shareholders.

IRR and NPV analysis is a useful tool for assessing the attractiveness of investment opportunities. Sensitivity analysis should also be performed on the likely IRR and NPV results.

ROIC versus cost of capital

Numerous textbooks attempt to find a link between ROIC and the value of a business. The trends in ROIC percentages and growth thereof are converted into complicated formulae and then linked to DCF valuations. This may be a futile exercise given that ROIC is calculated based on accounting values (instead of market values) and growth in free cash flows may be unrelated to this ratio.

Let's examine the calculated ROICs and earnings-based multiples for some South African listed companies. The companies selected are:

- Aspen Pharmacare Holdings Limited (Aspen), a global manufacturer of pharmaceutical products;
- Comair Limited (Comair), an airline business operating in sub-Saharan Africa;
- Oceana Group Limited (Oceana), a fishing business that also processes catch into fish products;
- Shoprite Holdings Limited (Shoprite), a retailer of groceries, liquor and furniture operating in South Africa and on the continent; and
- Steinhoff, referred to earlier in this chapter.

Various ratios were calculated based on the companies' published integrated reports and annual financial statements for the years ended 2010 through 2014. Adjustments were made for impairments, share-based payments and non-recurring items as reported in determining EBIT and EBITDA for ratio analysis purposes. EBIT multiples were based on year-end share prices and ROIC ratios on balance sheet information. Table 12.8 shows the companies' average ROIC and EBIT multiples over the period 2010 to 2014.

TABLE 12.8 Average ROIC and EBIT multiples, 2010 to 2014

2010 to 2014	Average ROIC	Average EBIT multiple
Aspen	13,3%	17.5
Comair	12,5%	12.3
Oceana	36,8%	8.6
Shoprite	39,1%	15.2
Steinhoff	6,9%	10.5

The results in Table 12.8 are somewhat surprising. Pharmaceutical companies like Aspen generally have high ROIC ratios. According to McKinsey research (Koller 2011), USA pharmaceutical businesses had an average ROIC of higher than 20 per cent over the period 1965 to 2007. Aspen, however, has been highly acquisitive globally and this may account for its slightly lower ROIC. Growing organically will result in increased asset investment. Acquisitions of businesses are likely to cost more than organic growth, so the capital employed on the balance sheet will be higher, resulting in declining ROIC. The group certainly had the highest EBIT multiple of the companies listed in Table 12.8.

Comair's ROIC and average EBIT multiple was also surprising. Airlines are capital intensive and generally deliver lower ROIC (±7 per cent in US dollar terms per the McKinsey research) than most other industries. The EBIT multiple seems generous given the cyclical nature of the business. Comair's reported EBIT in 2010 through 2012 was lower than in 2013 and 2014. However, its share price held up relatively well over this period. It follows that Comair's historic EBIT multiples in 2011 and 2012 were relatively high compared with other financial years; this skewed the average multiple over the period.

Oceana's ROIC was high relative to the other companies (except Shoprite) yet it traded on the lowest EBIT multiple of all of them. Shoprite's ROIC is generally high as is the case for most food retailers. These businesses mostly lease trading space, so their major 'asset' is not on their balance sheets.

Steinhoff's ROIC ratio seems very low. This could be due to the large acquisitions made in Europe over the past five years. Its logistics businesses (highly capital intensive with low margins) would also drag down its ROIC ratio.

It may be apparent that linking ROIC to earnings-based multiples is difficult in practice. Could there be more correlation between EBIT multiples and reported and expected earnings growth than ROIC? Refer to Table 12.9 for the companies' compound annual growth in EBIT and share prices over the period 2010 to 2014.

TABLE 12.9 Compound annual growth and share prices, 2010 to 2014

2010 to 2014	CAGR EBIT	CAGR share price
Aspen	31,0%	40,8%
Comair	29,9%	20,9%
Oceana	14,8%	23,3%
Shoprite	11,2%	16,6%
Steinhoff	23,2%	34,7%

Conclusion

Valuations are a pervasive skill in business – at some stage in your career you will be required to perform or review a valuation. The exciting part of valuations is that there is no single correct answer. Instead, the process is one of placing a value on an asset or a business for acquisition, disposal or merger purposes. Valuations draw upon multiple financial management skills and are inextricably linked to strategy and understanding business. Chapters 1 through 12 attempted to provide a sound theoretical base for performing valuations and practical tips to arrive at appropriate indicative fair value for assets, businesses, debt instruments and options. The next section of the book will deal with most aspects of mergers and acquisitions. Valuations are a critical part of this process as overpaying for a business can be highly value-destructive. In addition, knowing when to exit a business could unlock significant value for stakeholders.

References

Koller, T., Dobbs, R. & Huyett, B. (2011). *Value: The four cornerstones of corporate finance.* New Jersey: John Wiley & Sons Inc.

Part 2

MERGERS AND ACQUISITIONS

CHAPTER 13

Why consider mergers and acquisitions as part of your growth strategy?

LEARNING OBJECTIVES

Once you have worked through this chapter, you should be able to:

+ Understand the notion that mergers and acquisitions (M&A) is only one way of fuelling growth, and that it works best when it aims to meet a strategic objective
+ Identify some of the pitfalls of M&A
+ Identify some of the things you can do right in M&A
+ Understand drivers and risks associated with offshore investment
+ Discuss joint ventures (JVs) and strategic alliances as an alternative to M&A

Introduction

The strategy phase of the mergers and M&A process represents the high-level thinking that you need to do in order to start an M&A initiative off on the right foot. The individual steps include:

+ establishing why you want to make acquisitions
+ understanding causes of success and failure in M&A, and identifying ways of slanting the odds in your favour
+ considering the implications of going global as part of your growth strategy
+ considering alternatives to outright M&A as a way of meeting your growth objectives
+ defining what you are looking for in an acquisition, drawing up a list of possible targets, prioritising them and compiling a shortlist.

We'll look at these actions in in this chapter.

The strategic rationale of M&A

Establish why you want to make acquisitions

It has been said that all companies are in a process of either growing or dying. Even if growth is not an overall strategic objective, adaptation to change will certainly need to be, because change is as predictable and inevitable as death and taxes. Change comes from technological innovation and changes in consumer tastes, among many other causes. If you accept that reasoning, then growth and transformation can be seen as key business imperatives, and M&A is one way of addressing these.

CASE STUDY **Xerox and Kodak**

Two examples of the impact of responding or not responding to changes in the market follow.

Xerox is a company that is more than 50 years old. Halfway through its life it would have called itself a photocopying company, but adapting to technological change has led it to define itself as a business process and document management specialist – a much wider definition of its purpose than when it started doing business. Xerox grew its diluted earnings from continuing operations from 54 cents per share to 93 cents per share between 2009 and 2013, a compound growth rate of 14,5 per annum. Its change in strategy ensured its survival.

By contrast, Kodak started life in the late nineteenth century as an innovator in a new technology – photography. This specialisation served it well, to the point that its tagline – 'a Kodak moment' – came to epitomise the rewards of capturing and sharing a moment on film. But, in the 1990s, it failed to recognise the full implications of a new shift in technology to digital photography. It underestimated the impact of falling sales in high-margin film, which eventually led it to file for Chapter 11 (bankruptcy) protection early in 2012.

M&As can be seen as glamorous and exciting, and can appear to be a welcome respite from the daily grind of running a company efficiently, but these are not good reasons for considering going to the expense and effort of growing by merger or acquisition. The best basis for doing so is as part of a carefully considered growth strategy.

M&As are not the only way of meeting growth objectives. Equal consideration should be given to **organic growth** and entering into **joint ventures** (JVs) and **strategic alliances** as an alternative to outright acquisition. We will consider the merits of JVs and alliances later in this chapter. None of the three ways of achieving growth equates to a silver bullet that ensures success. Rather, the merits of each alternative need to be weighed at each growth phase in the entity's life.

Good reasons for growth through M&A

There are many reasons why growth by acquisition may be the right way to go. Table 13. 1 shows these.

TABLE 13.1 Good reasons for growth by acquisition

Objective	Using M&A to achieve the objective
Need for speed	In times of rapid technological change, organic growth may be too slow to address changes in the market, and new products and skills may need to be acquired by acquisition. Cisco, the US-based IT networking company, has grown and continues to grow by acquisition, rarely making fewer than five acquisitions a year. It recognises that its own research efforts will not be sufficient to keep abreast of customers' requirements.
Economies of scale	The acquisition of similar or complementary businesses may result in economies of scale, often due to the rationalisation of back-office costs. When two South African life assurance companies, Metropolitan Life and Momentum Life, merged in 2011 to form MMI, cost savings of R500 million per year were targeted. This level of saving was achieved in the two years following the acquisition.

Continued

Economies of scope	Acquiring new products to distribute though existing channels can add value. This is the thinking behind the bank assurance model (banks and assurance companies teaming up to promote one another's products). Nedbank and Old Mutual, and Standard and Liberty, are local examples.
Strategic shift	The company's strategy might dictate that it is time to move into new products or new markets with which it is not familiar. Acquiring existing expertise and/or products will provide a buffer against the riskiness of the new strategy. Running counter to perceived wisdom (conglomerates are treated with suspicion by the markets), South African conglomerate Bidvest has very successfully followed a strategy of diversification built on acquisitions.
Move into new markets	The fastest way to gain a foothold into new markets may be through acquisition, particularly if the new markets are in other countries. Two South African healthcare groups, Netcare and MediClinic, have both adopted this approach, investing in the UK and Switzerland respectively, among other countries.
Gain size/relevance in a given market	General Electric, in common with many companies, pursues a policy of being number one, two or three in the markets in which it participates. Management's objective is to have some element of control over the market. South African companies that have adopted a similar policy include Tiger Brands, which continues to make acquisitions in its areas of expertise, exemplified by its recent (2012) acquisition of a stake in Dangote Mills in Nigeria (unfortunately not a very successful acquisition, leading Tiger to impair a large portion of its acquisition price).

The lessons from these reasons are that acquisitions are most likely to succeed when a very specific strategic objective has been identified, and the risks and benefits of an acquisition have been carefully evaluated.

Skewed thinking in relation to M&A

The wrong reasons for entering into M&A transactions include the following:

TABLE 13.2 Incorrect reasons for M&A transactions

Incorrect reason for doing deals	Impact
CEO hubris (exaggerated self-confidence)	It's been said that the kiss of death for a CEO of a large company can be the point at which he or she features on the front cover of one of the prominent financial magazines. From that point on he or she is inclined to believe his or her own publicity, and his or her judgement becomes compromised. This can lead to making acquisitions for the wrong reasons.
Short-term pressure	In the US, the need to report positive results to the market on a quarterly basis leads to short-term pressure that can dissuade management from taking actions that make long-term, strategic sense, but that may impact the bottom line adversely in the short term. To make acquisitions to hype the share price in the short term would be to fall into such a trap.

Continued

Boredom	Managing operating costs downwards and controlling cash flows is hard work, and not very glamorous. It doesn't garner many headlines, whereas a juicy M&A deal does.
Fear of being left on the shelf	When markets run and industries are consolidating, and all your competitors are doing deals, it can be very tempting to enter into transactions in order not to feel left behind. This isn't a good reason for doing a deal. In 2001 AngloGold made an offer to acquire Normandy, the Australian gold miner. Newmont, its US-based competitor, made a counter-bid. AngloGold raised its offer after re-evaluating Normandy's prospects, and was again trumped by Newmont. This time AngloGold did not raise its offer price, because management could not see how an investment at that level could create value for Anglo shareholders. This is an example of a deal well left alone.
The quest for size	Although, as we have seen, size in relation to a particular market can produce competitive advantage, management can get caught up in chasing size for size's sake. This is particularly true if management is rewarded for top-line performance, rather than a more encompassing measure, such as return on invested capital.
Share market expectations	Management of companies that are highly rated on the stock exchange comes under pressure to do something to meet those expectations. A high price/earnings ratio signals an expectation by the market of value-adding growth, and executives may give in to the temptation to pursue acquisitions without there being sufficient strategic rationale to support them. In the mid-1980s, IT companies in South Africa traded at a PE of 60 or 70, leading to their making many acquisitions paid for by the issue of their overpriced shares. Many of these acquisitions did not create sustainable shareholder value.

There are plenty of right and wrong reasons for making acquisitions. Honest self-appraisal of your motivation and the strategic reasoning behind an acquisition is required before proceeding.

SELF-ASSESSMENT

- Which primary business need is fulfilled by M&A?
- Name three valid reasons why an entity might consider entering into an M&A transaction instead of growing organically.
- Name three inappropriate reasons why an entity might consider entering into an M&A transaction instead of growing organically.

Understanding causes of success and failure in M&A and identifying ways to improve success

Background

Many researchers have conducted studies into the effectiveness of M&A, and the broad consensus is that acquisitions fail to produce the value that was intended when the deal was conceived. The rough statistic that is often quoted is that one third fails outright, one third has limited success and one third can be regarded as successful.

A more optimistic view of M&A effectiveness

Given this apparently dismal track record, you might wonder why companies continue to persevere with an acquisition strategy. Bruner (2004) provides a contrarian review. In Chapter 3 of his book *Applied Mergers and Acquisitions*, titled 'Does M&A Pay?,' he reports on the findings of his review of 12 informal surveys and 120 scientific studies carried out by other researchers into M&A. Some of his key conclusions are set out below.

The risks of M&A are no greater than the risks of any other projects

Bruner (2004) argues that risk is inherent in any aspect of business. Starting up a new mine or developing a new shopping centre is not risk-free. The best the investor can do is to be aware of the risks and take a calculated guess that the project is likely to succeed. This is no different from entering into an M&A transaction, provided an equivalent risk-evaluation process is followed. But, we will see a little later that the field of behavioural finance teaches us how we can choose to delude ourselves when it suits us.

Conventional wisdom generalises, too readily, the findings of a single study

Bruner (2004) reports that most of the losses from 1980 to 2001 occurred in just 87 deals out of the 12 023 studied. In other words, it is the big value-destroying deals, such as Time-Warner's acquisition of AOL in the late 1990s, which hit the newspapers, whereas there is a large body of less spectacular but potentially value-creating deals that goes unreported. Bruner reminds us not to lose perspective or to be overly influenced by media reports.

There is a tendency to over-exaggerate failure

Bruner (2004) argues that we tend to ignore the context in which high-profile M&A failures occur. For example, while the Time-Warner/AOL deal did indeed wipe out a lot of shareholder value, a lot would have been wiped out in any case by the dotcom crash that occurred shortly after the deal was completed.

Pointers to likely M&A failure

Based on his research, Bruner (2004) provides the following list of factors that provide a strong indication of potential failure:

+ Your organisation enters into a fundamentally unprofitable industry, or refuses to exit from one.
+ Your organisation steps far away from what it knows.
+ The economic benefits of the deal are improbable or not incremental to the deal.
+ You fail to seek some economic advantage (you are doing the deal for the wrong reason).
+ Your organisation is not creative in deal structuring.
+ Your organisation has poor checks, balances and incentives (poor control over the acquisition process and the subsequent integration process).

Further insight into causes of deal failure is provided by Carrol and Mui (2008). Their observations include:

The synergies that supposedly justify the deal can be a mirage

The synergies might be there on the surface, but turning them into reality might be tougher than you think. As with many construction projects, the effort may need twice as much time as originally anticipated and the potential benefits may have been overstated.

Too much emphasis on financial engineering

For some groups of companies, a large portion of the value to be derived from acquisitions stems from clever structuring techniques, aggressive use of loan finance and aggressive tax planning. There is nothing wrong with this in itself, unless it is used to disguise flaws in the underlying business reasoning behind the acquisition.

Stubbornly staying the course

Management of some companies sets a course for their companies and never deviates from it, even though the environment in which their company operates is changing significantly. We have already looked at the Kodak example. Kodak management severely underestimated the impact of digital photography and, as a result, subsequently fought a rearguard action against it. Management, given its historic success with printing photographs, struggled to come to terms with a world in which many images may never get printed, but would be shared from smartphones and tablets or stored on social networking sites.

Betting on the wrong technology

It is easy to become mesmerised by technology, to the extent that a service or product that is not likely to capture the imagination of the market is pursued at all costs – to the point of destruction.

CASE STUDY Telkom

In 2011, Telkom lost $1 billion of its investment in Nigerian telecoms company Multi-Links. At least one reason for the loss of value was that Multi-Links and, by definition, Telkom, backed the wrong technology. Multi-Links invested in CDMA mobile telecoms technology, rather than the more common GSM technology. The resulting incompatibility meant that users of CDMA could not use their phones in many other countries. Reasons for the failure put forward by market commentators include poor market research, over-eager investing and weak leadership. Large markets can have a mesmerising effect on potential investors. As a valuer, you often hear the argument 'if we could just grab x per cent of the market we could do very well'. Unless this vision is backed up by very clear execution plans, the size of the market will remain a mirage.

Achieving success in M&A

So, if there are so many pitfalls along the way, what should you be focusing on to improve your chances of success in M&A? Bruner (2004) provides the following summary of situations in which M&A clearly pays:

- M&A clearly benefits the sellers of target firms. This is confirmed by movements in buyers' and sellers' share prices when a merger or acquisition is announced – on average, the buyer's share price goes down, while the seller's price goes up.

- Returns to shareholders of buyers and targets are positive in aggregate (a fact confirmed in an annual study by McKinsey).
- Value is conserved for at least two thirds of buyers.
- But the distribution of returns is very wide around those averages.

The implication of the last point is that in order to succeed at M&A, you need to develop an approach that will position you above the average.

Carroll and Mui (2008) argue strongly in favour of having an internal review process that provides a measure of objectivity to counterbalance the over-enthusiasm for the transaction that the negotiating executives may have developed. Pursuing an M&A transaction is both exhilarating and exhausting. It is easy to fall in love with a deal, especially after having sunk a great deal of energy into it. An objective review should help to restore a more balanced view of the possible outcomes.

Lessons from an M&A practitioner

Neville Crosse, the Chairman of Omnia Fertiliser, and a veteran of many acquisitions, cites the following reasons for disenchantment with deals that he has been involved in:

- Parts of the business looked good on paper, but were actually in bad shape.
- The reports of auditing firms or external consultants did not reflect the reality of the business going forward.
- The effort involved was much greater than anticipated, as were the costs.
- On reflection, the effort may have been better applied to the existing business.
- External economic or market changes were not anticipated in the price paid.
- The price paid was too high.
- The acquisition was done at the high point in the target company's life cycle.
- There were flaws in the basic strategy.
- Differences in culture between the acquiring and target companies were not overcome satisfactorily.

In his role as chairman, his preferred way of dealing with management introducing a potential transaction to the Board is the slightly whimsical recipe set out below:

- Say no.
- Ask for the alternatives.
- Understand the downside.
- Only when your tongue is bleeding from biting on it, say yes.

He also emphasises the importance of conducting a review six months after the effective date of the acquisition so that key lessons learnt can be incorporated into the next acquisition pursued. The review should include:

- checking that original objectives are being met;
- checking on cultural, people and management issues that may be problematic;
- reviewing outstanding compensation issues;
- dealing with the parts of the business that are not up to expectation; and
- checking that the existing business is not suffering from lack of attention.

Many other checklists of causes of failure and recipes for success exist. The issue to understand at this point is that M&As are risky in a way that is different from the risks encountered in the day to day activities of the company. Developing a robust strategy that may lead to an acquisition is an important starting point, followed by adopting a carefully crafted acquisition process.

SELF-ASSESSMENT

- Identify four factors that suggest that a particular M&A transaction is likely to fail.
- Identify five pitfalls that should be avoided in seeking M&A success.
- List five warning signs that a deal may go wrong.

Consider the implications of going global as part of your growth strategy

Moving into other markets, within Africa or beyond, can be an important part of your growth strategy, but it is one that carries a number of risks.

Why do South African companies choose to invest abroad?

Valid reasons include:

Capitalising on a core competency

Companies that have built up a distinctive competence that provides them with a competitive advantage often choose to exercise this competence in other markets. This is particularly the case when the local market is saturated.

The healthcare industry in South Africa provides a good example of this. Three major hospital groups – Netcare, Medi-Clinic and Life Healthcare – dominate the industry. There is little room for these groups to grow within the local market, so each of them has expanded overseas where they successfully apply the skills developed in South Africa.

Realising location economics

Where a company's competitive advantage relies on it being a low-cost producer, it makes sense to move to where manufacturing costs are lowest – provided, of course, that transport costs don't outweigh the manufacturing cost benefits. US-based fashion/sporting goods companies such as Nike maintain control over marketing and branding of their goods, but most of their manufacturing is carried out in Asia, where labour costs are lower. More recently, this has been seen to be a risky policy, as consumers in the US and Europe react to the poor labour policies in certain Asian countries.

Achieving experience curve economics

Industries that have high fixed costs need to establish a presence in many countries to generate sales that will lower the unit cost of this expenditure. This applies to the pharmaceutical industry (the cost of research and development to create new drugs) and the automobile industry (the length of time and the cost involved in getting a new model to market), among others.

CASE STUDY **Offshore investment and South African companies**

Successes include the following:

- SABMiller started off as a South African company with skills in brewing, logistics and understanding developing markets. SABMiller expanded into other parts of Africa, and then into Eastern Europe and China, before it made acquisitions in developed countries, culminating in its acquisition of Miller Brewing in the USA in 2002.
- Shoprite operates very successfully in Africa, whereas Pick n Pay's foray into Africa was short-lived. Shoprite's management believes it can manage the risks of trading in Africa, and can thus benefit from the higher rewards on offer. This belief is borne out in Shoprite's results.

Areas where offshore investment has not worked for South African companies include the following:

- South African retailers that have made acquisitions in Australia, such as Pick n Pay and Wooltru, have struggled to make them work.
- Discovery Health established Destiny Health in the US in 2000 in order to capitalise on Discovery's success in South Africa. The take-up was not what Discovery expected, and Destiny was wound down a decade later. Discovery's Vitality concept continues to prosper in the US, however.

What should you be thinking about?

Thoughts on what to do to improve your chances of success when investing offshore include:

- taking account of consumer tastes and preferences – what works in one country may not capture the market's imagination in another;
- making sure you have access to the necessary distribution channels – Discovery struggled with this in setting up Destiny;
- being aware of host government demands – any company wanting to enter the South African market needs a good understanding of the country's BBBEE policy; and
- considering taking a local partner as part of your entry strategy, as discussed in the next section.

SELF-ASSESSMENT

- Name three drivers of offshore investment.
- Which additional risks are brought about by investing outside of your home territory?
- Would you make your first offshore deal a large one?

Consider alternatives to outright M&A as a way of meeting your growth objectives

M&As are often compared to marriages, partly as a result of their failure rate, and partly as a result of the challenges involved in integrating two previously independent entities into a successful union. JVs and strategic alliances can be compared to the period of getting to know each other before getting married. They provide a chance for the parties to size each other up; of course, not all of these relationships end in marriage (M&A).

Types of relationship

JVs and strategic alliances should form part of your strategic planning in relation to your growth strategy. Figure 13.1 suggests that the types of relationship you might consider, from loosest to tightest, lie along a continuum:

FIGURE 13.1 Types of relationship, from loosest to tightest

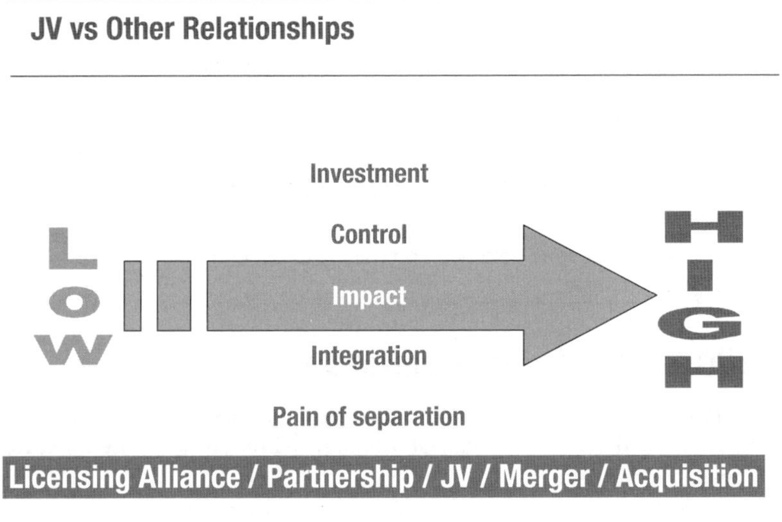

As you can see from Figure 13.1, the loosest relationship option is to enter into a licensing arrangement for a product or service, and the tightest option is to commit to a full acquisition, with various options in between. The factors that might drive your decision include:

- how much you are willing to invest;
- your need for control over the relationship;
- the importance of the relationship to your business;
- the challenges of integrating the two businesses; and
- the challenges of decoupling the businesses after a merger.

The authors of an article titled 'Launching a World-Class Joint Venture' that appeared in the February 2004 edition of *Harvard Business Review* (Bamford, Ernst et al. 2004) point out that organisational considerations often result in management failing to make a measured comparison of the three strategic options (organic growth, acquisition and partnering). The reason for this is that different executives are in charge of acquisitions and of expansion projects. Each executive is likely to argue the merits of his/her own area of expertise, without necessarily having an overall view of what is best for the organisation. Management also becomes grooved in its thinking. If an acquisition was good for the organisation the last time, then an acquisition will be favoured the next time, rather than equal consideration being accorded to each option.

JVs and alliances can take many forms. For example, they may involve taking up a minority equity stake, or they may merely involve an agreement to work together for each party's benefit, without any capital injection.

Typical reasons for entering into a JV or alliance include the following:

TABLE 13.3 Typical reasons for entering into a JV or alliance

Objective	Impact
Access	JVs and alliances are often the preferred route for a client to move into a foreign country, where local knowledge is important and can be provided by the partner. Even the mighty Wal-Mart partnered with local firms when it started to expand into South America in the 1990s.
Risk spread	The objective here is to share the fixed costs of research/product development. This has been seen in the motor industry, where the costs of getting a new model into the market are significant. Renault and Nissan, for example, have been strategic partners since 1999.
Learning	Companies with complementary skills may get together to learn from each other.
Critical mass	A JV or alliance may help two companies to become relevant in a particular market.

Success and failure in JVs and alliances

It would be a happy thing if JVs and alliances were an easier route to success than going the acquisition route, but unfortunately the statistics suggest that approximately 50 per cent of JVs/alliances fail. Some of the reasons for this are:

- The alliance can provide competitors with a low-cost route to technology.
- Control can become an issue, as the parties haggle over who is in charge.
- Going it alone in a globalisation programme can deliver benefits of location economics (manufacturing in the cheapest place possible) and moving up the experience curve (learning to become a low-cost producer on the global stage). These benefits will be diluted in an alliance.
- Alliances require a lot of attention to ensure they keep meeting the alliance partners' objectives. It is easy for the relationship to become more important for one party than the other, leading to breakdown.

When to ally and when to acquire

The *Harvard Business Review* article titled 'When to Ally and When to Acquire' (Dyer et al. 2004) provides some interesting insights into how to make the choice of entering into an alliance or making an acquisition. One angle the authors explore is the nature of the synergies expected from the relationship, as set out in Table 13.4:

TABLE 13.4 Synergies expected from a relationship

Nature of the synergy	Preferred route	Rationale
Modular	Non-equity alliance	Where the synergies arise independently for each partner, such as a relationship between an airline, a car hire company and a hotel group, then a loose alliance can achieve each party's objectives.

Continued

Sequential	Equity alliance	Where the synergies that are created for one party form the input for the other party, a tighter relationship is required, so an equity alliance should be entered into. Many of the motor industry alliances are equity alliances for this reason.
Reciprocal	Acquisition	Where the synergies pass back and forth between the parties and there is a high level of interdependence, then an acquisition will be the best route.

Source: Adapted from Dyer et al. (2004)

Dyer et al. (2004) also suggest that if the synergies are to be derived from hard assets, then an acquisition will be best, whereas if the synergies are to generated from soft assets - research, knowhow, etc. - then an alliance might produce better results. This is often the case in the pharmaceutical and IT industries, where rather than gobbling up entrepreneurial entities and forcing them to conform to their bureaucratic frameworks in an acquisition, the larger, established companies enter into alliances with the smaller, more nimble ones.

An alliance relationship is one of trust, but trust is easier to maintain when supported by contractual safeguards, such as:

+ designing the alliance in a way that makes it difficult to transfer technology;
+ including contractual safeguards in the alliance agreement to guard against the risk of opportunism by a partner;
+ both parties agreeing in advance to swap skills that the other party covets; and
+ both parties committing to a relationship of trust at the outset.

In this section we have taken a brief look at joint ventures and alliances as an alternative way of achieving your growth objectives. We have looked at some good reasons for entering into alliances and considered where the benefits from an alliance could arise. We have also looked at the reasoning you might use to choose between an alliance and an acquisition.

Alliances can involve significant advantages, but they can also easily disintegrate to the benefit of one partner. Vigilance is required to reduce the possibility of this happening.

SELF-ASSESSMENT

+ Name three valid reasons for entering into a JV or alliance.
+ Name three risks of doing so.
+ In what circumstances might you decide that an acquisition is better than a JV?

Conclusion

In this chapter, we considered reasons why companies might consider mergers and acquisitions as a means of meeting their growth objectives. We looked at both good and bad reasons for doing deals, and considered the statistics cited to support the accusation that the majority of M&As fail to create value. We looked at Bruner's (2004) arguments that counter the dim view of M&A success often reported in the press, and identified some causes of deal failure. We then considered some ideas on how to improve the chances of success, notably that:

+ Deals stand a greater chance of success if they are the outcome of a carefully crafted strategy; and
+ Success is encouraged if a robust process is followed.

We considered the additional risks of going global and outlined some of the benefits and pitfalls of joint ventures and alliances as an alternative to outright acquisition.

References

Bamford, J., et al. (2004). Launching a World-Class Joint Venture. *Harvard Business Review*. February 2004.

Bruner, R.F. (2004). Does M&A Pay? *Applied Mergers & Acquisitions*. New Jersey: Wiley Finance, pp. 30–65.

Carroll, P.B. & Mui, C. (2008). Seven Ways to Fail Big. *Harvard Business Review*. September 2008.

Dyer, J.H., Kale, P. & Singh, H. (2004). When to Ally and When to Acquire. *Harvard Business Review*. July–August 2004.

CHAPTER 14
Pricing the deal

LEARNING OBJECTIVES

Once you have worked through this chapter, you should be able to:

+ Consider the interplay between price and value
+ Analyse a conceptual diagram that will guide your thinking when setting a price for a transaction
+ Recall some of the valuation techniques relevant to M&A covered earlier in this book
+ Consider the steps in the price-setting process
+ Identify areas of behavioural bias that play a role when arriving at a price
+ Identify areas of corporate discipline that are important in getting the deal you want

Introduction

Warren Buffett, the chairman of Berkshire Hathaway, expressed the following viewpoint in a letter to shareholders in 2000:

> *Leaving aside tax factors, the formula we use for evaluating stocks and businesses is identical. Indeed, the formula for valuing all assets that are purchased for financial gain has been unchanged since it since it was first laid out by a very smart man in about 600 BC (though he wasn't smart enough to know it was 600 BC). The oracle was Aesop and his enduring, though somewhat incomplete, investment insight was 'a bird in the hand is worth two in the bush.' To flesh out this principle, you must answer only three questions. How certain are you that there are indeed birds in the bush? When will they emerge and how many will there be? What is the risk-free interest-rate (which we consider to be the yield on long-term government bonds)? If you can answer the three questions, you will know the maximum value of the bush – and the maximum number of birds you now possess that should be offered for it. And, of course, don't literally think of birds. Think dollars.*

Buffett, also known as the Sage of Omaha, is one of the world's most successful investors and is among the world's richest people. Despite this success, he keeps his philosophy simple – and amusing! – as can be seen from the above extract from one of his legendary letters to shareholders.

Buffett invests for the long term, ignoring the short-term ups and downs of the market, and he invests where he can see value being created over the long term. He invests where he believes more birds are likely to come out of the bush than he needed to give up to acquire the bush. In the terminology of the first 12 chapters of this book, he invests where he believes the long-term returns on the investment will exceed the cost of the capital used to make the acquisition.

Buffett's approach suggests that he is more interested in assessing value than price. As noted previously, price and value can differ as a result of the state of markets at a particular point in time. A period of 'irrational exuberance' – a phrase used by Alan Greenspan, former head of the Federal Reserve Bank in the USA – will lead to price exceeding value. In extreme bear markets, value may well exceed price and bargains may be had.

So, when should you invest? It comes down to backing your own assessment of long-term value. If the above observation on value exceeding price is valid, then you should be looking for bargains in bear markets. Surprisingly, analysis of M&A activity does not reveal a rush of bargain buying in bear markets. This is partly as a result of lack of resolve on the part of potential buyers, and partly because the expectations of potential sellers remain anchored in the prices they could have got for their businesses before the onset of the bear market.

If you agree with Warren Buffet, you shouldn't buy when price exceeds your assessment of value. In the short term you might choose to play a rising market with a view to getting out before it peaks, but this mindset is not appropriate for long-term investing.

SELF-ASSESSMENT

- Consider situations in which you have seen people pay more than something was apparently worth, such as at an auction. What led to this behaviour, do you think? Were they thinking of the long term or were they reacting to current circumstances?
- Do you think they were likely to be satisfied with their purchase in the long term?
- Are there sources of value that cannot be expressed in monetary terms?

A value-creation model for M&A

In the M&A environment, sticking to a clear investment philosophy may not be as easy as it sounds. The negotiation process provides plenty of opportunities to get carried away and to overpay. And the investment of time and effort may lead to the false conclusion that it is too late to back out. In order to avoid these traps, you will need a strong conceptual framework, such as the one set out in Figure 14.1:

FIGURE 14.1 Determining the true value of an acquisition

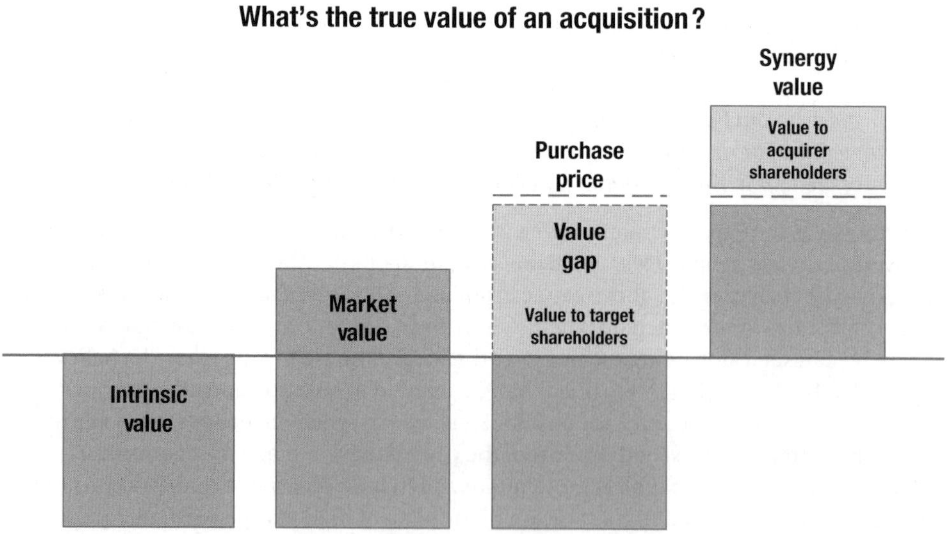

Source: Eccles et al. (1999)

The framework is drawn from an article published in the *Harvard Business Review* (Eccles et al. 1999). Although the framework is simple, it is also powerful in that it contains the key elements that you need to keep in mind when considering the value implications of an acquisition.

The elements of the model depicted in Figure 14.1 can be described as follows:

+ **Intrinsic value.** Before any deal activity is suspected, a company will trade at its intrinsic value, which is the value attributed to it primarily by minority shareholders trading on a stock exchange. These shareholders have little say in the running of the company – certainly less than a shareholder with a large voting bloc has. The price attributed to the share will reflect this situation – it is not the price that will be paid for the company in a takeover.
+ **Market value.** When a deal is announced, the share price will usually move upwards. If a price for the deal has been announced, the share price will move towards that price, but will be discounted to take account of the time lapse before money changes hands and to take the risk of the deal not happening into account. Even if an offer price has not been announced, the target's share price will tend to go up in anticipation of the buyer pricing some of the potential synergies into the offer. In the framework in Figure 14.1, this is depicted as the market value.
+ **Purchase price.** Negotiations will result in a price being paid that is almost certainly greater than the company's intrinsic value and may or may not match the market's expectations of the price to be paid. The price paid is also often greater than the initial offer price. SABMiller bought rival brewer Foster's Group in Australia late in 2011, but only after raising the price it was initially prepared to pay by 10 per cent. The difference between the purchase price and the target's intrinsic value, described in the third column in Figure 14.1 as the value gap, accrues to the selling shareholders.
+ **Value including synergies.** Many, if not most, M&As are justified by the value to be derived from synergies. In terms of this framework, the aim is to make sure that the value of these synergies is not inadvertently given away in the negotiation process. The fourth column in Figure 14.1 shows the desired outcome – some of the synergy value has been paid across to the sellers in order to secure the deal, but there is still value left over that accrues to the acquiring shareholders.

To tie the above approach back to Warren Buffet's philosophy and, indeed, to the valuation principles set out in the first 12 chapters of this book, the maximum amount that should be paid for an acquisition is the price at which the forecast returns from the investment exactly equal its cost of capital. If that were the only outcome of a company's acquisition, it would grow in size, but would not really create value for shareholders. Only if there is the potential for additional value, as depicted in the fourth column of Figure 14.1, can the deal be said to be value-creating for the acquiring shareholders.

SELF-ASSESSMENT

+ In terms of Figure 14.1, what justifies a buyer paying a premium to consummate an acquisition?
+ How is value potentially created for the acquirer's shareholders in an acquisition?

Summary of the technical valuations issues relevant to pricing a deal

We have already covered the following principles in this book:

- In Chapter 1, we pointed out that valuations are as much art as science. Your first objective is to remove areas of technical error from your valuation. Thereafter, you need to corroborate your primary valuation method with a secondary one. After pushing the numbers around for a while, a picture of the possible range of values will start to emerge.
- In Chapter 3, we demonstrated the role of debt in adding value to companies, but we cautioned that it is easy to overstate this value, particularly where companies are not able to sustain borrowings, rendering the WACC as a discount rate inappropriate.
- In Chapter 4, we looked at earnings-based valuations as a way of corroborating your cash-flow-based ones.
- In Chapter 6, we looked at the implications of applying the general valuation principles discussed thus far to private companies.
- In Chapter 8, we considered ways of testing the reliability of your calculations of continuing value, where DCF is your primary valuation method.
- In Chapter 10, we examined reasonability checks and sensitivity analysis, both extremely important considerations when calculating your value range.
- In Chapter 12, we introduced the idea of using the investor's IRR as the ultimate test when valuing an acquisition.

M&As do not introduce new valuation principles. Valuations for M&A purposes should be based firmly on the principles outlined in Chapters 1 to 12. It's just that the M&A process produces lots of temptations to stray from the general principles.

The deal-pricing process

Pricing a potential acquisition is an iterative process. You are likely to start by working with publicly available information, which should give you enough of a feel for the value of the business to allow you to engage knowledgeably with target management. Thereafter, your task - via steps such as due diligence and conversations with management - is to deepen your assessment of value and risk in the business.

One of the key objectives of due diligence, which we discuss in the next chapter, is to identify issues that may have a bearing on how much you are prepared to pay for the acquisition. Let's assume, for example, that in the course of due diligence you discover that some of the target's products are coming out of patent protection in the near future, but it seems as though target management has not taken this fact into account in the financial projections they have shared with you. You need to take a view on the likely impact on sales of the patents expiring and feed this view into your valuation model.

When you believe you have as much information as you are going to get in the time available, supplemented by educated guesses, you will be able to come up with a valuation range, using sensitivity analysis as we discussed in Chapter 10. You will use this range for negotiation purposes.

Before you finalise this exercise, it is always a good idea to stress test your valuation model using what may seem like unlikely assumptions, to test the effect of those assumptions on the target's value. Why do this? Because sometimes the unlikely happens! At the time of writing, the price of oil per barrel had halved over the last twelve months. For companies such as Sasol, which produces products priced according to the global oil price, this has had serious consequences, and its share price had reduced from a peak of R60 per share to R35 per share. The oil price is critical to Sasol but may be less so to other companies. Your task is to identify your target's value drivers and to stress test them to the point where you understand the value dynamics of the business.

Behavioural considerations in pricing M&A transactions

We have touched on the impact of human behaviour on market movements throughout this book, but it will be useful to summarise some of the issues here, when thinking about setting a price for a deal. Behavioural finance, or behavioural economics, is a subject that has become increasingly popular in recent times. The interest has been spurred on, perhaps, by seemingly irrational market behaviour before spectacular market failures, such as in 2008. One if its founding principles is that although we think of ourselves as rational investors, carefully balancing risk and reward, we are actually a lot less rational than we believe.

There are many examples of how we act irrationally in practice. Here are a few:

Loss aversion

Loss aversion, simplistically, refers to our **irrational fear of loss**: the possibility of loss 'hurts' more than the pleasure to be derived from an equivalent gain. For example, what choice would you make when offered the following options:

- Option A – winning a guaranteed R20 000; or
- Option B – standing an 80 per cent chance of winning R30 000?

Strict application of mathematical principles would require you to choose Option B, on which the pay-off is 80 per cent of R30 000 = R24 000: greater than the pay-off on Option A. However, most people don't make the 'rational' choice, and opt for A, the option with less perceived downside and higher certainty.

To extend the example into a business context, let's assume that your company has invested R50 million in a new project. Choose between the following options:

- Option A – investing a further R10 million with a 20 per cent probability that the project will be successful (80 per cent chance that you will have to write off R60 million); or
- Option B – discontinuing the project and writing off R50 million without any further investment.

Again, were you rigidly to apply mathematical principles you would follow Option A, wherein the potential loss is R48 million (80 per cent × R60 million), rather than face a sure loss of R50 million by canning the project immediately. Here, your corporate reputation plays a part and is likely to affect your judgement. Would you want to be known as the person who invested good money after bad should the project go sour?

You can see from the above examples that the key issue is one of grappling with uncertainty. For example, what if the probability of the project in the second example being successful is really only 10 per cent, rather than 20 per cent? Then the pay-off under Option A would be a negative R54 million (90 per cent × R60 million) and you would have been right to choose Option B. It seems that we are inherently uncomfortable in dealing with uncertainty, and that most people choose the option with the most definite outcome or build a margin of safety into the probability estimates.

Confirmation bias

In the *Harvard Business Review* article 'Deals Without Delusions' (Lovallo et al. 2007), the authors address several topics that create bias in an M&A context, including confirmation bias, which suggests that as we walk down a particular M&A road we start to seek out evidence to support our views rather than information to refute our opinions. In other words, we start to fall in love with the deal and subconsciously edit out information that will challenge our propensity to go ahead with the transaction. This crooked thinking is supported by the sunk-cost fallacy, which suggests that we have spent so much time and money on the transaction so far that we better go ahead with it at all costs.

The authors suggest that a conscious effort is required to offset confirmation bias, and that you deliberately need to collect disconfirming evidence. It may be helpful, for example, to brief someone outside of the acquisition team to perform this role. Accountants are often very good at playing devil's advocate, for example, although we also have to be careful of knowing the price of everything but the value of nothing. A broader, more enlightened view is required, rather than instinctively shooting everything down in flames.

It is also extremely important that you brief your advisors appropriately in this regard. Due diligence as a means of controlling risk, examined in the next chapter, is an essential component of the M&A process, but is most effective if your advisors feel that any bad news they bring you will be heard and acted upon.

Anchoring

Anchoring is the psychological phenomenon in terms of which the **initial value** introduced into a conversation serves as a **mental benchmark** or starting point for estimating an unknown quantity. It has an amazingly powerful impact on the receiver. For example, say you are trying to sell your old car, the market value of which is around R100 000. You find a potential buyer and your opening comment is, 'I am selling this car for R125 000.' Immediately, the potential buyer starts evaluating his or her own assessment in relation to the anchor (R125 000): 'How can this person be asking for R125 000 when I know the market value is only R100 000? I must be missing something otherwise he or she wouldn't have the gall to ask such a high price? Perhaps this car isn't like similar cars?'

One caveat is that the first number mentioned must, at least, be capable of being true. If you start by saying, 'I'm selling this car for R1 million,' the potential buyer will simply walk away.

Anchoring is a useful principle to adopt in M&A negotiations. If you think the buyer of your business is going to beat you down in negotiations, then introduce your high, but still realistic, expectations into the conversation at an early stage, then leave the buyer with the problem of moving away from the anchor.

There are many more types of bias that have been identified in the fascinating field of behavioural finance, but for now all that is required is to recognise that neither you nor your counterpart in negotiations is operating off a purely rational base. Beware of falling into traps such as confirmation bias, but use the irrationality to your benefit by 'anchoring' your opponent in negotiations.

SELF-ASSESSMENT

- After reading the information about behaviour in this chapter, do you believe that we act rationally 100 per cent of the time?
- Can you identify ways in which you could use irrationality to your advantage in negotiations?

Maintaining discipline when pricing a transaction

Justifying the price

The justification for entering into a transaction is sometimes given as, 'It's the last deal of its kind and we have to have it. We need to do the deal for strategic reasons.' Eccles et al. (1999) point out that when some bankers hear that reasoning, they close their files and walk away. Any reasoning that supports a decision to go ahead with a deal must be capable of being turned into numbers, however inexact those numbers might be. And if the numbers don't stack up, the deal should be abandoned.

CASE STUDY **AngloGold**

We alluded in Chapter 13 to AngloGold's desired acquisition of Australian gold miner Normandy, an acquisition that competitor, Canadian miner Newmont, thwarted. Events proceeded as follows:

- AngloGold's initial bid in November 2001 valued Normandy at A$1,43 a share.
- Newmont arrived on the scene shortly thereafter with a bid of A$1,70 a share.
- The AngloGold board went back to the drawing board to review their original offer. After further analysis, they concluded that they could raise their offer to A$1,65 per share, including a cash component of A$0,20 per share. The board justified the increase on the basis that:
  - full value had not been offered in the first round; and
  - Normandy's recent financial results were better than anticipated.

AngloGold waived minimum acceptance levels by Normandy shareholders for the deal, indicating their keenness for the deal to go ahead.

- Newmont's reaction was to increase their offer to A$1,90 per share, including cash of A$0,40, also without a minimum acceptance requirement.
- Once again, the AngloGold board put their thinking caps on, but this time all they could do was increase the offer by A$0,10 per share, based on the perceived financial impact of a co-operation agreement with Barrick Gold for operations in Australia and Tanzania.
- Newmont reacted again, increasing their offer to A$1,93 per share, including cash of A$0,50 per share. At this point, AngloGold's bid was valued at A$1,81 per share.
- Even though the bid spread fell over the next few weeks, all that AngloGold management felt they were able to do at this point was to extend their offer by a week. They saw no basis on which they could justify a higher offer.
- The outcome of the above was that Newmont's bid was successful.

Faced with a bidding war against an international opponent, it would have been very easy for AngloGold management to get carried away in the auction, but they didn't. They retained their trust in their valuation calculations and only increased their offer when they could point to specific factors that they had evaluated and built into the offer price. On this basis, walking away from the deal was a correct and courageous decision by AngloGold management.

Maintaining discipline in the bidding process

It's one thing to have carefully applied a range of valuation techniques gleaned from this book in coming up with an acceptable valuation range, but it is another to make sure that you come out of the negotiation room with the deal you want. The bidding situation lends itself to ego potentially trumping rational thought, as we've seen from the AngloGold example, but you need consciously to put safeguards in place to prevent this.

Eccles et al. (1999) recommend a discipline of the front-line negotiating team working within a pre-agreed negotiating range. Should the negotiating team believe there is reason for the bid to be raised, they need to discuss the possibility with an executive back at head office who has remained out of the day-to-day conduct of negotiations, and who thus has maintained his or her objectivity about the deal. This creates a firebreak that stops the negotiating team from getting caught up in the excitement.

The authors also refer to the role of financial objectives in maintaining corporate discipline. This is the approach used by conglomerates such as Bidvest, where management is decentralised but financial targets are set by the Centre. Discipline is easily enforced when the money required to fund acquisitions has to be obtained from a central treasury function. The Centre then has control over the cost of that capital. Financial targets might take any form, but it should be clear by now from this book that the authors advocate targets based on cost of capital and measurement of returns achieved on capital employed, rather than measuring growth in EPS and other accounting-dependent measures.

Conclusion

This chapter dealt with the art of valuation, rather than the science that Part 1 covered. We have examined the issues involved in applying valuation techniques appropriately in an M&A situation. We have seen that there are many opportunities for self-delusion in the heat of an M&A battle, and we have considered a few helpful safeguards that encourage keeping a level head during a competitive process. As with any other element of the M&A process, there is no substitute for experience, but starting the journey with a mental roadmap will undoubtedly be helpful.

References

Eccles, R.G., Lanes, K.L. & Wilson, T.C. (1999). Are You Paying Too Much for That Acquisition? *Harvard Business Review*. July–August 1999, pp. 136–146.

Lovallo, D., Viguerie, P., Uhlaner, R. & Horn, I. (2007). Deals Without Delusions. *Harvard Business Review*. December 2007.

CHAPTER 15

Managing risk: Do you really understand the business you are buying?

LEARNING OBJECTIVES

After working through this chapter you should be able to:

- Explain the different roles of due diligence and warranties in managing risk in M&A
- Understand how due diligence is organised in practice
- Understand the roles and responsibilities in a due diligence investigation
- Recognise the anticipated outcomes of the due diligence exercise
- Explain what a vendor due diligence is

Introduction

Prior to embarking upon a due diligence investigation you would normally have:

- decided upon your growth strategy and how M&A will form part of that;
- found a potential target company that meets your M&A criteria;
- performed a preliminary desktop valuation of the target company; and
- held preliminary talks with the target's management.

So, what do you do next? At this stage, you need to focus on identifying and managing the risks associated with the transaction – which is not to say that you are trying to manage away the risks completely (if that was your intention, you would be better off investing in government bonds), but rather that you are building an understanding of the risks that you are taking on so that you can make an informed choice about whether to proceed with the investment. Certain risks can be mitigated through deal structuring, such as by only acquiring specified assets and liabilities of the target firm.

The target's management will surely know their business better than you do, so your objective is to find out as much as you can in the time available. You do this by conducting a due diligence exercise. To cover any risks that remain undetected, you will ask for warranties to be included in the Sale and Purchase Agreement (SPA) – the agreement that records all the terms and conditions of the acquisition.

Due diligence

Due diligence from the acquirer's perspective

Due diligence (DD) is the name given to the process by which the acquirer is given access to information about the target company in order to gain a deeper understanding of what is being acquired.

Lesson 1: DD is not an audit!

Whereas an audit's primary focus is to look backwards in order to sign off on a company's financial statements at a point in time, the DD is aimed at identifying current and potential risks and opportunities. This is a creative process. Your interest lies in uncovering the unknown. Done correctly, it will allow you to gain an informational advantage in negotiations with the target. It will also help you to refine your preliminary valuation. All of the valuation expertise you have learnt in the first half of this book will count for nothing if you do not have confidence in the numbers with which you are working.

What areas does a DD cover?

You will plan the scope of the DD according to the risks you are trying to manage, but it is likely that the DD will cover issues under the following headings:

+ Financial, including taxation
+ Legal
+ Operational
+ Environmental
+ Human resources
+ Cultural issues
+ Business processes and information technology systems
+ Other relevant issues.

The first three points in this list are standard in DDs. Environmental issues have become very important over time due to the increased scrutiny by regulatory authorities and legislation covering responsibilities and liability for environmental damage and rehabilitation. It is important to involve specialists in this area if the target company's business is exposed to environmental liabilities.

One of the key reasons cited for M&A failure is that insufficient attention was paid upfront to cultural issues. People are often a key asset in a business. Understanding the people dynamics in a business is critical. Differing corporate cultures can prevent effective integration of businesses after acquisition.

Who is responsible for the DD?

It is fairly likely that the acquiring management will outsource some of the DD tasks. For example, the financial DD may be outsourced to an accounting firm and the legal DD to a law firm. Operational DD will, in all likelihood, be kept in-house, particularly where the acquirer and the target operate in the same industry.

But even if tasks are outsourced, it is important for acquiring management to retain overall responsibility for the exercise. A poorly briefed professional firm is likely to produce a poor or unfocused result. More than that, professional services firms are expensive, so you will want to focus them on areas in which they are most likely to deliver value. For example, tax is a highly specialist area that needs careful investigation if you are planning to acquire shares in a company. The value of the information unearthed in a tax DD can easily outweigh the cost of gathering it.

How should you go about planning a DD?

There is often a strategic element to planning a DD. One of the rules of the Takeover Regulation Panel is that equal rights to information must be accorded to all bona fide bidders, so in a competitive bidding situation you might elect to make do with less information if you think it will put your fellow bidders at a disadvantage.

CASE STUDY Nedbank

In 2002, when Nedbank was considering acquiring The Board of Executors (BOE), there was speculation in the market that one of the large international banks was also considering making a bid for BOE. Nedbank management felt that their knowledge of the local banking market and their competitors gave them an informational advantage over any foreign bank. Therefore, they deliberately limited their information requests in their DD on BOE. Given that any foreign bank would thus be limited to the same level of information in their own DD, it was felt that they would be relatively more disadvantaged by the lack of detail than Nedbank would. Nedbank closed the deal!

Another way of looking at DD planning is to consider the required level of detail in terms of Figure 15.1:

FIGURE 15.1 The level of detail required in a DD

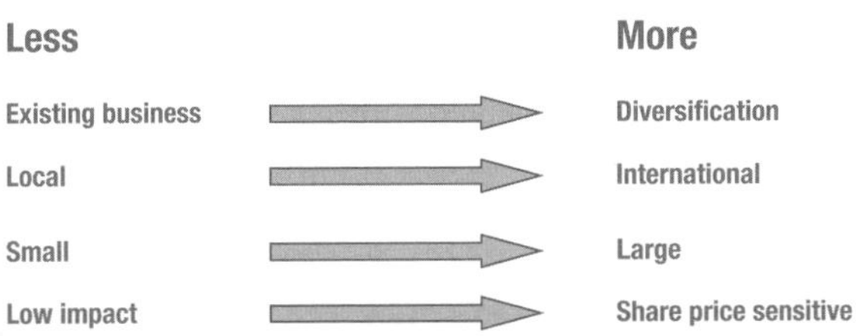

Where you are investing in a familiar industry you might opt for a less detailed DD, whereas if you are investing in a new industry, or one with which you are not totally familiar, you might go into a lot of detail. Similarly, risk is higher in an international investment than in a local one, or one that is large in relation to the acquirer's size, or that is high-profile enough potentially to impact the acquirer's share price.

How is a DD organised in practice?

Two questions arise in answering this question:

- How much information will be made available in Round 1?
- How will the information be divulged?

The vendor has the upper hand in terms of how much information to divulge. One tactic used by vendors hoping to muddy the waters is to divulge vast quantities of unnecessary information, such as old product brochures and price lists. For the acquirer, it is important to establish a list of critically important information that is necessary to form a view on risk and value. If the information has not been supplied, the acquirer can ask for it, on the understanding that the information will be made available to all potential bidders in a competitive situation. Access to the information is for a limited time only, so potential bidders need to act quickly and effectively.

Even in a friendly deal, it is unlikely that all information will be disclosed in the first round of a DD. The information release process went as follows in a recent sale transaction that came to the author's attention:

- Phase 1 – submit an expression of interest (EOI) based on very high-level information. The EOI was to contain a single value indicating how much the interested party might be prepared to pay for the target firm. This amount would not be binding and, being based on

such limited information, would probably not indicate anything other than the buyer's ability to consider a transaction of a certain size.
- Phase 2 – the successful interested parties from Phase 1 would, after signing a non-disclosure agreement (NDA), be provided with an information memorandum (IM) setting out more detailed information, following which they would again be required to submit a non-binding offer.
- Phase 3 – interested parties making it through Phase 2 would be given a vendor due diligence or VDD report (this will be described later in this chapter), access to a virtual data room, site visits and an additional question-and-answer session. At the end of this process the interested parties would be required to submit a binding offer to acquire the business.

You can see that the release of information is a slow process aimed at:
- Establishing the credentials of the interested parties – are they really bona fide bidders?
- Retaining control over sensitive information, such as client lists and profit margins, until the very end of the process, once credibility has been established.

The Reunert case study that follows shows that M&A is a game played within a set of very complex rules, of which seasoned dealmakers know how to take advantage. We will look at some of the relevant regulations in Chapter 17.

CASE STUDY **Reunert**

In 1999 Reunert's share price was under pressure and, as a result, Brait Capital Partners expressed an interest in acquiring the business. Reunert management allowed Brait to conduct a detailed DD, but the resulting offer was below Reunert management's expectations and the offer was rejected. As is often the case when an initial offer is made, Reunert was now 'in play', and a consortium comprising Altron – a direct competitor to Reunert – and BOE popped out of the woodwork and asked for rights to the same information as had been given to Brait. Reunert management refused, and the Altron consortium appealed to the Securities Regulation Panel (SRP), the forerunner of the Takeover Regulation Panel, which sided with Altron in terms of SRP rule 16.4, which deals with 'equality of information to competing offerors'. Reunert successfully appealed the SRP's decision in the High Court, on the basis that Altron and Reunert were direct competitors, and that in any case Reunert management were of the opinion that the Altron offer did not represent Reunert's true value. Reunert then declared a cash dividend to shareholders, possibly making it a less attractive target. No deal between Altron and Reunert took place at the time.

What is a virtual data room?

A data room is the place in which information that is being disclosed to bidders is gathered. Whereas in the past this would have involved placing physical documents in a room, this is more commonly now achieved on a virtual basis. Electronic versions of documents are made available on a dedicated website. Access to the site and requests for additional information are managed by the data room controller.

Reasons for having a data room include:
- Confidentiality – the flow of information can be controlled and the target's staff will not find out about the transaction until there is a reasonably high chance of it going ahead;

+ Convenience – all relevant information can be found in one place; and
+ Focus – the risk of being sidetracked is lessened.

What are the key objectives of a DD?

Why should an acquirer conduct due diligence at all?

TABLE 15.1 The aim of due diligence

Aim	Description
Make sure you are getting what you think you are getting.	For example, if the value of the target lies in its brands, you need to make sure that the company has title to the trademarks supporting those brands. As surprising as it may seem, this is not always the case.
Avoid surprises should the deal go ahead.	After the deal is done is not the time to find out that product warranties have not been adequately provided for, or that the defined benefit pension fund is underfunded. DD provides you with an opportunity to uncover this information before concluding the deal.
Confirm what you think you know.	When you created your acquisition strategy and identified your shortlist of targets, you were looking for an acquisition that would meet one of your company's strategic objectives. That is where the value of the deal potentially lies. If you think a company has particular abilities or assets that are important to you, you need to confirm this through the DD process.
Gather information with which to update your preliminary valuation.	In getting to this point you came up with a preliminary valuation that was based on publicly available information. One objective of the DD is to identify information that needs to be fed back into the valuation before you commence final negotiations. For example, an analysis of historical trends might lead you to realise that the margins you have used in your forecasts are not achievable. There should be a strong link between the DD and the valuation.
Quantify synergies and feed them into the valuation.	The DD will help you to identify and quantify potential synergies that may arise out of the acquisition. We saw in, the first part of this book, that understanding and valuing the synergies is an important part of the overall process. This is the point at which you can gain some comfort that the synergies are realistic.
Identify risks to be addressed in negotiations.	As you conduct the DD you will become aware of risks that you would like covered in the Sale and Purchase Agreement. Again, there should be a strong link between the financial DD and the legal team drawing up the agreement.
Identify potential integration issues.	This is also a good time to foresee any post-acquisition integration issues. These may be as big as non-aligned IT systems or as small (relatively speaking) as their people flying business class whereas your company's policy is to fly economy class.

What are the practical outcomes of a financial DD exercise?

In broad terms, you are seeking to establish the following:

+ Are assets overstated?
+ Are liabilities understated?
+ Are all liabilities recorded in the financial statements?
+ Are reported profits sustainable?
+ Are accounting policies appropriate?

The list that follows is not exhaustive, but it sets out categories of information you may wish to obtain during the course of an effective DD:

Business insight

- Corporate details
- Business overview
  - History
  - Markets
  - Products
  - Customers
  - Suppliers
- Sources of competitive advantage
- Key business drivers
- Key business risks
  - Internal
  - External
- Growth opportunities.

Operating issues

- Manufacturing operations
- IT systems
- Logistics
- Health and safety
- Environmental issues.

Financial information

- Current trading performance
- Consolidated balance sheets
- Potential adjustments to historical EBITDA
- Forecasts
- Potential synergies
- Capital expenditure
- Working capital requirements
- Free cash flow.

Human resources (HR) issues

- Management
- Workforce issues
- Salary scales and incentivisation of key executives.

Legal environment

- Material contracts
- Intellectual property
- Any litigation in progress or on the horizon
- Regulatory compliance.

Some warning signs for DDs that will reduce effectiveness

The process:

- does not start at a high level, questioning whether the deal will add value to the acquirer;
- is driven by standard checklists, resulting in extensive enquiries into non-critical areas;
- does not focus on identifying key risks;
- does not lead to an understanding of key value drivers; and
- focuses on 'known unknowns', rather than providing the possibility of uncovering 'unknown unknowns'.

In other words, a process that is formulaic, compliance-orientated and pedestrian is unlikely to produce valuable results. The process needs to be creative, with a constant focus on the objectives of the exercise.

In summary, from a buyer's perspective the DD is a way of improving the information you have about the target so that you can negotiate a deal that will create value for your shareholders. This is the point at which you obtain information that is critical to your negotiations; is where you empower yourself to reduce the risks of the transaction; and where you start to plan how to implement the deal.

Due diligence from a seller's perspective

The sale process and information flow

The seller is able to decide on the sale process and, as a result, the information flow to interested parties. Options include the following:

- **Sale by treaty.** This describes a situation in which the seller and the buyer are already known to each other and there is a period of exclusivity while the buyer gathers the information necessary to formulate an offer. In this situation, access to information will be decided by mutual agreement.
- **Sale by auction.** This option will be selected when it is perceived that the business for sale will attract a lot of attention in the marketplace and that a higher price could be achieved as a result. In this case, access to information will take place along the lines of the formal process described earlier in this chapter.

Due diligence by the seller

DDs are not only performed by the buyer:

- As a seller that is going to receive shares in the acquiring company as payment, you should be thinking about performing a DD on the buyer to make sure you are getting value for your business. This will be particularly important in the merger of two companies of equal sizes.
- As the seller, you should also consider conducting your own vendor due diligence (VDD) before inviting offers for your business. A VDD is an independent review of the business commissioned by the seller on which competing bidders will rely. The objective is to make sure that they buyers do not pick up any negative information about which the seller is not already aware. Once again, information superiority could play an important role in obtaining the highest value for the business.

CASE STUDY **Edcon**

Before Edcon was acquired by Bain Capital in 2007 in a process that involved more than one interested party, Edcon management performed their own VDD to make sure that they were not surprised by issues raised about Edcon by the potential buyers.

A final thought on due diligence

The article 'Deals Without Delusions' (Lovallo et al. 2007) introduces us to another element of behavioural finance, namely confirmation bias. As you saw in Chapter 14, this is the typically human inclination subconsciously to weed out data that does not support a preconceived outcome. Make sure that you are open to finding information that could refute what you know or believe about a business and/or industry. In fact, actively seek out such information!

SELF-ASSESSMENT

- How would you define the difference between a DD and an audit?
- Should a DD be limited to financial and legal issues or are there other areas that should be covered?
- Who carries final responsibility for the DD?
- Describe three reasons why you might choose to set up a data room.
- Name four key objectives of a DD.
- Name five practical outcomes of a DD.
- As a seller, why would you consider commissioning a VDD?

Warranties and indemnities

As a buyer, despite having conducted detailed due diligence, you may still be looking for more comfort that what you see is what you are going to get. The additional comfort that you seek is available in the form of warranties and indemnities.

Warranties

A warranty is a contractual statement of fact made by the warrantor to the acquirer that is recorded in the SPA. Issues that the seller will be required to warrant are a matter of negotiation, to be agreed between the parties with the help of legal advisers. The seller, having awarded you the right of due diligence, will be keen to limit the warranties provided. Warranties can be limited or extensive, depending on the circumstances. They can also be a deal-breaker, so sometimes a cool head is required in the negotiating room.

Examples of common warranty clauses are as follows:

- The sellers are able to give free and unencumbered title to the transfer assets to the purchaser.
- The sellers are the sole owner of the transfer assets.
- None of the transfer assets are subject to any hire purchase or credit agreement, lease, pledge, lien, hypothec, mortgage, material bond or other encumbrance, except as disclosed.
- No person other than the purchaser has, or will have, on the effective date, any right or option to acquire the businesses or to acquire any of the transfer assets.

- The sellers are not a party to, nor threatened with, any litigation or arbitration in respect of the business and are not aware of any facts that may give rise thereto.
- There is no underfunded liability in respect of any defined benefits or contribution fund or medical aid of the businesses.
- All employment contracts with transferring employees have been entered into in the ordinary course of business and do not contain any unusual or abnormal terms or conditions.
- The seller will not, without the consent of the purchaser, vary the terms and conditions of employment or working conditions of any of the transferring employees and warrant that they have not done so prior to, and in anticipation of, this agreement.
- The seller has, to the best of their knowledge and belief, made a full and complete disclosure to the purchaser of all material information relating to the business.
- The seller has fully disclosed and provided for any environmental liabilities.

The remedy for a breach of warranty is that the buyer can sue the seller for the damages resulting from the breach, but the breach does not usually invalidate the contract. Rather, the buyer will calculate the financial effect of the breach and sue the seller accordingly. It can be seen, therefore, that caution needs to be exercised when relying on warranties to manage risk. At the time of wanting to sue the seller, the seller may not have sufficient funds to compensate the buyer. Warranties are therefore not a complete alternative to conducting a DD.

It is often useful for the acquirer to require the seller to deposit a portion of the purchase price into an escrow account to cover any potential breaches of warranties. It may be easier to recover damages if an amount is set aside upfront.

Warranties are generally for a period of time. It is unlikely that the seller will agree to be responsible for a breach of warranties forever. Rather, sellers would prefer to be liable for any breaches discovered within three years of the effective date of the acquisition. Thereafter, the acquirer would have no claim against the seller. This is a tricky situation in practice. For example, Competition Commission offences discovered five years after the deal may be punitive, but the seller would not be liable for fines and penalties paid to Competition Commission authorities.

Indemnities

According to a Quickguide titled 'Warranties and Indemnities' published by Ashurst LLP attorneys in March 2010 on their website (https://www.ashurst.com/publication-techguide.aspx?id_Content=5974):

> *indemnities are appropriate for matters which are specific and known and which clearly fall outside the responsibility of the buyer. They often deal with the issues such as environmental risks, litigation and product liability matters. It is also common for tax liabilities relating to the seller's period of ownership to be dealt with in the tax deed of indemnity.*

The remedy where an indemnity has been granted to the purchaser is that the purchaser can claim the specific loss arising from the indemnified situation from the seller. In other words, if an environmental risk that takes R10 million to fix is discovered, the R10 million can be claimed back from the seller. The quantum of damages is easier to establish under an indemnity than under a warranty.

The objective of this sub-section has been to provide a very broad indication of the scope of warranties and indemnities. It is, however, important to note that his is a technical legal subject, and you should not proceed without seeking advice from your legal advisers.

SELF-ASSESSMENT

- Would you see warranties and indemnities as replacing a DD?
- What do you think are the essential differences between warranties and indemnities?

Conclusion

This chapter focused on risk management in M&A and looked at the roles of due diligence and warranties and indemnities in limiting the purchaser's risk. As mentioned at the start of the chapter, the intention is not to eliminate risk entirely, but rather to increase the purchaser's awareness and understanding of the risks involved before proceeding with the investment. Paying attention to this process is an important way of preserving the potential value to be created from the transaction.

References

Lovallo, D., Viguerie, P., Uhlaner, R. & Horn, I. (2007). Deals Without Delusions. *Harvard Business Review*. December 2007.

CHAPTER 16

Effective deal structuring and funding

LEARNING OUTCOMES

After working through this chapter you should be able to:

- Explain the role of deal structuring in preserving value in M&A transactions
- the reasons for considering buying shares in a company versus buying the business (assets and liabilities) out of a company
- the issues surrounding the use of cash or the issue of shares as consideration in a transaction
- the role of earn-outs in deal structuring

Introduction

So far, you have done a lot of work to ensure that the transaction has the potential to create value:

- You have established an M&A growth strategy and identified targets that are consistent with that strategy.
- You have conducted preliminary due diligence on the target to minimise your risks.
- You have arrived at a negotiating range by applying the valuation principles set out in Chapters 1 to 12 in this book, guided in your thinking by Chapter 14.

Now you need to ensure that you preserve that value-creating potential by carefully structuring the transaction. Key issues that need to be addressed include:

- Should you buy the shares in the company or should you buy the business out of the company?
  - What are the tax implications of each method?
- How should you pay for the acquisition? Should you use shares or should you pay in cash?
  - What impact will your chosen method of funding have on the company's balance sheet?
  - If you plan to issue new shares, how will that impact your existing shareholders?
  - What impact will your chosen method of funding have on the sellers (do you want them to stay in the business for a period and be motivated, for example)?
- Should you hold back a portion of the purchase price that will only be released once certain profit or cash generation targets have been met by the acquiree?

Buy shares or buy the business?

The first decision that needs to be made in terms of structuring an M&A transaction is whether to buy the shares in the target company or to buy the business out of the company. How would you go about making that decision?

It is important to recognise that the buyer and the seller sit on different sides of the fence when it comes to choosing:

- The buyer is not anxious to take on hidden liabilities in the target company, and would therefore prefer to buy the business (operations and assets) out of the company.

- The seller is probably more inclined to do a clean deal by selling the shares in the company. The structuring decision is also impacted by tax considerations, such as tax on recoupment of wear and tear allowances previously granted and capital gains tax (CGT).

The basic rules of tax applying to the transaction-structuring operations are set out in Tables 16.1 and 16.2. A worked example follows these tables.

TABLE 16.1 Option 1 – the target company's shares are the subject of the transaction

Party	Tax implications
Buyer	For the buyer, this is a capital transaction. The cost of the shares will become the base value for CGT purposes in any future transaction. Previously, the interest on any borrowings used to fund the transaction would not have been tax deductible, because of the capital nature of the transaction. However, as of 1 January 2013 a new provision allows a deduction of interest in the hands of a company buying at least 70 per cent of the shares of another company if that company is an operating company, i.e. it provides good or services on a continuous basis. In your planning, you would also have to be sure that the acquiring company has the tax base to make use of the interest deduction. Those considerations aside, this is a significant tax concession that makes buying the target company shares more feasible.
Seller	The seller is the owner of the shares in the company. In most instances, this would be a capital transaction, and would therefore attract CGT. For individuals, one third of the taxable gain on the sale would be taxable; for companies, two thirds of the gain would be taxable. The shareholders who are disposing of their shareholdings would be responsible for paying the CGT.

TABLE 16.2 Option 2 – the target business is the subject of the transaction

Party	Tax implications
Buyer	For the buyer, this is a revenue transaction – the purchase of an asset in pursuit of the production of income. The assets acquired need to be recorded in the buyer's books at fair value, in terms of the accounting standard IFRS3. The tax values of those assets must also be recorded at fair value. Where applicable, the buyer will be able to claim wear and tear allowances on the tax values of the acquired assets. Interest on borrowings used to fund the transaction will be deductible for tax purposes, given the revenue nature of the transaction. Provided that the business is being sold as a going concern, the transaction will be zero-rated for VAT purposes (but the transaction must comply with the VAT Act's definition of a going concern, as tested in the courts).

Continued

Seller	The seller is the company, not the shareholders. The sale of the company's assets may trigger a recoupment of previous tax allowances, up to the total amount previously claimed (in other words, the recoupment will not exceed the difference between the original cost and the current tax value). Should the sale price of an asset exceed its original cost, then CGT will be payable on the excess. As noted from the buyer's perspective, if the transaction complies with the definition of the sale of a business as a going concern, then the transaction will be zero-rated for VAT purposes (but if the sale agreement is silent on this point, the transaction will be deemed to be subject to VAT at 14/114 of the selling price – at current VAT rates). For the shareholders to receive the cash, it will, in most instances, need to be paid to them as a dividend, thus attracting dividend withholding tax (DWT) at a rate of 15 per cent on dividends declared after 1 April 2012.

EXAMPLE 16.1

The buyer and the seller (an individual owning the shares) have entered into negotiations and agree that the value of the underlying business in a company is R100 000. The company has no debt. It operates in the service industry, so has little in the way of fixed assets, but it has R10 000 invested in working capital. Its balance sheet looks like this:

Opening balance sheet	
Equity	10 000
Assets (working capital)	10 000

The company was started after the introduction of CGT in 2001, so the base value for CGT purposes is nil. How should the transaction be structured?

From the buyer's perspective the choice is simple – his or her preference would be to buy the assets, in order to take advantage of the interest deductibility and possibly to claim wear and tear allowances on the stepped-up value of assets (although the seller would be fighting in the opposite direction not to trigger recoupments in the company's hands).

It is the seller that has the problem.

If the shares are sold for R100 000, there will be no base value for CGT purposes, and the proceeds will attract CGT at the rate for individuals, which is currently 13,3 per cent (one third of maximum marginal personal tax rate of 40 per cent). The net proceeds to the seller will be as follows:

Proceeds of sale	100 000
Less CGT at 13,3%	(13 300)
Net proceeds to the seller	**86 700**

However, if the business is sold out of the company, the transaction will proceed as follows:

Assets in the company exchanged for cash	100 000
CGT payable at company rates (18,6% – two thirds of corporate tax rate of 28%) on 100 000 – 10 000	(16 740)
Net cash in the company	83 260
Dividend withholding tax at 15%	(12 489)
Net proceeds = dividend to seller	**70 771**

You can see from Example 1 that the seller will be disadvantaged in cash terms by selling the business rather than the shares (proceeds of R70 771 versus R86 700), and will be reluctant to do so. This is an extreme example - companies with a proportionately higher CGT base would pay less CGT and thus the gap would close, and rollover relief may be available and so on - but it demonstrates the issue.

So, given the differing orientations of the buyer and the seller, how can this issue be resolved? As with many other aspects of M&A, the answer is by negotiation, where the views of the negotiator with the strongest negotiating position are likely to prevail, and the party most anxious to do the deal will be prepared to give up most in the negotiations.

And, of course, tax is not the only consideration in deciding whether to buy shares or the assets out of the company. Buying assets will require:

+ vehicles to be re-registered in the name of the new owner;
+ business licences, such as a licence to sell alcohol, to be issued in the new owner's name;
+ renegotiation of important contracts, such as supplier contracts (this may be required even where shares in the company are bought, when the contract has a grandfather clause which is invoked on change of control in the company); and
+ many other possible administrative implications.

The cost and risk of these requirements - principals may find this a convenient time to find a different agent with which to work - must be set off against any potential benefits of buying the assets.

SELF-ASSESSMENT

+ Which factors would influence your decision to buy the shares in the company or to buy the business out of the company?
+ How would the existence of contracts that would need to be renegotiated if the business was sold out of the company influence your decisions?
+ Which reservations would you have about relying on warranties from the vendors to cover any concerns you might have when buying shares in a company?

Settle the purchase price using shares or cash?

This is the next important decision you need to make. Options available include:

+ Paying cash
    + Using existing cash resources
    + Borrowing cash to fund the acquisition

- Issuing new shares
  - Issuing shares to the vendors
  - Issuing shares to third parties, using the cash proceeds to fund the acquisition (known as a private placement)
- Using a combination of cash and shares.

Each of these options has implications for the buyer and the seller. These will be examined in the sections that follow.

Evaluating the options from the buyer's perspective

Option 1: Using existing cash resources

In this example:

- a price of R900 million has been negotiated for the acquisition of the target's assets;
- the target will deliver an additional R150 million of EBIT to the acquirer;
- the acquirer has R900 million of cash on its balance sheet, currently earning interest at 6 per cent per annum;
- the acquirer has 100 million shares in issue that trade at R57 per share; and
- before the acquisition, the acquirer's earnings per share (EPS) were 471 cents.

		Before		After
Rmillions		**Acquirer**	**Target**	**Acquirer**
Income statement				
EBIT		600	150	750
Interest on excess cash	6%	54		-
PBT		**654**		**750**
Tax	28%	-183		-210
PAT		**471**		**540**
Balance sheet				
Net operating assets		3 100	900	4 000
Excess cash/(Borrowings)		900		–
Net equity		**4 000**		**4 000**
Market capitalisation		**5 700**		**5 700**
Shares in issue (m)		100		100
Price per share (R)		57		57
EPS (cents)		471		540

After the acquisition:

- cash has been exchanged for the new asset;
- EBIT is the sum of the EBIT of the two entities prior to the transaction;

+ interest received has been reduced to nil as all the cash has been used;
+ there is no change in the book value of the acquirer's net equity – all that has happened is that cash has been swapped for new assets;
+ the market is indifferent to the deal – no change in value per share – on the assumption that fair value has been paid for the new assets; and
+ the acquirer's EPS has risen from 471 cps to 540 cps.

So, why has the acquirer's EPS increased? Because the investment in the new assets will produce a higher return than interest on surplus cash – PBT increases from R654 million to R750 million, the net of new EBIT gained and interest income given up. In general, the markets punish companies for retaining surplus cash on their balance sheets, unless shareholders are convinced that management has value-creating investments in its sights. If not, the shareholders would like the money to be returned to them by way of a dividend or share repurchase.

So, the impact of the Option 1 transaction is as follows:

+ On the acquirer's gearing – none, but surplus cash has been redeployed
+ On the acquirer's shareholders – none, assuming that fair value has been paid for the assets
+ On the sellers – they have been paid in cash and therefore have no further interest in the business that they have sold.

Option 2: Use existing cash and then borrow more to fund the acquisition

In this example:

+ a price of R1 800 million has been negotiated for the acquisition of the target's assets;
+ the target will deliver an additional R300 million of EBIT to the acquirer;
+ the acquirer has R900 million of cash on its balance sheet, currently earning interest at 6 per cent per annum;
+ the acquirer has 100 million shares in issue that trade at R57 per share; and
+ before the acquisition, the acquirer's earnings per share (EPS) were 471 cents.

In this example, the target business is worth exactly twice that in the previous example. As a result, the acquirer not only uses its existing stockpile of cash but has to borrow a further R900 million.

		Before		After
Rmillions		**Acquirer**	**Target**	**Acquirer**
Income statement – before				
EBIT		600	300	900
Interest on excess cash/ (Borrowings)	6%	54	9%	-81
PBT		**654**		**819**
Tax	28%	-183		-229
PAT		**471**		**590**

Continued

Balance sheet – before				
Net operating assets		3 100	1 800	4 900
Excess cash/(Borrowings)		900		-900
Net equity		**4 000**		**4 000**
Market capitalisation		**5 700**		**5 700**
Shares in issue (m)		100		100
Price per share (R)		57		57
EPS (cents)		471		590

After the acquisition:

+ cash of R900 million has been replaced by borrowings of R900 million;
+ EBIT is the sum of the EBIT of the two entities prior to the transaction;
+ interest received has been reduced to nil and has been replaced by interest paid on the new loan;
+ there is no change in the book value of the acquirer's net equity – cash has been swapped for new assets, partially funded by new borrowings;
+ the market is indifferent to the deal – no change in value per share – on the assumption that fair value has been paid for the new assets; and
+ the acquirer's EPS has risen from 540 cps to 590 cps.

The EPS has risen even further in this example. Why? Because the return on the investment is higher than the cost of the new debt raised.

So, the impact of the Option 2 transaction is as follows:

+ On the acquirer's gearing – borrowings have risen to R900 million in relation to the market cap of equity of R5 700 million, a debt/equity ratio of 16 per cent. This is not a high level of gearing but is an important ratio that will need to be monitored when considering the funding of future acquisitions
+ On the acquirer's shareholders – none, assuming that fair value has been paid for the assets
+ On the sellers – they have been paid in cash and therefore have no further interest in the business that they have sold.

Option 3: Issue new shares to fund the acquisition

In this example:

+ a price of R1 800 million has been negotiated for the acquisition of the target's assets;
+ the target will deliver an additional R300 million of EBIT to the acquirer;
+ the acquirer has R900 million of cash on its balance sheet, currently earning interest at 6 per cent per annum;
+ the acquirer has 100 million shares in issue that trade at R57 per share;
+ before the acquisition, the acquirer's earnings per share (EPS) were 471 cents; and
+ the value of the business is the same as in the previous example, but instead of borrowing to pay the balance of the purchase price, the acquirer has issued new shares at current market value – R57 per share.

		Before		After
Rmillions		**Acquirer**	**Target**	**Acquirer**
Income statement – before				
EBIT		600	300	900
Interest on excess cash	6%	54	9%	-
PBT		**654**		**900**
Tax	28%	-183		-252
PAT		**471**		**648**
Balance sheet – before				
Net operating assets		3 100	1 800	4 900
Excess cash/(Borrowings)		900		–
Net equity		**4 000**		**4 900**
Market capitalisation		**5 700**		**6 600**
Shares in issue (m)		100		116
Price per share (R)		57		57
EPS (cents)		471		560

After the acquisition:

- cash of R900 million has been reduced to nil;
- EBIT is the sum of the EBIT of the two entities prior to the transaction;
- interest received has been reduced to nil as all the cash has been used;
- the acquirer's net equity has increased by the value of new shares issued – R900 million;
- the number of shares in issue has risen by 16 million – R900 million at R57 per share;
- the market is indifferent to the deal – no change in price per share – on the assumption that fair value has been paid for the new assets; and
- compared with Option 2, the acquirer's EPS after the transaction reduces from 590 cps to 560 cps, but this ratio does not tell the whole story. The original body of shareholders now has title to 100/116 * R648 million of earnings, being R558 million. This is higher than their pre-deal earnings entitlement of 100 per cent of R471 million. This indicates that the deal is good for the company, despite the reduction in EPS. Be careful of basing a decision to go ahead with a deal on its impact on EPS and NAV. The essential issue is whether the deal is likely to create value for shareholders.

So, the impact of the Option 3 transaction is as follows:

- On the acquirer's gearing – borrowings are nil, but this may not be an ideal situation, given that it results in an important source of value being ignored, namely the tax deduction that can be claimed on interest paid
- On the acquirer's shareholders – new shares have been issued. Whether they have been issued to the sellers of the business, or to third parties in a private placement, the outcome will be the same – the acquiring shareholders' interest in the company will have been diluted
- In the sellers – if the new shares have been issued to the sellers, they will now have an economic interest in the acquirer's business

In Option 3, consider what happens if the market likes the deal and, a few months later, pushes the acquirer's share price up to R65 per share in anticipation of new value to be created in the future:

+ The company's market cap will increase to R7 526 million (65/57*6600)
+ The original shareholder's portion of that value will be R6 488 million (100/116*7526)
+ This is a 14 per cent increase on the R5 700 million of value with which they started.

But, of course, if the acquirer's share price drops to R50 per share, the converse will apply, and the above figures will become:

+ Acquirer's market cap – R5 790 million
+ Original shareholders' portion – R4 990 million
+ Proportion of original value lost by acquiring shareholders – 12 per cent.

But the loss of value borne by the acquiring shareholders is less than would have been the case had the deal been financed in cash, leading to the following principles for deciding on the use of shares or cash in acquisitions:

+ Where it seems likely that the acquiring company's shares are overpriced, or where the likely benefits of the deal are dubious, use shares to acquire so that the sellers share the risk of a possible share price downgrade.
+ Where it seems likely that the acquiring company's shares are underpriced, or where there is strong belief in the potential benefits of the deal, use cash to acquire, so that all potential gains accrue to the acquiring shareholders.

CASE STUDY **Nedbank**

Dilution of existing shareholders is also an issue when choosing to finance an acquisition by issue of shares. When Nedbank acquired BOE (a rival but smaller bank) in 2002, the price was around R7,7 billion and Nedbank would have liked to have made it an all-share transaction. However, Old Mutual was (and still is) Nedbank's controlling shareholder, with a holding at the time of over 50 per cent. Old Mutual did not wish to own less than 50 per cent of Nedbank, so the deal was funded by the issue of new shares to the value of R1,3 billion and cash of R6,4 billion. The cash portion was funded by raising subordinated debt and issuing preference shares.

CASE STUDY **Adcorp**

Adcorp made two acquisitions in 2014 that it funded by a combination of existing cash resources and a private placement to selected existing shareholders. It raised no debt. A problem with this approach is that it allowed some shareholders to benefit by increasing their holdings in Adcorp at the expense of others. At some future stage Adcorp will consider a rights issue that will allow shareholders to increase their interest in the company proportionate to their interest at the time, but the dilutionary effect of the private placements will remain.

Option 4: Use existing cash, raise a loan and issue new shares to fund an acquisition

This option is a combination of the previous three options.

		Before		After
Rmillions		**Acquirer**	**Target**	**Acquirer**
Income statement – before				
EBIT		600	450	1 050
Interest on excess cash	6%	54	9%	-81
PBT		**654**		**969**
Tax	28%	-183		-271
PAT		**471**		**698**
Balance sheet – before				
Net operating assets		3 100	2 700	5 800
Excess cash/(Borrowings)		900		–900
Net equity		**4 000**		**4 900**
Market capitalisation		**5 700**		**5 700**
Shares in issue (m)		100		116
Price per share (R)		57		46
EPS (cents)		471		603

SELF-ASSESSMENT

Test your understanding of the principles in the three options above by following the calculations through and providing reasons for the outcomes.

Linking the structure of the deal to the overall deal objective

Perhaps the most important planning consideration when deciding whether to issue shares or pay cash for an acquisition is considering how the funding mechanism will contribute to the likelihood of success of the deal.

Research by Bouwman et al. (2003) indicates that deals that are funded from cash are more successful than deals that are funded by the issue of shares. There is something about using existing cash resources that focuses management's attention more than issuing shares. The temptation to use shares to fund deals of dubious value will be stronger when the stock markets are in a bull phase (a period of over-optimism).

But while the use of cash for funding is associated with the success of the deal, it is also important to consider the impact of the method of payment on the sellers. Settling the purchase price in cash may be appropriate when the sellers are not required for the ongoing running of the business and are likely to exit immediately. More often, though, a handover period is required, in which case it is better to settle at least part of the purchase price in shares, with a stipulation that they may only be sold after a period of time, such as three years. The objective is to align the interests of the sellers and the acquirer during this handover period.

Another consideration to be taken into account in determining whether to settle using cash or shares is how likely it is that the synergies priced into the transaction will be realised in reality. If acquirer management is confident that the synergies will become a reality, then it will want to retain that value for their shareholders by paying cash for the deal. Where there is uncertainty about the synergies being achieved, issuing shares will divide the risk proportionately between the acquirer and the sellers receiving shares as part of their total consideration.

At what price should shares be issued?

Finally, if shares are issued, at what price should they be issued? Options are to:

- issue a fixed number of shares; or
- issue a fixed value of shares.

If a fixed number of shares is issued, the acquirer is able to calculate with precision how much the company's existing shareholders are going to be diluted. But the sellers take a risk on what happens to the acquirer's share price between the time of negotiation and the time of the deal being finalised. For example, in a R1 billion deal the sellers might agree to accept 100 million shares in the acquirer, currently trading at R10 per share. However, if the market doesn't like the deal and the acquirer's share price reduces to R9,50, then the sellers will have disposed of their business for R950 million, not R1 billion.

CASE STUDY Facebook's acquisition of Whatsapp

Facebook acquired WhatsApp in the first half of 2014 for a massive $19 billion, which was to be settled as follows:

- US$4 billion in cash
- US$12 billion in Facebook shares
- US$3 billion in restricted stock units.

Clearly the sellers were taking a big risk on the market's reaction to the transaction; in fact, at first Facebook's share price declined before rebounding.

By contrast, if a fixed selling price is to be settled by the issue of shares at market value on closure, the sellers have certainty on the proceeds of the sale, but the acquirer is not in control over the dilution of existing shareholders that will follow. As per the above example in which the share price dropped from R10 to R9,50, just over 105 million shares would need to be issued to settle the R1 billion purchase price, resulting in existing shareholders being diluted by an additional 5 per cent.

Share for share exchange

Where shares are to be issued by the acquirer in exchange for shares in the target, an appropriate exchange ratio needs to be calculated. This will be based on the relative value of each entity's shares.

EXAMPLE 16.2

The target has a market value of R100 million and has 100 million shares in issue. The value of each target share is thus R1.

The acquirer has a market value of R500 million and has 1 000 million shares in issue. The value of each acquirer share is thus 50 cents.

Ignoring synergies for the moment, the exchange ratio is based on the following formula:

$$ER = \frac{\text{Value per target share}}{\text{Value per acquirer share}}$$

The exchange ratio is thus R1/R0,50 = 2,0. In other words, 2 acquirer shares will need to be issued to acquire 1 target share. So, the acquirer will need to issue 200 million new shares to complete the acquisition, and existing shareholders will be diluted to owning 83 per cent (1 000/1 200) of the company.

Now let's introduce the possibility of synergies arising from the deal, estimated at R20 million. The purchase price should never be more than the target's market value plus the full value of synergies – in this case, R120 million. At a value of R120 million, the bid price for the target's shares would be R1,20 (R120 million ÷ 100 million), and the exchange ratio would become:

$$ER = \frac{R1{,}20}{R0{,}50}$$

$$= 2{,}4$$

Thus we have established a feasible negotiating range of 2,0 to 2,4. At the lower end of the range, as the acquirer we retain the full value of the synergies. At the upper end of the range, again as the acquirer, we pay the full value of the synergies to the sellers. Negotiations will often lead to an exchange ratio somewhere in the middle of the range.

Where both parties are listed, It is common for limits to be set on the movement in the exchange ratio. It will be agreed up front that if the limits are exceeded, the aggrieved party can cancel the transaction on the basis that the value exchange originally envisaged is no longer possible.

You can see that the decision to use cash or shares to fund the acquisition is a trade-off between the interests of the parties that will need to be settled by negotiation. For further insights into this important topic, read Rappaport and Sirower (1999).

SELF-ASSESSMENT

- Summarise the issues that would influence your decision to use shares or cash to settle the purchase price.
- How would being sceptical about the projected synergies being achieved influence your decision?
- If the share markets are running and your share price is continuing to climb, would you fix the number of shares to be used to settle the purchase price or would you rather fix the value of the shares to be issued?
- As the seller in the above situation, which alternative would you choose?
- In a share-for-share swap, how would you calculate the exchange ratio between the shares in the two companies?

When should you hold back a portion of the purchase price to be paid out against future performance?

It often happens that the buyer and the seller have very different ideas about the future prospects of the target company and, therefore, about price. This is particularly the case in relatively young companies, when the sellers believe the sky is the limit for their company but the buyer is more sceptical. One way of addressing this issue is to agree on an upfront payment that both parties can live with, and then make future payments subject to achieving the forecast results.

In fact, this approach is widely used by serial acquirers such as EOH Holdings Limited. In one example known to the writer, one-third of the purchase price was paid to the seller in EOH shares upfront, with two tranches of EOH shares to follow at yearly intervals thereafter, subject to profit targets being met. The price at which the future tranches of shares would be issued was determined upfront, based on a growth percentage on the EOH share price at the time. Given that EOH's share price has risen rapidly, the seller stands to gain more than his notional selling price should he meet his targets and should the EOH price rise at a faster rate than the growth rates applied when setting the future issue price of the remaining tranches. But, of course, the reverse also applies should the EOH share price decline! The seller in this case is happy to bet on EOH's share prices continuing to rise rapidly, while EOH management is happy that in this way it will only pay for value that has already been earned. From their perspective, this form of structuring represents a risk mitigation strategy.

While useful, this approach has pros and cons. Pros include a reduced risk of overpaying, while cons include the following:

- It limits the ability of the newly acquired business to be integrated into its new parent. In order to measure the achievement of the targets set by the acquired business, it has to be left substantially intact over the earn-out period. This may not be the most efficient way to run the business.
- Management may adopt-short term thinking in the earn-out period, rather than making strategic moves that may jeopardise their ability to meet the earn-out targets.
- The arrangement may set up conflicts of interest between the acquirer and sellers.

This is an area of creativity in deal-making. Sometimes provision is made for an additional payment if the targets are exceeded, and it is reasonably common to allow a shortfall in the first year's target to be met in the second year. The nature of the final arrangement will depend on the objectives of the parties, after they have been thrashed out in the course of the negotiating process. For practical purposes, earn-outs don't usually last for longer than two years.

SELF-ASSESSMENT

What are the pros and cons of using earn-outs as a protection mechanism in a deal?

A practical example of deal structuring

This example is based on a real example that dates back a few years but is still very relevant. For convenience we'll refer to the parties as Acquirer and Target, even though the information was public at the time.

Background

Both the Acquirer and the Target were in the IT industry. The Target was a young entrepreneurial company that was forecast to grow very fast, having already turned the corner in terms of making a profit. The Acquirer was prepared to pay for the anticipated growth, but wanted to protect itself should the growth not materialise.

The offer structure

The offer incorporated the following features:

- The value of the transaction was set at R80,7 million.
- An amount of R45,7 million was due to be paid on fulfilment of the conditions precedent, as follows:
  - A cash payment of R4,0 million, which was to be raised through the issue of 96 386 shares to be placed on behalf of the vendors with institutions at an issue price of 4 150 cents per share; and
  - A further payment of R41,7 million, which was to be settled through the issue of 1 089 806 shares to the vendors at an average issue price of 3 826 cents per share.
- A further R15,0 million was to be settled through the issue of 405 405 shares at an issue price of 3 700 cents per share if the audited profit before tax (PBT) was not less than R7,5 million for the 12-month period from 1 April xx08 to 31 March xx09. In the event that the audited PBT was less than R7,5 million, the 405 405 shares would be adjusted appropriately downwards.
- The balance of the purchase price of R20,0 million was to be settled, at the election of the acquirer, either in cash or through the issue of shares at the weighted average market price over 30 trading days prior to settlement, provided the PBT was not less than R11,5 million for the 12-month period from 1 April xx09 to 31 March xx10. In the event that the PBT was less than R11,5 million, the amount to be paid was to be adjusted appropriately downwards.

The purchase consideration was subject to an appropriate adjustment upwards by an amount limited to a maximum of R15,0 million. The adjustment was to be determined based on the audited PBT achieved by the Target in excess of the warranted profits for the years ending 31 March xx09 and xx10.

Commentary on the offer structure

- A firm price was established at the outset, namely R80,7 million, to which a potential performance bonus of R15 million could be added.
- Profit performance hurdles were set, which, if not met, would result in the purchase price being adjusted downwards. The announcement did not specify how this would be done, but the price would generally be adjusted by a multiple of the shortfall.
- The offer included a sweetener for performance beyond the earn-out hurdles, as an additional incentive.
- The initial payment included a small cash amount, with the balance in the Acquirer's shares.
- The cash element was to be raised by private placement of shares.

- Restrictions would usually be placed on the vendors' ability to trade in the consideration shares during the earn-out period.
- The price at which the shares for the first earn-out payment would be issued was fixed in terms of the offer. The implication is that the vendors were taking a risk on any downward price movements in the Acquirer's shares until payment was effected. As it happens, the vendors achieved a significant benefit from this structure, for two reasons:
  - The Acquirer's share price had historically traded well above the R37 at which the shares would be issued; and
  - IT shares were running hard at the time, and the Acquirer's share price had risen by the time the first tranche of shares was issued.
- The shares for the final tranche would be issued at market value.

This approach had the advantage of allowing the vendors to capitalise on the growth they had helped to create. The Acquirer's objective had been to ensure that the vendors remained motivated throughout the earn-out period, by which time – hopefully – they would continue to contribute to the group's broader growth objectives.

SELF-ASSESSMENT

- Do you think the acquirer protected itself appropriately in the above situation, or was it too generous?
- As a vendor, how do you think your behaviour would have been influenced by the above deal structure?

Conclusion

Giving careful consideration to the structure of a deal as a means of capturing the maximum amount of value from the transaction is as important as establishing an appropriate value for the transaction. Application of insightful valuation techniques will mean nothing if value is leaked through a weak structure. In this chapter, we have examined various techniques that can be employed when structuring a deal.

References

Bouwman, C.H.S, Fuller, K. & Nash, A.S. (2003). Stock market valuations and mergers. *MIT Sloan Management Review*, Fall 2003.

Rappaport, A. & Sirower, M.L. (1999). Stock (Shares) or Cash – Trade-offs for Buyers and Sellers in Mergers & Acquisitions. *Harvard Business Review*, November–December 1999.

CHAPTER 17

Learning the rules of the game: Regulatory requirements that govern M&A transactions

LEARNING OUTCOMES

Once you have worked through this chapter you should be able to:

+ Have a broad understanding of the regulatory requirements that govern M&A transactions
+ Understand where valuation techniques need to be applied to satisfy the regulations
+ Understand some of the jargon associated with M&A
+ Appreciate that this is an area in which you will be dependent on experts for guidance
+ Understand where such experts can be found

Introduction

A complex web of regulations controls mergers and acquisitions. The purpose of these regulations is to ensure fair play amongst shareholders, consumers and other stakeholders who might be impacted by a potential M&A transaction.

This chapter will not make you an expert on these regulations. Rather, the intention is to provide you with a broad overview so that you know when to call for help and from whom.

Our understanding of the regulations that apply to M&A transactions in South Africa is made a great deal easier by studying the diagram on the next page devised by Professor Johan Brink, Extraordinary Professor of Mercantile Law at Unisa and partner at law firm Webber Wentzel.

Figure 17.1 shows that the process starts with a structuring phase during which management:

+ defines its growth strategy and the part that M&A will play in it;
+ defines the sort of targets it is aiming for to fuel this growth; and
+ identifies potential targets and makes preliminary contact with them.

Should one of the targets show interest in taking the idea of doing a deal further, then further practical steps include:

+ valuing the target business and formulating a bidding range (Part 1 of this book);
+ conducting due diligence to be forewarned about the risks involved in going ahead (Chapter 15);
+ structuring the transaction in a way that limits the risks identified (Chapter 16);
+ planning how the deal will be financed (Chapter 16); and
+ assessing the tax implications for all parties to the deal (Chapter 16).

Mechanisms for implementing a transaction, such as a scheme of arrangement or a general offer to shareholders, are provided by the Companies Act. The mechanism to be adopted is selected during the offer phase depicted in Figure 17.1. We will look at these mechanisms in greater detail later in this chapter.

FIGURE 17.1 South African regulatory framework for mergers and acquisitions

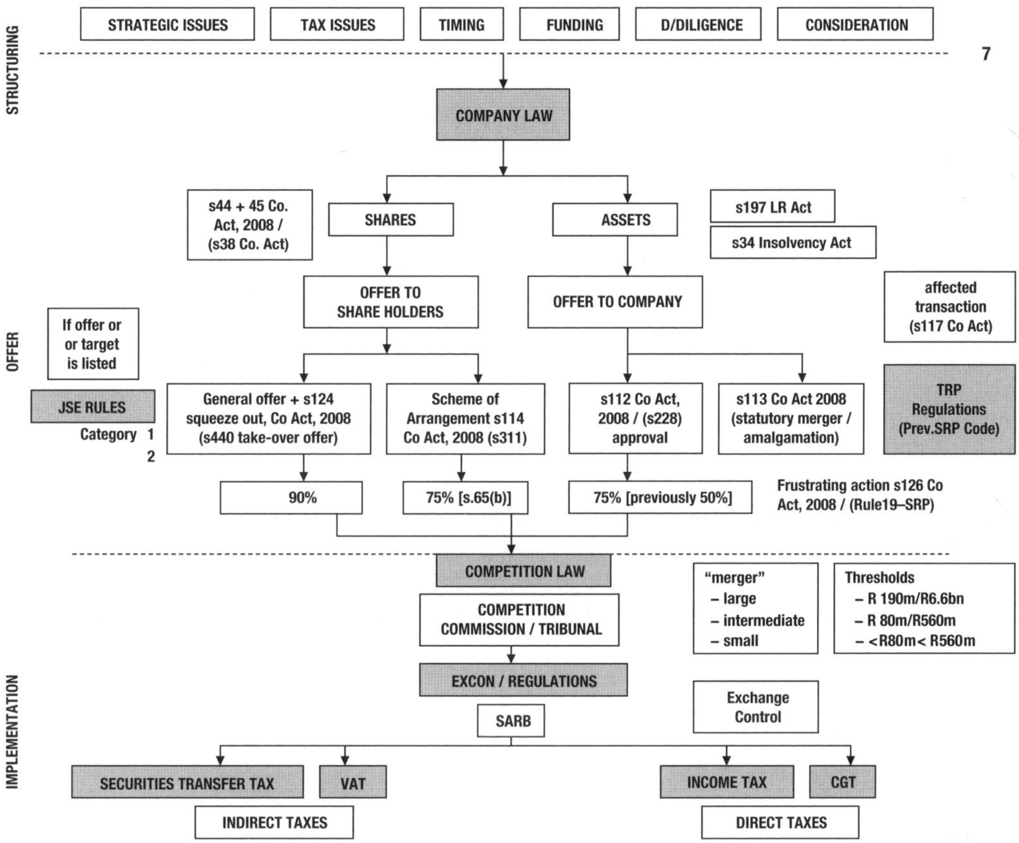

Source: Professor Johan Brink, partner, Webber Wentzel

The Companies Act is also concerned that minority shareholders are treated fairly in the course of a transaction. The Takeover Regulation Panel (TRP) is a watchdog body established in terms of the Act that governs behaviour during the course of transactions that fall within its sphere of control. We will look at the functions of the TRP in greater detail later in this chapter.

In M&A situations, the JSE is concerned with ensuring that appropriate protective steps are in place when related parties are involved. We will also look at the JSE's requirements in greater detail in a later section.

All of the above will help to ensure that agreement is reached between the parties in an acceptable and fair manner. Part of the oversight exercised by the TRP and the JSE is in the form of fairness opinions compiled by suitably qualified, independent experts, which you will learn more about in Chapter 18.

The last approval hurdle is to satisfy the Competition authorities that the deal does not create a distortion in the market to the detriment of consumers.

The key elements of the relevant statutes for M&A transactions in the South African environment, then, are as follows:

- Companies Act - Mechanisms available to effect takeovers
- Companies Act - Protections provided by the Takeover Regulation Panel
- JSE rules affecting takeovers
- Fairness opinions required by the JSE and the TRP (Chapter 18)
- Competition law in relation to takeovers.

The Companies Act: Mechanisms available to effect takeovers

As noted earlier, the Companies Act provides mechanisms by which the buyer can either buy the shares of the target company (amalgamations and mergers) or the assets of the company.

Buying shares or assets is an important decision you will need to make. Tax considerations may drive the seller to push for one or other method (the tax implications of the methods were discussed in Chapter 16 under structuring considerations). One of the key reasons why buyers might prefer to buy assets out of the target company is to avoid taking on any of the selling company's unrecognised liabilities or its liabilities that are difficult to quantify. Examples of such liabilities include outstanding tax issues with the South African Revenue Service and product warranties on current or discontinued products.

In the sections that follow, we expand on the two mechanisms provided by the Companies Act to facilitate the purchase of shares in the target company, namely a scheme of arrangement and a general offer to shareholders. We also look at the process outlined in section 112 of the Companies Act that needs to be followed before the assets can be bought directly out of the target company.

Option 1: Buying the shares of the target company using a section 114 scheme of arrangement

If the directors of the target company support the proposed transaction, they can propose to shareholders that it be implemented by way of a scheme of arrangement (if the directors do not support the deal, a would-be buyer could still approach shareholders directly - a process known as **going hostile** - but this is a more difficult route with a relatively low likelihood of success). In terms of the scheme, the target's shareholders will be asked to exchange their shareholdings in the target company for shareholdings in the acquiring company and/or cash (where cash is offered as part of the purchase price). While schemes can be used to effect other types of transactions, these are not discussed in this section as they are not relevant to M&A transactions.

In accordance with section 114 (2), the board of directors of the target company supporting the proposed scheme must appoint an independent expert to report to the board on the value of the scheme and its effect on the rights and interests of the holders of the affected classes of securities. In due course, this information must be made available to the target company's shareholders. The independent expert's opinion is known as a fairness opinion, discussed in Chapter 18.

The scheme has to be approved by 75 per cent of the shareholders in attendance at the scheme meeting, either in person or by proxy, subject to a quorum being present (currently 25 per cent of shareholders entitled to vote - certain shareholders may be unable to vote as a result of a conflict of interest).

Unlike schemes carried out under section 311 of the previous Companies Act (No. 61 of 1973), current legislation does not require schemes to be approved by the Court unless 15 per cent of the votes cast were cast against the resolution, even though the resolution was, in fact, passed. If that is the case then one of the shareholders who voted against the resolution may, within five business days, require the company to seek the Court's approval.

In a review process, a Court may only set the resolution aside if:

- it is manifestly unfair to any class of holder, or
- voting was materially compromised because of conflict of interest, inadequate disclosure and failure to comply with the Act or memorandum of incorporation or other procedural irregularity.

In summary, the legislation protects the target's minority shareholders in an M&A transaction by requiring:

- 75 per cent of the shareholders eligible to vote to approve the deal;
- a quorum of shareholders to be present;
- an independent expert to evaluate the fairness and reasonableness of the proposed transaction; and
- a review of the transaction by the Court prompted by aggrieved shareholders under specified circumstances.

CASE STUDY **Bidvest**

When a Bidvest-led consortium acquired 34,5 per cent of Adcock Ingram in the first half of 2014, it did so by way of a scheme of arrangement, despite initial resistance from the Adcock Ingram directors. This has become the most popular way of structuring M&A transactions as a result of the lower approval ratio (75 per cent vs 90 per cent) and the tighter timeline in comparison with general offers to shareholders.

Option 2: Buying the shares of a target company using a general offer to shareholders in terms of section 124

The buyer can also choose to make a **general offer to the shareholders** of the target company to buy all or part of their shares. If the intention is to buy 100 per cent of the shares, then the offer will be worded accordingly.

Section 124 of the Companies Act provides a mechanism for forcing out minority shareholders who have not accepted the offer (perhaps because they could not be traced). In terms of section 124, the buyer can give notice to **expropriate** the shares of those shareholders who have not accepted the offer, provided that 90 per cent of a class of shareholders accept the offer within four months of the offer being made. Minority shareholders who are aggrieved by this process may apply to court within 30 business days of this notice for an order to prevent the expropriation going ahead.

Monies due to untraced shareholders must be paid into the Guardian's Fund (a fund that falls under the jurisdiction of the Master of the High Court and which is used to house monies that cannot be paid out immediately and which may belong to unidentified persons).

As mentioned earlier, the lower approval level of a scheme compared with a general offer (75 per cent approval versus 90 per cent approval) has made a scheme the most popular way of structuring M&A transactions. The general offer is best left to situations in which management is confident that all or most of the offerees will accept the offer.

CASE STUDY Growthpoint

When Growthpoint Properties acquired 100 per cent of the shares in Paramount Property Fund in 2006, it did so by way of a general offer. This is in contrast to the Metboard transaction that Growthpoint implemented by way of a scheme at about the same time. The implication is that Growthpoint management was more confident that it could gain broad acceptance of the Paramount offer than it was in the Metboard offer.

Option 3: Buying assets of the target company

If the buyer would like to buy the target company's assets, then the target company (i.e. the seller) must be authorised to sell its assets, which requires a special resolution of shareholders in accordance with section 115. A special resolution requires approval by at least 75 per cent of the shareholders of the selling company. The company's assets must be disposed of at **fair value**, as per section 112 (4).

Such a transaction forms part of the definition of a **fundamental transaction** that falls under the aegis of the TRP. Section 115 (2) stipulates that approval of fundamental transactions requires a quorum of 25 per cent of all of the voting rights that are entitled to be exercised on the matter. Those shareholders who are aggrieved during this process and who voted against the resolution can use the protection processes afforded them by section 115 of the Act, provided that at least 15 per cent of the votes cast on the day were against the resolution.

DID YOU KNOW?

In looking for help in this area, consider consulting:

- international investment banks, such as Goldman Sachs and Deutsche Bank;
- local investment banks, such as the investment banking arms of the Big Five commercial banks;
- departments within legal firms dealing with corporate transactions;
- the Corporate Finance sections of accounting firms; and
- boutique corporate finance firms.

Often the size and complexity of the transaction will determine the appropriate expert to use. Fees for using international investment banks are high; therefore, it is likely that it will only be economical to consult them on very large transactions, or those with a significant international leg.

SELF-ASSESSMENT

- What do you understand by the terms 'scheme of arrangement' and 'general offer to shareholders'?
- What factors would you take into consideration in deciding whether to pursue a transaction via a scheme or via a general offer to shareholders?
- As a buyer, why would you prefer to buy the business out of a company rather than the company itself?
- Which of the three implementation options discussed so far are most likely to be used in a hostile takeover?

The Companies Act: Protections provided by the Takeover Regulation Panel

The Takeover Regulation Panel (TRP) derives its authority from sections 117 to 120 of the Companies Act. Under the previous act, this panel was known as the Securities Regulation Panel.

The TRP is there to control the behaviour of management and shareholders in relation to **affected transactions**. Affected transactions are defined in section 117 and include schemes of arrangement, general offers and asset buyouts. The TRP's overall objective is to create a situation of fair play between majority and minority shareholders. While the TRP's broad mandate is contained in the Companies Act itself, the panel's specific practices are set out in the Companies Regulations that accompany the Companies Act.

One of the TRP's key duties is to set the threshold for triggering a compulsory offer to shareholders. The threshold is currently set at 35 per cent of the target company's shares. The threshold has remained unchanged for a number of years and is similar to the threshold in other countries, such as Australia. What this means is that once a buyer acquires an interest of more than 35 per cent in a company, a **compulsory offer** to all the remaining shareholders on the same terms and conditions as the best offer made over the last three months will be triggered. This is why you will often see announcements to the effect that buyer A has bought 34,9 per cent of the shares in Company B. Falling short of the 35 per cent threshold allows the buyer to have considerable influence over the affairs of the target company without triggering a compulsory offer to shareholders.

Other issues addressed in the Companies Act and Companies Regulations with respect to M&A transactions and the TRP's sphere of control include the following:

- The Companies Act, together with the Regulations, contains rules for the treatment of **concert parties**, namely parties that can be assumed to be working together in a particular M&A situation.
- The **offer period** is the period between the first cautionary announcement being published and the closing date for acceptance of the offer. The directors of the offeree company (the target company) may not take any **frustrating actions** to block the deal during the offer period. Frustrating actions are defined in section 126 of the Act and include:
  - taking actions that could result in a bona fide offer being frustrated
  - issuing new securities (shares)
  - issuing options in respect of unissued shares
  - selling material assets other than in the ordinary course of business
  - entering into contracts other than in the ordinary course of business
  - making a distribution that is abnormal as to timing and amount (such as a massive dividend to denude the company of cash).

The TRP requires the offeree company's board of directors to appoint an independent expert to provide a fair and reasonable opinion on the value and price of the offer.

The TRP regulations apply to all public companies and to private companies in which more than 10 per cent of securities have been transferred between non-related or inter-related persons within 24 months prior to the offer being made.

The details of affected transactions must be set out in circulars to the shareholders of the offeror and offeree. The TRP must be notified about affected transactions.

DID YOU KNOW?

The experts to consult in this area would be the same as for Options 1 to 3 discussed earlier in this chapter. The chief requirement of an appropriate advisor is a keen understanding of procedural issues affecting M&A transactions. Where necessary, advisors will obtain rulings from the TRP before going down a particular line of transaction implementation. This can save time and effort.

SELF-ASSESSMENT

- What is an affected transaction?
- What are the implications of buying 36,5 per cent of the shares in a listed company?
- How do you think the takeover threshold would be applied in relation to concert parties?
- Are the directors of a company that has received a takeover offer entitled to do anything they like to repulse the suitor?

JSE rules affecting takeovers

The JSE's concern in relation to M&A transactions is to promote the necessary flow of information to create and maintain an orderly market that is fair to all shareholders, in particular where one of the parties to a transaction is a **related party**, implying a potential conflict of interest. The JSE is concerned with **price-sensitive information**, which it defines as unpublished information that would be likely to have an effect on the price of a listed company's securities if it were made public.

Price-sensitive information could, therefore, include information about a deal that is being contemplated by a listed company. As soon as it appears that the market has started to react to knowledge (real or suspected) of the deal and confidentiality becomes hard to maintain, the directors of each listed company involved in the transaction must publish a **cautionary announcement** disclosing that they are in talks that could affect the company's share price. This announcement needs to be refreshed every six weeks for as long as negotiations continue, until a deal is announced or negotiations are terminated.

Once heads of agreement have been signed, a detailed cautionary announcement must be published, disclosing the main terms of the proposed transaction. The JSE regulates the need for further communication with shareholders by categorising the M&A transactions in terms of the following two percentage ratios:

- The **market cap percentage** – the value of the purchase consideration against the listed holding company's equity market capitalisation (excluding treasury shares and shares in a share incentive trust); and
- The **dilution percentage** – the number of shares issued for the purchase consideration versus the number of listed equity securities prior to the transaction (again excluding treasury shares and shares in a share incentive trust).

M&A transactions are categorised by the JSE as follows:

- Category 1 – either percentage ratio is equal to or greater than 25 per cent
- Category 2 – either ratio is equal to or greater than 5 per cent, but less than 25 per cent.

The JSE stipulates certain communication protocols for each category of M&A transactions.

For Category 1 transactions, the larger transactions, management is required to make an announcement in the press as soon as possible after the parties agree on terms (a terms announcement). Management is required to include the following details in the terms announcement:

- The subject of the transaction (e.g. assets, shares and so on)
- The vendors or purchasers
- Conditions precedent
- Other significant terms agreed upon
- Description of the target's business
- The consideration and terms of settlement
- Effect of the transaction on the entity's net asset value per share and net tangible asset value per share, if the effect is significant (i.e. greater than 3 per cent)
- Effect of the transaction on the entity's earnings per share and headline earnings per share if the effect is significant (i.e. greater than 3 per cent)
- The rationale for the transaction.

For Category 1 transactions, management of a listed acquiring company is also required to send to each shareholder a circular that includes the notice of the general meeting to be held to approve the transaction. Approval for the transaction is required by way of special resolution, which requires 75 per cent of shareholders present and voting to vote in favour of the resolution. The requirement for shareholder approval is a check and balance on management's actions.

For Category 2 transactions, management is only required to make a terms announcement. Approval by shareholders is not required.

DID YOU KNOW?

Communication with the JSE must be conducted through the listed company's Sponsors, if the company is listed on the main board, or its Designated Advisor (DA) if it is an AltX company. Sponsors and DAs are staffed by Approved Executives, employees who have gone through the training on the JSE's Listing Requirements and who have qualifying experience. A company may appoint a sponsor to carry out its day-to-day work – dividend and results announcements, for example – but may also appoint a different sponsor to deal with its M&A transactions.

South Africa has something in excess of 25 sponsor and DA firms.

For more information about fairness options required by the JSE and TRP, see Chapter 18.

Competition law

Management needs to take competition law into account when thinking about and structuring an M&A deal. What follows is a broad overview of South Africa's competition law, starting with the legislation's objectives, powers and thresholds and concluding with a summary of the timelines associated with investigations of M&A activity that are carried out in terms of this legislation.

Objectives, powers and thresholds

The Competition Act No. 89 of 1998 as amended (the Competition Act) was promulgated to:

> *promote the efficiency, adaptability and development of the economy;*
> *provide consumers with competitive prices and product choices;*

promote employment and advance the social and economic welfare of South Africans; expand opportunities for South African participation in world markets and recognise the role of foreign competition in the Republic; and
ensure that small and medium-sized enterprises have an equitable opportunity to participate in the economy, and promote a greater spread of ownership, in particular to increase the ownership stakes of historically disadvantaged persons.

Source: http://www.compcom.co.za/who-are-we/

The powers set out in the Competition Act are exercised through two bodies, namely the **Competition Commission** and the **Competition Tribunal**. The Competition Commission exercises its powers in respect of M&A transactions by investigating and evaluating transactions above a specified size. Table 17.1 sets out these thresholds.

TABLE 17.1 Thresholds for investigation of M&A transactions

Merger thresholds as at 1 April 2009 (still in force)		
Thresholds	**Combined turnover/asset value**	**Target turnover/asset value**
Lower threshold	R560 million	R80 million
Higher threshold	R6 600 million	R190 million

Source: DTI (2013a)

Management of the acquiring company is required to notify the Competition Commission of an **intermediate merger or acquisition** if the value of the proposed merger equals or exceeds R560 million (calculated by combining the annual turnover of both entities **or** the values of their assets, whichever is the greater), and either the target entity's annual turnover **or** asset value is at least R80 million.

If the combined annual turnover/asset value calculation is equal to or above R6.6 billion, and the target entity's annual turnover or asset value is at least R190 million, the acquiring company's management must notify the Competition Commission that it has effected a **large merger or acquisition**.

The Commission has the power to rule on intermediate mergers. It makes recommendations on large mergers to the Competition Tribunal, which is not obliged to follow the Commission's advice. Possible rulings include:
+ Do not allow the transaction to proceed;
+ Allow the transaction to proceed; or
+ Allow the transaction to proceed, but with conditions.

The last option has become popular, with conditions often including a ban on merger-related retrenchments for a specified period, such as a year.

Timing

While the legislation sets a reasonably tight deadline for the Competition Commission to complete its work on small and intermediate mergers, large mergers are likely to have wider economic implications and the Commission is allowed to apply for extensions to allow it to complete its work. The timeline for large transactions will generally be much longer than for small and intermediate deals. Table 17.2 shows the timelines of these investigations.

TABLE 17.2 Timeline for investigation of M&A transactions by the Competition Commission

Period of investigation			
Category of merger	**Initial period**	**Extended period**	**Refer to Competition Act**
Small or intermediate	20 business days	Once only for 40 business days. The Commission has sole discretion to extend the period of investigation.	Section 13 (5)(a) or section 14 (1)(a)
Large	40 business days	One or more extensions of a maximum of 15 business days. The Commission requires the merging parties and the Tribunal's consent to extend the investigation.	Refer to section 14 (1)(b), 13 (5)(a), 14 (1)(a) of the Competition Act and Rule 34 (2)(a) of the Commission's Rules.

Source: DTI (2013b)

DID YOU KNOW?

Competition advice seems to be the domain of the large legal firms, although it is possible that the larger accounting firms also offer this advice. Where necessary the legal firms will appoint economists or other relevant experts to investigate conditions in the market in which the transaction is going to take place. A written submission is required to be given to the Competition Commission in support of the transaction. Two words of warning:

- Start planning the submission sooner rather than later, to avoid unnecessary delays in the transaction process.
- Put an appropriate level of effort into the submission. Your objective is to get the transaction approved in the minimum time; the effort will be worth it.

SELF-ASSESSMENT

Categorise the following transactions in terms of the Competition threshold criteria:

- Large company buys small company

Rm	Turnover	Assets
Acquirer	1 000	250
Target	70	40
Combined	**1 070**	**290**

- As above, but with higher target company turnover

Rm	Turnover	Assets
Acquirer	1 000	250
Target	85	40
Combined	**1 085**	**290**

Continued

+ Merger of equals

Rm	Turnover	Assets
Acquirer	3 500	1 000
Target	3 100	1 000
Combined	**6 600**	**2 000**

Other issues to be addressed

Section 197 of the Labour Relations Act No. 66 of 1995 determines that when a business is acquired, the staff are taken over by the acquirer with all their existing benefits of employment intact. Benefits include pension provisions, accumulated leave, perks, etc. Where remuneration systems differ widely between the acquirer and the target - which would often be the case - the value of the salary packages of the acquired employees will need to be assessed, and that value will need to be recreated in terms of the acquirer's remuneration system. This is a complex process that is usually handled by Human Resources experts.

When a business is sold out of a company, Section 34 of the Insolvency Act No. 24 of 1936 requires a notice to be published in two national newspapers alerting the selling company's creditors to the sale to make sure they are not prejudiced as a result.

Conclusion

It should be apparent from this section on South Africa's regulatory framework that M&A transactions take place within a complex set of rules. Falling foul of a rule can cause costly delays in the process; therefore, very careful planning is required to make sure that the proposed transaction complies with the relevant legislation and rules in all respects. Obtaining expert advice is essential.

References

Competition Commission. (n.d.). Who we are. Available at http://www.compcom.co.za/who-are-we/. [Accessed 22 June 2015].

DTI. (2013a). 4. When must the Competition Commission be notified of a Merger? The Competition Commission. Available at http://compcom.co.za.www15.cpt4.host-h.net/file-a-merger/.

DTI. (2013b). 13. How long does it take to process a merger? The Competition Commission. Available at http://compcom.co.za.www15.cpt4.host-h.net/file-a-merger/.

CHAPTER 18

Fairness opinions required by the JSE and the TRP

LEARNING OBJECTIVES

Once you have worked through this chapter, you should be able to:

+ Distinguish between the concepts of fairness and reasonableness
+ List the circumstances under which fairness opinions are required by the JSE and the TRP
+ Describe the differing requirements of each body in relation to fairness opinions
+ Understand the procedures to be followed when preparing and disseminating such opinions
+ Integrate valuations theory into the preparation of these opinions

Introduction

Fairness opinions are a protection mechanism for shareholders called for by the JSE in relation to listed entities and by the Takeover Regulation Panel (TRP) in relation to Affected Transactions (mergers, schemes of arrangement, offers and so on). Both bodies require suitably qualified and independent experts to prepare their own estimates of the value of the transactions taking place, but there are fundamental differences between the requirements of the two bodies. The JSE only requires that the expert opine on the fairness of a transaction (although it would allow the expert to opine on the reasonableness, provided detailed disclosure is made in this regard), whereas the TRP looks for assurance that the transaction is both fair **and** reasonable in relation to the minority shareholders.

These terms require definition:

+ Fairness is a quantitative evaluation – if the value of the consideration received is equal to or greater than the value given up, the transaction is considered to be fair.
+ Reasonableness is a qualitative evaluation – when all the circumstances surrounding the transaction are taken into account, it may be reasonable for the shareholders to proceed with the transaction, even though the transaction may not be fair on a quantitative basis.

In forming the above opinions, experts can arrive at the following conclusions in relation to the proposed transactions:

+ Fair and reasonable;
+ Fair, but not reasonable;
+ Reasonable, but not fair; or
+ Not fair and not reasonable.

In the following paragraphs we will examine the requirements of the two regulatory bodies.

The JSE's requirements in relation to fairness opinions

JSE-listed entities are regulated through the provisions of the JSE Limited Listings Requirements (LRs). Integral functions of the JSE are:

- to provide the exchange's users with an orderly market for trading;
- to ensure that full, equal and timeous public disclosure of price-sensitive information is made; and
- to ensure that all holders of the same class of securities are accorded fair and equal treatment in respect of their securities.

When is a fairness opinion required?

In terms of the LRs, a fairness opinion would be required when the following are being contemplated:

- **A voluntary delisting** from the JSE (paragraph 1.14(d) of the LRs);
- **Transactions involving a related party:**
  - **Specific issues of shares for cash**, where a related party is involved and the discount to 30-day VWAP is greater than 10 per cent (paragraph 5.51(f) of the LRs);
  - **Specific issues of options and convertible securities granted/issued for cash**, where a related party is involved (paragraph 5.53(b)(i) of the LRs);
  - **Specific repurchase of shares** where a related party is involved and where the repurchase is at a premium to the 30-day VWAP of more than 10 per cent (paragraph 5.69(e) of the LRs); and
  - **Transactions** (principally acquisitions and disposals) with related parties (paragraph 10.4(f) of the LRs).
- A **general issue of options and convertible securities granted/issued for cash** when the strike or conversion price of the options/convertible securities are at a discount that exceeds the maximum discount contemplated of 10 per cent (paragraph 5.53(b)(ii) of the LRs); and
- When **determining the size of a transaction** in relation to the listed entity's market capitalisation for transaction categorisation purposes (Category 1 or Category 2), if the JSE is of the opinion that such an opinion is called for (LR 9.7).

Fairness opinions are not required in the following circumstances:

- For **property transactions**, where property valuations have been prepared by a suitably qualified and independent property valuer; and
- For **mining transactions**, where a Competent Person's report has been produced by a suitably qualified and independent mining expert.

The JSE retains its right to ask for a fairness opinion under circumstances other than those set out above.

Related parties

You can see from the requirements that the primary concern is to make sure that transactions are priced on an arm's-length basis. A related party is defined as follows in section 10.1(b) of the Listings Requirements:

> *'related party' means:*
>
> *i. a material shareholder;*
>
> *ii. any person that is, or within the 12 months preceding the date of the transaction was, a director of the issuer or its holding company. For the purpose of this definition, a director includes a person that is, or within the 12 months preceding the date of the transaction was, not a director, but in accordance with whose directions or instructions the directors are or were accustomed to act;*
>
> *iii. any adviser to the issuer that has, or within the 12 months preceding the date of the transaction had, a beneficial interest, whether direct or indirect, in the listed company or any of its associates;*
>
> *iv. any person that is, or within the 12 months preceding the date of the transaction was, a principal executive officer of the issuer, by whatever position he may be, or may have been, designated and whether or not he is, or was, a director;*
>
> *v. the asset manager or management company of a property entity, including anyone whose assets they manage or administer.*
>
> *vi. the controlling shareholder of the persons in paragraph 10.1(b)(v);*
>
> *vii. an associate of the persons in paragraph 10.1(b)(i) to (vi) above.*

Notwithstanding the above definitions, the JSE may, in its sole discretion, determine that a transaction is a related party transaction if extraordinary conditions exist.

Governance procedures

Fairness opinions must be prepared in accordance with the requirements of Schedule 5 of the LRs (Schedule). In terms of paragraph 5.1 of the Schedule:

> *A fairness opinion must:*
>
> *a. be prepared by an independent professional expert, acceptable to the JSE, who has no material interest either in the transaction or in the success or failure of the transaction;*
>
> *b. make appropriate disclosure where the independent professional expert has any existing or continuing relationship with the issuer and/or any other parties involved in the transaction; and*
>
> *c. set out all of the material factors and assumptions taken into account in the preparation of the statement [...]*

All communication between the JSE and a company listed on the Main Board must be conducted via the company's Sponsor, and for a company listed on Alt-x the communication must be via the company's Designated Advisor (DA). The Sponsor/DA will submit the following forms to the JSE in relation to the independent professional expert:

- Schedule 2 Form B1 - Expert's confirmation of independence;
- Schedule 2 Form B2 - Expert's declaration of competency; and
- Schedule 2 Form B3 - Declaration by the issuer (the listed company).

Schedule 2 Form B3 attests, among other things, that:

- a particular expert has been approached and selected;
- directors with a potential conflict of interest in the selection process have not been involved;
- the expert has been or will be provided with all the necessary information on which to base his or her opinion; and
- the issuer has not negotiated a price with the expert at which he or she would be prepared to declare the transaction fair.

The JSE may pre-approve an independent professional expert for a period of up to two years, on application, provided the expert's team, their roles within the team and area of expertise or industry remain unchanged from the date of initial application. In this instance, Schedule 2 Form B1 and Schedule 2 Form B2 will not be required and the expert will be required to consider its independence in respect of each mandate and confirm its independence from the JSE, and also to confirm that its team and roles have not changed since the date of pre-approval.

Manner of preparation

In terms of paragraph 5.5 of the Schedule, the independent professional expert must perform a valuation of the issuer and/or the subject of the transaction. The manner in which the valuation is carried out is not prescribed in terms of the Schedule. In other words, the valuation will be carried out in terms of the general valuation principles debated in the first half of this book. Although not specified as a requirement, it may be wise to take into account the definition of fair value as set out in the accounting standard IFRS 13:

> *This IFRS defines fair value as the price that would be received to sell an asset or paid to transfer a liability in an orderly transaction between market participants at the measurement date. (Clause 15)*
>
> *A fair value measurement assumes that the transaction to sell the asset or transfer the liability takes place either:*
>
> > *a. in the principal market for the asset or liability; or*
> >
> > *b. in the absence of a principal market, in the most advantageous market for the asset or liability. (Clause 16)*
>
> *An entity shall measure the fair value of an asset or a liability using the assumptions that market participants would use when pricing the asset or liability, assuming that market participants act in their economic best interest. (Clause 22)*

Nature of the opinion

Where the independent professional expert comes to the conclusion that the transaction is not fair, he or she must provide his or her reasons for coming to that conclusion.

Although the JSE only requires an opinion on fairness, it will allow the expert to support reasons for suggesting that the transaction is reasonable, if not fair.

The basic elements of the content of the report are set out in paragraph 5.8 of the Schedule. It is not sufficient for the expert merely to deliver an opinion that the transaction is fair. The expert must report on his or her reasoning and the information on which the opinion is based.

Note that although the expert attests to the fact that he or she has performed a valuation, there is no requirement to disclose the value or value range arrived at.

Dissemination of the opinion

The manner in which the opinion is to be made available to shareholders depends on the size of the transaction.

For acquisitions and disposals with related-party transactions (consideration to market capitalisation is more than 5 per cent), issue of securities for cash to related parties, the repurchases of securities from related parties, etc., shareholder approval in general meeting is required. The fairness opinion is therefore included in the circular to shareholders. The circular provides shareholders with information regarding the proposed transaction and incorporates the notice convening the general meeting.

For small related-party transactions (consideration to market capitalisation is between 0,25 and 5 per cent), an announcement providing details of the transaction must be published. Confirmation must be provided in the announcement that an independent expert has been appointed, that the transaction has been declared to be fair, and that the fairness opinion will lie for inspection at the issuer's registered office for a period of 28 days from the date of announcement. Should the transaction be found not to be fair, shareholder approval in a general meeting would be required.

Recent examples of transactions requiring a fairness opinion to satisfy the JSE's requirements

Related-party transaction

Sun International announced on SENS on 2 July 2014 that it had, on 30 June 2014, reached agreement with Novomatic and Chilean Enterprises to acquire an effective 98,9 per cent of Monticello shares, as well as shareholder loans and cash. Monticello is a casino complex based outside Santiago, Chile. At the time, Novomatic was a material shareholder in a Sun International subsidiary, namely Novosun S.A.; as a result, Novomatic was deemed to be a related party to Sun International. Investec was appointed to provide the fairness opinion, which was published in Sun International's circular to shareholders. Approval of the related party transaction was required by 50 per cent of shareholders entitled to vote (Novomatic was not allowed to vote).

Small related-party transaction

One Logix Group (OLG) published on SENS on 23 April 2014 that OLG, through a wholly-owned subsidiary, OneLogix Proprietary Limited, had concluded an agreement with Robert Ian Lockett (the seller) to acquire the seller's shareholding (10 per cent) in and claims against OneLogix Projex Proprietary Limited for a purchase consideration of R7 500 000.

As this was classified as a small related-party transaction, a vote from shareholders was not required, provided an independent expert deemed the transaction to be fair to OLG shareholders. The opinion to this effect was provided by Merchantec Capital and was made available for inspection by shareholders at OLG's offices for a 28-day period.

SELF-ASSESSMENT

- What is the JSE's chief concern in calling for fairness opinions?
- Does the JSE prescribe the valuation approach to be followed?
- What governance procedures must be carried out to underpin the quality of the fairness opinion?
- How is the opinion communicated to shareholders?

The Companies Act requirements in relation to fair and reasonable opinions

The Companies Act is concerned with protection of minority shareholders. Fair and reasonable opinions are one of the mechanisms used to achieve this.

When is a fair and reasonable opinion required?

Fair and reasonable opinions are required in the following circumstances:

- When a company proposes a scheme of arrangement in terms of section 114 of the Act, sub-section (2) requires the company to appoint an independent and suitably qualified expert to compile a report that, among others:
  - states all prescribed information relevant to the value of the securities affected by the proposed arrangement
  - identifies the type and class of security holders affected by the arrangement
  - describes the material effects that the proposed arrangement will have on the above
  - evaluates any material adverse effects of the proposed arrangement
- When a company enters into a fundamental transaction defined in section 117 of the Act, such as the disposal of all or the greater part of its assets or an amalgamation or merger, the offeree-regulated company must request a ruling from the TRP in terms of regulation 90 of the Act as to whether an independent expert must be retained to report on the proposed transaction. Regulated companies are defined in section 118 and include public companies, state-owned companies in certain circumstances and private companies in certain circumstances. Note that a public company need not be listed to fall within the ambit of section 118.
- In terms of section 86 (4) of the Companies Regulations, 2011, a transaction is exempt from the obligation to make a mandatory offer if the independent holders of more than 50 per cent

of the general voting rights of all issued securities of the regulated company have agreed to waive the benefit of such mandatory offer. A waiver requires a fair and reasonable opinion to be included in the circular.

The manner of preparation

Regulation 90 of the Act sets out the framework within which the opinion must be prepared, including the following:

- The valuation must be performed in accordance with generally accepted valuation approaches used in the market from time to time, including:
  - capitalisation, income or cash flow approach in terms of the value-in-use principle
  - comparative or market approach
  - cost approach.

The relevance of these approaches was discussed in the first half of this book. The authors have expressed a preference for using a discounted cash flow approach where possible. However, the reference to value-in-use is interesting.

CRITICAL THINKING

Value-in-use means what it says – the value based on current use, rather than the use to which a market participant would put the asset. Consider the situation where a valuable piece of land in the heart of Sandton is currently being used to house a flower nursery. The value based on the current use would be significantly lower than if a market participant, such as a property developer, were to buy the property. The returns on a high-rise office block would be significantly higher than those on a nursery. In such circumstances, would an opinion based on value-in-use be fair to the selling shareholders?

The contents of the opinion

Regulation 90 (5) of the Act mandates the contents of the opinion, including the following:

- The date of the opinion
- Permission to include the opinion in communication with shareholders
- A clear expression of opinion dealing with the fairness and reasonableness of the offer consideration in regard to holders of relevant securities, excluding the offeror
- Source documentation used and work done
- The valuation approach adopted and material assumptions made
- A range of possible values and a most likely value used as the core number for purposes of the expression of the opinion
- The corroborating valuation approaches used
- The fee payable to the expert and confirmation that it is not contingency-based
- A declaration of independence and competence of the expert.

You can see that the work to be done is exactly in line with the approach recommended in the first half of this book. Note that in contrast to an opinion required for the JSE's purposes, explicit values must be disclosed in the opinion. If the range of values is too wide, the TRP will ask the expert to narrow it. There are no guidelines as to how wide the range can be, but a swing of 5 per cent above and below the most likely value is unlikely to be contested. Note, also, that the expert in this circumstance is required to express an opinion on both fairness and reasonableness, whereas the focus of a JSE opinion is on fairness.

Consideration of the offer by the independent board of the offeree

The fair and reasonable opinion is addressed to the independent board of directors appointed for the purpose of providing governance over the transaction. The independent board comprises independent directors of the company.

The independent board must, in terms of Regulation 110, express an opinion to the security holders impacted by the transaction on its fairness and reasonableness. In doing so it must deal with value and price in relation to the consideration received.

The independent board can either perform its own valuation or, as is far more common, it can take cognisance of the opinion received from the independent expert. Regulation 110 provides some interesting guidelines in relation to fairness and reasonableness:

- If the value of the offer consideration falls within the value range it can generally be considered to be fair.
- An offer in which the value of the offer consideration is above the offeree company's traded price at the time the deal was announced will generally be assumed to be reasonable.

Where the offer consideration includes offeror shares, then the offeror board must procure a fair and reasonable opinion on the value of the offeror shares.

The boards' opinions and the experts' opinions will be included in notifications to shareholders.

Recent examples of fair and reasonable opinions

One of the largest transactions to take place in the period before writing was the acquisition by Woolworths Holdings of a 100 per cent stake in Australian retailer, David Jones, in the first half of 2014. In terms of Australian takeover regulations, which are similar to South Africa's, the independent board of David Jones was required to obtain a fairness opinion from an independent expert. They did so, from specialist valuers Grant Samuels and Associates. Grant Samuels supported the transaction in an 80-page opinion circulated to shareholders. This underlines how seriously these opinions are taken in other jurisdictions.

On 22 May 2014, Telkom announced its intention via the Stock Exchange News Service (SENS) to acquire the entire issued share capital of BCX. One of the conditions precedent to the finalisation of the deal (Clause 6.1 of the announcement) was:

> *by not later than 23h59 on 22 May 2014, BDO Corporate Finance Proprietary Limited (**'Independent Expert'**), appointed by the independent board of BCX as constituted in terms of Regulation 108 of the Takeover Regulations (**'Independent Board'**), has delivered the independent expert report required in terms of section 114 of the Companies Act and the Takeover Regulations (**'Independent Expert Report'**).*

SELF-ASSESSMENT

- In what circumstances does the Companies Act specify the need for a fair and reasonable opinion?
- Does the Companies Act specify any unusual valuation approaches to be adopted?
- Does the reference to value-in-use change your opinion on the approach to be adopted?
- Note one significant difference between the reporting of the outcome of the valuation exercises undertaken for the JSE in fairness opinions and the Companies Act in fair and reasonable opinions.

Conclusion

Fairness opinions form part of the governance structure under which M&A transactions are entered into. The JSE and the Companies Act each have different requirements as to when these opinions are required and what is to be reported on. The JSE's chief concern is to ensure that transactions with related parties are reported on in a transparent manner in order to protect shareholders. The Companies Act requires confirmation by an independent expert that the proposed values of M&A transactions are fair and reasonable in relation to shareholders. The valuation approaches to be followed are not specified in anything other than general terms, and therefore the principles set out in Chapters 1 to 12 of this book will need to be followed.

References

Johannesburg Stock Exchange. *JSE Listings Requirements*, as at May 2015. Johannesburg: Lexis Nexis.

IFRS Foundation: IFRS 3, IFRS 13.

CHAPTER 19

Accounting for the transaction (IFRS 3)

LEARNING OBJECTIVES

Once you have worked through this chapter, you should be able to:

- Recognise the basic requirements of accounting standard IFRS 3 – Business Combinations
- Understand the process required to identify intangible assets acquired in the course of the transaction
- Discuss the approach to valuations required by the standard
- Understand two valuation techniques not discussed earlier in this book – the relief from royalty method and the multi-period excess earnings method (MEEM)
- Understand how accounting for intangible assets impacts the company's earnings in the long term
- Form a viewpoint about whether the effort required in terms of IFRS 3 is worthwhile

Introduction

IFRS 3 – Business Combinations – was introduced in March 2004 with the objective of:

- improving disclosure to shareholders in relation to business combinations (mergers and acquisitions); and
- aligning the approaches of the International Accounting Standards Board (IASB) and Financial Accounting Standards Board (FASB) on this topic.

The key innovation brought about by the adoption of IFRS 3 was that the difference between the purchase price in a transaction and the value of tangible assets acquired would no longer be treated as a globular figure allocated to goodwill. Rather, in terms of IFRS 3, the fair value of all identifiable assets – both tangible and intangible – has to be assessed, and their sum deducted from the purchase price in arriving at a goodwill figure or a gain on acquisition (should you have acquired a business at a bargain price). This process is referred to as purchase price accounting (PPA). The focus of this chapter is on the valuation of intangible assets rather than tangible assets.

The accounting treatment of goodwill over the years has flip-flopped between requiring goodwill to be amortised and subjecting goodwill to an impairment test on a periodic basis. By reducing the overall level of goodwill arising from acquisitions, it is hoped that anomalous impacts on the income statement will be reduced.

A word of warning

This chapter is included here as it covers the last piece of valuation work required in relation to an acquisition transaction – accounting for what we received versus the value we gave up in a transaction. But the word of warning is that unlike setting the price for the transaction, which was based on the business or economic principles espoused in this book, and unlike producing fairness opinions, where the JSE and the TRP rely on the valuation expertise of the independent experts in arriving at their opinions, this is an exercise in accounting compliance.

Despite its good intentions, IFRS 3 does not reflect the thinking process that businesspeople follow when considering a merger or an acquisition. For example, unless there is a very specific reason to do so, businesspeople would generally not perform a sum-of-the parts valuation when calculating an offer price. IFRS 3 also requires some esoteric valuations to be performed, such as valuing customer relationships, using some unusual valuation methodologies that will be demonstrated later in this chapter.

In complying with IFRS 3, you are likely to work with two sets of experts, namely:

+ valuations experts; and
+ accounting technical experts.

The purpose of this chapter is to provide you with a very high-level view of the requirements of IFRS 3 so that you are in a position to work effectively with these experts.

What does IFRS 3 require you to do?

IFRS 3 requires you to account for business combinations, which it defines as occurring when the assets acquired and the liabilities assumed constitute a business. By contrast, if individual assets were acquired, such as items of machinery on their own without any accompanying inventory or work in progress, this would be considered to be an asset purchase. As noted above, there will certainly be situations in which you will need an independent opinion as to whether the transaction can be construed as the acquisition of a business.

Once it has been decided that a business has been acquired, the following four steps need to be completed in terms of IFRS 3:

+ Identify the acquirer
+ Determine the acquisition date
+ Recognise and measure identifiable assets acquired, the liabilities assumed and any non-controlling interest in the enquiry
+ Recognise and measure goodwill or a gain from a bargain purchase.

In terms of the standard, 'for each business combination, one of the combining entities shall be identified as the acquirer.' This judgement needs to be made in conjunction with IFRS 10. In most cases, the identity of the acquirer should be fairly obvious, but in the case of exceptions, expert opinion will be required.

Again, in terms of the standard, 'the acquirer shall identify the acquisition date, which is the date on which it obtains control of the acquiree.' This would generally be the date on which the acquirer legally transfers the consideration, acquires the assets and assumes the liabilities of the acquiree; in other words, the closing date of the transaction. But, again, individual circumstances need to be examined on each transaction. For example, Competition Commission and/or other conditions precedent have to be met before the acquirer can account for the transaction.

Recognising the identifiable assets acquired, the liabilities assumed and any non-controlling interest in the acquiree

As noted previously, this requires the identification of both tangible and intangible assets acquired. The process to be followed is set out in Figure 19.1:

FIGURE 19.1 Identifying tangible and intangible assets acquired

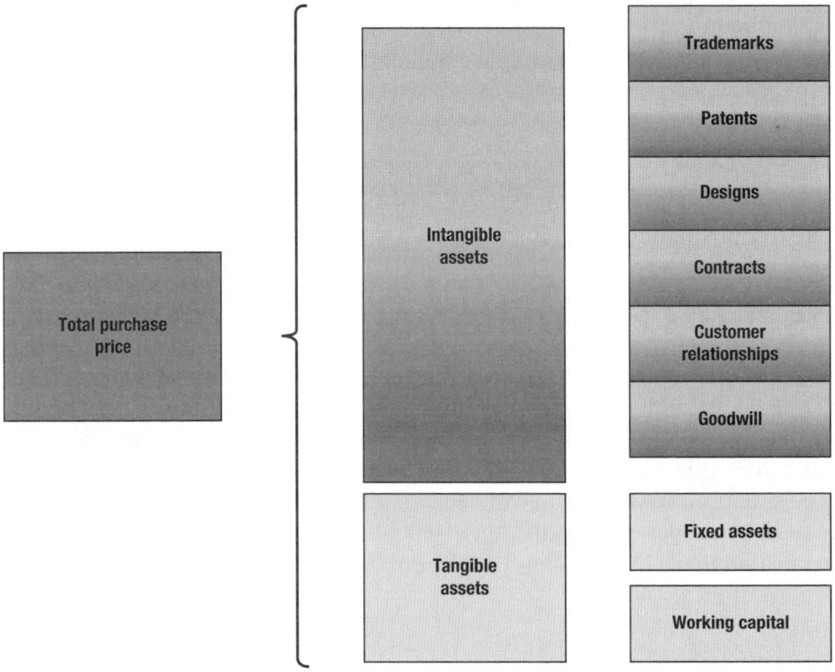

Source: Author's own construction

Identifying the intangible assets acquired will require a bit of detective work. You will need to understand management's objectives in entering into the transaction in the first place. What advantage did they want to gain from the transaction? What elements of the acquiree were likely to satisfy that objective?

For example, earlier in this book we referred to the transaction in which SABMiller gained control over Australian brewery Foster's. What do you think SABMiller's management wanted to achieve by making this acquisition? Possibilities include:

- the Foster's brand itself, which is a global beer brand that had been extremely popular but whose popularity had recently waned;
- other brands owned by the Foster's Group;
- a customer base of Australian buyers of Foster's products that could be introduced to SAB-Miller's other products;

- access to a distribution network in Australia that could help SABMiller to distribute its other products into the Australian market;
- management with knowledge of the Australian and Asian markets;
- brewing assets; and
- brewing expertise.

In order to complete an IFRS 3 exercise, you would need to consider each of these possibilities as potentially representing assets acquired by SABMiller in the course of the transaction. How would you go about doing so? You would start by examining available documentation that would reveal management's intentions and thinking, such as:
- minutes of SABMiller board meetings;
- papers presented to the board by SABMiller management to persuade the directors to support the proposed transaction;
- the sale and purchase agreement;
- newspaper coverage of the transaction, including speculation of the benefits of the deal to both parties;
- meetings with management; and
- press releases issued to the market.

The press coverage on the deal included the following quote from the late Graham Mackay, at the time SABMiller's chief executive:

> *Foster's will become an important part of our business, and through the application of our commercial capabilities and global scale, we expect to build on the initiatives that Foster's management has put in place, further enhancing Foster's performance and creating value for our shareholders.*
>
> *Source: http://dealbook.nytimes.com/2011/09/21/sabmiller-to-buy-fosters-for-10-15-billion/?_r=0*

This is a bland statement that does not really provide much insight into management's thinking. Fortunately, the journalist who wrote the article provided the following helpful paragraph:

> *With the acquisition of Foster's, SABMiller will gain exposure to a market with high margins but sluggish growth. Foster's has a 50 percent share of the Australian industry, with 7 of the top 10 brands, including the No. 1 beer, Victoria Bitter.*
>
> *Source: http://dealbook.nytimes.com/2011/09/21/sabmiller-to-buy-fosters-for-10-15-billion/?_r=0*

We now see that, at least in the view of one person, a significant part of the value received by SAB Miller was in the form of Foster's brands, including the very popular Victoria Bitter. This would provide a good starting point for your investigation and subsequent discussions with management.

IAS 38 provides guidelines for what constitutes an intangible asset. It specifies two elements that need to be present for an intangible asset to exist:

- The asset must be separable. In other words, it is 'capable of being separated or divided from the entity and sold, transferred, licensed, rented or exchanged, either individually or together with the related contract, asset or liability'; or
- It must arise from 'contractual or other legal rights, regardless of whether those rights are transferable or separable from the entity or from other rights and obligations.'

It may also be helpful to divide the intangible assets into categories for identification purposes, as set out as follows:

1. Customer-related intangibles
   - customer lists
   - customer contracts
   - customer relationships
2. Technology-based intangibles
   - patented and unpatented technologies
   - software
   - databases
   - secret formulae and processes
3. Contract-based intangibles
   - licensing, royalty agreements
   - leasing agreements
   - broadcasting rights
4. Marketing-related intangibles
   - trademarks
   - Internet domain names
   - non-competition agreements
5. Artistic-related intangibles
   - plays
   - books
   - pictures.

What if you know that management is not going to use all of the intangible assets it has acquired? For example, you may have seen in the board papers somewhere that SABMiller was intending to slowly to phase out the Foster's brand itself and replace it with Castle. How should that impact your identification exercise? The answer is, it shouldn't! In terms of IFRS 3, you will recognise and value the asset as being part of the purchase price, and then you will impair the Foster's brand as soon as it becomes clear that it is no longer worth what was paid for it.

The last step in the identification process is to agree the list of assets to be valued with the acquirer's auditors. The auditors will be required to sign off on the values of the assets and liabilities acquired, and will therefore need to be happy with the process that was followed. Note that independence considerations mean that the acquiring company's own auditors are not allowed to perform the business combination valuations. They are not allowed to audit their own work. The valuations are the responsibility of the acquiring management and would generally be outsourced to experts other than their own auditors.

Measuring the value of the identifiable assets acquired, the liabilities assumed and any non-controlling interest in the acquiree

In terms of IFRS 3, all assets and liabilities acquired must be accounted for at fair value. We have seen earlier in this book that IFRS 13 defines fair value as 'the price that would be received to sell an asset or paid to transfer a liability in an orderly transaction between market participants at the measurement date'.

The key principles are that agreement has been reached without duress between market participants - rational and knowledgeable parties.

The first step in this process might be to tackle the valuation of the tangible assets. The methodologies to be applied would be fairly obvious and routine. For example:

+ If a property has been acquired, a property valuation specialist should be appointed to value the property at the acquisition date.
+ The valuation of other plant and equipment might require valuations by a specialist plant and machinery valuer.
+ An intelligent review of current assets and liabilities will be required. For example, are the receivables amounts really recoverable? Has the policy for creating provisions for bad debts been consistently applied? Are the trends in bad debt experience consistent with what is happening in the market? A similar process would need to be followed in relation to inventory and payables.
+ Provisions, such as for leave pay, would need to be assessed for adequacy.

IFRS 13 - Fair Value Measurement, which is referred to by IFRS 3, suggests that valuations of assets should be completed as follows:

+ Market approach
  + Similar transactions method
+ Income approach
  + Multi-period excess earnings method
  + Relief from royalty method
+ Cost approach
  + Replacement or reproduction cost method.

The market approach assumes that it is possible to identify similar transactions for the purposes of valuation. Unfortunately, intangible assets are very rarely sold on their own, so establishing a value in this way is difficult. Occasionally, pharmaceutical companies will sell the rights to some of their products, which is helpful, but in most cases this method will be difficult to apply in practice.

We will look at examples of the income approach later in this section.

As we saw in the first part of this book, the cost approach to valuation only has limited applicability as cost only rarely equals the fair value of an asset.

Having identified the methodologies available, you also need to determine the sequence in which the assets will be valued, based on their interdependence. Figure 19.2 explains this concept:

FIGURE 19.2 Valuation of intangible assets

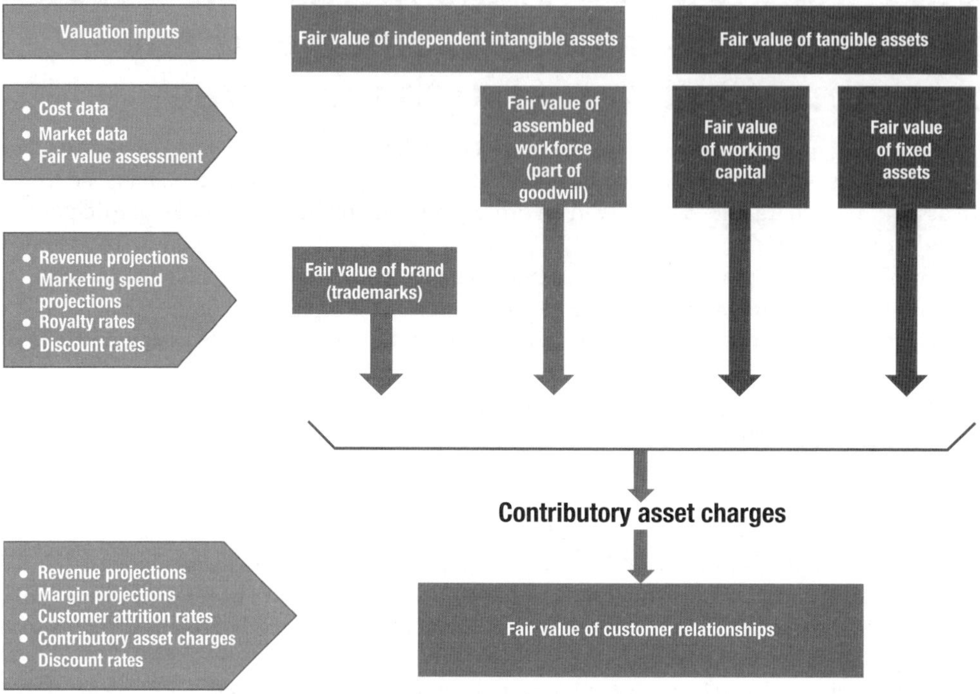

Source: Author's own construction

In Figure 19.2, the assets that can be valued without taking interdependencies into account are valued first, namely:

+ fixed assets
+ working capital
+ assembled workforce
+ brands/trademarks.

The treatment of the assembled workforce asset needs some explanation. Its fair value is based on the cost of assembling an equivalent workforce with the same skill set as the existing one. Costs include placement fees, sign-on bonuses etc. Although the cost or fair value of the assembled workforce can be established in this manner, ultimately the assembled workforce is not treated as a separate asset in terms of IFRS 3. The value ultimately falls into goodwill. In Figure 19.2, the value of the assembled workforce is being recognised as a necessary component in arriving at a value of customer relationships.

The other independent intangible asset value that can be arrived at is that of the company's brands/trademarks. This will be demonstrated in the next section. Note that trademarks are the subject of legal protection if they are registered, but the concept of a brand is somewhat wider. A brand is a driver of customer behaviour that benefits from the legal protection afforded to trademarks, but also includes the brand promise that the company offers – quality and reliability if you are Woolworths, for example – and reflects the company's investment in market image and product support.

Once the fair value of these items has been established, the value of dependent intangible assets, such as customer relationships, can be established. Again, the manner of doing so will be demonstrated in the next section.

Intangible asset valuation techniques

Valuing brands: The relief from royalty method

The relief from royalty method is a form of income approach that is based on the expected annual royalty savings attributable to ownership of the subject intangible asset. In other words, by owning and using the asset, the owner is giving up the opportunity to rent out the use of that asset to another market participant. The rent, or royalty, that the owner could earn by renting out the asset provides input into the valuation of the assets. This approach is primarily applied to the value of brands or trademarks, but can also be applied to the value of patents and technologies.

The key variables required in order to apply this approach are:

+ revenue projections;
+ royalty rates;
+ brand support projections; and
+ discount rates.

Revenue projections

The challenge here is to isolate the revenues to be generated from the sale of the particular product that benefits from the brand. For example, if you were trying to value the Coca-Cola brand, you would need to identify sales from all of the products that depend on the Coca-Cola brand. The obvious sales to identify are the sales of canned and bottled Coke, but what about sales of peripheral items branded Coca-Cola, such as towels and umbrellas? In other words, you would need to think carefully about the role that the Coca-Cola brand plays in generating revenue throughout the company.

Once you have decided on the basis of projecting revenues, you need to decide how those revenues are going to grow over time, and how long the forecast period should be. For example, Coca-Cola has been in existence for over 100 years - but, soon after the company started up in the early 1900s, could you have made the assumption that its brand would still be in existence 100 years later? Almost certainly not! And the problem hasn't gone away. Is Coca-Cola going to be in existence for another hundred years? There is significant pushback against obesity throughout the world, and the consumption of sugar is a significant contributor to that obesity. Does this mean that Coca-Cola's life is limited? It's a difficult question to answer, but it is one that you would have to turn your mind to in valuing the Coca-Cola brand.

By contrast, it's interesting to note that it is a lot easier to estimate the life of technology. The current pace of change suggests that the life of technology is getting shorter and shorter as competition increases in intensity. So, whereas the Apple brand may last for years, provided that it continues to read the market correctly and to provide innovative new product offerings that the market wants, individual products will be short-lived.

Royalty rates

The relative power of the brand is encapsulated in the royalty rate that could be earned from somebody else using that brand. You can access databases – such as RoyaltyStat and Royalty Source – that provide comparative data that can be helpful in establishing royalty rates for use in valuations. The royalty rate would be influenced by the characteristics of the underlying product, such as

- market share
- consumer recognition
- longevity
- leverage
- product differentiation
- barriers to entry
- advertising and promotion.

Marketing people refer to the combination of the above as the product's brand strength. The higher the brand strength, the higher the royalty that can be charged for the use of the brand.

Another way of getting a feel for the royalty rate is to think about the role the brand plays in encouraging consumers to pay a higher price for the product. For example, let's say that a no-name brand cola product sells at $0.95 a can. Coca-Cola's advertising promises a unique experience – a feeling of joy and connectedness with the global Coca-Cola drinking community – when drinking its product. The implication is that the consumer will be prepared to pay a premium to obtain that additional enjoyment.

Let's assume, therefore, that Coca-Cola prices its cans at $1. The implication is that the additional five cents, or 5 per cent, that Coca-Cola is able to charge is attributable to the value of its brand. If you are happy with this thinking, then the royalty rate to be used in valuing the Coca-Cola brand will be 5 per cent.

Brand support projections

Brands require significant ongoing support to maintain their place in the market. The cost of this support is a charge against the value of the brand. Brand support costs can be assessed from a review of the company's marketing expenditure and expressed as a percentage of brand sales.

Discount rates

You need to select an appropriate discount rate to be applied to the after-tax earnings generated by the brand. Intangible assets are, by definition, more vulnerable to risk than the company itself. Think of the technology and social media companies that are so highly priced today, such Uber, Facebook and Twitter. A significant portion of their value is attributable to their intangible assets – brand name, reputation, sizzle factor, clever technology, etc. But, if the management of those companies makes an incorrect strategic move or if their reputations are compromised in some way, those high values will come tumbling down, and the first category of asset to lose value will be intangible assets.

Therefore, in selecting a discount rate to be applied to the notional royalty flows, one would expect this rate to be higher than the cost of the company's capital.

EXAMPLE 19.1

Here is an example of the relief from royalty valuation method applied to the value of a brand. In it, we have made the following assumptions:

- Revenue growth is 5 per cent per annum;
- 80 per cent of total revenue is relevant to the brand valuation;
- The royalty rate has been set at 5 per cent;
- The cost of brand support has been set at 1 per cent of relevant revenue;
- The income tax rate on the notional revenue stream is 28 per cent;
- The discount rate has been set at 17,5 per cent, whereas the WACC for the business as a whole is 15 per cent; and
- The valuation is being performed in perpetuity and the ongoing growth rate is 5 per cent per annum.

TABLE 19.1 Calculating fair value

		Year 1	Year 2	Year 3	Year 4	Year 5	Year 6
Total revenue		**1 000 000**	**1 050 000**	**1 102 500**	**1 157 625**	**1 215 506**	**1 276 282**
Revenue base relevant to brand value	**80%**	795 500	835 275	877 039	920 891	966 935	1 015 282
Royalty rate		5,0%	5,0%	5,0%	5,0%	5,0%	5,0%
Avoided royalty pretax		39 775	41 764	43 852	46 045	48 347	50 764
Brand support expenses (advertising etc)	**1%**	(7 955)	(8 353)	(8 770)	(9 209)	(9 669)	(10 153)
Income tax expense	**28%**	(8 910)	(9 355)	(9 823)	(10 314)	(10 830)	(11 371)
Avoided royalty after tax and expenses		**22 910**	**24 056**	**25 259**	**26 522**	**27 848**	**29 240**
Present value factors	**17,50%**	0,8511	0,7243	0,6164	0,5246	0,4465	0,3800
Present value of after-tax avoided royalty		**19 498**	**17 424**	**15 570**	**13 914**	**12 434**	**11 111**
Terminal year value	**5%**						93 332
Present value factor							0,3800
Present value of terminal year value							35 465
Present value of discrete period cash flows		89 951					
Present value of terminal year value		35 465					
Calculation of fair value		**125 416**					

Source: Author's own construction

You can see that the resulting value before taking any tax amortisation benefit into account is roughly R125 000. In jurisdictions where it is possible to amortise the value of the intangible for tax purposes, an additional value arises from this tax shield. This is not the case in South Africa.

It is difficult to check intangible valuations for reasonableness, given the lack of comparable transactions. Later in this chapter we will outline the reconciliation process that you can apply to business combination valuations to provide a sense check.

The multi-period excess earnings method (MEEM) valuation approach

The MEEM approach is the most common approach for the valuation of customer- and technology-related assets. The asset value is estimated through the sum of the discounted future excess earnings attributable to the acquired customers or technologies over their remaining lifespan. In order to apply this approach, all other intangible assets not forming part of the customer relations or technology asset being valued (the contributory assets) must have been correctly identified and valued.

In terms of the illustrative examples in IFRS 3, customer relations must be valued in the following circumstances:

- 'If an entity establishes relationships with its customers through contracts, those customer relationships arise from contractual rights. Therefore, customer contracts and the related customer relationships acquired in a business combination meet the contractual-legal criterion even if confidentiality or other contractual terms prohibit the sale or transfer of a contract separately from the acquiree.'
- 'Customer relationships also meet the contractual-legal criterion for identification as intangible assets when an entity has a practice of establishing contracts with its customers, regardless of whether a contract exists at the date of acquisition. A customer relationship acquired in a business combination that does not arise from a contract may nevertheless be identifiable because the relationship is separable.'

Without going into detail, material customers who buy on a regular basis from the company and who can be identified through the receivables records or some other means, such as loyalty cards, would fall within the definition of an intangible asset to be valued.

Further discussion of this topic will focus on the valuation of customer relations, but do not lose sight of the fact that you can also use the approach to value technology assets, such as software developed in-house.

Once the contributory assets have been identified and valued, the expected cost of the capital invested in these assets can be computed and deducted from the cash flows estimated to be generated from the customer relations. Only excess earnings attributable to the customer relations should be included in the calculation. Excess earnings can be defined as the difference between:

- the after-tax operating cash flows attributable to the existing customers at the acquisition date; and
- the return required on the contributory assets necessary to deliver a finished good or maintain the customer relationship.

Figure 19.3 illustrates the concept:

FIGURE 19.3 Calculating the value of customer relationships

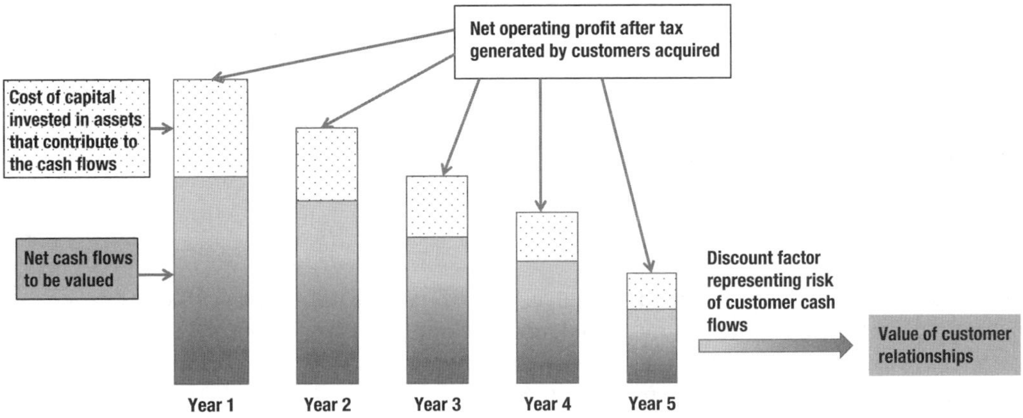

Source: Author's own construction

Let's consider each of the elements of the calculation in Figure 19.3 in turn.

Net operating profit after tax (NOPAT) generated by customers

The NOPAT to be included in the calculation is the future after-tax operating profit to be generated by the existing body of customers taken over at the time of the acquisition with whom the company has a contractual relationship, as discussed earlier. Cash flows to be generated by customers won in the future are not included in the valuation of customer relationships.

You will see from Figure 19.3 that NOPAT (the full height of the columns) diminishes over time as a result of the initial body of customers no longer buying from the organisation – or customer churn, as this is known. In order to establish the rate of customer attrition, you need to analyse historical attrition rates and apply that rate going forward, assuming that the rate is not likely to change in the future.

You also need to consider the rate at which existing customers will continue to buy from the organisation (will they increase their purchases or is there a declining trend?) and feed that into the NOPAT projections.

The length of the forecast period will be determined by the rate of customer attrition.

Cost of the capital invested in contributory assets

As Figure 19.2 shows, the ability to conduct customer relationships is based on the existence of tangible assets, such as fixed assets and working capital, and intangible assets, such as brands or trademarks (the contributory assets). The business needs to earn a return on the contributory assets that is equal to their cost of capital. This assessment will need to be made in the context of the company's overall cost of capital. If a large part of the contributory assets is in the form of property, with relatively lower risk than the business itself, then the required return on the contributory assets could be lower than the company's WACC. The cost of the capital invested in contributory assets is a charge against the NOPAT generated from customer relations.

Return required on the customer relations asset

Similar to calculating the value of brands, we have to make an assessment of how risky the customer relations are in relation to the overall risk of the business. The value of customer relations can easily be affected by negative experiences with the company. It seems likely, therefore, that the return required on an investment in customer relations will be higher than the return required on an investment in the company as a whole. The return is therefore likely to be higher than the company's cost of capital. Exactly how much higher will depend on the specific circumstances of that business.

EXAMPLE 19.2

In this example:

+ we have attributed 30 per cent of total revenue to the top 15 customers with whom we can say we have an ongoing contractual relationship;
+ we have assumed that one in five of those customers will no longer do business with the company annually, implying a five-year valuation period;
+ operating expenses are allocated to the revenue from top customers at the average rate of expenses to revenue from all customers, namely 65 per cent;
+ income tax has been levied at the rate of 28 per cent;
+ charges for the use of the contributory assets have been calculated at a rate that provides for a risk-related return on those assets over the forecast period; and
+ the discount rate has been set at 18,5 per cent, higher than the WACC of 15 per cent for the company as a whole.

TABLE 19.2 Calculating fair value

		Year 1	Year 2	Year 3	Year 4	Year 5	Year 6
Total revenue		**1 000 000**	**1 050 000**	**1 102 500**	**1 157 625**	**1 215 506**	**1 276 282**
Revenue attributable to the top 15 customers							
- Percent		30%	30%	30%	30%	30%	30%
- Absolute rands		300 000	315 000	330 750	347 288	364 652	382 884
Retention rate		100%	80%	60%	40%	20%	0%
Expected revenue, top 15 customers		300 000	252 000	198 450	138 915	72 930	-
Operating expenses	**65%**	(195 000)	(163 800)	(128 993)	(90 295)	(47 405)	0
Operating income		**105 000**	**88 200**	**69 458**	**48 620**	**25 526**	**0**
Income tax expense	**28%**	(29 400)	(24 696)	(19 448)	(13 614)	(7 147)	0
Net income (loss)		**75 600**	**63 504**	**50 009**	**35 007**	**18 378**	**0**

Continued

Charges for the use of contributory assets							
- Working capital		(1 425)	(1 140)	(855)	(570)	(285)	0
- Fixed assets		(7 410)	(5 928)	(4 446)	(2 964)	(1 482)	0
- Trademarks		(6 563)	(5 250)	(3 938)	(2 625)	(1 313)	0
- Developed technology		(6 563)	(5 250)	(3 938)	(2 625)	(1 313)	0
- In-process technology		(5 100)	(4 080)	(3 060)	(2 040)	(1 020)	0
Assembled workforce		(4 000)	(3 200)	(2 400)	(1 600)	(800)	0
After-tax cash flow		**44 540**	**38 656**	**31 373**	**22 583**	**12 166**	**0**
Present value factors	**18,50%**	0,8439	0,7121	0,6010	0,5071	0,4280	0,3612
Present value of after-tax cash flow		**37 586**	**27 528**	**18 854**	**11 452**	**5 207**	**–**
Calculation of fair value		**100 628**					

Source: Author's own construction

As for the valuation of brands, it is difficult to perform a reasonableness check on the resulting value of R100 000, but the reconciliation covered later in this chapter helps to provide comfort that the value is reasonable.

Recognition and measurement of goodwill

Goodwill is calculated as the residual between the value of the business as a whole (the purchase price) and the sum of values estimated for other identifiable tangible and intangible assets of the business, as set out in this chapter. Intangible assets included in the amount recognised as goodwill might include:

- customer service capability;
- presence in geographic markets or locations (market power/influence);
- non-union status or strong labour relations;
- ongoing training or recruiting programmes;
- outstanding credit ratings and access to capital markets;
- favourable government relations; and
- an assembled workforce.

In other words: elements of the business that contribute to its value but that did not fall within the definition of intangible assets that are capable of separate valuation.

Goodwill calculated as above may be a positive or a negative figure. Where it is a positive figure it is an asset that is not subject to further analysis but must appear on the acquirer's balance sheet.

Where the calculated goodwill is a negative figure, the fair value of assets acquired as a result of the transaction exceeds the value given up. In other words, the transaction represents a bargain. At this stage, you need to be very sure of your ground and need to be confident that you have, indeed, obtained a bargain. If the circumstances surrounding the transaction suggest that there was little prospect of a bargain being achieved, then you will need to go back and check your valuations. Should you finally come to the conclusion that a bargain was, indeed, obtained, then the negative goodwill figure will be credited to the income statement, but will not impact headline earnings per share.

Reconciling the business combination valuations to the purchase price

Now that you have stated all the tangible and intangible assets at fair value and, by deduction, have calculated the fair value of goodwill, you are in a position to check whether your results make sense. You do this by reconciling the external approach to assessing the required return on capital - the WACC - to an internal approach of assessing the required rate of return on each class of asset (WARA), as demonstrated Figure 19.4:

FIGURE 19.4 WACC and WARA

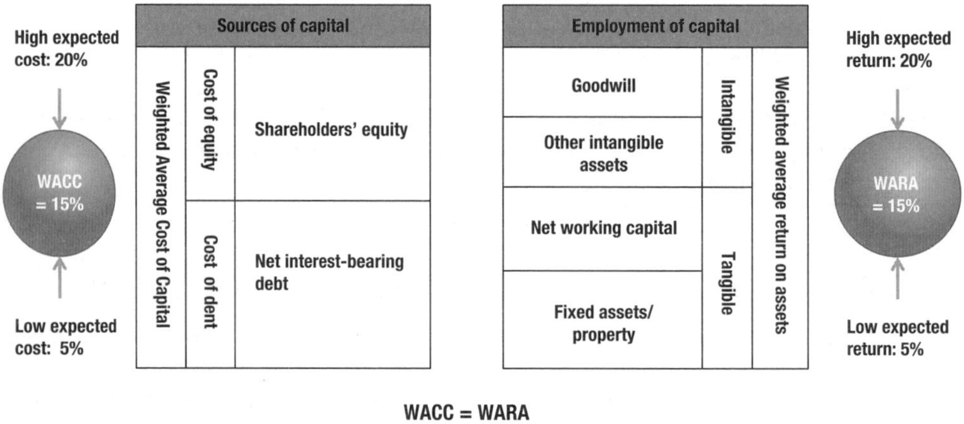

Source: Author's own construction

WACC and WARA are defined as follows:

- Weighted average cost of capital (WACC)
  - After-tax cost of equity
  - After-tax cost of debt
  - Capital structure (% equity and % debt)
- Weighted average return on assets (WARA)
  - After-tax returns by asset class
  - Asset classes
    - Net working capital
    - Tangible assets
    - Intangible assets
    - Goodwill.

If your calculations are correct, WACC and WARA will be the same. Example 3 shows a WARA calculation.

EXAMPLE 19.3

In this example, the WACC used to value the business as a whole was 15 per cent, a fairly average WACC for a South African company.

- Start by listing the fair values calculated for each asset class. In this example, the total fair value on a sum-of-the-parts basis is R1 million.
- Calculate the proportion of the value of each asset class to the total value.
- Estimate a required rate of return for each asset class, taking the relative risk of each asset class into account; you can see that tangible assets require a lower rate of return than intangible assets, and that goodwill has the highest required rate of return, being the most vulnerable of the intangible assets.
- Calculate the WARA as set out in the right-hand column of Table 18.3.

TABLE 19.3 Calculating the WARA

Asset class	Fair value	Proportion of total	Required return	Weighted average
Working capital	95 000	9,5%	5,00%	0,5%
Net property, plant and equipment	247 000	24,7%	10,00%	2,5%
Identified intangible assets				
- Trademarks	125 000	12,5%	17,50%	2,2%
- Developed technology	125 000	12,5%	15,00%	1,9%
- Customer relationships	100 000	10,0%	18,50%	1,9%
- In-process technology	85 000	8,5%	20,00%	1,7%
Goodwill	223 000	22,3%	20,00%	4,5%
	1 000 000	**100,0%**		**15,0%**
Weighted Average Return on Assets (WARA)				**15,0%**

Source: Author's own construction

In this instance WARA = WACC, which is the desired outcome. However, you can also see that with a bit of deft manipulation of the required rates of return, particularly the return required on goodwill, you could easily manipulate WACC and WARA to be the same. This is nothing more than a high-level reasonableness test and should not be seen as anything more than that. Note that the required returns on brands or trademarks and customer relationships are at the levels used in the examples supplied earlier in this chapter.

Subsequent accounting for intangible assets and goodwill

Goodwill and intangible assets are accounted for differently.

Intangible assets that have been valued over a finite period must be amortised over that period. Intangible assets valued over an infinite period must be subjected to impairment review annually, as per IAS 36. Amortisation of intangible assets impacts headline earnings per share, whereas impairment does not.

Positive goodwill is no longer amortised, but is subject to impairment review, either annually or when an impairment trigger, such as losses being incurred, occurs. In practice, the goodwill will not be valued in isolation, but the cash generating unit to which the goodwill belongs will be valued as a whole and compared to the original purchase price. Value diminution will affect goodwill first, then intangible assets and possibly tangible assets.

Goodwill impairments are debited to the income statement but do not affect headline earnings per share. Subsequent increases in value of the business unit do not result in a reversal of previous amortisation of goodwill.

Negative goodwill, as pointed out earlier, is credited to the income statement, but does not affect headline earnings per share.

What does it all mean?

The introduction of IFRS 3 was intended to improve communication with shareholders in relation to acquisitions. Details of the purchase price allocation values per IFRS 3 are set out in notes to the company's financial statements, and the basis of arriving at the fair values is explained.

The intention was also to move some of the amorphous value of goodwill to specific categories of intangible assets. In theory, this should provide comfort to shareholders that their money has been well spent.

Whether the information provided by purchase price accounting for business combinations is of use to management is moot. In the writer's experience, management does not portray a great deal of interest in the value of customer relations acquired in the course of an acquisition. The basis on which they arrived at a price for the acquisition was top-down and not bottom-up, and that is how they are going to measure the progress of the company going forward.

One implication of IFRS 3 accounting is that, in looking at the balance sheet of any company, you need to recognise that a hybrid system of accounting was used to arrive at the numbers. For example, the value of internally generated brands does not appear on the balance sheet, whereas the value of acquired brands does.

The hybrid nature of accounting is more evident in relation to accounting for non-controlling interests acquired as part of an acquisition. The accounting options are the fair value method and the proportionate share of assets method and, to add to the confusion, either of the options can be selected to account for additional tranches of shares acquired.

Recognising the impact of IFRS 3 is important when setting out to understand any company's financial statements.

Conclusion

In this chapter we have presented a very high-level picture of the operation of business combination accounting. In reality, tricky technical points to achieve compliance with IFRS 3 need to be addressed at each point along the journey. We have warned that working with accounting technical and valuations specialists is therefore mandatory in this area. The purpose of this chapter has therefore been to raise awareness within the broad topic of valuations and M&A, not to produce specialists. As always, having a high-level understanding of the issues should enhance your ability to manage the specialists charged with preparing the work. Like it or not, IFRS 3 is compulsory and you need to pay attention to it.

References

IFRS Foundation: IFRS 3, IAS 38.

Werdigier, J. (2011). SABMiller to buy Foster's for $10.15 billion. *The New York Times*. Available at http://dealbook.nytimes.com/2011/09/21/sabmiller-to-buy-fosters-for-10-15-billion/?_r=1. [Accessed 11 June 2015].

CHAPTER 20

Post-merger integration: Do not lose the value you have just created

LEARNING OBJECTIVES

Once you have worked through this chapter, you should be able to:

- Understand where value can get lost once the deal has been finalised
- Understand the influence of people issues on this value leakage
- Recognise the basic elements of culture and how culture can be measured
- Make suggestions for people focus areas during the transition
- Recognise warning signs that the transaction is not bedding down as it should be
- Take steps in post-merger evaluation six months after the deal is finalised

Introduction

So far we have looked at value creation in M&A:

- at the strategy-setting stage – by being clear in your objectives
- at the implementation stage – by not overpaying
- at the implementation stage – by managing risk
- at the implementation stage – by mastering the regulatory environment.

Now, we get to the final stage of the process – bedding the deal down and harvesting its value potential. This is the post-merger integration (PMI) phase. The integration phase of M&As is extremely important, but often receives insufficient attention. It is estimated that one third to one half of merger failures are attributable to 'employee problems'.

Merger integration is a subject on its own, and one that is largely outside of the scope of this book, but it is important that M&A practitioners have at least a high-level understanding of the issues that are likely to be encountered. The aim of this chapter is merely to raise your awareness of these issues. In practice, you would work with human resources professionals to plan and execute the implementation process.

Areas of value loss

One reason that this phase may not receive sufficient attention is that there is insufficient involvement by the team responsible for the deal. The strategy-setting and implementation may be handled by a senior team and their advisors, but as soon as the ink is dry on the agreement the responsibility for implementation is handed to another team. Companies that have developed a reputation for being skilled acquirers, such as Johnson & Johnson in the US, make sure that senior executives remain involved in the transition until the acquisition is fully bedded down (see the MMI case study later in this chapter for a good example of this).

Figure 20.1 depicts how value can slip away in M&A transactions.

FIGURE 20.1 The value gap

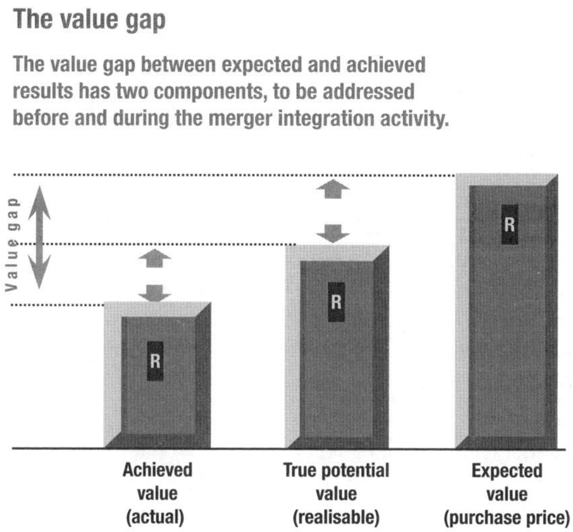

Source: Ernst & Young

The transaction gap

The transaction gap is the gap between the expected value (the purchase price paid) and the true potential value (the value that was unlikely ever to be exceeded). Factors contributing to this gap are listed in Table 20.1. They revolve around the deal execution process having been handled badly, resulting in too much having been paid for the acquisition.

TABLE 20.1 Factors contributing to the transaction gap

Issue	Underlying reason
Managerial hubris	Management's belief that, having successfully concluded acquisitions before, they can now succeed at any acquisition to which they turn their hand. As a result, they pay insufficient attention to the implementation issues.
Lack of clear vision and strategy on the part of leadership	Muddled thinking on the benefits of the transaction; failure to consider other growth options, such as organic growth or strategic partnerships
Multiple agendas and perspectives	Corporate politics; not all executives agree with the CEO's thinking; executives batting for their own teams rather than seeing the bigger picture

Continued

Improper selection of the target	Flawed strategy or misreading the acquirer's strategic fit with the target
High premium paid	Irrational exuberance to get the deal done leads to overpayment; poor understanding of the valuation principles dealt with in the first part of this book
Internal and external time pressure	Deal done in a hurry to 'scoop' the market or beat competitors to the acquisition
Limited access to information	An informed guess about how much information was necessary to formulate an offer price turns out to be flawed
Lack of human resources or cultural due diligence – ignoring people issues in M&A	The nature of business has changed to the point where the key asset to be acquired in a business is often people, including their creativity, their know-how and their corporate memory. The key question to be addressed at this stage is, What will I be left with if the deal goes ahead? This requires a critical look at the target's stock of human capital and an assessment of areas of vulnerability to people walking out. Further, an assessment needs to be made of the compatibility of the target's culture – understanding the way things are done in the target company and its compatibility with the acquirer's way of doing things (see the section on people issues for more detail)
Failure to assess implementation considerations	A blind eye is turned to the challenges of merging the two organisations, involving people issues or possibly technical issues, such as incompatibility of IT systems. Time and cost of implementation is underestimated and the impact on the overall economic justification for the transaction is ignored.
Lack of prior experience in acquisition analysis and negotiation	No track record in acquisitions; poor use made of advisers

Source: Luiza Dehrmann, Managing Director, Eversheds Consulting SA (Pty) Ltd

The transition or transformation gap

The transition or transformation gap results from the true potential value not being achieved in practice as a result of the implementation phase being poorly handled. At this stage, people are likely to be nervous and unsettled, and wondering whether they are likely to lose their jobs. The leakage of value in this stage can often be attributed to poor handling of people issues.

TABLE 20.2 Factors contributing to the transition or transformation gap

Issue	Underlying reason
Lack of leadership	Having finished the deal, the leaders fail to take responsibility for the implementation phase, possibly handing this responsibility down to a more junior team
Lack of involvement of middle management	Allied to the above point, there is a lack of operationalisation of the broad strategy behind the acquisition; the grand vision has not been passed down to the next level of management

Continued

Lack of a plan for Day 1	No plan for how to proceed with the implementation, such as defining the new organisation chart, announcing which executives are to assume which roles in the new organisation, or publicising a roadmap that employees can use to understand how the implementation is progressing
Organisational confusion and division	Roles in the new organisation are not clearly defined; there is jockeying for new positions among executives
Poor internal communication	Seasoned acquirers remind us to communicate, communicate and communicate. And if there is nothing to communicate about, communicate that there is nothing to communicate!
Inability to create and celebrate early wins	In M&A transition there is the concept of the 90-day plan, a plan that prioritises the actions that are to take place and the wins aimed for immediately after the transaction is signed. Wins over this period act as a morale booster and create confidence that there will be a good outcome to justify the current feeling of insecurity.
Loss of momentum	Integration badly project-managed, possibly run by management that is too junior or does not have sufficient authority; resources drafted to help with the implementation return to their own departments; progress falters
Loss of control	Responsibilities are not clearly defined in the implementation plan; there is a lack of accountability
Cultural clashes	People issues are not dealt with effectively
Neglect of customers	Internal focus prevails; no one is minding the store
Flight of key talent and knowledge	Insufficient attention paid to getting buy-in from key staff

Source: Luiza Dehrmann, Managing Director, Eversheds Consulting SA (Pty) Ltd

SELF-ASSESSMENT

- What is the essential difference between the transaction gap and the transition gap?
- Name three elements of the transaction gap.
- Name three elements of the transition gap.

People issues and value leakage

As noted earlier, people issues are extremely important in the transition phase. If badly handled, they can lead to a loss of value.

Resistance to change

It is a natural human instinct for people involved in an M&A situation to ask, How is this going to impact me? For key personnel, this is a question that needs to be answered as soon as possible. Human resources professional Luiza Dehrmann, managing director of Eversheds Consulting SA (Pty) Ltd, points out that people have a natural resistance to change. Their reactions to impending change are not that much different to the stages of reaction identified by Elizabeth Kübler-Ross in relation to impending death as the result of a fatal disease, namely:

+ disbelief and denial;
+ anger;
+ bargaining;
+ depression; and
+ acceptance.

For M&A purposes, the list has been refined as follows and has been dubbed the change curve:

+ Denial
+ Resistance
+ Exploration
+ Commitment.

People start off by wishing that the change were not happening. This is followed by a period of resistance to change. Then, when reality sets, in they might start to explore the potential of the new situation, finally ending up with commitment to the new way of things. Leaders who understand this process are more likely to manage the situation effectively.

The impact of culture

What is culture?

Formally, culture is defined as a set of norms, values and assumptions that govern how people act and interact every day. Informally, culture is 'the way we do things around here'. Sometimes culture is palpable; you can pick it up immediately when you go for an interview, for example. At other times culture is subtler, and requires experience to become aware of.

CASE STUDY **Culture**

The CEO of a low-cost airline in the US was visiting the CEO of another company with a view to setting up a business relationship together, possibly leading to a merger/acquisition. Talks proceeded well until the CEO of the airline noticed that the CEO of the other company was amusing himself by tearing sheets off a desk pad of expensive-looking paper, scrunching them up and throwing them into a wastepaper basket, basketball style. In that instant, the airline CEO realised that the two organisations could never be compatible in terms of attitude to cost control, and he terminated the discussions.

How can we establish the likelihood of a cultural fit?

To establish the likelihood of a cultural fit, we can ask the following questions:

+ Are the missions and values of the two companies compatible?
+ Do we know which elements of each culture we are going to keep?
+ When speaking about similar topics, do both companies use the same language?

- Are their meetings like our meetings?
- Do we have the time and resources to allocate to understanding both companies' cultures?

As noted at the outset of this chapter, this area is the domain of human resources professionals on whom you will rely for their expertise, but this does not imply that your own experience and common sense is irrelevant. We saw, in Chapter 15, that what we are often looking for is the 'unknown unknowns'. Keep an open mind when you are assessing the likelihood of people issues in an acquisition.

CASE STUDY **Daimler-Benz and Chrysler**

The merger of German car manufacturer Daimler-Benz and US automobile manufacturer Chrysler in 1997 was designed to be a transformative deal for both organisations. The intention was that it would be a merger of equals. This intention was underpinned by the fact that Jurgen Schrempp and Bob Eaton, the CEOs of Daimler and Chrysler respectively, were appointed as joint CEOs of the new combine. While the combine was intended to produce an organisation of unrivalled strength, that promise was eroded by cultural issues:

- Appointing joint CEOs, instead of choosing a single, outright leader, turned out to be unworkable in practice.
- Daimler was a producer of premium vehicles, while Chrysler's offerings were seen as blue collar, which stood in the way of a single identity.
- German thoroughness meant that Daimler board meetings were formal, with long agendas, whereas Chrysler prided themselves on a more nimble, creative approach that involved less bureaucracy.
- The fact that Chrysler executives arrived for meetings in their corporate jets did not fit well with the Germans' more self-effacing style.
- American workers were paid more than German ones, which was a cause of friction.
- Germans smoked, drank wine and beer with lunch, and worked late hours, while Chrysler banned smoking and alcohol at their facilities and worked round the clock for deadlines, but did not work late as a routine.

By 2000 the façade of a merger of equals was dropped, and Jurgen Schrempp took over as sole CEO. The deal was unwound in 2007 and Chrysler was sold off to a private equity company. The impact of the differences in culture had been badly underestimated.

People issues requiring attention after the deal

Once the deal has been signed, management needs to pay attention to the following issues in order to preserve and create value:

TABLE 20.3 People issues

Issue	Action
Communication	To offset the inevitable feelings of insecurity once the deal has been announced, it is important that management communicates regularly with staff in as transparent a manner as practical.

Continued

Leadership	Management needs to show a united front in its optimism for the outcome of the deal and its commitment to an effective transition process. It should be sharing the same message as well as displaying and promoting the same values and vision.
Inclusion of employees	Where possible, management should look to employees for ideas on how to proceed with the transition and on ideas on what a transformed business should look like. Practical wisdom can be found on the shop floor and a consultation process should help to offset the anxiety that accompanied the deal announcement. This process will further encourage employee buy-in.
Dealing with retrenchments	Human resources experts acknowledge that this is an issue that should not be ducked. People will read that one of the justifications for doing the deal in the first place is the ability to create synergies, and synergies often imply job losses. The important thing is that the process is seen as logical and fair. The basis on which retrenchments will be handled needs to be communicated transparently. (It has become commonplace in South Africa for the competition authorities to approve transactions subject to there being no merger-related retrenchments for a period of time, such as year. Whether this is doing anything more than delaying the unfortunate day is arguable, but can be understood in relation to the social context of our country.)
Psychological contracts	It is important to re-establish trust with employees. One of the features of a retrenchment process is survivor guilt – people ask why the person next to them was retrenched and not them. This feeling of unworthiness needs to be replaced by a clear understanding between management and employees as to what is expected of them going forward and how they are likely to benefit from the situation.
Creating security and providing career direction and guidance	If the merger or acquisition achieves its objectives it should create new opportunities for staff. Forward-looking conversations along these lines need to be held as soon as possible in the transition period.
New merged entity should know its culture and values	The overall objective is a transformed organisation that has benefited from the strengths of both sides of the deal.

Source: Luiza Dehrmann, Managing Director, Eversheds Consulting SA (Pty) Ltd

Warning signs that the transition is not going as it should

Dr Theo Veldsman, Professor of Industrial Psychology and People Management at the University of Johannesburg, suggests looking for the following signs that the transition is not progressing smoothly:

+ Ambiguity/confusion about the identity and profile of new organisation
+ Integration efforts that are confined to top management

+ Preoccupation with consequences of integration
+ Widely fluctuating mood or climate swings
+ Unrealistic expectations
+ Widespread and constant firefighting and crisis management
+ Clear signs of an inability or unwillingness to perform or counter-perform
+ Widespread insecurity, anxiety, fears and stress
+ A strong 'scoreboard' mentality
+ Severe and rampant personality and culture clashes
+ High absenteeism and turnover
+ A rising frequency of customer and supplier complaints.

SELF-ASSESSMENT

+ How does resistance to change play out in an M&A situation?
+ How would you go about assessing cultural compatibility between two companies?
+ Name three areas of people management that you would focus on after a merger.
+ List four warning signs that indicate that a merger transition process is not proceeding smoothly.

Post-merger evaluation six months after deal finalisation

Once you have completed the deal, it is important to learn something from the process that you underwent and to determine whether the merger is on track in terms of delivering the value that it should:

+ Are you achieving your financial goals and operational goals?
+ Are schedules on target and changes being implemented according to plan?
+ Do employees understand and support the need for change?
+ Are managers taking steps to minimise negative reactions and building positive feelings?
+ Is productivity and work quality being affected?
+ Do people understand the new roles and what is expected of them?
+ Do leaders, managers and employees understand the business culture and values, and do they conduct themselves in accordance with this culture and these values?

The objective is to harvest the learning from this transaction to improve the outcomes on the next one.

CASE STUDY **MMI**

Insurance giant MMI was created in 2010 by the merger of Momentum Life and Metropolitan Life. One of the justifications for the deal was that it would lead to synergies, quantified as R500 million per annum. Nicolaas Kruger, group CEO of MMI and previously CEO of Momentum, announced as follows in MMI's 2014 financial results:

> *In our chairman's letter to shareholders he refers to the successful completion of the MMI merger. The merger integration has been an exciting journey of three years, culminating in the creation of a much stronger entity than its individual component*

parts. I am very pleased that the merger integration is complete and that we achieved our annual merger-related expense savings of R522 million (R22 million above target). The MMI management team is equally as excited about the opportunity to focus on the stronger new entity's future prospects.

On the face of it, therefore, this has been a very successful merger. One of the major contributors to this success was the fact that Wilhelm van Zyl, previous CEO of Metropolitan, stayed on for three years after the deal was finalised to oversee the successful implementation of the deal. At the time of writing he had left MMI only recently, having successfully completed this project.

The significance of this story is that:

- two CEOs potentially fighting for the same position were able to work together constructively for three years after one of them got the top job;
- the position of new group CEO was announced shortly after deal completion, thus avoiding unnecessary speculation and gossip-mongering;
- a senior executive was devoted to overseeing the integration process – this task was not left to a junior manager; and
- The synergies from cost savings were achieved.

Conclusion

While there are many practical aspects of the implementation of a merger or acquisition, such as rationalising IT systems or selling off surplus production facilities, organisations are driven by people and people issues can lead to a great deal of value being lost. In this chapter, we argue for the integration phase receiving as much attention as – if not more attention than – the strategy-setting and implementation phases. While we recognise that this is an area in which a heavy reliance will be placed on human resources professionals, that does not mean that management can abdicate responsibility for people decisions that need to be made.

References

Luiza Dehrmann, Managing Director, Eversheds Consulting SA (Pty) Ltd

Dr Theo Veldsman, Professor of Industrial Psychology and People Management, University of Johannesburg

Index

Page numbers in *italics* refer to figures and tables.

D

E

F

T

V

W

Y